Intercultural and Interreligious Pastoral Caregiving

sipcc
society
for *intercultural*
pastoral care
and counselling

Intercultural and Interreligious Pastoral Caregiving

The SIPCC 1995-2015

20 Years of International Practice and Reflection

Edited by
Karl H. Federschmidt and Daniël J. Louw

Published for
Gesellschaft für Interkulturelle Seelsorge und Beratung /
Society for Intercultural Pastoral Care and Counselling (SIPCC)
Düsseldorf, Germany

by Books on Demand GmbH, Norderstedt

2015

Intercultural and Interreligious Pastoral Caregiving
The SIPCC 1995-2015
20 Years of International Practice and Reflection

Published for
Gesellschaft für Interkulturelle Seelsorge und Beratung e.V. (SIPCC)
c/o H. Weiß, Friederike-Fliedner-Weg 72, D-40489 Düsseldorf,
Web site: www.sipcc.org

Design and text processing by Karl Federschmidt
Cover artwork by Hubert Begasse

A catalogue record is available from Deutsche Nationalbibliothek

Bibliografische Information der Deutschen Nationalbibliothek:
Die Deutsche Nationalbibliothek verzeichnet diese Publikation in der Deutschen Nationalbibliographie, detaillierte bibliographische Daten sind im Internet über http://dnb.dnb.de abrufbar.

Herstellung und Verlag:
BoD – Books on Demand, Norderstedt, Germany

ISBN 978-3-7386-3515-7 2nd rev. print

Contents

PART C

INTERRELIGIOUS REFLECTIONS AND DIALOGUES ON PASTORAL CAREGIVING

APPENDIX

Foreword and Acknowledgements

When in 1986 Howard Clinebell was invited to an "International Seminar on Pastoral Care and Counselling" in Germany, the organisers hardly expected that this meeting would turn out to be an intercultural encounter. But that was exactly what happened and what was experienced there.[1] Indeed, this seminar started a tradition of yearly seminars, in which the intercultural aspect in pastoral caregiving more and more was made an explicit focus of reflection. In 1995, this resulted in the foundation of the "Society for Intercultural Pastoral Care and Counselling", SIPCC.[2]

For the last 20 years now, SIPCC has been an international "learning community"[3], with seminars, studies, publications and networking activities – thereby becoming a catalyst (and in some respect a forerunner) in the reflection of intercultural aspects in the field of pastoral care and counselling. And step by step, this focus was widened from the intercultural to the inter-religious field.

This book contains essays that reflect the work and the "learning course" of SIPCC:

- Serving as *Introduction*, in the first essay Helmut Weiß discusses the hermeneutics of intercultural and inter-religious encounters, based on the experiences of SIPCC's 20 years history.
- The essays in *Part A* tackle – albeit starting from their specific contexts or challenges – general questions for a hermeneutics of pastoral caregiving in intercultural and interfaith perspective. The authors in this part approach

---

[1] For the story of this seminar and the follow up until the founding of SIPCC, see Helmut Weiß and Klaus Temme, "Reviewing the Journey", in *Intercultural Pastoral Care and Counselling, 1*, 1996, 6-13. See also the list of seminars in the appendix of this book.

[2] For actual information about SIPCC, see http://www.sipcc.org.

[3] Cf. the essay of Helmut Weiß in this book.

pastoral caregiving from a Christian perspective. The intention is not to create an exclusive approach, but to enhance theory formation in pastoral caregiving in line with the very old tradition of the care or cure of human souls (*cura animarum*). This has been done with the vision that pastoral caregiving should explore new frontiers and take up the challenge to be inclusive, taking into consideration the connection between pastoral care, spiritual care and wholeness in healing and helping.

• *Part B* focusses on themes and challenges of caregiving in concrete contexts. Thus, the emphasis is on local issues on grassroots level within different cultural and religious settings. It is clear that the themes that are tackled here are by no means exhaustive, but exemplary in character.

• *Part C*, finally, takes up the challenge of inter-religiosity. For SIPCC, this challenge was present right from the beginning,[4] but it took some time to find ways to approach it methodologically. The essays in this section show steps to do that without neglecting the fact that religions like e.g. Judaism, Christianity or Islam are (in their self-understanding and in their empirical phenomenology) more than just "cultural expressions of different spiritualities".

Most essays in this book have been presented and discussed at one of SIPCC's seminars, and later been published in SIPCC's magazine *Intercultural Pastoral Care and Counselling.*[5] Some were specially written for books of SIPCC and are published here by courtesy of Neukirchener Verlag.[6] All contributions have been reviewed and selected according to their contribution to the field of caregiving, helping and healing; to their representativeness for the different areas of discussion and the intercultural profile of SIPCC's work; and, finally, to their availability in English.

---

[4] In the first seminar of SIPCC 1995 already, a Buddhist monk participated with a lecture.

[5] This series (ISSN: 1431-8954) is published since 1996 by SIPCC, Düsseldorf, with a parallel series in German: *Interkulturelle Seelsorge und Beratung* (ISSN: 1431-8962). All issues are also online available at http://www.sipcc.org/schriftenreihe. The lectures of the seminar 2013 have been published in: E. Begic, H. Weiß, G. Wenz (eds.), *Barmherzigkeit. Zur sozialen Verantwortung islamischer Seelsorge*, Neukirchen-Vluyn: Neukirchener Verlag 2014.

[6] See K. Federschmidt, E. Hauschildt, Chr. Schneider-Harpprecht, K. Temme and H. Weiß (eds.), *Handbuch Interkulturelle Seelsorge* [Handbook on Intercultural Pastoral Care and Counselling], 2002; H. Weiß, K. Federschmidt and K. Temme (eds.), *Ethik und Praxis des Helfens in verschiedenen Religionen* [Ethics and Practice of Helping in Different Religions], 2005; H. Weiß, K. Federschmidt and K. Temme (eds.), *Handbuch Interreligiöse Seelsorge* [Handbook on Inter-Religious Pastoral Care and Counselling], 2010; all books published by Neukirchener Verlag, Neukirchen-Vluyn.

As is appropriate for an intercultural publication, the styles of language in the different contributions show the different backgrounds of the authors. The style of bibliographical references in the footnotes was unified, in order to assist readers who do further research. All references to internet resources have been checked and, if necessary and possible, have been updated.

As any selection remains arbitrary to some extent, we want to give thanks also to all those colleagues and co-workers, who have valuably contributed to SIPCC without being explicitly present in this book.

Especially we want to acknowledge the input and insight of the following members of SIPCC for their assistance in the editorial process: Dr. Dominiek Lootens, Belgium, who helped reviewing essays and was willing to scrutinise the final document; Prof. Dr. Kathleen Greider, USA, who helped clarifying communications and translations in a number of essays; Prof. Dr. Solomon Victus, India, and Prof. Dr. Martin Walton, Netherlands, who offered their consultation in the setup phase.

Karl Federschmidt and Daniël Louw

August 2015

Relationship in Difference: The SIPCC as a Learning Community

Helmut Weiß
Germany, 2015

Abstract: The article aims to summarise essential features of intercultural and inter-religious learning based on the 20-year history of the association *Gesellschaft für Interkulturelle Seelsorge und Beratung - Society for Intercultural Pastoral Care and Counselling (SIPCC)*. Interpersonal encounter is presented as the most important way of learning. Intercultural and inter-religious encounters challenge us to develop a hermeneutics, formulated here as "relationship in difference" and "translational work". Through various kinds of SIPCC meetings and processes of understanding the skills for intercultural and inter-religious care and counselling are enhanced. SIPCC is described as an "open space" where these skills and competences can be developed.

Introduction

When on 17 October 1995 56 people from several countries around the world formed the *Gesellschaft für Interkulturelle Seelsorge und Beratung – Society for Intercultural Pastoral Care and Counselling (SIPCC)* as a legal association in Düsseldorf, the combination of "intercultural" and "counselling" was a novelty in Germany. Many other adjectives were set in combination with care and counselling: kerygmatic (preaching); therapeutic (healing); pastoral psychological; feminist; Biblical and others. Care and counselling were connected to depth psychology, human sciences and sociology, but what they might have to do with culture or interculturalism, had hitherto been hardly considered.

In other disciplines it was different: education, social work, economics were talking of "inter-culture". In other countries colleagues were dealing with "cross-cultural counselling", e.g. in the United States. But in Germany and other European countries the question was raised, "Why should we bring together culture and pastoral care?" Culture might be the business for missiology, but not for counselling. And the 56 people who included "intercultural pastoral care" in the name of this new association could vaguely explain what was meant and where the road would go with this society. But they were sure that pastoral care must be seen in the context of different cultures. For one thing was clear: the respective cultural environment determines people's lives to a great extent – and therefore also pastoral work. Beside the inner dynamics that are at the core of pastoral care oriented toward psychology and therapy, the "external dynamics" of the cultural (and therefore social, political and economic) environment has to be recognised and understood in caring and counselling encounters with people.

Today, 20 years later, the situation is completely different. Almost every aspect of life in our multicultural world has to be viewed *inter-culturally* and that is so for care and counselling too. This is a development not only in the so-called "advanced" countries of the "western" hemisphere, but all over the world in varying degrees. Everywhere the knowledge of diversity of cultures and religions grows, as part of the improvement in modern communication. Care and counselling cannot negate these phenomena. Care and counselling must learn anew to understand the culturally influenced life-situations of people and to deal with various "cultures of care and counselling", that is, with the diversity of concepts and practices of care and counselling.

In 1995 it did not come into our minds to put into the name of our association "intercultural and *inter-religious* care and counselling". Only through an intensive examination of inter-culturality did we become more and more aware that the diversity of cultures and the diversity of religions are mutually dependent. Therefore the editors of the first SIPCC book in German, *Handbuch Interkulturelle Seelsorge* (Handbook of Intercultural Pastoral Care and Counselling), published in 2002, wrote in the introduction: "We want to say that there is a desideratum in this book – meaning a separate thematic treatment of inter-religious aspects of our subject. Intercultural encounters are often simultaneously inter-religious encounters, and the question of different 'pastoral cultures' could also be extended to the question of forms and traditions of pastoral care outside the Christian range of culture and religion." [1]

In SIPCC we speak now of "intercultural and inter-religious care and counselling" with one breath, and we see that they are closely related and depend on each other, without being identical.

In the last two decades, a lot has happened in the field of intercultural and inter-religious learning. It is interesting to examine these developments and to explain them not only for care and counselling but for social

---

[1] K. Federschmidt, „Introduction", in: K. Federschmidt, E. Hauschildt, Chr. Schneider-Harpprecht, K. Temme and H. Weiß (eds.), *Handbuch Interkulturelle Seelsorge,* Neukirchen-Vluyn: Neukirchener Verlag, 2002, 14.

activities and the living together in diverse societies. To illustrate these processes, allow me to present key findings within SIPCC.

SIPCC – an open space for encounters and relationships

Encounter as a basis for intercultural and inter-religious learning

SIPCC is an association which creates and designs "open spaces" in which interaction among people from different countries, cultures and religions can take place in order to promote learning of intercultural and inter-religious care and counselling. In the already mentioned "Handbook of Intercultural Care and Counselling", I wrote an article "The Discovery of Intercultural Care and Counselling" describing the pathway from internationality to inter-culturality.[2] Already between 1986 and 1995 we had International Seminars with people from East and West, North and South, as well as rich and poor countries. Those were times of world conflicts between capitalism and communism, the time of the danger of war and the peace movement in Europe, the time of the so-called *Conciliar Process for Justice, Peace and Integrity of Creation* – a strong movement in Eastern and Western Europe. During that time many connections and relationships started through SIPCC, and the conviction was growing that they have meaning and importance for our common work in care and counselling. Through the foundation of SIPCC as a legal body these connections became stronger: members took responsibility to involve themselves in this movement.

In the many years of the activities of SIPCC in several countries of the world, these relationships have continued and new encounters with new groups have arisen. There are now about 280 members from 35 countries, participants are both practitioners and educators, and there are people from different professions; there are not only Christian members of various sorts, but also Jews and Muslims as members and participants. SIPCC is trying to be international, intercultural, inter-religious and interdisciplinary.

This principle of promoting encounter and exchanges is featured in all the activities of SIPCC: not only the previously mentioned International Seminars (in 2015 we shall conduct the 27th)[3] but also other meetings and conferences, study tours and training courses. SIPCC has done such training courses in Hungary, Romania, Indonesia, Slovakia, Poland, Tanzania and Germany (a course in Islamic pastoral care in hospitals). Additional courses are planned for the future.[4]

---

[2] H. Weiß, "Die Entdeckung Interkultureller Seelsorge", ibid., 17-37.

[3] Cf. the list of these seminars in the appendix of this book.

[4] For the activities of SIPCC, see http://www.sipcc.org.

In SIPCC, *personal encounters* are understood as *the* basis for dealing with intercultural and inter-religious issues. Encounters challenge and stimulate new ways to deal personally and professionally with foreigners and otherness in a sensitive, understanding and open way. Encounters enable us to see people in a differentiated manner, to enjoy this diversity, to offer more respect, value and dignity. Personally, I find that I am strengthened in my faith by realising that God is showing himself in the many faces and acts of humanity in our world. The encounters with people from other cultures and religions are often joyful as we experience each other, though sometimes it can be painful and hurtful, for such conversation discloses our limitations – so enabling us to learn humility and modesty.

Intercultural and inter-religious encounters become alive in *storytelling:* the meetings have a narrative feature and character. People meet each other and they begin to share. And in sharing they give each other a part of their own life. In this exchange, cultural characteristics immediately stand out. By sharing with people from other cultures and religions, one realises that in communicating with others, "understanding" cannot be taken for granted. One is invited to pause, to reflect and to think about the assumptions and conditions of myself and of my counterpart. As we experience that both of us start at different points, we question ourselves and others.

Intercultural and inter-religious encounters become alive by *becoming open for questions*. How does the other person live? Why does she/he live this way? How does he/she manage his/her everyday life? What makes him/her happy? What drives him/her to behave in such a way? What questions can I ask without embarrassing her/him? What can he/she understand when I tell him/her about myself? In being open for questions I show my interest, but by asking questions I expose myself to others and at the same time I show my borders and limitations.

There are many ways to learn about other cultures and religions and to move into their worlds. One can study them, read about them and acquire knowledge about them, so to speak, one can learn by looking and observing from the outside – without personal involvement. But it is different to encounter "*living human documents*" of cultures and religions and to experience life and faith in an unmediated and direct contact with people. When we engage in a personal encounter, intercultural and inter-religious learning has a direct, even a physical and bodily basis – and that has a lasting effect. The *inter-subjective encounter* can be described as the "royal way" of learning about other religions and cultures. If members of different religions meet on an equal level and live together as community for a while, memorable and sustainable cultural and religious learning occurs. In a dialogue of humans, mutual strangeness is breaking up, they become more and more open to challenge each other, fear is vanishing, and conflicts can be solved. In the meetings of SIPCC, people of different cultures and religions perform a "*dialogue of life*" where people are of equal worth and dignity and still keep their differences.

This principle that intercultural and inter-religious learning needs personal encounter as a basis has been used by SIPCC from the beginning and continues today. In order that a *dialogue of life* can take place, most SIPCC events are planned and carried out over five or more days so that the participants have the opportunity to live together and share over some time.

Personal and institutional relationships for intercultural and inter-religious learning

If encounters become significant, they leave an impression in memory, so relationships grow. The more people open themselves and share with each other, the less they fear each other. Strangeness may continue – but it does not frighten or bother so much as it did before. There might be a lot I cannot agree with – but the difference does not prevent the strengthening of the relationship. An emotional bond of perpetual mutual discovery can be created.

Again and again I have been impressed that through these new relationships, I perceive with fresh eyes what happens in the world. After getting to know a person from another country, news from that part of the world takes on a different quality for me. The events there – far away – come much closer, have a "face", and become connected to specific persons. When in February 2015 a colleague from Eastern Ukraine in Morning Prayer at a conference prayed for peace, the bitter struggles and conflicts far away came much closer than even when I watch TV and see the fighting. When a Lutheran Pastor from Palestine presented in an international seminar his pastoral work with Christians and Muslims, the conflicts in the Middle East gained a different "taste" than that given by a television report of a few minutes. When in 2012 we organized a SIPCC Seminar in Tanzania with the theme *Caring for Creation - Caring for People: Climate Changes and Natural Disasters as Challenges for Care and Counselling* and the participants travelled for hours by bus through the parched land, then the problem of global warming becomes a more personal challenge to each one of us. When participants sit in a Seminar in Mainz in the New Synagogue, and admire that beautiful building and hear about the fate of the Jewish community there through many centuries, the question of inter-religious dialogue is much more urgent than when we meet in "theological circles" and discuss at an intellectual level.

In immediate personal – physical and bodily – encounter, relationships are formed that are inescapable. They set the life and the surrounding of persons in a new light. Intercultural and inter-religious learning needs this incarnational (born into) "corporality" so that encounters and relationships take place not only on an abstract and intellectual level, but in a physical, sensory, and emotional manner. SIPCC offers safe and open spaces for such relationships and for learning processes of care and counselling in an intercultural and inter-religious framework.

Our association conducts all events in cooperation with other institutions and agencies. As an example: the annual International Seminars take place each year at diverse locations (2009 Israel, 2010 France, 2011 Hamburg, Germany, 2012 Tanzania; 2013 Mainz, Germany; 2014 Netherlands, 2015 Poland) with organizations from that country. We want to build up relationships on institutional levels too and to enhance the learning of institutions. Preparations with these organisations mean sharing and crossing structural boundaries without abandoning our respective institutional identities. These processes between organisations offer many opportunities of intercultural and inter-religious exchange and dialogue. But in SIPCC we always have a common interest and goal: to enhance care and counselling and to become aware of and engage to the needs of the people. We orient ourselves in our cooperation to a "third reference point" outside of ourselves and the respective organisations: people in need. They are our common objective.

Not only as individuals, but also as a Society we want to learn. That is why we have set up what we call a Study Group and a Research Network to reflect on and develop this common institutional learning. At the same time, we offer our experience and expertise to other institutions. The collaboration is usually done without much difficulty, but sometimes conflicts may show up. They can begin with language differences (for example, different understanding of "Seelsorge", "cure of souls" and "spiritual care"), different ideas about the title of the seminar, or how the social and political specificities in different countries can be taken into account (for example, differences between pastoral activity in hospitals in the Netherlands as compared to Germany). This raises again the question of how we can work together with all the existing institutional differences and interests and how we can foster communal learning.

Areas of learning

In intercultural and inter-religious context – in personal and institutional encounters and relationships, but also in intercultural and inter-religious care and counselling – we have to adapt to new perspectives on a wide range of topics. From the experience of our activities in the SIPCC, we have learned that many issues are at stake: language, family, gender roles, authority, power, work and economic conditions, violence, values, religion, health and disease, to name only a few. All of these issues are closely tied to specific cultural and religious meanings; there is a great variety how these terms can be understood and these different understandings must be discovered and explained in conversations. All of these words are complex in meaning, and that is marked by the context. Only in context are words spoken and and only through the context do words become fully alive. Out of these many areas of learning I would like to give a short outline of just three examples: Language – Family – Religion.

Language

Language is not the only one, but an essential element of interpersonal communication. Again and again it is necessary to reflect the on linguistic issues in communication. This is even more urgent when people of different cultures and religions meet and have to speak in foreign languages. All who have to speak in foreign languages know that translation is an art form that succeeds more or less. Present day needs for understanding have improved the effectiveness of translation. But still: what are we talking about when we use certain words? Does the equivalent in the other language – and sometimes there is none – really match or does it transport a foreign "world"? What images do certain words produce in speaker and hearer, if they come from different linguistic and cultural contexts? Are the images compatible in speaker and listener? In SIPCC meetings we operate mostly in two languages, and it is interesting to observe the linguistic misunderstandings and how they affect the emotions. Many times it happens that misunderstandings do not originate through errors in translation, but from different interpretations of terms in the other language. Language is not static, it moves.

As in care and counselling listening plays a major role in intercultural and inter-religious exchange. Both sides have to have the chance to express themselves, and tell their stories from different sides until the listener gets the impression of coming close to the meaning of the words. And the speakers have to direct themselves to the listeners; they have to stay in contact to them, relating to them. That is a good exercise and needs a lot of patience.

Family

Human beings like most animals start their life in families – and they live in one or another form through their whole life in families. But there are different family models shaped by culture and living conditions that make it difficult simply to talk about *the* family. When people from India, Africa or the United States are speaking about "my family," what is on their mind? When Turkish patients in a German hospital expect the visit of "the family," who will come? When a German patient in the hospital is telling the chaplain that he has good relationships to "his family," whom does he include? Care and counselling with people from our own, but especially from other, cultures have to understand the respective family structures of people to understand the person: how she or he is living in community, who is sustaining him or her not only emotionally but economically and spiritually. Of course, there is the possibility that certain family structures are poisonous and destructive, that traditional structures have become outdated, and care and counselling has to deal with that too. Quite often counselling an individual is at the same time a sort of family counselling. And family counselling in different contexts has to take many different forms and methods. Systemic and intercultural approaches are supporting each other in care and counselling.

Religion
When you meet people from other religions, you will encounter persons with convictions that are essential to them and part of their identity. For religious people, these beliefs are ultimate truths that are non-negotiable. How can we converse on religion and deep conviction when people hold theirs as fundamental? You can inform each other about your faith, but for most it is what is done that shows "faith". It is very valuable to exchange information about our own religion, the contents, rituals, ethical standards and the everyday practices and how all of that was formed through tradition and how it can be understood today. But it would still be talking "about". To go into a personal encounter about religion and truth means to share with others one's own spiritual life, with all its joys and doubts, opening one's own heart intimately, sharing confidence and hope, unrest and despair. We could share how faith shapes our lives. We could show what role religion plays in our personal biography, how it has become a resource for life and the points where we struggle with religious traditions. Such exchange not only requires mutual respect for the religious experiences of the other, but mutual appreciation. This is not easy because religious truths always have a claim of "personal certainty". Certainty is not meant as an ultimate "security" in oneself. Certainty and confidence is formed in dialogue and in relation to the "ultimate reality" of each religion, that is, in relation to what concerns us ultimately. These certainties become "truths" only in relationship. If truths, certainties, confidence and claims of ultimate concerns (even if we call them divine) are perceived as expression of relationships to our "ultimate reality", they can become fruitful for inter-religious communication.

SIPCC – an open space for the development of a hermeneutics of intercultural and inter-religious care and counselling

The encounters of different people with their life and faith stories, with their beliefs and cultural and religious influences, always develop a dynamic that can be full of strangeness, tension, surprise, pain and blissful togetherness. Encounters in this – especially emotional – diversity with openness and respect are often accompanied with uncertainty and in some cases even with unconscious harm. It is therefore necessary to reflect again and again on the processes of encountering. They require an intercultural and inter-religious hermeneutics. During the many meetings and discussions in SIPCC we have found this to be a key question to understand what is going on in encounters with others: how can we, being strange to each other, go into relation? How can relationship take place in difference? Our answer: in each situation of encountering, we have to build up "relationship in difference". We have to start with recognizing that we are Others to each other. From there we can try to come closer to each other emotionally or in finding a common third point to which we can relate together. Schleiermacher (the theologian and translator of Greek philosophers) said: normally we misunderstand each other, because we come from another "world", and we have to bring these worlds into a dialogue to come closer to each other.

In SIPCC we are offering open spaces for this "translation work": to learn to "read" the signs and the communication of others and to search for their meaning – despite diversity. Intercultural and inter-religious encounters clearly reveal what is constitutive of all work in care and counselling, namely, to become open to others and to meet them with one's own personal being. This hermeneutical principle of *difference in relationship* provides an important clue for human encounter and caring action. SIPCC offers learning experiences in many forms: International Seminars and other conferences, study trips and courses and through reflecting on our experiences in a variety of publications.[5] In order to promote intercultural and inter-religious learning and to develop the hermeneutics and theory building in our field, as mentioned earlier, we have established a Study Group for enhancing the processes in our meetings and a Research Network to do interdisciplinary research on intercultural and inter-religious care and counselling.

Understanding culture

When we talk about "culture" and "religion," some explanation is needed regarding what these terms mean in our context, since both are understood in many ways. For care and counselling and for communication it seems to me that the description of Clifford Geertz, a U.S. anthropologist and ethnologist, is very helpful. He states that *cultures* are "networks of

[5] See http://www.sipcc.org/publikationen&tl=en.

meanings".[6] Without these networks of meaning, people remain animals, because we need guidance and control mechanisms for our behaviour, which are not genetically given to us as they are to animals.[7] Humans "spin a web of meaning" to communicate and to have orientation to appropriate behaviour.[8] Culture as a system of signs and symbols and as a net of meaning is continuously changing. A continuous discourse has to go on about meaning under ever-changing circumstances. Since the circumstances are different from person to person, from country to country, from tradition to tradition and so on, the search for meaning is an intercultural search in all fields of life: we have to go into relationship with others to listen to their expressions and needs and to tell them what we need ourselves. "Culture as network" means: being with others, being in communion and taking responsibility for social developments.

Intercultural hermeneutics understands the expressions (words, gestures, behaviour, etc.) of others not only as individual expression, but as embedded into a collective "sign system", which he/she shares with some others and which has become a "second nature". But at the same time his/her expressions have to be taken individually and even if they can be understood by all humans to some extent. The "system of signs" always includes different levels and is plural in itself. Even my own expressions are to be understood as a system of signs that is ambiguous and plural. In intercultural communication we encounter diverse complex "worlds" that can only be understood when we reflect on them and go into communication with them.

Understanding of religion

Religion can be viewed as a particular "culture", as "socially established structures of meaning". However, culture and religion have to be distinguished. The theologian *Gerd Theißen* helps us to understand the difference when he writes: "Religion is a cultural system of signs that promises

---

[6] Cf. C. Geertz, *The Interpretation of Cultures: Selected Essays*, New York: Basic Books, 1973, 5: "Believing, with Max Weber, that man is an animal suspended in webs of significance he himself has spun, I take culture to be those webs." And on page 12: "Culture consists of socially established structures of meaning."

[7] Ibid., 49: "Without men, no culture, certainly; but equally, and more significantly, without culture, no men."

[8] Ibid., 44: "Culture is best seen not as complexes of concrete behavior patterns – customs, usages, traditions, habit clusters – as has, by and large, been the case up to now, but as a set of control mechanisms – plans, recipes, rules, instructions (what computer engineers call 'programs') – for the governing of behavior... Man is precisely the animal most desperately dependent upon such extra-genetic, outside-the-skin control mechanisms, such cultural programs, for ordering behavior."

fulfilment of life by correspondence to an ultimate reality."[9] He continues: "What is so special about the religious system of signs? It can be characterised as a combination of three forms of expression that are coming together only in religion: myth, ritual and ethics."[10] However, religion is not fixed, but is formed in living myth, ritual and ethics. Every religion is based on basic stories, rituals and practice of behaviour, but religion becomes meaningless when it is not "practiced". Religion is an interpretation of reality and life that helps us to reflect on the significance of our daily lives, provides an overall context and supplies meaning and purpose. If we accept this understanding of religion, we discover that pastoral care is a form of religious communication: it strives to bring to everyday reality of life the context of the "ultimate reality" – in Christian terms: to connect life with God, who revealed himself to us in Jesus Christ.

Steps of understanding in intercultural and inter-religious communication

Intercultural and inter-religious communications indicate complex dynamics in the encounter between people of different cultural and religious systems. To promote cultural and religious understanding in all difference, I propose the following steps:

a) sharing stories of our *existential situations* (i.e. not talking that is detached from the reality of life, but understanding such existential situations as a starting point for encounter;

b) exploring *cultural and religious interpretations* of these situations and the meaning of them;

c) reflecting on the *background of these interpretations* (this includes addressing the cultural and religious traditions and resources and dialogue with the "fathers, mothers, brothers and sisters" who are involved);

d) *verifying* what interpretations are currently applicable to the situations described (reality check);

e) if needed, looking for new, *more helpful interpretations*;

f) listening to *how people from different religious* and cultural traditions interpret the situation;

g) entering with them into an *open conversation*, even if the interpretations are controversial.

In such processes, relationship takes place – even if differences and misunderstandings remain.

---

[9] G. Theißen, *Die Religion der ersten Christen*, 4th ed., Gütersloh: Gütersloher Verlagshaus, 2008, 19. (Revised and expanded version of G. Theißen, *A Theory of Primitive Christian Religion*, London: SCM, 1999).
[10] Ibid., 21.

SIPCC – a learning experience in intercultural and inter-religious competence

The activities of SIPCC enhance intercultural and inter-religious competencies. Emotional, rational and spiritual learning grows through encounters, reflections and understanding the interpersonal dynamics of people who are different from ourselves. The aim is to teach identity and relatedness as basic means of care and counselling and living together in societies. Personal and spiritual confidence and trust of oneself and the appreciation of cultural and religious convictions of others come together. In an open discourse, changes and learning become possible.

To improve intercultural and inter-religious competencies means learning how to deal with the familiar and foreign, with individual and cultural weaknesses, with regressive and sometimes aggressive impulses in dealing with strangers and what is strange to us. It is about unbearable feelings of powerlessness, fear of failure, hurts and pain in oneself and in others and, if possible, to use the crises experienced in encounters with others in productive and creative ways. Crises, uncertainty and helplessness can be understood as a challenge and an opportunity of understanding and relationship. Communication becomes sensitive to intimacy and distance, to closeness and defence and to understanding and not understanding. All persons involved in intercultural and inter-religious situations can reasonably be expected to remain in conversation, even if it runs on different levels of interaction and communication. When faults occur, they do not revoke either the conversation or the relationship; if we keep talking and relating,, it is possible to make the disorder itself the subject of communication. This may create a joint effort that aims to bring the process to a mutual understanding again. The aim of SIPCC is to reinforce such abilities and make them useful for care and counselling.

Summary

SIPCC understands itself as a *"learning community"*. Our association sees its task as helping people to develop their cultural and religious identity and to relate to people with identities different from our own. In an open and at the same time protected space people may experiment in dealing with others, may learn and test themselves. It is important that others may remain different from us, they do not have to adapt and to resign - and yet those others may change in the exchange with us. In this way, diversity is lived, the exercise of power is reduced and togetherness is strengthened. Differences can be seen, endured and appreciated. At the same time, it is important to seek understanding and interpersonal similarities, to show that people are equal in dignity and share valuable experiences. Thus, integration and inclusion can be learned and the cohesion of societies promoted.

The learning community focuses its activities on *care and counselling*: Concern for people in their concrete life is the connecting reference point. The specific living conditions of people form the fundamental point of reference, which helps us not to circle around ourselves but see what is going on "outside". Concern for others becomes the common task. The perception of the respective contexts of people and their impact on the physical and psychological conditions of those people are essential in order to go into relationship and to be helpful to them. Intercultural and interfaith care and counselling is learning with concrete people and their specific needs, difficulties, problems – and joys.

Through including cultural, religious, economic, social and historical contexts, *care and counselling becomes a socially relevant activity* and reinforces learning in civil responsibility and participation.

Inter-religious and intercultural care and counselling is *learning in spirituality*. It occurs in relation to an "ultimate reality" that can be named and believed in differently, but can be seen as a creative force that seeks and donates confidence in life. Caring for people is connected with this ultimate reality in practice and its spiritual and theological grounding. This leads to realising one's own human limitations and to humbleness towards the power that "is greater than ourselves" and to the people who seek help and give help.

Part A

Towards a Hermeneutical Approach to Pastoral Caregiving in Intercultural Perspective

Intercultural Exchange: A Discovery of Being Different *

Julian Müller
South Africa, 1996

Personal experience as a South African

The earliest story of my life that I can remember is a birthday story. It must have been either my third or fourth birthday, I am not sure. On that birthday I received as birthday present from my parents a box with a few toy cars in it. I remember that I was overjoyed and that my first intention was to show this wonderful present to my best friend. We lived on a farm and my best and only playmate at the time was Daniel, a black boy, a little older than me. He and his parents lived on the farm and they were our servants. So, I ran outside to show my present to Daniel. I remember that he was sitting on a little bench in a room in the backyard. Proudly I showed him the cars. He looked and admired, and then after a while, chose the two most beautiful ones and gently pushed them on their wheels, underneath his bench, backwards. With this act, he said to me without words: "I'll take these, thank you!" The rest I do not really remember. There must have been a commotion, but I got my cars back. Perhaps my parents intervened. The fact is that I got the cars back.

This is a personal little story from my childhood and I would like to use it as a basis of reflection on the South African society.

1. The story of South Africa is one of involvement and even enmeshment of black and white people. Like the little boy who ran to share his birthday joy with his best friend, most people in South Africa would be able to tell stories of how they shared moments of joy and sorrow with someone of another race.

Black and white South Africa don't exist as two completely separated and isolated worlds. Although the apartheid policy was a form of social

---

* Lecture presented at the 10th International Seminar on Intercultural Pastoral Care and Counselling, 1996, in Ustroń, Poland. Published in *Intercultural Pastoral Care and Counselling*, 2, 1997, 4-8.

engineering which forced people apart in different neighbourhoods, different schools, different churches, etc., it couldn't stop people's involvement with each other. Economical realities forced people towards each other, at least in the work situation. And today South Africa is very rapidly changing towards a totally integrated society – a process which started gradually long before the laws of segregation were repealed.

2. A second point of reflection on my childhood story: As in Daniel and my relationship, most South Africans grew up with definitive and even rigid role distinctions and expectations. Although Daniel was my friend, he knew and I knew that he was the servant and I was the boss. And because of historical reasons all the bosses are white and all servants are black in the South African community. Therefore we grew up with the stereotype that a person's colour equals his/her value and status in society. When people are framed into these roles because of stereotypes which developed in our minds from childhood, one cannot easily get rid of such presuppositions. I must admit that within the South African context, it is up to this day not easy for me not to put myself in the boss-role when communicating with a black person. I think that I and many other South Africans try hard, but find it still an effort, a struggle to become free from the roles inflicted on us through our upbringing.

3. These are structures of society with a long history. The roles into which Daniel and myself fitted so easily from childhood, were the inheritance of generations before us and the way in which they structured society. The way in which the South African society developed was not the result of a criminal government which one day sat down and made a list of vicious laws. It developed through centuries and what the Nationalist government wrote in the law books from 1948, was only the legalising of social practice through many years. The development of this legalisation process represents indeed the deepest point of inhuman and unchristian discriminatory practices. But the fact is that it is deeply rooted in the history of our community.

4. This story represents most probably also a difference between the African and Western experience of personal property. According to the western capitalistic mind, personal belongings and property are individualistically earned. The African, on the other hand, has primarily a communalistic mind. The riches which were developed on African soil by western industries and capital, are seen as the corporate riches of all the people. Prosperity and poverty must be shared by all. That is why issues such as the private ownership of land and the rights of inhabitant workers on farms are the most difficult ones to handle in the negotiation processes.

It is against this background of personal bias, a history of social injustices, and conflicting cultural expectations in the South African context, that I would like to try and contribute to the development of theory which can be of value in our praxis of intercultural interaction, especially in the field of pastoral family therapy.

Approaches to culture in the social sciences and in family therapy

In recent literature, a number of different possible approaches to intercultural therapy were described:

The essentialist view: According to this view[1] cultural differences are considered to be much like other differences, i.e. differences based on gender and age. Culture is seen as an overwhelming influence which determines the individual's behaviour and thought. According to this view, the individual does not really operate as an agent constructing and making choices about his/her own life.

The essentialist definition of culture would have us think about culture as one great organism in which all parts are connected to all other parts. You have to take either the whole lot or none of it, for only in this way could culture have the iron hold on individuals required to form and mould their bodies and their minds. If, however, we combine a generative notion of culture with an interactive one then it becomes possible not only to consider some cultural differences more important than others but also to talk about them cross-culturally.[2]

The universalistic view: The universalist approach[3] takes the position that persons and families of different cultures are more alike than different. This school of thought argues that there are basic similarities which are to be found in all cultures, for instance the concept that all children need love and discipline and that parenting always involves a combination of nurturing and control.

The problem with this view is that the perception of what is considered to be normative, may be local knowledge or beliefs based on a certain cultural experience. It also follows that adherents of this position have little use for training in cultural differences.

---

[1] I. Krause, "Personhood, Culture and Family Therapy", in *Journal of Family Therapy, 17,* 1995, 363-382.
[2] Ibid., 365f.
[3] C.J. Falicov, "Training to Think Culturally: A Multidimensional Comparative Framework", in *Family Process, 34,* December 1995, 373-388, see p. 373.

The particularistic view: This position is the opposite of the universalistic one. According to this approach persons and families of different cultures are more different than alike and no generalisations are possible. The uniqueness of each family is stressed and often idiosyncrasies of a certain family are referred to as "a culture unto itself". As was said by Falicov: "In the particularist position, then, the word *culture* is tied to the internal beliefs of each particular family rather than to the connection between the family and the broader sociocultural context."[4]

As is the case with the universalist view, this approach also doesn't regard cultural training as very important, because the family's interior, which is always unique, is held solely responsible for all of the family's distress. In discussing this view, Inga-Britt Krause calls it: culture as an idiom of differences. The popular use of the word "culture" shows a preoccupation with diversity, choice and identity. "Culture becomes an idiom for the expression of all kinds of individual differences and appears to encompass everything." [5]

The ethnic-focused approach: According to this position families differ, but the diversity is primarily due to the factor of ethnicity.[6] The focus here is on thought patterns, behaviours, feelings, customs, and rituals that stem from belonging to a particular cultural group. This school of thought would see culture as a symbolic expression, and "a symbol is some form of fixed sensory sign to which meanings has been arbitrarily attached. Persons within a cultural tradition share common understandings. Those outside this symbol system take great risks in inferring the meanings of symbols from the outside of their own system."[7]

In this position there is a real danger in oversystematising and stereotyping the notion of shared meanings. It might be assumed that ethno-groupings are more homogeneous and stable than they actually are. We are actually talking here of an epistemological error: "...clients are seen as their culture, not as themselves." Bateson warns also that "The map is not the territory, and the name is not the thing named."[8]

Ethnic values and identity are influenced by various factors. There are variables within the group (education, social class, religion, etc.) and then there are the phenomena of cultural evolution and the effect of influences

---

[4] Ibid., 374.

[5] Krause, "Personhood", 364.

[6] Falicov, "Training", 374.

[7] D.W. Augsburger, *Pastoral Counseling Across Cultures*, Philadelphia: Westminster Press, 1986, 61.

[8] G. Bateson, *Mind and Nature: A Necessary Unity*, New York: E.P. Dutton, 1979, 30.

stimulated by contact with the dominant culture. Perhaps the most important limitation is the assumption that the observer, the person who describes the other culture, can be objective and has no effect on the conclusions being made about the group observed.

A narrative approach to intercultural pastoral therapy

Over and against these four approaches, I want to propose the narrative model of intercultural understanding and communication. The narrative approach implies that the therapist places him or herself in a not-knowing position. And that position calls for "...a kind of conversational questioning that leaves room for the client's story as told by the client in the client's own words, unchallenged by preconceived therapeutic knowing."[9] "The process of therapy is not to reveal the truth or to impose a reality, but to explore through conversation, through languaging, realities that are compatible with a particular client's unique tendency to attribute meaning and explanation in his or her own life."[10]

In spite of the well intended and well phrased theories introduced by Augsburger in his good book, concepts like *interpathy* and *transspection*[11] are too much coloured by a knowing position and do not reveal the same epistemological position to be found in the not-knowing position of the narrative approach. The idea that a therapist is capable of moving over to persons of the other culture in a process of transspection, is already arrogant and knowing. It reveals something of an asymmetrical communication, of a messianic role instead of a partnership role. It consists of a movement initiated form here to there, while the narrative approach wants to experience the sensation of being drawn into the other's world, of being drawn over the threshold of a cultural difference.

The narrative approach to therapy is clearly and in detail described by authors like Anderson and Goolishian and Michael White.[12] Anderson and

---

[9] G.E. Boyd, "Pastoral Conversation: A Social Construction View", in *Pastoral Psychology, Vol. 44 No. 4*, 1996, 215-225, see p. 220.

[10] H.A. Goolishian and H. Anderson, "Language Systems and Therapy: An Evolving Idea", in *Journal of Pschotherapy, 24*, 1987, 529-538, see p. 536.

[11] "Transspection is an effort to put oneself into the head (not shoes) of another person... Transspection differs from analytical 'understanding.' Transspection differs also from 'empathy.' Empathy is a projection of feelings between two persons with one epistemology. Transspection is a trans-epistemological process which tries to *experience* a foreign belief, a foreign assumption, a foreign perspective, feelings in a foreign context, and consequences of feelings in a foreign context, as if these have become one's own." Maruyama et al., quoted by Augsburger, *Pastoral Counseling*, 30.

[12] H. Anderson and H. Goolishian, "Human Systems as Linguistic Systems: Preliminary and Evolving Ideas About the Implications for Clinical Theory", in

Goolishian describe the therapeutic conversation as "...a slowly evolving and detailed, concrete, individual life story stimulated by the therapist's position of not-knowing and the therapist's curiosity to learn." [13] Seen from this point of view, intercultural therapy seems no longer a complex and rather impossible task, as long as the therapist is honestly willing to learn from the person from the other culture. "The kenotic pattern of Philippians 2:25ff describes the Christ-conversation and makes clear that our position must be one of service rather than domination or social control. A stance of agape-listening places the pastoral conversation in the realm of mutual co-authoring of a new story for the one in need of healing by valuing the unique reality of the other while continually striving for a stance of openness and humility."[14]

The "tools" which fit this approach to therapy are: responsive-active listening; a not-knowing position; conversational questions. The aim, as in all therapy, is change, but change within this perspective can be defined as "...the evolution of new meaning, new narrative identity, and new self-agency."[15] The narrative approach has a capacity to "re-relate" events in the context of new meaning. We can refer to this kind of therapy as "being in language".[16]

When working in this school of thought, it becomes increasingly difficult to view culture on the basis of the previously mentioned approaches. Culture must be seen as a much more immediate and ongoing process and not as something static which is handed down unaltered from generation to generation. The broad definition which Falicov gives, is perhaps one which fits into this paradigm: "...those sets of shared world views, meanings and adaptive behaviours derived from simultaneous membership and participation in a multiplicity of contexts, such as rural, urban or suburban setting; language, age, gender, cohort, family configuration, race, ethnicity, religion, nationality, socioeconomic status, employment, education, occupation, sexual orientation, political ideology; migration and stage of acculturation." [17]

When the combinations of "simultaneous memberships" and "participation in multiple contexts" are seriously taken into account, the groups that emerge are much more "fluid, unpredictable and shifting, than the groups defined by using an ethnic-focused approach."[18] It thus becomes much

---

Family Process, Vol. 27 No. 4, 1988, 371-393; M. White, *Re-authoring Lives: Interviews and Essays*, Adelaide: Dulwich Centre Publications, 1995.

[13] According to Boyd, "Pastoral Conversation", 221.

[14] Ibid.

[15] Ibid., 220.

[16] Anderson and Goolishian, "Human Systems", 377, use concepts like "language", "in language", and "languaging" to refer to the process of the social creation of the intersubjective realities that we temporally share with each other.

[17] Falicov, "Training to Think Culturally", 375.

[18] Ibid., 376.

more difficult to make generalisations about culture groups and much more necessary to take on a not-knowing position.
In discussing the phenomena of cultures, cultural similarities and differences, Falicov refers to two important concepts:[19]

Cultural Borderlands, a concept which refers to the overlapping zones of difference and similarity within and between cultures. This gives rise to internal inconsistencies and conflicts. On the other hand, it is the borderlands that offer possibilities of connectedness. Falicov refers to the poet, Gloria Anzaldua who describes the "new mestiza" (a woman of mixed Indian and Spanish ancestry born in die USA): She "copes by developing a tolerance for ambiguity. She learns to be Indian in Mexican culture, to be Mexican from an Anglo point of view. She learns to juggle cultures. She has a plural personality."

Ecological Niche refers to the combination of multiple contexts and partial cultural locations. We can think of a family narrative which encompasses multiple contexts rather than a single label (Mormon, African, Afrikaner, Boer). The philosophy here is to emphasise large categories – a philosophy that supports inclusiveness and a diversified unity.

With these concepts in mind, I again want to strongly argue the not-knowing position of the narrative approach as the only acceptable approach in an intercultural therapeutic situation. I agree with the approach and words of Dyche and Zayas: "We argue that one should begin cross-cultural therapy with minimal assumptions, and that one way to learn about a culture is from the client. This argument seeks to balance the cognitive model of preparation with a process-oriented approach by exploring two therapist attitudes: cultural naiveté and respectful curiosity."[20]

The ideal is for therapists to be participant-observers. Rather than working with historically constructed descriptions only, the therapist should learn from a present and current cultural community.[21] As is shown by Goolishian and Anderson, all human systems are linguistic systems and are best being described from inside by those participating in it, than by so called objective observers.[22]

---

[19] Ibid.
[20] L. Dyche and L.H. Zayas, "The Value of Curiosity and Naiveté for the Cross-Cultural Psychotherapist", in *Family Process, 34*, 1995, 389-399, see p. 389.
[21] Falicov, "Training to Think Culturally", 385.
[22] H. Goolishian and H. Anderson, "Strategy and Intervention Versus Nonintervention: A Matter of Theory?", in *Journal of Marital and Family Therapy, 18*, 1992, 5-15.

Narrative pastoral counselling: a social constructionist approach

Narrative therapy can be described as the rewriting of history and autobiography.[23] And this rewriting takes place through the mutual conversational co-creation of new stories. This is a view of pastoral counselling which takes seriously our "radical embeddedness in history and language." "Such a view takes for granted the creative and creating power of language. In the Judeo-Christian tradition, the God who is active in history is also active in language. Consider the powerful *dhabar* of the Old Testament creation narratives and the *logos* of John's gospel and the early Church Fathers."[24]

To focus on conversation in this way directs our attention away from the inner dynamics of the individual psyche or events in the external world.[25] Instead, we are more free to be attentive to *words in their speaking*, words we create and by which we are created.

With reference to an article by Gergen, Boyd summarises the social construction orientation as follows:[26]

- what we take to be experience of the world does not in itself dictate the terms by which the world is understood,
- the terms in which the world is understood are social artifacts, produced of historically situated interchanges among people,
- the degree to which a given form of understanding prevails or is sustained across time is not fundamentally dependent on the empirical validity of the perspective in question, but on the vicissitudes of social processes (e.g., communication, negotiation, conflict, rhetoric), and
- forms of negotiated understanding are of critical significance in social life, as they are integrally connected with many other activities in which people engage.

To take a narrative approach is to look for a "negotiated understanding". When a new negotiated understanding is reached, a new narrative has been constructed. By taking this approach, culture is no longer seen as a determining factor, but as an interesting "borderland" from where new "ecological niches" can be developed. Then human beings become inventors of and inventions of culture. The prerequisite is of course that we take on the risks of the borderlands and give ourselves for intercultural interaction. As Augsburger puts it: "This change comes from encounter, contact, and interaction, not from programmic education or social engineering. It occurs on the boundary, not in the cultural enclave. ... The capacity not only to 'believe' the second culture but to come to understand it both

[23] Boyd, "Pastoral Conversation", 215.
[24] Ibid.
[25] Ibid., 216.
[26] Ibid., 218.

cognitively ('thinking with') and affectively ('feeling with') is necessary before one enters cross-cultural counselling."[27]

The way we interpret our world, the rights and wrongs of our life, the good and bad, are all products of our social (and therefore cultural) embeddedness. "There is no recounting of the history of a country ... apart from a narrative loaded with interpretations of interpretations which are by-products of human relationships."[28]

The South African context

Although things have changed much for the better during the past few years, the poem by a black South African, Oswald Mtshali, still describes the situation in our country:

WALLS

Man is
a great wall builder
The Berlin Wall
The Wailing Wall of Jerusalem
But the wall
most impregnable
Has a moat
flowing with fright
around his heart

A wall without windows
for the spirit to breeze through

A wall
without a door
for love to walk in.

Oswald Mtshali, Soweto poet

These walls of fear are part and parcel of the South African scene and history. The following story shows how in an ironic, but tragic way, it shapes our lives: "This is a parable of fear obscuring fear that occurred a long time ago, in a small town called Bulwer, in 1906 – the year of the Bambatha rebellion, the last Zulu uprising. Bulwer lay close to Zulu territory, and white farmers in the district feared the local Zulus might join Bambatha's rebel army and butcher their masters in bed. So the whites called a meeting and formulated a plan of action: if the Zulus rose, all

[27] Augsburger, *Pastoral Counseling*, 25-26.
[28] Boyd, "Pastoral Conversation", 218.

whites would rush to Bulwer and barricade themselves inside the stone courthouse.

A few days later, someone cried wolf, and the whites panicked. They loaded their guns and children onto wagons and abandoned their farms, leaving meals on the tables and leaving cows unmilked in the barns. They barricaded themselves inside the courthouse, loaded their guns, posted lookouts, and sat back to await the barbarians. By and by, they saw dust in the distance. Peering out through chinks in the barricade, the whites beheld a vision from their worst nightmares – a horde of Zulus approaching on foot. The crowd halted a few hundred yards away. A deputation detached itself and approached the courthouse. The Zulus knocked on the door. The wary whites opened a window, expecting to hear an ultimatum. Instead, the black men said 'Why have you forsaken us? We see there is a terrible danger coming, because our masters have fled into this fort, and we are frightened, for we don't know what it is. So we came to ask if we could also come inside, to be under the protection of our masters' guns.' "[29]

Stories like this one which tell of misunderstandings and fear between cultural groups in Africa are actually very common. Language and other cultural differences are part of our community. To communicate across these borders is not always easy, but it remains fascinating. For those among us who are willing to listen and willing to be drawn into the stories of others, new worlds of understanding emerge almost daily. The difficulties sometimes bring us to the verge of despair, but with a narrative, not-knowing attitude we can make growing progress in the "borderlands" and develop new "ecological niches" where being different can be experienced as the most fulfilling part of existence. This is the joy of becoming part of someone else's story – like it is to know the joy of fish in the story of the old Chinese philosopher Chuang Tzu:

Chuang Tzu and Hui Tzu were crossing Hao river by the dam.

Chuang said: "See how free The fishes leap and dart: That is their happiness."

Hui replied: "Since you are not a fish, how do you know what makes fishes happy?"

Chuang said: "Since you are not I, how can you possibly know that I do not know what makes fishes happy?"

Hui argued: "If I, not being you, cannot know what you know, it follows that you, not being a fish, cannot know what they know."

Chuang said: "Wait a minute! Let us get back to the original question. What you asked me was 'How do you know what makes fishes happy?' From the terms of your question you evidently knew I know what makes fishes happy. I know the joy of fishes in the river through my own joy, as I go walking along the same river." [30]

---

[29] R. Malan, *My Traitor's Heart*, London: The Bodley Head, 1990, 226.

[30] Quoted from p. 41 of R. Rosenbaum and J. Dyckman, "Integrating Self and System: An Empty Intersection?", in *Family Process, 34*, March 1995, 21-41.

Reflections on Intercultural Pastoral Caregiving and the Seminars of SIPCC *

Karl Federschmidt
Germany, 1997

Looking back on her experience in the realm of international conferences on pastoral care, Liesel-Lotte Herkenrath-Püschel who has done a lot by way of interconnecting various international pastoral care movements writes the following: "...when members from different systems try in earnest to reach mutual understanding it is inevitable that they hurt each other's feelings...; and naturally clashes between very close systems hurt the most." One feels so, because it is from closer systems where one would expect it the least and because the sudden experience of non-understanding and of being like strangers is most painful and irritating and particularly disconcerting. According to Herkenrath-Püschel "such offences are almost typical of intercultural dialogue and occur when the concerned suddenly become aware of a deep rift between their cultures."[1]

The above words could be taken as a commentary on the meanwhile ten "International Seminars on Intercultural Pastoral Care and Counselling" the last of which was held in Ustron/Poland. The above-mentioned experience seems to have been made many times and in different ways over and over again. And it was exactly this experience of feeling hurt and not understood which led us to explore deeper the cultural dimension of pastoral care and counselling and which – at least in relation to the pastoral care movement in Germany – awakened our interest in the issue of "intercultural pastoral care" as such.[2] This is not at all surprising. As a matter of fact, culture normally envelops us like the air we breathe but take no notice of until something disturbing happens – shortness of fresh air or sudden

* First published under the title "Intercultural Pastoral Care and Counselling" in *Intercultural Pastoral Care and Counselling*, 2, 1997, 8-12.

[1] L.-L. Herkenrath-Püschel, "Kulturelle Faktoren im seelsorgerlichen Dialog", in *Wege zum Menschen*, *40*, 1988, 50-64, see p. 54 (my translation).

[2] Cf. H. Weiß and K. Temme, "Reviewing the Journey: The 'Intercultural Seminars' 1986 to 1995", in *Intercultural Pastoral Care and Counselling*, *1*, 1996, 6-12.

changes. We become aware of the existence of air for instance if there is a draft, so it causes a twinge – and the same can be said of our culture.

It is also very interesting that – at least with us – the question of culture did not emerge at first from dealing with multicultural settings in practice, but rather from "within": from experiences of being different within our (supposedly) own and secure environment, among ourselves as women and men working in pastoral care and counselling, among ourselves who believe to have so much in common, even as far as having equal standards of training. I think this is a very important point. It makes me realise that that which is strange and of different culture need not necessarily be exotic, it may wait for me just across my own garden fence. Even in the closest area of my own tradition I have to be prepared for the different and for culturally based alienness – for difficulties in understanding and acts of offence which do not result from malevolence or an unwillingness to understand each other, but are rooted in the variations of cultural colouring which distinguish me from my neighbour.

As for the specific elements which the intercultural aspect adds to our practical work – once we have become aware of it – the first realisation simply is that once again things have become a little more complicated than expected. With encounters in the field of intercultural pastoral care still more aspects and factors have to be taken into consideration and paid attention to as having an effect on the encounter. It is no longer enough to concentrate on the encounter on a personal level, in fact, the social, political, and even spiritual backgrounds of the people gain importance;[3] group processes become increasingly more complex – and in the end, there will be even more things of which I must admit that I did not understand these. So I simply carry on alongside the things I understood as well as those I did not, and try to deal with both in the most sensible manner (both as a human being and as someone engaged in pastoral care).

Again, let us listen to Liesel-Lotte Herkenrath-Püschel: "Only if we acknowledge the limitations of understanding between members of different cultures can we succeed to some extent. This also means to refrain from over-expectations on both sides." [4]

---

[3] In our seminars, we tried to dispose the relevant aspects under tree headlines, which then formed a kind of "circle" to be worked through when analysing a situation of intercultural pastoral care and counselling:
a) Interpersonal Communication: biographical situation, biographical processes, emotional links, roles, etc.
b) Personal Context: historic conditions, economic factors, social and political conditions, cultural values, etc.
c) Experiences of Faith: religious symbols, religious and church traditions, life schemes and faith statements, religious and spiritual forces, etc.

[4] L.-L. Herkenrath-Püschel, "Kulturelle Faktoren", 56 (my translation).

Possible forms of encountering the alien

In the last decades, the context in which pastoral care and counselling occur in Western Europe has changed considerably. Cultural diversity has become a visible aspect of our everyday life, manifest in the changed streetscape of our towns and cities. How do I meet people from different environments, different cultures, in a world that has turned multicultural? Which is the attitude to be adopted towards them?

There are many destructive forms of dealing with people. If we leave those aside and concentrate on a more positive approach, we will discover a multiplicity of other possibilities. Below, I would like to try and outline a few possible attitudes – "ideal type" ones and not by any means exhaustive:

A supposed world citizen

I can choose to meet the alien with a universalistic attitude, the attitude of a world citizen. In that case I accept the differences as a given fact, as something that might make an encounter more difficult at first, but – in principle – could be overcome by increased background knowledge, through studies and more contacts. This is partly what I have experienced myself: Things which felt alien to me first grew more familiar once I got to know these better. However, if the fact that something is "alien" is basically something temporal, something that has to be overcome – then this approach results in the end in a negation of the alien within the alien. Viewed from a higher plane, there is no such thing as "being alien" at all; and if something feels alien to me, this only gives proof of my own limited horizon. I think that the conception of pastoral care within the church is still predominantly based on this universalistic ideal. Our demand reads: Closeness and understanding are always possible, in principle, and therefore have to be striven for. However, reality often draws a different picture. Even some optimistic models of a multicultural society are based on this conception: To overcome "being alien" is only a question of learning. And often this learning programme is coupled with considerable moral pretensions.

The alien as a foil to set off myself

Negating the alien: this can happen in a much more subtle way. Many of the fashionable things which come under the name "postmodern" even seem to search for what is alien or different, demonstrate and emphasise it. But this is done in such a way as to "alienate" the alien elements from their contexts. To me this seems like turning the whole world into a collage or a museum in which I can experience myself. The alien detached from its hereditary context becomes a projection area for myself, the alien is made into something exotic which stimulates me but has stopped to stir me. The corresponding pastoral-care model would be an attitude of arbitrariness which prefers to let all forms of verbal expression, all forms of religion or culture exist amicably side by side.

A variation of this can be found in the role the culturally alien played in the art of painting in the first decades of this century. Among expressionists for instance, African sculptures were *en vogue* for quite some time. Even Picasso collected such items. Gauguin went to live on Tahiti – but not with an idea to share the existence of the people there! The alien was experienced as a counter-image and was interesting because it reflected experiences of alienation, differences and rifts in one's own society.[5] This, I feel, is along the lines of pastoral-care models or therapy approaches which reduce the issue of "feeling alien" to the problem of the "alien within myself". The alien which irritates me is thus reduced to an expression of the unconscious, the suppressed parts of myself. Such models of interpretation are well known from analytically-oriented psychological definitions. I should think that these explanations offer many valuable insights, but they do not suffice as a sole pattern of interpretation.

Hermeneutics of the alien

It may sound old-fashioned: But I feel that the classical approach of hermeneutics is more helpful here than all the above models. The point is to try to "understand" the alien without eliminating its being alien or different. The point is not to give in to generalisation too quickly, but to perceive my vis-à-vis in her or his singularity and within their particular context - while at the same time hoping (and to a certain extent expecting) that understanding is possible even across borders.

I am in no way concerned with the high standards of hermeneutic virtuosi who claimed that by proceeding methodically they could understand an author better than he or she could themselves. What I have in mind is to remind us that our occidental hermeneutics originates from the exegesis of the Holy Bible and therefore, at least in its origins, is committed to certain theological fundamentals. Exegesis must be seen as an attempt to understand a vis-à-vis which I know I will never have understood fully, which will always remain one step ahead since it confronts me with words of divine revelation unfathomable to me. As a matter of fact, hermeneutics, viewed from the point of exegesis, does not start from the assumption that "only like knows like," as Aristotle and the classical philosophers have put it. On the contrary, confronted with a biblical text I always discover things unsuspected, new things which are nevertheless important for myself and

---

[5] Cf. Th. Sundermeier, *Den Fremden verstehen: Eine praktische Hermeneutik*, Göttingen: Vandehoeck & Ruprecht, 1996, 40-42.

for my conception of myself as well as for my life. Significantly enough, the founding father of the pastoral care movement, A. Boisen, developed the theory of encounter in pastoral care along the lines of an exegesis: he describes the vis-à-vis as "a living human document" which deserves to be read applying the same methods as when reading the Holy Bible. This means: Boisen must have been consciously aware of this tension existent also in pastoral care work: A successful encounter holds something divinatory, can be characterised as a kind of revelation to me - and it may happen without ever totally removing any last trace of feeling alien towards my vis-à-vis. This illustrates how my own conception of a God-human relationship determines the options I have in my relationships to other people.

What matters to me in these reflections is the following: An encounter must include both, becoming closer as well as reserving the alien. And another point: Successful understanding sets off a process and changes occur, in fact on both sides. The issue is to get involved in an encounter as a never-ending process.

In concrete terms: problematic areas in intercultural pastoral care and counselling

Is there anything like a basic "inter-cultural" attitude in pastoral care? David Augsburger whose book *Pastoral Counseling Across Cultures* (1986) is still a standard work with regard to our topic distinguishes between three different positive attitudes in an encounter:[6]

- *"Sympathy"* as a spontaneous and in most cases unreflected way of feeling with the vis-à-vis, which means that I simply project my own feelings upon the other person or recognise these in her or him.
- *"Empathy"* (in the way this term is known from client-centred therapy and from pastoral care training): Feeling with the other person as a conscious and affective attitude towards my vis-à-vis, an emphatic understanding, as "active imagination" of her or his emotions – making a distinction between my own emotions and those of the other person.
- *Thirdly: "Interpathy"* which D. Augsburger understands as a form of conscious empathy, too, but making an effort to let oneself in for the emotions, standards of values and mentality of the other person all of which are different from mine so that my own beliefs will somehow be temporarily ignored and shoved to the background. What we talk about here is something more than empathy; for if I acknowledge the existence of

---

[6] David W. Augsburger, *Pastoral Counseling Across Cultures*, Philadelphia: The Westminster Press, 1986, 27-32.

different values and standards, the question arises anew of what is normal, what is the aberration? What is healthy, what is sick?

Some issues which came up during the last Intercultural Seminars may point to what is at stake here, and may show how great the differences possibly are:[7]

The question of our world view

Which is the world view, the cosmology I assume? Not reflecting on it philosophically or theologically, but in my everyday talking and doing? At the seminar two years ago, Robert Solomon from Singapore illustrated the great importance attached to a peculiar area of experience in his country, placed somewhere between the given and the transcendent: An "in-between sphere" which on the one hand is fully present in the everyday doing and on the other hand is not subjected to the law of nature; an area having religious aspects and at the same time being independent of concrete images of God and a particular religion and which is therefore experienced as real by many Buddhists, Muslims and Christians alike. In this sphere, spirits for instance play a big role. According to him, it is from this area where most of the questions that come up in pastoral care originate from – and those involved in pastoral care should take this seriously if they did not want to miss the people concerned. I have also come across such questions working as a pastor in pastoral care – may be this "in-between sphere" plays a much bigger role with us than we generally assume.

Looking at the question of cosmology (of a world view), we must also take into consideration that there are cultures and religions which are not theistic, i.e. do not have a personal God. This is particularly true of Buddhism. Studies about dying processes in Japan show that mourning phases are experienced there, too, similar to those described by Kübler-Ross. But the phase of "bargaining" as part of the dying process seems not to occur there.[8] If no personal vis-à-vis exists, no God or any kind of personal fateful power, who is there to bargain with? This difference is all the more interesting in so far as we often find that (in the West) even such people who view themselves as irreligious, as agnostics, start to "quarrel with their fate" once they are confronted with severe strokes of fate – as if there did exist some sort of a vis-à-vis, however vague it might be. Obviously these are cultural characteristics which lie much deeper than any conscious profession of religion!

---

[7] For some of the following examples cf. *Intercultural Pastoral Care and Counselling, 1,* there especially: Robert Solomon, "Pastoral Counselling in Asian Contexts", 22-25, and Nalini Arles, "Counselling in the Indian Context", 26-28. [R. Solomon's essay is reprinted in this book, pp.141-150.]

[8] Cf. Augsburger, *Pastoral Counseling*, 66.

The concept of person

A different cosmology also means: a different concept of person. In certain respects, the relationship between the individual and society is of a totally different nature in other cultures. At our last seminar, Nalini Arles from India explained how difficult it was to transfer fundamental conceptions of client-centred therapy to her country. Therapeutic goals such as "strengthening of the ego" or "development of the Self" will catch only in a very limited way; the only "Self" existent in the cultural tradition of India is "jiva", the individual soul, which incidentally happens to be regarded as something temporary, something which needs to be overcome in order to reach identification with the "atman" or world soul. Of course, cosmological axioms will not be found in a philosophically perfected form with most people there either; and still they have a very subtle bearing on the thinking and feeling of the people.

The individual and society

On the societal level, a difference is made between "individual-centred" and "community-centred" societies. Most of the non-Western societies are much less individual-oriented than ours. Guidance by traditions, the individual embedded in the extended family, all these play a much bigger role – with the result that the pastoral care worker or counsellor must take on a different role, too. Our Indian colleague told us that while it is common practice in the psychological therapy setting in the West to limit the establishment of a relationship to the counselling set-up, this pattern will hardly work in India. When she builds up a relationship in pastoral care, for instance to a student (she works at a Christian college), it will naturally be expected of her to accompany and encourage the student during exam times, to attend family events etc. It would be regarded as a breach of confidence if she did not do so; she would create the impression that her "acceptance" of her vis-à-vis was not really worth that much. As counsellor she is also given the role of a personal mentor – and she is expected to fill this role even to the extent of placing her client in a job. This certainly is a very holistic model of pastoral care as compared to the professionally set-up therapy (in the West). On the other hand, it is much less emancipative as regards the individual. However, the textbook model of a client-centred counsellor who develops action models together with the client and in doing so remains deliberately non-directive, leaving the part of decision-taking totally to the client – this is a model hardly conceivable in an Indian context; there, a counsellor, as the mentor, also gives advice, even to the extent of direct instructions.

In this context, many questions arise with regard to the goal which is to be achieved by pastoral care or therapy. For instance: Given a certain conflict situation, is it my aim to strengthen the individual in her/his independence as against their community (family) – or do I try to help her/him adapt themselves?

If inclusion within a group – and acceptance via the role the group assigns to an individual – plays such a dominant part, this will also bring up methodical questions. While we prefer to use role-play, even bibliodrama, in order to help the individual experience various possibilities of action, understand and live through them, this method might not have a liberating effect on people who are anyway strongly governed by the expectations towards them from their society, and might rather have a restricting effect on them.[9]

The issue of religion

"Interpathy" as a means of letting myself in for the standards and world view of a different culture - this will inevitably take me to the area of religiousness. Issues like cosmology or the concept of person, all these have a religious aspect, too. Drawing a clear line between culture and religion as we often do is quite impossible with regard to Asia or Africa. Even with us, there is a closer connection between the two than we like to admit. I first realised this when colleagues from Eastern Europe happened to ask me at some of our seminars: In your work, how does your faith, your religion come to the fore? – In part, I felt this was a justified question to ask. On the other hand: In the environment in which we work as pastors (or as counsellors in church institutions) we can afford to leave questions of faith unmentioned; this is to say that in our work we quietly feed on the set-up of the ambient church life and of the Christian faith. It is self-evident that a pastor belongs to the Church, this needs no particular mentioning. God's name may remain unmentioned, because in a certain way God is implicit in our thinking. However, the situation is quite different in many other countries.

When I meet somebody from a different culture, of a different faith – how about my own faith? How far am I prepared or able to let myself in for the other person's faith if I try to let myself in for her/his culture? I think each of us will have to find their own distinct and theologically founded positions. In intercultural pastoral care, in fact, the inter-religious issue always arises; and inter-religious dialogue – not on an abstract academic level, but embedded in the facts of everyday life - certainly is at the core of intercultural pastoral care. There are still many unsettled points with all of us in this field.

When founding our "Society for Intercultural Pastoral Care and Counselling", there was a strong controversy about a certain formulation in our

---

[9] Cf. L. Herkenrath-Püschel, "Kulturelle Faktoren", 61.

statutes. How important is the fact that we are rooted in a Christian tradition if we want to encourage intercultural pastoral care and counselling? Obviously, we want cooperation with people coming from other religious traditions. But how important is the fact that the majority of us administer pastoral care as Christians and that this is where our motivation comes from? If we show our own identity, this may cause friction – but it can also produce more clarity.

Two years ago, a Buddhist monk came to our seminar as a speaker. It was extremely interesting to listen to his discourse on his pastoral care work in Thailand. One evening, he offered to hold a meditation, just to give a first impression. Of course, we Western Europeans took part – where else could we learn about something like that in a more authentic way? However, the reaction of some of our Asian and African colleagues I happened to talk to was quite different. They were aware of the fact that Buddhist meditation was not just another cultural phenomenon, but quite a determined form of religious practice – a kind of religious practice which was not theirs (and as a matter of fact neither mine). Certainly, I do not wish to put up dividing lines, but I think each of us will have to find their own position here, a position which is clear and responsible in its theological consequences. For naive openness would mean that I do not take the other person seriously in just her/his separate religiousness.

The issue of politics

In the same way as intercultural encounters touch on the issue of religion they also lead to the issue of politics. This became quite obvious in many workshops in Ustron. As some of the contributions from there are part of this documentation it must be enough to just mention this here. Let me only say the following: When, as it happens, traditional social structures collapse in Papua New-Guinea eventually resulting in the destruction of families as a consequence of accelerated modernisation, then there emerges a task for pastoral care which cannot be tackled on an individual level but only on a political one. And what is more, this is not a question of government politics in Papua New-Guinea only, but rather of developments in world economy. The political dimension of pastoral care – what do we make of it?

Some strategies to reduce complexity

Realising that in intercultural pastoral care so many factors come into play and everything is so much more complex, the question arises: Are encounters and understanding at all possible? It is simply impossible to have in mind all the various aspects however relevant they may be. Fortunately, experience tells us that this is not necessary. Deep encounters across cultural barriers are possible (and have been so during our seminars). Building up a contact to another human being can succeed – and, thank God, has been doing so again and again, even though one might not have fully understood all the aspects of the other person's culture.

Cross-cultural fundamental experiences

In my everyday practice I am forced to somehow diminish intercultural complexity. Most of the time this will happen unconsciously, which is good. However, some methodical proposals can be made. Quite obviously, one can draw on fundamental human experience which is cross-cultural. I take John Foskett's considerations on "the unknown in intercultural communication", mainly his recourse to our individual birth experiences, as an important suggestion in this context.[10] Experiences of one's own birth, of joy or death are essentially human in such an elementary way that it will certainly be impossible to ever "pin them down" to one single culture. Taking in a glimpse of the horrors of Oswiecim /Auschwitz was such an elementary experience which had its own effects, however complex they were. It united – and divided.

In a well-known German-language journal of the pastoral care movement, Albrecht Grözinger recently suggested to draw on human "fundamental symbols" and basic "gestures".[11] Among others he mentions the symbol of water to which is attributed a sense of being threatening as well as healing in many religions and cultures – even in modern literature. Can we use such fundamental symbols in a cross-cultural context?

I think we had better not be over-enthusiastic in this regard. I would like to recall the unexpected effect the uniting symbol of "soil from the Holy Land" had on one of the participants during the closing service at a former seminar. A woman, wife of a pastor, whose ancestors came from the Carribean left the service crying. Later she explained: "In the Caribbean, if we get involved with soil, we get involved with the evil – if someone puts soil into our hand, the evil is present."[12]

With regard to basic gestures – as for instance the gesture of blessing – the situation may not be any different. How much physical closeness or distance does the other person need or can she/he take without feeling embarrassed? That is very different from one culture to the next. Our body language, mostly uncontrolled by ourselves, is strongly influenced by our

---

[10] J. Foskett, "The 'Unknown' in Intercultural Communication", in *Intercultural Pastoral Care and Counselling, 2,* 1997, 13-15.

[11] A. Grözinger, "Seelsorge im multikulturellen Krankenhaus", in *Wege zum Menschen, 47,* 1995, 389-400.

[12] Quoted from: Weiß and Temme, "Reviewing the Journey", 10.

culture. Does it make any difference which of my two hands I use to welcome an African? Yes, it does – there have been interesting encounters at seminars also in this respect!

Tolerance

We have to admit that it is impossible to fully avoid offence to occur in intercultural encounters. To see this matter-of-factly can also be a relief. We need to practise enduring such acts of offence, which means: practise tolerance (*tolerare* in Latin means to stand or endure something). Hence, two things are needed to make intercultural encounter a success: On the one hand, to practise tolerance with regard to others and to ourselves; and on the other of course, to find ways to keep these offences small.

With regard to the latter, I have learned to appreciate anew the importance of social manners through our intercultural seminars. Among those engaged in pastoral care, frankness and directness during arguments as well as a preparedness to quarrel are considered high objectives in dealing with one another. The way Germans or Britons for instance tended to act out their individual tensions or frustrations during intercultural seminars was very impressive. It used to leave Asians, Africans, and even Eastern Europeans perplexed: "Is this the way you treat each other?" they asked.

In Chinese culture, in all my dealings with other people, I must be very careful not to let the other person lose face. Save my face, allow the other person to save face – in dealing with one another this is very important. In Ustron, a colleague from Ghana said: In a conflict situation, we would always put the interest of the group above our personal interest. None of the two are ideals I should like to follow. But what I found worth thinking about was the sensitivity of my colleague from Ghana when he commented on social manners in his tradition, as for instance the different meanings given to one's right or left hand, respect of old age and similar things (matters which, as far as I could see, were immediately understood and acknowledged by the people present from Asia) – and above all the complexity of his sensitivity in these issues. And I realised: Social manners are not always mere symbols of social repression. They are also a high cultural good – and a great help when dealing with anything alien.

Intercultural Pastoral Care as a Model for a Theory of Radically Interactive Pastoral Care *

Eberhard Hauschildt
Germany, 2002

A general theory of pastoral care has to clarify also the practice of intercultural pastoral care. Thus, intercultural pastoral care is a test case for the quality of poimenic theorizing. A theory of pastoral care must hold together three perspectives:

- We are all human (and in so far all the same);
- groups of people are different;
- each individual is special.[1]

It is obvious that intercultural pastoral care motivates the theory building of pastoral care to work out the meaning of the second sentence as carefully as the other two. How do present concepts of pastoral care deal with the structure of these three sentences? How do they clarify the constellations of intercultural pastoral care?

---

* Shortened version of "Interkulturelle Seelsorge als Musterfall für eine Theorie radikal interaktiver Seelsorge," first published in K. Federschmidt et al. (eds.), *Handbuch Interkulturelle Seelsorge*, Neukirchen-Vluyn: Neukirchener Verlag, 2002, 241-261. Translation to English by K. Federschmidt.

[1] "Every individual is, in some respects, like all others, like some others, and like no other." D.W. Augsburger, *Pastoral Counseling Across Cultures*, Philadelphia: The Westminster Press, 1986, 49. This principle of intercultural pastoral care is also discussed in E.Y. Lartey, *In Living Colour: An Intercultural Approach to Pastoral Care and Counselling*, London: Cassell, 1997, 12ff. The notion was first expressed by C. Kluckhohn and H. Murray, *Personality in Nature, Society and Culture*, New York: Knopf, 1948, 35.

Intercultural pastoral care and the deficits of the theory of pastoral care

Confidence in global adjustments?

The pastoral care movement is the first case of a clearly globalized practical theology. So far it was always argued that practical theology, even as a theory, could only be designed for a particular church. Taking into account different ecclesial situations, e.g. in the United States as compared with Germany, this was quite plausible. But with the modern, psychologically professionalized ministry, this changed. Along with western modernization, the religious situation of individuals was more and more conformed, and in fact, there remained hardly any difference, whether the pastoral care-seeker lived in a German national church situation or in the U.S. situation of plurality of denominations. Starting from the United States, the theory and practice of the pastoral care movement took hold in more and more countries. This resulted, mainly since the late 1970s, in international conferences of the pastoral care movement. They showed that, in fact, adjustments had taken place, beyond the borders of languages and continents, and also beyond the boundaries of denominations.

In this context, the problem of different traditions of pastoral care appeared to be only the problem of the still trailing past: of course, there were still some underdeveloped countries and people in terms of pastoral care, but that would change in the wake of time. The pastoral care movement developed a deep understanding that each individual person is a singular case and that generalizing ethical norms could and should always be renegotiated in the individual pastoral care situation. The principles for leading a counseling conversation, it was assumed, have universal validity for all people. But the insight that groups of people are different remained rather in the background.

The meanwhile ever-increasing globalization in the fields of economy, information and media is in fact a good argument for even further adjustments in terms of individual religiosity: everywhere, religion will more and more become a matter of individual choice or at least affiliation, with many and diverse alternatives globally. The relationship between religion, religious community and the individual has to be designed individually, and can be handled differently according to individual situations. With the binding force of traditional values and norms diminishing, in case of conflict individuals are increasingly faced with the task to solve these conflicts individually. All this predicts that there will be even more global alignments also in the ministry of pastoral care. And the international conferences of the pastoral care movement, with participants from many different parts of the world, prove it outright.

And yet, precisely at these international conferences the opposite was experienced. It turned out that not even the chaplains and pastors in the pastoral care movement were so much the same as they had thought themselves to be. Liesel-Lotte Herkenrath-Püschel was one who developed an early sensitivity for this.[2]

It became visible: the so-called pre-modern practice of pastoral care remains present, particularly in non-Western cultures. The process of globalization does not simply lead to an equalization of pastoral care, it also brings into consciousness the cultural and regional characteristics of different worlds of pastoral care.[3] There is not only the one pastoral care, there are different cultures of pastoral care. And in a globalized world, these different cultures of pastoral care clash more often.

Confidence in the archaisms of the caregiver's own tradition?

If the pastoral care movement could not eradicate the pre-modern pastoral cultures, and if these cultures are now increasingly taken into account by pastors and chaplains in the modernized West, can a common ground be found in a return to pre-modern pastoral care? Will intercultural pastoral care become possible by rediscovering pre-modern traditions in pastoral care?

This seems to be the logic of the new model of pastoral care recently published by Manfred Josuttis as "energetische Seelsorge"[4] ("energetic"[5] pastoral care). Josuttis advises German pastoral care to turn back: "from identity to conversion," "from the self to the soul," "from meaning to blessing," and "from the theologian to the spiritual guide."[6] Pastoral care, according to Josuttis, is not about development and growth, it is about the experience of an overwhelming power; and divine powers and energies act – this is particularly important for Josuttis – even independent from consciousness.[7] "Pastoral care would then consist in ... realizing the force field

---

[2] L.-L. Herkenrath-Püschel, "Seelsorge – transkulturell", in *Pastoraltheologie, 71*, 1982, 288-295.

[3] Concerning this double development and its relevance for practical theology as a whole, see E. Hauschildt, "Die Globalisierung und Regionalisierung der Praktischen Theologie. Beschreibung und Plädoyer", in *Praktische Theologie, 29*, 1994, 175-193.

[4] M. Josuttis, *Segenskräfte: Potentiale einer energetischen Seelsorge* [Blessing Forces: The Potentials of an Energetic Pastoral Care], Gütersloh: Kaiser Verlag / Gütersloher Verlagshaus, 2000.

[5] Translator's note: The neologism "energetische Seelsorge" was coined by Josuttis in order to point to a "powerful" and "energy-based" aspect of pastoral care. Josuttis refers to the Greek word "energeia" (energy, power) that is used in the New Testament to describe the acting of Jesus as acts in spiritual power/energy, opposing evil powers.

[6] These are the subtitles of chapter 2 in Josuttis' book, pp. 65-124.

[7] Ibid., 89.

of the Holy Spirit in such a way that harmful forces are eliminated and healing currents create new structures."[8] In this way, Josuttis gains a connection to the pre-modern concepts of pastoral care; he re-mythologizes pastoral theory. He recommends that Christian pastoral care return to the idea of pastoral care as the exorcism of evil powers by good powers.

By this, all intercultural communication problems of Western Christian pastoral care in dealing with foreign cultures of pastoral care seem to be solved in one swoop. A common language seems to be found. But the price would be that chaplains and pastors turn away from scientific theories and practices of healing, emigrate from the world of medicine, of depth psychology and behavioral therapy. The price would be an artificial distancing from modern culture. In this way, the intercultural contact with modern culture is finished.

This approach of "energetische Seelsorge" breaks free from concentration on the individual case. Attention is not directed to identity formation in the individual but to trans-psychic processes common to all people. Specifically, all human beings are understood as being exposed to good and bad powers. Similarly, attention is not directed to differences between groups of people. Rather, all possible differences of a culturally determined consciousness are relativized by one decisive difference: that either the sanctifying effect of the Spirit is experienced, or the effect of evil powers remains. The Holy Spirit (as understood by the Christian faith) is perceived as energy. Other energies and ideas of other religions about energetic effects, and thus also the corresponding cultures that represent these ideas, remain marginalized.

Therefore, what initially looked like a general basis for effective cross-cultural encounter – going back to the archaic traditions of Christian pastoral care – turns out to be the re-setting of a single occidental Christian concept-pattern, which is made a precondition for the theory of pastoral care. Pastoral care is once again nothing but the mediation and enforcement of one understanding of pastoral care. A truly intercultural encounter, one that does not want to cancel the otherness of the other person, is missing in this concept.

Intercultural pastoral care as a highly interactive process of interpretation

In the more recent debate on pastoral care, increasingly criticism is raised against models that suppose one single specific frame of theory, because

[8] Ibid., 39.

this creates and maintains an imbalance of power in the pastoral encounter.[9] Here, the concept of "conversation," which was basic for the pastoral care of the "word-of-God-theology" (Thurneysen)[10] and the German pastoral care movement of the late 20th century (Scharfenberg)[11] likewise, is not taken seriously enough. A "conversation" as a specific form of communication implies that both sides have a say of their own, both are entitled to raise the word, to hear and to talk, implying an equivalence of both interlocutors (and thus also an equivalence of their possibly different cultures). So it is not only intercultural pastoral care, but it is already the need for a conversation among equal partners, that shows the shortcomings both of the classic modern movement of pastoral care, that makes a therapeutic psychological framework a precondition of any pastoral encounter, and of the model of "energetic" pastoral care, which wants to refer to "powers" acting independently from any communicative bargain.

Not coincidentally, it was women who have pointed out that pastoral theory must not be limited to a theory of individual subjects (psychology) but has to take into account the social situation, the belonging to social constellations and groups, and that, therefore, pastoral theory is well advised to take a look at sociological theorems. Human groups are different, men and women are different in the way they are socialized in our society.[12] The "feminist view"[13] has shown: in the pastoral relationship, such affiliation plays a role that has to be recognized. Pastoral relationship happens between a man and a woman, or between men and women. Pastoral theory cannot do without a theory of the larger social context.

The experience of intercultural pastoral care shows once more how inevitable it is to conceptualize the interaction of both sides radically: in pastoral care not only do both sides have to have their say with their individual ideas and values, they have to be recognized also with their culturally shaped understanding of the words and actions and with their

---

[9] See M. Nicol, *Gespräch als Seelsorge*, Göttingen: Vandenhoeck & Ruprecht, 1990, 107ff.; Th. Henke, *Seelsorge und Lebenswelt*, Würzburg: Echter, 1994, 70-73; R. Schieder, "Seelsorge in der Postmoderne", in *Wege zum Menschen, 46*, 1994, 26-43.

[10] See E. Thurneysen, *Die Lehre von der Seelsorge*, Zürich: TVZ, 1948 [*A Theology of Pastoral Care*, Richmond: John Knox Press, 1962], chapter 5: "Seelsorge als Gespräch" [pastoral care as conversation].

[11] J. Scharfenberg, *Seelsorge als Gespräch* [pastoral care as conversation], Göttingen: Vandenhoeck & Ruprecht, 1972.

[12] U. Pohl-Patalong, *Seelsorge zwischen Individuum und Gesellschaft*, Stuttgart: Kohlhammer, 1996; I. Karle, *Seelsorge in der Moderne*, Neukirchen-Vluyn: Neukirchener, 1996, 173-192.

[13] See also: U. Riedel-Pfäfflin and J. Strecker, *Flügel trotz allem: Feministische Seelsorge und Beratung*, Gütersloh: Gütersloher, 1998; R. Bons-Storm, *The Incredible Woman: Listening to Women's Silences in Pastoral Care*, Nashville: Abingdon, 1996.

own conception of what pastoral care is about and how it works. In the relationship of a pastoral encounter itself, there has to be clarified, what this pastoral care can be for those involved, and how it can proceed. Therefore, the task of a theory of pastoral care is not only to understand the processes of interpreting certain statements in the pastoral encounter. It has also to explain, how "worlds of interpretation" can come into interaction. In intercultural situations we experience that "worlds of interpretation" are so radically different that a chaplain or counselor cannot expect his/her counselees simply to adopt his/her framework of interpretation (be it therapeutic psychological, "energetic", or traditionally dogmatic) and to give up their own. With such a supposition in mind, a Christian pastor would not be able e.g. to "talk" with a Muslim, a counselor would not helpfully accompany a German-Tunisian couple, and an African pastor would not come into conversation with a German chaplain about their pastoral care. Pastoral theory, therefore, has to conceptualize how in pastoral care a real exchange becomes possible between the "cultural worlds."

It is still too early to present a complete theory for this. But important aspects for such a radically interactive pastoral paradigm can be named.[14]

Pastoral care as a hermeneutics of a helping conversation

I suggest to conceptualize pastoral theory as hermeneutics: a theory of how understanding between individuals – or, more precisely, between individuals with their respective worlds of interpretation (i.e. cultures) – is going on. And further clarified: a theory of pastoral care should be understood (and thereby also distinguished from other scholarly theories) as a hermeneutics of "helpful conversation." Its task is to clarify what goes on in this special interaction of a conversation, a conversation that is helpful prior to action. More exactly, the conversation is helpful *because* action is not yet undertaken, because the possibilities for action are played through and alternative actions are tested. Then – after and outside the pastoral care – acting will start and the conversation will no longer interrupt this acting, but only eventually accompany it.[15]

[14] Cf. pp. 66-70 in E. Hauschildt, "Seelsorgelehre", in *Theologische Realenzyklopädie, Vol. 31*, 2000, 54-74.

[15] Christoph Schneider-Harpprecht in his essay "Was ist interkulturelle Seelsorge?", in Federschmidt et al. (eds.), *Handbuch Interkulturelle Seelsorge,* 38-62, notes that the praxis of intercultural pastoral care is "wholistic" and "open for social work" (ibid., 43). The difference between social welfare and pastoral care is not a difference of subject: is counseling *still* pastoral care? is debt counseling *only* social work? The difference lies in the interpretation of the subject: is the conversation a disruption of acting, different from social work (and therefore a helping conversa-

How does understanding happen in an intercultural conversation? M. Nicol, in accordance with many other concepts of pastoral care, states as a prerequisite for the encounter of pastoral care a certain unity, namely the common Christian understanding.[16] Compared to this, Hans-Georg Gadamer's thinking was already much more complex, if not paradoxical. True, Gadamer did emphasize that there must be something common that precedes the conversation. But at the same time he did express that this common thing becomes visible or even emerges in the conversation itself.[17] Intercultural hermeneutics will be even more careful than Gadamer in supposing such a common thing, and even more skeptical towards a "fusion of horizons." In the relationship of pastoral care, the commonality of the two sides (the two individuals, including the cultures involved in them) has to be found during the conversation.[18] Or even more pointedly: intercultural pastoral care has to construct a commonality as part of the process of intercultural understanding.[19]

---

tion = pastoral care), or is it interpreted as a preparation for action (and therefore part of a helping action = social work)?

[16] Cf. Nicol, *Gespräch*, 164ff.

[17] "Every conversation presupposes a common language, or better, creates a common language. Something is placed in the center, as the Greeks say, which the partners in dialogue both share, and concerning which they can exchange ideas with one another. Hence reaching an understanding on the subject matter of a conversation necessarily means that a common language must first be worked out in the conversation. This is not an external matter of simply adjusting our tools; nor is it even right to say that the partners adapt themselves to one another but, rather, in a successful conversation they both come under the influence of the truth of the object and are thus bound to one another in a new community. To reach an understanding in a dialogue is not merely a matter of putting oneself forward and successfully asserting one's own point of view, but being transformed into a communion in which we do not remain what we were." H.-G. Gadamer, *Truth and Method*, rev. ed., London/New York: Continuum, 2004, 371 [Wahrheit und Methode, rev. ed. 1965].

[18] For reasons for this understanding of hermeneutics (which relies on Schleiermacher), and for a correlative rather than unifying understanding of hermeneutics of pastoral care (that was elaborated in the 1980s in the United States by Charles Gerkin and Donald Capps), cf. E. Hauschildt, "Seelsorge und Hermeneutik: Vom Verstehen helfender Gespräche", in U. Körtner (ed.), *Glauben und Verstehen: Perspektiven hermeneutischer Theologie*, Neukirchen-Vluyn: Neukirchener, 2000, 75-96. For developing a theory of intercultural hermeneutics, it is in my opinion very promising to deal with constructivist concepts.

[19] In my opinion, constructivism is a highly relevant theoretical approach, both for intercultural hermeneutics and for understanding pastoral care. For a critique of so-called "cultural psychology" against the universalism of "cross cultural psychology" see Chr. Schneider-Harpprecht, *Interkulturelle Seelsorge*, Göttingen: Vandenhoeck & Ruprecht, 2001, 154. On the role of constructivism in systemic pastoral care see

Talks – talks in pastoral care, talks in intercultural pastoral care – are ventures. And they can easily fail. At stake is not only whether or not the pastoral caretaker will prove to be helpful. At stake is the whole world of interpretation of the pastoral caretaker, be it psychological, therapeutic, "energetic" or traditionally dogmatic. This is the deepest uncertainty, which for a pastor might arise in any serious pastoral care encounter; and this becomes particularly evident in intercultural ministry.

In the theological debate this uncertainty is articulated in the question of what is *Christian* counseling – in contrast to other helpful conversations. In the model of radically interactive pastoral care, one surely cannot and will not any longer say that (as argued by Thurneysen in his theology of pastoral care)[20] the counselor should take the lead in the conversation and he/she should lead it to a certain liturgical form of conversation (Bible word, confession, prayer) – in order to recognize it as "Christian." Such an objective prevents radical interactivity. Also, one cannot and will not any longer say that the pastor or chaplain must stick to the rules of therapeutic communication and convince his counterpart to do likewise, because only thereby a relation of true acceptance could be created that corresponds to the Christian doctrine of justification.[21] But then: what really makes a helping conversation with someone who comes from another "culture of helping relationships" and perhaps from a different religion than Christianity, a "Christian" conversation? I want to propose the following: the question of whether a certain conversation is a form of Christian care and counseling or not, is, right from the beginning, not adequately addressed if we expect an answer in terms of a clear logic of either/or. In this case, the decision about the Christian character of pastoral care is imagined in a spatial logic, in the image of an allotment garden, so to speak: is it within or is it outside the Christian territory, *my* Christian territory? A conversation, however, develops; and what is contributed from both sides develops over time and disappears. To examine this process with an either/or-logic is inappropriate. More adequate for pastoral care is the logic of "more or less": pastoral care is only gradually Christian. At a moment it may be particularly Christian, and later less. It may be perceived as more Christian from the perspective of the one participant in the talk, and less from that of the other. If pastoral care is defined as the hermeneutics of helping conversation, then this conversation can be seen as Christian to the extent that

P. Held, *Systemische Praxis in der Seelsorge*, Mainz: Matthias-Grünewald, 1998, and Chr. Morgenthaler, *Systemische Seelsorge*, 2nd ed., Stuttgart: Kohlhammer, 2000.

[20] See Thurneysen, *Die Lehre von der Seelsorge*.

[21] For an example of this often unspoken assumption in the pastoral care movement, see D. Stollberg, *Wahrnehmen und Annehmen: Seelsorge in Theorie und Praxis*, Gütersloh: Mohn, 1978.

Christian interpretations play a role in it.[22] In a cross-cultural contact, especially an interreligious contact, this will be the case only partially. But the aim of intercultural pastoral care will be for a Christian pastor/chaplain to bring Christian interpretations and interpretations of the other person with his/her other religion into a relationship, as close as possible. Surely this is a very exciting, instructive, and horizon-expanding matter also for the Christian pastor himself/herself! Thus, a common mosaic of interpretation is evolving, connecting both cultures without leveling their contradictions.

In the context of a radically interactive model of Christian pastoral care and the experiences of intercultural pastoral care, there are certain issues that need particular attention. And there are already some developed theorems, to which we can turn.

The relationship between power and interpretation in pastoral care

When pastoral care is oriented by a model of interactive equality, instead of petrifying the power-difference between pastoral care practitioners and pastoral care seekers, it is obvious: pastoral care does not find its interpretations in a power-free zone. In talking together, always power is exercised, too.[23] The concept of "energetic pastoral care" has once again strengthened the notion of the exercise of power in the context of pastoral care. However, its focus on trans-subjective powers has distracted the attention from the power manifesting itself *between* the parties in the conversation (wherever this power may come from). In contrast to that, the pastoral care movement stressed the ideal that the caregiver should, in a controlled way, abstain from his/her power of lead, to make room for the feelings and associations of the client. The power of interpretation, however, was shared only under the premise that the client agrees to the caregiver's interpretative framework of what pastoral care should be. In this way, the culture of the caregiver remained dominant. Compared with the dogmatic traditionalism of "Dialectic Theology" (i.e.: the baptized pastoral-care-seeker should understand himself/herself as a sinner before God, who is justified by God), it was only expanded in a secular way: the client (the care-seeker)

---

[22] More precisely: as far as the recourse to transcendent instances, or the theological statements, or the fact that actions have a religious function, are perceived as something that can be seen in a perspective related to Christ or that is related to the Christian church. And Christian pastoral care will be "protestant," when and insofar the Christian interpretations are interpretations of *sola scriptura*, *solus Christus*, *sola gratia* and *sola fide*. Cf. Hauschildt, "Seelsorgelehre", 69f.

[23] This is, for instance, shown by socio-linguistic studies about the changing right to speak (the so-called "turn-taking") in a conversation. Cf. H. Sacks, E. Schegloff, and G. Jefferson, "A Simple Systematics for the Organization of Turn-Taking for Conversation", in *Language, 50*, 1974, 696-735.

should understand himself/herself as a person within a psychic conflict, that could be solved by the means of therapeutic counseling. In a radically interactive care, as it evolves in intercultural pastoral care, precisely this affiliation of both parties to their respective cultures is taken into view. "Cultural analysis" means: to recognize that (and where exactly) different cultures meet; to agree that (and how exactly) these cultures are related to each other in terms of power; and, to find a reconciliation despite this constellation of power.

The relationship between projections and interpretations in care/counseling

One of the significant psychological findings about the process of conversation that was made fruitful for pastoral care by the pastoral care movement is the existence of projections in a helping conversation. In the construction of interpretations, the pastoral care seeker tends to project his/her world (of early childhood) to the current pastoral relationship. The early father/mother-relationship is actualized with the care giver. This transference on the part of pastoral care seeker corresponds to the dynamics of countertransference from the other side.[24] In depth psychology, these processes in conversation are considered inevitable and conducive for healing, as long as the therapist engages them in a therapeutically controlled way.

In intercultural pastoral care, not only projections of individual biographical relationships take place, but also projections of cultural links. The clients who culturally differ from the pastoral care giver will inevitably project interpretations that are plausible in their own culture into the interpretative patterns that are offered to them by the modern western caregiver. They may take on the modern therapeutic psychological vocabulary and behavior externally, but nevertheless, for the clients these may mean something entirely different.

Analogously, modern Western pastors have an idea of the culture of their counterparts, an image that is characterized by their own modern Western perspective; and so the foreign culture of the other person may be devalued as particularly unscientific or idealized as particularly holistic. Helpful for intercultural pastoral care are then the insights of intercultural psychology or ethno-psychoanalysis,[25] in order to perceive the indigenous psychology of the counterpart in as undistorted a way as possible.

---

[24] The pastoral care movement has insisted that this is an indispensable insight for any theory of pastoral care. Cf. e.g. J. Scharfenberg, *Seelsorge als Gespräch*, 65ff., and H. J. Thilo, *Beratende Seelsorge*, Göttingen: Vandenhoeck & Ruprecht, 1971, 45ff.

[25] Cf. Schneider-Harpprecht, "Was ist interkulturelle Seelsorge", especially pp. 53-56.

In order to deal with the psychologies of cultures different from those of caregivers, theories of pastoral care need to learn from research in indigenous psychologies of different cultures, especially seeking to understand the patterns in those psychologies. Above, we have critically discussed two such patterns in western pastoral care, used to engage diversity in psychologies: relying on global adjustments in the pastoral care movement and archaization of Christian pastoral care in the concept of "energetic" pastoral care. The aim of an intercultural pastoral care relationship is, then, after transference and countertransference of the respective psychologies, to come to a transference that is adjusted to reality – a reality for which the relation with the conversational partner in the process of conversation stands surety. According to Augsburger, the aim would be to reformulate one's own categories in the language of the other person.[26] Ethno-psychoanalysts are a bit more cautious. They assume that a pluri-theoretical technique of consultation may modify the theories both of the counselor and of the client.

The relation between system and interpretation in pastoral care

Systemic counseling[27] has shown us how much pastoral care interacts and has to work with the systems of action and interpretation of the immediate environment of the care-seeker, especially the family-system. In the horizon of intercultural pastoral care, a theory of pastoral care will, in addition, pay attention to the larger cultural systems that are present in the immediate social environment. Interpretations have their place within a system, and they serve to maintain their own (cultural) system. Interpretations that come from outside the (family) system – and a relationship of pastoral care will always come along with such interpretations – are perceived as a difference. This is even more true when interpretations come from outside the cultural system, as in intercultural pastoral care. Systemic pastoral care teaches us to work productively with such experiences of difference.[28] Intercultural pastoral care needs, above that, an explicit "multi-systemic" perspective.[29]

Dialogue on interpreting the phenomenon "soul"

For this last aspect it is especially true that the theory of pastoral care is still at a beginning point. Following the scientific destruction of any

[26] D. W. Augsburger, *Conflict Mediation Across Cultures*, Louisville KY: Westminster Press, 1992, 38.
[27] Cf. Morgenthaler, *Systemische Seelsorge*.
[28] For the techniques cf. ibid., 141-159.
[29] Cf. Schneider-Harpprecht and H. Weiß, in *Handbuch Interkulturelle Seelsorge*, 56-59 and 268-273, with cases.

material/substantial conception of the soul, which happened at the beginning of the 19th century, in the 19th century the theory of pastoral care ceased to design a concept of the soul. In the Dialectic Theology of the 20th century, the "soul" is nothing but an equivalent for the human being standing in front of God, and in the pastoral care movement, talking of "soul" is completely replaced by talking of the "self" and of "identity".

Manfred Josuttis' demand to move "from the self to the soul" in pastoral care corresponds with the observation that the "soul" has not entirely vanished from everyday language, and that post-modern religiosity shows new interest in it. In intercultural pastoral care, we inevitably encounter different interpretations of the soul. Therefore, a theory of Christian pastoral care, that has gone through the turn of modernity, indeed has to answer the question, what to do with the term "soul."

Here the systematic theologian Konrad Stock recently has presented an interesting answer:[30] According to him, the term "soul" indicates a Christian ontology, i.e. the Christian understanding of the human being as a creature. "Soul" refers to the "inside" of the human nature, and to the knowing of this "inside" as well. In accordance with the tradition of the reformation, "soul" is understood as a strictly relational term,[31] relational in a threefold way: we experience soul in relation to others, in relation to God, and in relation to our selves. According to Schleiermacher, the human being realizes his/her soul in his/her self-awareness: the awareness of one's freedom and at the same time of one's being defined by a foundation, that is, the condition of the possibility of one's freedom. The soul becomes aware of itself in reason, it is experienced in acting, and it always has affective connotations. With such a concept of soul, religious emotions are not only understood as projections of my self-relation and my world-relation, because the God-relation is seen as an instance of its own, and in the logic of the soul, as the fundamental instance for the shaping of my affections.

In this way, the relationality of the ego is grounded even more deeply and the role of feelings and affections becomes even more fundamental than in common modern psychologies (because the aim cannot be to simply transfer feelings into consciousness). At the same time, there is a possibility to connect to substantial concepts of the soul: the idea that the soul can "suffer," and all the religious imagination that goes along with such concepts. But for this, it is not necessary to negate the modern insight

---

[30] Cf. for the following: K. Stock, *Gottes wahre Liebe*, Tübingen: Mohr Siebeck, 2000, especially the chapter "Die interne Struktur des Seelischen" (118ff.), and K. Stock, "Seele VI", in *Theologische Realenzyklopädie, Vol. 30*, 2000, 759-773.

[31] M. Weimer, "Die Seelsorgerolle als offenes System", in *Pastoraltheologie, 90*, 2001, 2-16, puts it bluntly: "Seele gibt es nur zu zweit" ("Soul is available only in pairs"), p. 13.

into the psychophysical continuum and in the role of self-consciousness for psychic processes.

If the theory of pastoral care continues to work along these lines as a practical theological discipline, it will help modern Christian pastoral care to take part in intercultural dialogue about the soul.

In summary

Intercultural pastoral care is a model for a theory of pastoral care, sharpening our understanding of pastoral care as a process of interpretation. In genuine dialogue, with awareness of the processes of transference and of systemic connections, it serves analysis of the constellations of relationships and power structures, and their transformation.

New Perspectives and Challenges for Pastoral Care and Counseling in a Globalizing World *

Emmanuel Y. Lartey
Ghana, 2005

Because the practice of pastoral counseling is closely related to people's everyday life experiences, pastoral counselors have historically had to employ cultural analytical skills. The experiences we have and the interpretations we make of them are deeply informed by culture. Understandings of personhood, health, illness and appropriate forms of healing are all socially and culturally configured.

Pastoral care and counseling, therefore, are informed by culture at every point. Pastoral counselors face the challenges of exploring cultural realities today with the added realization of the particular challenges facing the multicultural and multi-faith world in which we live.

The world, of course, has always been multicultural and pluralistic. However, it is only now as a result of rapid technological developments and the realities of the movement of people across national and cultural borders, that we are able to face squarely the challenges and opportunities of this reality.

The world of today throws people of very different social, cultural, economic, religious and ethnic backgrounds into close proximity with each other in very many places. The challenges of communication across linguistic and cultural barriers face us more intensely now. We can no longer assume that our neighbors speak the same language or share the same beliefs with ourselves. Moreover, people of different cultures who are in contact with each other influence each other in subtle and at times overt ways. The power of the Media is considerable in this regard. The influence of a radio in a remote village community can be phenomenal. Political and even national revolutions have been traced to the power of the Media either in sowing seeds or else giving the oxygen of publicity to little known causes. We no longer live, anywhere in the world, in communities that are

---

* Lecture presented at the 18th International Seminar on Intercultural Pastoral Care and Counselling, 2005, in Düsseldorf-Kaiserswerth. Published in *Intercultural Pastoral Care and Counselling, 13*, 2006, 68-73.

completely closed or impenetrable. Computer technology invades even the most inaccessible terrain. The pastoral care provider's task is made even more intractable by the dynamic nature of all cultures. Not only do we have to deal with varieties of experience, background, culture and faith, but also we are called upon to respond to these differences whilst they are in a baffling state of flux and change through interaction and influence.

How are we to proceed with pastoral counseling in this situation? What does Christian pastoral counseling mean in today's circumstances? How are Christian pastoral counselors to relate to Muslim or Sikh clients? What happens when the chaplain available in the hospital at the crucial moment of critical care is a Buddhist or Hindu and the patient Muslim or Christian? How do different religious faiths come into play in pastoral counseling? How are Christian pastoral counselors to counsel persons of Generation X or else the Millennial, for whom postmodernism is already beginning to be outdated? Pastoral counselors and care providers face immense challenges in our globalizing world.

The realities of multiplicity and plurality

We live increasingly in contexts in which the pre-modern, modern and post-modern (and what is already beginning to be described as the post postmodern) are juxtaposed. These three are no longer historical epochs separable from each other. They exist together and are in constant interactive relationship.

The postmodern disillusionment with ambitious total explanations such as offered by science, religion, economic or political ideologies is already fracturing into extremism on the one hand and nihilism on the other. Violence against self and others born of religious fundamentalism and desperation, stalk the world. "Cutting" and other forms of self-injury, suicide of teenagers and retreats into the fantasy world of drugs, altered states of consciousness and nihilistic self-absorption, are commonplace. At the same time, and often in the same neighborhoods it is possible to find people living with "affluenza" (the intoxicating and debilitating effects of affluence) in close proximity with those suffering the effects of abject poverty and disease. While many have access to computers and the World Wide Web, others in our environment can barely read and write. Hurricane Katrina most recently exposed this reality in New Orleans, LA, USA to the whole world.

Varieties of religious faith and practice are now taken for granted in many places. Interfaith dialogue and respect were dealt a severe blow on Sept 11th 2001 in the US and March 11th 2003 in Europe. In some places 9/11 spurred efforts in interfaith dialogue on. In many other places interfaith dialogue has given way to mutual suspicions and recriminations. The philosophy of tolerance long maintained in Europe is under great strain. This is a very fragile and turbulent time for people who believe in peace, ecumenism, co-existence, and good neighborliness among people of different faiths. Atrocities committed against members of other religions in "ethnic cleansing" operations are coming to light in Europe and other unexpected locations. Targeted killings of high profile persons who appear in the eyes of some radical fundamentalists to have in some way violated their sacred faith are a chilling reminder of the lengths to which some will go in defense of their religious values.

Following widespread disenchantment with first civilian and then military regimes in various African and other so-called "Third world" countries which promised independence, freedom, redemption, liberation, revolution, and progress, postcolonial discourses are increasingly critical of the neo-colonialist governments and societies that emerged. Civil society continues to be non-partisan if not completely a-political and deeply skeptical of calls for "democracy" and "freedom", especially when they emanate from powerful, militaristic forces.

Perspectives on "pastoral" counseling

The need for renewed forms of pastoral counseling which embody values of communal as well as personal wellbeing is clear. The characteristics of such new forms of pastoral counseling are contained in a description of pastoral care I first wrote in 1993 and revised slightly in 2003. The description is as follows: "Pastoral care consists of helping activities, participated in by people who recognize a transcendent dimension to human life, which, by the use of verbal and non-verbal, direct or indirect, literal or symbolic modes of communication aim at preventing stress, relieving anxiety or facilitating persons coping with anxieties. Pastoral care seeks to foster people's growth as full human beings together with the development of ecologically and socio-politically holistic communities in which all persons may live humane lives."[1]

In my view, pastoral counseling, which in essence involves intensive psychotherapeutic and theological attention to individuals and small groups, needs to be set within a framework of pastoral care which is broad, inclusive and pluralistic. Pastoral counseling can be compared to surgical intervention whilst pastoral care functions as public or community health care. Pastoral counseling is an intensifying and focusing of the general skills and aims of pastoral care, upon an individual or small group of persons-in-

---

[1] See Emmanuel Y. Lartey, *In Living Color: An Intercultural Approach to Pastoral Care and Counseling*, 2nd ed., London/New York: Jessica Kingsley Press, 2003, 30-31.

relation. For pastoral counseling to be healthy it needs the framework and context of the wider ministry of pastoral care. Moreover, pastoral counseling is premised upon recognition of transcendence. This is a way of affirming that it has to do with spirituality, significance, structures of meaning and faith.

Pastoral counseling is a form of religious or spiritual practice. To further explore the challenges faced by this practice it is instructive to pay attention to different ways in which the adjective pastoral is used to qualify and illuminate the nature of the counseling that is on offer through pastoral counseling.

In spite of protests from practitioners and teachers, by far the most common understanding which seems to be evoked by the expression "pastoral counseling" is that it is counseling of or by ordained clergypersons. Here pastoral counseling means counseling *of* pastors or simply put, talking with pastors to help them with their problems (pastors also do have problems!). Along similar lines, pastoral counseling may be understood as counseling by pastors or simply as pastors talking with other people about their personal, family or relational problems. Howard Clinebell described pastoral counseling as "the utilization by clergy of counseling and psychotherapeutic methods to enable individuals, couples and families to handle their personal crises and problems in living constructively."[2] In this way of understanding pastoral counseling the focus is on the one who receives (recipient) or else gives the counseling – (the agent) namely, the pastor. This "clerical" paradigm continues to shape the practice of pastoral counseling in many places.

Such pastoral counseling takes religious issues seriously. Exploring and analyzing faith development, taking religious histories, and gauging theological sensibilities are important features of it. For some pastoral counselors, religious verbiage indicates the pathological or transferential material that is the focus of therapeutic work. That is to say that religion has a place in the transference and counter-transference between counselor and client the exploration of which is crucial for effective therapy. For others faith talk when properly and directly attended to, can help the therapeutic process move forward in helpful ways. In either case, though in very different ways, issues of faith are not dismissed. Instead there is a serious engagement and attempt to integrate theology with psychology, both in diagnosis and treatment. However, religion is not only notoriously difficult to define, it is also hard to categorize. As such some, who would wish to retain the designation "pastoral" counseling as demarcating a religious interest, seek to include within it any matters of faith or ultimate

[2] In Alastair V. Campbell (ed.), *A Dictionary of Pastoral Care*, London: SPCK, 1987, 198.

concern and not merely religious affiliation.[3] This approach seeks to address the fact that many who "believe" do not belong to any religious community.[4] Moreover, various participants in communities of faith hold what may be described as unconventional or unorthodox beliefs. Pastoral counseling on these terms would include any and all matters of faith and ultimate concern or "spirituality" however defined or described.

The clerical paradigm, nevertheless, has been criticized especially in western European circles as individualistic, patriarchal, encouraging magical thinking, promoting dependence, and having an intrinsic tendency towards the abuse of power. Theologically it is seen as allied to a monarchical view of God that can and has been associated with oppressive, paternalistic, imperialistic and colonial practices. Moreover, it is recognized that pastoral care is more often communally and unofficially ministered through the agency of unrecognized women and unlicensed lay people.

Another way of looking at pastoral counseling is to see it as arising out of and occurring within a community of faith. In this view pastoral counseling is communal counseling that is engaged in, by and within community. The whole community is the counselor and individual counselors see themselves as representatives of the community. Here team work and collaboration is vital. Different persons have different forms of expertise within the community and they offer these skills in concert and with consultation. The critiques of the clerical and later the clinical-pastoral models, the rise of feminist, womanist and various forms of liberation theologies, and the advent of post-modernism have all contributed to the emergence of the communal-contextual paradigm. Practitioners employing this model seek to restore these disciplines to their roots within communities of faith.

It is communal because it challenges individualism and encourages communal and ecclesial formation and practice. The church as a relational and corporate community is both the base and the agent of care. Communities of faith are the loci of pastoral care and pastoral theology properly understood and practiced. The "clientele" is also communal – whole communities become the focus of pastoral strategies. It is contextual because it pays much more attention to the historical, social and cultural contexts of the communities that mediate pastoral care. It argues that attention needs to be paid to the wider social environment for effective care of persons to occur. Under girding this model are four interconnecting and mutually reinforcing core values that inform this model: first, the centrality

---

[3] Cf. e.g. J. Foskett and M. Jacobs, "Pastoral Counselling", in Windy Dryden et al. (eds.), *Handbook of Counselling in Britain*, London: Tavistock/Routledge 1989.

[4] See Grace Davie, *Religion in Britain Since 1945: Believing Without Belonging*, Oxford: Blackwell Publishers, 1994; Gordon Lynch, *After Religion: Generation X and the Search for Meaning*, London: Darton, Longman and Todd, 2002.

of relationality and community; second, that human development is a relational process which occurs within a social context; third, individual differences and cultural diversity are highly valued; fourth, mutuality and reciprocity.[5]

An "ecclesial-prophetic" model has emerged as a further development of the communal contextual model. This model emphasizes the unique characteristics of ecclesial communities in which practices of care are rooted. The insights of recent developments in Trinitarian theology and ecclesiology are used to ground a vision of the church as a "web of interwoven relationships" which is characterized by love, commitment, acceptance, forgiveness, and intimacy. This model also calls the church to fulfill its calling to be a prophetic, transformative, and healing community.[6]

The intercultural paradigm, which extends the communal-contextual model into a global nexus and asks questions concerning issues of global justice specifically including matters of race, gender, class, sexuality and economics, is the most recently developed of the emerging theories. Its intercultural ethos expresses a "nonreductive, open, creative and tolerant hermeneutics" which is democratic in a global sense and argues that wisdom does not belong only to one group, race, ideology or faith.[7] This approach is polylingual, polyphonic and polyperspectival. Many voices need to be spoken, listened to and respected in our quest for meaningful and effective living. On the intercultural route all totalizing structures and systems are critiqued and challenged in recognition of the complexity, plurality, fragmentation and pluriformity of our post-modern and post-colonial times. Interculturality stands for an attitude that rejects both extreme relativism and exclusive absolutism. It inhabits different cultures but also seeks to transcend their narrow limits. The intercultural paradigm is increasingly influencing the pastoral disciplines through many avenues, not least encounters across cultures, social groups, religious faiths, gender and sexualities. For these newer models of pastoral care, the metaphor of the "the living human web" has replaced the "living human document," as the primary metaphor.[8]

---

[5] Karen Scheib, "Contributions of Communion Ecclesiology to the Communal-Contextual Model of Care", in *Journal of Pastoral Theology*, 2002.

[6] Karen Scheib, *Challenging Invisibility: Practices of Care with Older Women*, St. Louis: Chalice Press, 2004.

[7] Ram A. Mall, *Intercultural Philosophy*, New York/Oxford: Rowman & Littlefield Publ., 2000, 6.

[8] B.J. Miller-McLemore, "The Living Human Web: Pastoral Theology at the Turn of the Century", in J. Stevenson-Moessner (ed.), *Through the Eyes of Women*, Minneapolis: Fortress Press, 1996, 16.

Two other approaches to pastoral counseling seem to me to offer much of value to a faithful practice of pastoral counseling in the midst of the liminality, uncertainty and multiplicity of the globalizing world.

Counseling for whole communities

In the first pastoral counseling is envisaged and practiced as counseling for the whole person-in-community. The passion of pastoral counselors who envision their practice in these terms is for what I call "relational holism." The aim of their practice is not the isolated, tough, self-directed, self-regulated individual of Enlightenment rationalism but rather "emotionally intelligent"[9] persons, who are in touch with themselves, relate effectively and compassionately with others and seek the wellbeing of whole communities. The genius is leaning to relate well with self and others. These counselors do not work in isolation. They respectfully engage the expertise and practice of other health care professionals and expect in these teams to be treated in the same way. Matters of faith and belief are important to them not as impositions from without but as emanations from within persons in relation with a self-giving and responsive God. Matters of faith are not solely the preserve of active participants in communities of faith. Whoever wishes to ponder their life circumstances through lenses of significance may find help and support from pastoral counselors. The desire is to help persons find internal and inter-personal wholeness.
Many in this day and age seek such wholeness and do not find it because almost everyone is trying to sell them a product with their own stamp on it. Pastoral counseling that aims at promoting relational holism eschews any attempts to make people after our own image. Rather the skills acquired by the counselor enable her to accompany persons on their own journey in quest of personal wholeness.

Here an important distinction between "individual" and "person" may be helpful. The term "individual" derives from the idea of there being a unit of life substance (e.g. previously believed to be and called, the atom) that cannot be further subdivided. The individual is the unit of society that cannot be broken down any further i.e. the smallest unit of society. "Person" on the other hand derives from relationship. The Zulu saying "A person is a person by reason of other persons" captures this sense beautifully. We become persons from before the time of our birth, through an interactive process with other persons. No one achieves holistic development without the challenges and joys of inter-personal interaction. As such the term person, unlike individual, is a relational term. Many pastoral counselors have found a combination of the psychodynamic Object

[9] Daniel Goleman, *Emotional Intelligence*, New York: Bantam Books, 1997.

Relations Theories, the socially engaged theories of Family Systems therapies and the socio-historical ideas of Narrative Therapy useful in responding to realities and challenges of our social nature as persons.

Pastoral counseling which aims at facilitating the growth of whole communities does so through journeying with persons as they navigate the deep waters of internalized oppression, societal devaluing and cultural denigration. Pastoral counseling in quest of relational holism develops out of models not only of illness, disease and deprivation, but also from the wells of wisdom, strength and courage one finds in communities that have undergone trauma and hardship. Wholeness and holiness go together. There is an important shift taking place in psychotherapeutic and psychological studies from an exclusive focus on pathology to more study of human strengths and virtues. In the end there needs to be more balance so that we benefit from both. As Schipani has argued, "as providers of a special form of pastoral care, pastoral counselors are primarily concerned with helping people live more wisely in the light of God as they face life challenges and struggles."[10]

"Worldly" pastoral counseling

In Great Britain there is a decidedly secular usage of the term pastoral counseling which may seem strange to other nationals but which offers much in the climate we have been describing. The term is used within educational circles. Pastoral Care in schools in Britain has to do with the discipline, personal welfare and well-being, and academic achievement of students. It has the following four dimensions:

- Discipline and order
- Welfare and personal well-being
- Curriculum and academic achievement
- Administration and organization.

Pastoral care in educational circles in Britain though it may attend to "spirituality" has nothing overt to do with religion or religious belief. Teachers, tutors, guidance and career counselors, academic advisors and supervisors all have, among other things, a "pastoral" responsibility towards their students. It is significant to me that the term "pastoral" has been retained. In this way "pastoral" has been reframed so that its essential functional referent is brought out. "Pastoral" here is not so much about "who is doing it" as it is about "what is done and how". Pastoral counseling on this view is counseling that promotes or enables well-being, good order,

---

[10] Daniel S. Schipani, *The Way of Wisdom in Pastoral Counseling*, Elkhart IN: Institute of Mennonite Studies, 2003, 29.

disciplined living, and achieving of potential in a well structured environment.

Facing the challenges of a globalizing world

In the face of the plurality, liminality and uncertainty of our globalizing world I pose the following as characteristics of the art of pastoral counseling necessary to operate in this world.

First, the concerns of pastoral counseling need not be narrowly parochial. Pastoral counseling in this day and age needs to rise above being merely an inner dialogue between persons of the same faith or attempts to recruit along faith lines. It needs to be broader than that. Anyone, regardless of religious tradition or the lack of it should find some benefit from the careful, thoughtful practice of pastoral counseling. This means that pastoral counselors need a multi-faith orientation which is familiar with different faiths in a nonthreatening, non-defensive manner. Pastoral counselors need to be able to be respectful of all faiths no matter how different they may be from what they are familiar with. Security in one's own faith is a prerequisite, for where there is fear and insecurity dialogue and openness is difficult. Openness presupposes such inner security. Pastoral counselors need to serve communities beyond their faith group.

Second, pastoral Counseling in this globalizing context lends itself both to the sacred and the secular – the unexpectedly sacred as well as the "holy" secular. Pastoral counseling in the current environment needs to be at home with and "recognize transcendence" in various forms. An age of multiplicity needs the flexibility of a faith that recognizes God in unexpected spaces and places. Taking faith seriously requires attention to theology and how it has developed in particular people's experience. It also means attention to unconventional and uncharted forms of religious experience – and secular experience which is invested with sacred value. The expertise that pastoral counselors bring will be that of exploring the significance of conscious and unconscious ideas, images and relationships. These will include overtly religious symbols as well as nonreligious and secular ones.

Third, the forms of pastoral counseling that will be relevant in our current context will make respectful dialogue with and between a wide range of religious and non-religious persons possible. I have personally gained much through studying and living closely with persons of Islamic faith. The wisdom of mystics like Khalil Gibran, Rabindranath Tagore, the Dalai Lama, among others, have illuminated my own as well as many other Christians' personal journeys. In the quest for wise living it must be acknowledged that persons from many different religious faiths have made very significant contributions. There is a rich and broad literature of wisdom of the ages drawn from many different religious faiths that could enrich the theory and practice of pastoral counseling, if the practitioners could rise above our exclusive weddedness to particular psychologies, theologies and traditions. Pastoral Counseling needs an interfaith orientation of respect and interaction. In this regard it is instructive that the gospels portray Jesus as having much to say in commendation of the faith of non Jews, even of despised Samaritans and Romans. (e.g. Matt 15: 21 - 28, the Canaanite woman; Luke 7: 1 -10, the Roman centurion; Luke 17:15-19, the Samaritan leper who was the only one of the ten who returned thanks for his healing). Jesus' sharpest rebukes were reserved for those of his own faith (the Scribes and Pharisees) who refused to recognize God outside of their own narrow schemes.

Fourth, pastoral counseling now must continue to emphasize relationality above technique. Along with a theological re-discovery of the richness of the Doctrine of the Trinity has gone a realization of the fact that a more adequate way of talking of the "Persons" of the Godhead is to talk of Relations. God the Blessed Trinity is a movement of relations that interpenetrate and interact within and among each other. The language of relations is very dear to the heart of pastoral counselors because so much of our practice has to do with exploring the impact of past and present significant relationships upon our emotional and psychological health and well-being today. There is thus much to be gained by exploring what is meant by relations within God to see what may be learned for relations among and within human beings created in the image of God.

A hallmark of pastoral counseling in the new circumstances in which we find ourselves must be a deeper and more thoughtful theological analysis. Pastoral counseling cannot and must not merely be a sprinkling of a psychological baby with cold theological water or the overlaying of a thin veneer of shallow theology upon a psychological product. In this regard Trinitarian relationalism could be a helpful model.

Fifth, pastoral counseling now has to be oriented towards a balance between a disease model and a health and strength model. So much of the discipline of pastoral counseling has followed the disease model embedded in medical practice. As with psychology the main interest has been in diagnosis and treatment of pathology. Whilst this has clearly been valuable and will continue to be so, there is a steady increase in recognition of the importance of the more "positive psychology" that studies strength, virtue and ability. The cultivation of virtues and strengths has long been a practice associated with spiritual direction. Spirituality has tended in the direction of the practices that empower and enhance strengthened relations with the divine. As Len Sperry has argued[11] much of value could result from an

[11] Len Sperry, *Transforming Self and Community: Revisioning Pastoral Counseling and Spiritual Direction*, Collegeville, MN: The Liturgical Press, 2002.

integrative approach that draws together the practices of spiritual direction, moral education and pastoral counseling.

Sixth, pastoral counseling as argued above increasingly draws upon a rich and varied theological heritage. Pastoral counseling needs to be theologically astute in attempting consciously and unconsciously to mirror God's presence in the world, which is framed in Christian understanding as self-giving (kenotic), self effacing, unobtrusive, non-threatening and life-giving. "Secular" pastoral counseling in particular holds potential for such mirroring. In recognition of the God who though self-disclosing, invites all humans to "search for him and perhaps grope for him in the hope that they might find him – though indeed he is not far from each of us" (Acts 17: 27), pastoral counseling may by its very activity engage in such invitational practice. God's presence in the world is subtle and most often unrecognized or celebrated. Similarly the most effective forms of care and counseling are unannounced. It seems to be the way of the Holy Spirit to woo and lure rather than to overwhelm and compel. The God "in whom we live, move and have our being" (Acts 17: 28) does not seem anxious to constantly make her presence felt overtly. In Christ God gives God's self to humanity in faith and trust that the divine self-giving will eventually be discovered. Pastoral counseling mirrors such self-giving love.

Seventh, pastoral counseling needs now more than ever before to pay close attention to persons-in-context. As we learn just how much we are impacted by the contexts in which we live and grow, we recognize the need for pastoral counselors to be cultural analysts if our practice is to be of any significance for the persons and communities in which we practice. It is as pastoral counselors become aware of and sensitive to the changing cultural circumstances which are at work within and around our clients that we become more able to be authentically present with them. This contextual analysis is inclusive of the historical, social, political and economic dimensions of communal life. The world, as it were, is closing in on us in the global village. As the West has influenced others with language and cultural products so are we now subject to the influences that exist and arise from different regions of the world. Potentially we are humanized by empathic relations with all humankind no matter how different culturally and ethnically. We are called upon to be faithful and reflective practitioners of care by paying close attention to a world in flux.

Emotional Upheaval and Relational Refugeism in Contemporary Indian Experience:

An Intercultural Exploration and Proposal for Pastoral Therapy *

Joseph George
India, 2005

The SIPCC's 18th International Seminar on Intercultural Pastoral Care and Counselling focuses on Intercultural and Interfaith Communication in Pastoral Practice with a view to encourage new models and to learn from each other new directions in therapeutic endeavours in different cultural contexts. The therapeutic community in the recent times, including pastoral counsellors, recognizes the significance of contextual realities in responding to personal and interpersonal stress, dysfunctional traits, and demoralizing human experiences. The difficulty is, in my opinion, how pastoral counsellors discern the issues in a culturally sensitive manner, identify indigenous insights and tools, and respond pastorally and clinically to these issues and concerns without losing their professional integrity as analytically oriented clinical pastoral counsellors and informed theologians. The title of the paper suggests emotional upheaval and relational inequality that are significant concerns for all care professionals. The term "relational refugeism" is employed to show the depth of emotional upheaval or bankruptcy and unequal relational equations visible at all levels of living.

The focus of this paper is to highlight a few of the contemporary challenges and their impact on personal and relational experience in the context of doing pastoral counselling in mufti-faith, multi-ethnic, multi-linguistic and multi-cultural India. It has been a struggle for me to coin a name to the type of clinical pastoral approach that I have developed over the years for practicing pastoral counselling in India.

The primary focus of this approach is to bring the totality of human experience within the purview of pastoral psychotherapeutic practice while employing the tools and insights of the analytically oriented therapies. I am convinced that pastoral counsellors are not mere experts of intrapsychic

* Lecture presented at the 18th International Seminar on Intercultural Pastoral Care and Counselling 2005, in Düsseldorf-Kaiserswerth, first published in: *Intercultural Pastoral Care and Counselling, 13*, 2006, 90-96.

processes but enablers, who deal with issues, concerns, and challenges that have personal, functional, and relational impact. Though there is a theoretical acceptance of this insight among pastoral theologians, little change is noticeable in the modes of pastoral practice. Hence, I am proposing a Strategic Analytical Pastoral approach that allows the therapists to be cultural sensitive, strategic in addressing issues and concerns, analytical in method, and pastoral in therapeutic mission and spiritual direction.

This is in line with what the SIPCC proposes to achieve through the interactions and learning experiences during the Intercultural Seminars as it seeks to enhance a mutual holistic learning process among the participants, to strengthen personal skills in intercultural interactions, and to advance their skills in providing professional pastoral counselling in a culturally sensitive (empathy) manner. The SIPCC statement says:

The International Seminars want to enhance a mutual holistic learning process among the participants:

- the participants encounter people from other cultures and exchange various cultural experiences
- they give and receive new impulses for new lifestyles
- they give and receive new impulses for their spiritual and communal living
- they reflect on cultural, social, political, economical and religious contexts of people
- they challenge their own cultural and religious assumptions and presuppositions
- they present their practice in care and counselling and reflect upon them from various perspectives
- they extend their professional knowledge in dealing with the theme of the seminar,
- they enter into a process of theory-building of intercultural pastoral care and counselling. [1]

Contextual issues and therapeutic concerns in India

In formulating adequate theoretical framework and developing contextually relevant skills one needs to be culturally sensitive and discerning. There are numerous factors that could be highlighted in the discussion of contextual realities in India, demanding some sort of intercultural dialogue, learning, and action – at personal, social and political levels. For this presentation I focus on four different major areas within which one could also trace specific concerns and issues.

[1] Quoted from the SIPCC's "General Learning Goals". The section is well formulated and indicates the commitment of SIPCC to encourage persons in therapy to develop culturally sensitive insights and to acquire skills in dealing with personal and interpersonal issues in therapy. I am not aware of any other care providing professional organization that has an intentional agenda to discuss and to develop cultural competence in therapeutic practice.

Politics, religion, community, violence

There is a general agreement among social scientists on the influence of political processes on religion and the influence of religion on politics and community experience, though they may disagree on the nature and the degree in which this impact could be measured. The recent political trends in India, both at the national and regional levels, vividly indicate the ways in which political processes influence religious thought and interactions in India. It is also true that religions influence political processes. In the recent decades it has become difficult for a single political party to gain power at the National level, and in most of the States in India, besides the national parties, there are innumerable regional parties who are officially or unofficially sponsored by religious or ethnic groups. The regional parties are brought into the coalition governments in order to maintain a majority in the Houses. These regional parties with their religious affiliations continue to have a major role in Indian politics. Each of these regional parties represents specific cultural, religious or ethnic identities and they demand the fulfilment of their political expectations. In the given situation, then, the political process in India today is an encounter of different cultures, each one waiting to benefit from their political bargaining. What is to be noted in this bargaining is the emotional upheaval, identity crisis, personal and collective insecurity, and relational disturbance. The impact of such confusing and disturbing process could be seen at all levels – from the elected leaders to the common people in the villages. Further, at the personal and interpersonal level such processes thrive to create either relational dependency and refugeism or dominating the other in political relationships, hindering healthy political process. This could also be true of other nations where coalition governments are formed.

Religious groups that support regional political parties also gain by exerting their influence and power in administration and policy-making. For example, the previous national government in India, lead by the Bharatiya Janatha Party (BJP), was supported by other political parties with religious affiliation. Hence, religious groups advocating cultural and national integration under "one culture" formulae deeply influenced the government and justified whatever happened during this time in politics. The 2003 Gujarat violence and mass killing and large scale destruction of public and private property was/is justified as their right to do in order to protect India and its culture. The majority community brought tremendous amount of pain and agony on the minority community in this instance. Such experiences at the grass-root level create fear, pain, insecurity, and rejection of the other because the other is different and not to be trusted.

Alongside, one also needs to recognize the emergence of fundamentalist organizations of political nature with confused religious agendas, such as "cultural integration" or "national integration". There are also fundamentalist approaches from the Christian communities that deeply disturb social ethos and harmonious living. For example, the independent churches who focus on converting people of other faith as they see "Jesus as the only Saviour".

The history of India indicates the high tolerance among the Indians to "tolerate" the other that made the multicultural existence possible without forcing social, emotional, and physical termination of the other. However, the India-Pakistan divide and the events immediate before and after, point to intolerance and aggression towards the other, which still exists. Further, what has happened during the last two decades is highly disappointing and painful in terms of intercultural existence and interaction. The series of violence sanctioned by religious communities or their political organizations in different parts of the country brought widespread destruction, loss of lives, and long-lasting pain on persons, families, and groups. We encounter the victims of such experiences in therapy who have undergone deep pain and live with suspicion and fear of the other. Such situations also lead to social and psychological distancing – isolation and withdrawal – hindering the fullness of life and the meaning of living together. What does these religio-political events and dynamics mean for the intercultural discussions at the SIPCC?

Diminishing presence of nurturing communities

The long historical traditions in India – including the structure of family, kinship, village communities, and religious groups – indicate the presence of structures or agencies that had nurturing and therapeutic functions, irrespective of ethnic, cultural or faith background. For example, in an extended family set up (earlier to this was the joint-family system) there is a larger network of people, led by the eldest male, who were responsible for decision making and implementing. Hence, there was a feeling of support and guidance even at the most difficult decision-making process and in encountering the unknown and the unexpected. Whenever there was a personal or relational difficulty, there were "resource persons" within the set up, in a hierarchical order, to handle the issues and find a solution. There was a wisdom-sharing group that guided the thoughts and actions of its community members. Edward P. Wimberly, Professor and Dean at the Interdenominational Theological Centre, Atlanta, laments the loss of nurturing communities resulting in the development and domination of therapeutic communities in the West.[2] He was quite impressed with the sharing of wisdom and enlivening life in the African communities in Zimbabwe, as against the narrow individualism and related practices that he

---

[2] Edward P. Wimberly, *Relational Refugees: Alienation and Reincorporation in African American Churches and Communities*, Nashville: Abingdon, 2000, 16.

noticed and encountered in the United States. Elevation of individualism led to the death of caring institutions.

India is considered as one of the countries that still keep some of its traditional family and cultural features. However, this is not true in every situation of life. The influence of living in a technologically advanced world has touched not only the urban Indian communities but also the rural. There is a growing individualism that propagates personal freedom, competition, and excellence. Right from childhood, persons are initiated, directed, and motivated to be successful in that competitive world in order to be "somebody". This trend is noticeable in the areas of education, career choice, financial management, and interpersonal relationships. In a world of freedom, competition, and excellence many accomplish their dreams and ideals without even taking care of their own personal needs and psychic nourishment, resulting in emotional disruption and relational bankruptcy. Those who fail to reach their goals continue to live in bitterness blaming themselves and others for what has happened to them. Hence, personal experience in highly success-oriented urban Indian communities creates emotional upheaval and relational disturbance, whether one is an achiever or non-achiever. In the context of such emotional turmoil and displacement in relational experiences, the nurturing institutions have a natural place in caring and sustaining. However, the disappearance of such institutions leaves the people in turmoil without any genuine assistance. Emotional disturbance, relational dependence, and relational deprivation hinder the development of fully functioning persons. Does it in some way point to the need of intercultural openness and learning? The old and the new, urban and rural; indigenous and foreign, advanced and the non-advanced features of culture continue to be a point of friction and anxiety. What kind of intercultural dialogue is possible in this context?

Globalization and glocalization [3] – intercultural conversion?

The process of globalization has led to major changes in socio-economic and cultural situations influencing life-styles, gender relations, attitudes, belief systems and practices, primary relationships, and specific behavioural patterns. Globalization is encounter of cultures and in many ways a complex process. At the surface level, the encounter is between the cultures of the developed, developing, and underdeveloped countries in the areas of trade, employment, and financial transactions. One of the leading

[3] With *glocalization* is meant: the networking of local communities and the particularity of regional cultures within unique contexts. Glocalization is a reaction over against the pressure of global networking, and the danger to ignore local issues as related to interests of particular communities on grassroots level. It is an attempt to voice the needs of specifically poor and developing countries, over against the expansionism of the big economic enterprises.

sociologists in India, Professor Yogendra Singh highlights the five features of globalization and their direct or indirect impact on the community:[4] (1) Revolution in communication technology and the widespread use of it even by the non-professionals (2) Circulation of financial capital demanding large scale modernization in technology and demand in labour market (3) Homogenization of consumer products luring the common people to become the consumers – causing a change in lifestyle, behaviour, and world views (4) enlargement of the scope of the electronic media in communication that has changed the pattern of knowing, relationship, and informed action (5) Large scale circulation of professionally trained persons in the world market, changing the very concept of employment in India. The large-scale geographical mobility of persons coming to India and Indians going to other countries on a short or long term basis forces intercultural exposure, demanding response or reaction. This mobility influences not only the ones moving but also the people around them, both in home country and in the new destination. However, the encounters go much deeper than what is visible at the surface level – causing personality change and encouraging life-styles that are not genuinely one's own. Even one's view and practice of primary interpersonal relationships undergo noticeable changes resulting in a new emotional environment. There are demands and expectations that would make one competent in the job market. They do not have a choice of the nature of work, schedule, and life-style. Even the name is changed in some employment contexts in order to make them suit for the job.[5] Yogendra Singh notes the link between the globalizing process, market economy, career opportunities and the intellectual and emotional process that has impacted the world community, especially the developing nations. He remarks:

> It seems that a massive ideological transition is slowly taking place in our society. There is a manifest pull towards values of achievement and entrepreneur adventure. With increased global networking of economy, modes of consumption and cultural styles, a new resurgence of aspirations is taking place. It affects the career preferences of people and their perception of the life-world.[6]

---

[4] Yogendra Singh, *Cultural Change in India: Identity and Globalization*, Jaipur: Rawat Publications, 2000, 71-72.

[5] The people hired for Call Centres (BPO) managed by the MNCs undergo a period of rigorous training in personal appearance, communication, voice, and the skills of understanding 'the other' who is in the USA or UK. They are also given a name that would make them suit to the taste of the customers in the West. For example, one of my counselees has undergone such a name change in order to increase her professional competence. Of course, this process comes under intercultural competence! Sharmila Damedaran became Sheila in doing business with the company's target population. What does this change mean to the person is not a matter of concern for anyone?

[6] Singh, *Cultural Change in India*, 251.

The trends of globalization deeply influence local communities in their life-styles, values, attitudes, and patterns of relationships. This is the globalization. The wide range impact of globalization on local communities is widely discussed by professionals in every field. This is an area of interest to pastoral counsellors too in order to discern what is happening in the life of persons and their communities and to plan adequate methods of reaching them. Even theologians and theological communities have given thought in formulating the impact of such process on the lives of the people and their relationships. Further, what is the task of pastoral theologians and counsellors in dealing with issues arising from the intercultural interactions between specific communities around the world? While discussing the trends of globalization and its impact on the local communities, J. Jayakiran Sebastian, a professor of systematic theology at the United Theological College, points out the trend of transformation globally and locally. He remarks:

> At this point we need to recognize that those of us who are partners in this discourse on globalization are in many ways the Glocalized beneficiaries of the "rewards" that are on offer. In terms of our social and economic location and status, our clothing, our means of transformation, our access to communication facilities, our admittance to systems of knowledge, are reflected in what we have become... we should not try to locate the "glocal" outside ourselves but honestly and realistically interrogate ourselves in trying to understand how best we can continue to allow ourselves to be transformed... and what this transformation is doing to us in terms of what we believe and practice.[7]

Alienation in the midst of Globalization and Economic Development is an aspect of human experience that none can disregard. The non-inclusion of the less advantaged people to benefit from the economic development is a serious intercultural mistake. This trend can only create relational refugees and emotional death. Alienation of the Poor and the Marginalized cannot lead to developing communities with justice. How do we bring our intercultural learning in understanding and discerning the issues in this context?

Tsunami, Katrina, Rita, who is next... ?

Several unexpected and painful events in the last years have increased the amount of tension and feeling of insecurity all over the world, especially in the Western world. Are we safe in our "fortified cities"? Natural disasters

---

[7] J. Jayakiran Sebastian, "Security, Risk and the Consequences of Grace: Reading a Letter of Cyprian of Carthage in Today's Glocalized World", in Joseph George (ed.), *The God of All Grace: Essays in Honour of Origen Vasantha Jathanna*, Bangalore: Asian Trading Corporation and United Theological College, 2005, 220-221.

and unnatural disasters (human made calamities) have deeply disturbed the global community in its experience of handling suffering, disorientation, loss, and helplessness that many experienced due to natural calamities: Tsunami, Katrina, Rita, who is next? The Tsunami has totally destroyed coastal communities in many parts of Asia. The well meaning people everywhere, East and the West, responded immediately with assistance. Yet, at some point of time there was discussion indicating the technologically advanced countries could have provided adequate warning in order to control the destruction and loss. For millions in Asia, such discussions did not mean anything as they were in the process of grieving, counting the loss, dealing with injuries, adjusting to temporary shelters, and eagerly waiting for further help.

The way in which Katrina created havoc in the United States indicates a different picture. Whether you have the information or not, whether you are prepared or not, you are touched by the hand of "the unexpected". Of course, there was a better preparation for Rita! What does all this mean? Even in the most secured places, with all advanced technologies, we are not safe as we have not attained the mastery over controlling the nature, though at times one it is comforting to imagine (illusory world) that we are in control of everything.

Since September 11, there is a global interest in tracking and tackling violence and terrorism. Does that mean there were no violence and disturbing scenes before September 11? Even if there were, the global community (including the mental health professionals) have not given due attention! Asian community has witnessed and experienced violence and terrorism in different ways. India has been pleading with the world community the depth of its suffering due to religious fundamentalism, violence, and terrorism. During 1995 - 2001, there were over a dozen school related acts of violence in the United States (I was in the US during this period) resulting in loss of lives and creating panicky situation in the schools and the communities around. Did the world community listen? Did the mental health professionals and pastoral counsellors listen? I doubt it very much! Violence is always disturbing and needs to be addressed using the insights from depth psychologies. How can we address the issues of aggression, violence, and terrorism without genuine intercultural dialogue, respectful learning, and action with discernment? India had series of natural disasters in the last decade causing destruction and damage to persons, communities, and the State. In the same manner India suffered much from violence and terrorism. One of the contextual issues in discussion is providing professional care in the midst of destruction and death. Whether it is helping in the context of a natural disaster or taking care of persons victimized by violence and terrorism, there is a level of intercultural engagement, sharing, and relating. Healing and strengthening the emotionally disturbed, sustaining the lesser advantaged, and incorporating the relational refugees into the mainstream life are unavoidable therapeutic objectives, especially from the Indian scenario. It is in this context I share with you the following thoughts regarding the pastoral counselling approach.

Exploring pastoral therapeutic paradigms in India

The pastoral counselling practices in India have been highly influenced by the Western Clinical Pastoral Education and Pastoral Counselling approaches. In my view various factors contributed to this Western influence among the pastoral professionals in India. Western missionaries with specialization in counselling not only practiced but also trained pastoral counsellors in India, certainly within the purview of their own cultural context and training. The Indians who have benefited from advanced level of pastoral training practices from the Western context come back with what they have learned "new" without adequate tools to discern the validity of what they have learned for understanding Indian realities. The literature used in pastoral clinical training and counselling practices in India is mostly of Western origin. Hence, the therapeutic trend in the West has influenced the Indian pastoral practitioners. Given this context, let me also highlight various trends and paradigms existing among pastoral counsellors, professionally trained or not. This is very similar to tracing the historical paradigms in pastoral counselling in the West. While discussing culturally informed practices in pastoral counselling, Professor Emmanuel Y. Lartey of the Emory University makes a historical review of different paradigms that impacted the pastoral counselling profession. He details four different paradigms, based on the works of John Patton and Nancy J. Ramsay, that seem to cover the theoretical and clinical domains in pastoral psychotherapeutic practice. These are the classical-clerical, clinical-pastoral, communal-contextual, and intercultural paradigms.[8]

The *classical-clerical paradigm* reflects the traditional theological understanding and practice of pastoral therapy, primarily focused around the ordained persons who are the care providers. In this approach the caregivers and care-receivers view the process primarily as religious – a religious context, religious practitioners, and religious resources. It seems to promote the idea that religious experiences can lead to therapeutic process, This approach is found among the trained and untrained professionals in

[8] Emmanuel Y. Lartey, "Widening the Scope, Increasing the Depth: Developing Culturally Informed Practices of Pastoral Care and Counseling", A paper presented at the 8th Asia Pacific Congress on Pastoral Care and Counselling, Hong Kong, August 2000, 8-12.

therapeutic enterprise. The Roman Catholic, the Orthodox, a section of the mainline Churches, and the independent Churches adhere to such practices. Spiritual regeneration, salvific experience, and mental health are all interrelated in this approach. Though at times it focuses on community experience, mostly this approach is individual and "spiritually" oriented, thus lacking focus in contextual realities and inadequate approach to "non-religious" issues in life.

The *clinical-pastoral paradigm* is primarily influenced by modern psychological theories (mostly individual) and therapeutic practices. Lartey rightly points out that this model has widely influenced the Western pastoral psychotherapy.[9] The influence of this model is predominantly seen in clinical pastoral education, pastoral counselling training, and practices. In this approach an attempt is made to integrate psychology and theology, but one partner overcoming the other. The psychological influence is much greater than theological insights in such approaches. This resulted in an over identification with psychology while losing the ground of theology and missing the resources of the faith community in care and counselling. The counselling centres, church or institution sponsored, made their presence in India almost following the same line of clinical-pastoral paradigm. Such approaches are highly individual oriented with a view to strengthen the person. Hence, the approach is highly intrapsychic and less concerned about external realities in which the person lives and others who are suffering with this person.

The *communal-contextual paradigm* emerges as a reaction against the clericalization, clinicalization, and individualization[10] in pastoral counselling with a focus to bring community dimension to care and counselling. The approach not only recognizes that community is the context in which pastoral services are practiced and received but also gives primary attention to cultural, economic, political, and social environment and its impact on the suffering persons. While this approach proposes a radical shift in care and counselling, it fails to see the dynamics of human experience in its totality. This approach also lacks the universal global perspective in understanding issues and practical wisdom integrating human growth, community experience, and the insights of depth psychology. This is evident in the formulation of a number of "new theologies" in India, including liberation theology. There is no space for integrating the classical-pastoral features into therapeutic actions. What hinders the progress of

---

[9] Ibid., 10.
[10] Ibid.

such ideologies to become truly experiential is a matter of question for all professionals, especially for pastoral counsellors.

The *intercultural paradigm* while making use of the communal-contextual paradigm goes beyond the immediate community in order to address issues of the global community. This perspective addresses concerns relating to race, gender, caste, class, poverty, and minority struggles. It criticizes the therapeutic enterprise for being on the side of the privileged and being silent on the issues of minorities, women, and the outcastes. Like the earlier paradigm, it analyzes the social, economic, and political structures with a view to advocate justice for all. While focusing on the global community issues, the approach fails to see the strengths of earlier approaches and their appeal among the masses, especially the classical-clerical model.

Though historically traceable, each paradigm is prevalent in one form or another even today. Each of these paradigms has salient features that could help the professionally trained pastoral counsellors. The trend of adopting one and rejecting others is a rejection of people adhering to those trends. There is a need for integration – an integration that would bring tradition and modernity, lay and the ordained, religious and non-religious, local and global, professional and non-professional, faithful and the non-faithful, and developed and lesser developed into order to develop a sound approach to pastoral practice. A truly intercultural approach is learning from all in order to enrich and to minister the people of God – facilitating healing, sustaining, guiding, reconciling, nurturing, and empowering the people of God in all communities and faith orientations. It is in this context that I propose the "Strategic Analytical Pastoral Therapy" to deal with contextual and intercultural issues and concerns. We are different in many ways: tradition, language, faith, food, dress, values, attitudes, behaviour, and relationship patterns. In many respects we are not same and not equals. We are so strong and rigid that we do not want to change drastically what we believe as good, ideal, and the ultimate. Though quite often we talk about "unity in diversity" we practice diversity in diversity without recognizing the value and strength of diversities. Diversities and differentness can be our strength and resource. Will our intercultural explorations encourage each other and the human communities at large to come in terms with and fully utilize the strength of "diversity" in our diversities? What we need today in our therapeutic endeavours is a strategic analytical pastoral therapeutic approach in which there is respectful interaction and learning from each other and strive together to make life better in the global community – as individual, community, and diverse groups.

From therapeutic community to communities of care

While maintaining the integrity and professionalism in pastoral counselling, the pastoral caregivers must extend the professionalism to cover the needs of families, groups, and the community at large. Hence, the pastoral care and counselling actions must reach out beyond the therapy room, mostly with individual psychotherapy sessions. The contextual realities, group dynamics, ideological process, personality formation call the pastoral professionals to not only reach out to individuals in stress (intrapsychic or interpsychic) but also communities, religious groups, and the society at large. The programmes and processes that would lead to the wellbeing of all should be a burden of the caring communities and its professionals. This is an area of great importance to enhance the vitality of the faith communities and to experience the fullness of God as revealed in the cultural experiences of everyone, discerning what is life-giving and what is life-destroying. It is in this context, in my opinion, that we should be considering a shift from "therapeutic communities" to "communities who care". How will that experience emerge unless we pastoral counsellors engage in intercultural interaction and dialogue? How can that come true unless the pastoral professionals engage in dialogue with what they have learned from their therapy training and what is going on in the lives of the people – bringing the culture of people in dialogue with the therapeutic culture? Commitment to dialogue, learning, and action should make us think of becoming a different sort of therapists – moving away from "feel good" therapeutic agenda to the real needs of the community at large.

Identity and Care in Times of Change:

Is the Idea of Identity Meaningful for Pastoral Care and Counseling?*

Mary Rute Gomes Esperandio,
Brazil, 2008

Abstract: This text discusses the notion of identity, arguing that in times of rapid changes both in social configurations and in the constitution of existential territory, traditional understandings of identity are no longer adequate to conceptualize contemporary subjectivity. Especially, problematic are identity references that function as "identity traps" that prevent recognition of multiplicity in human subjectivity and ways of life. The essay underlines that one of the challenges for pastoral care and counseling today is the necessity of seeking ways of thinking and exercising pastoral care that escape from such identity traps. In this sense, pastoral care and counseling should support the destabilization of subjectivity for the purpose of promoting the process of healing and creation of modes of existence that affirm and expand life.

The idea of identity

When we refer to the word identity, what comes to our minds? Name, personal identity number, marital status and other family characteristics, nationality, occupation... We use these elements to "identify" ourselves. These elements can say who we are. They express something about our "essence."

We have the feeling that everybody knows what we are talking about if we mention the word "identity." But what do we really mean by identity? Identity, from the Late Latin *identitas*, means *the same,* identical. From a psychological perspective, it refers to our inwardness, our substance. The idea of identity implies some regularity, some permanency. It refers to the essence of an individual who is self aware and whose self understanding is consistent with this essence. This essence makes the individual identifiable also by others - traceable by the law and classifiable by rules, moral stan-

---

* Lecture presented at the 20th International Seminar on Intercultural Pastoral Care and Counselling, 2008, in Bratislava, Slovakia. A German translation was published in *Interkulturelle Seelsorge und Beratung, 15*, 2009, 7-12.

dards and social identification. That is why there is "cultural identity," "religious identity," "professional identity," "gender identity" and many others. Paradoxically, even though it is identity that allows one to identify, define, and differentiate the form of an individual, group, or nation, there seems to be something always missing, omitted from stated identities. Besides, the constantly changing modern world requires from us a constantly changing identity as well. How do we deal with the identification and recognition issue – which is connected to our sense of continuity – considering that the world is in constant movement? Not only is there something in the idea of identity that needs to be apprehended and perceived – something difficult to grasp – but one feels unsettled without understanding exactly why. How can we reflect on identity in a world of constant change? What challenges does the topic carry for pastoral care and counseling? Would a more precise definition of identity contribute effectively to the practice of care and counselling? What is the connection between identity and changing times?

I reflect on these issues from my Brazilian perspective and cultural context. The first section situates my reflections in relation to the global nature of this crisis in the notion of identity as exemplified by a Dutch artist. Next, I examine how a specific Brazilian religious group has been responding to the current identity crisis. From my perspective, the way this religious group offers pastoral care points toward some important elements regarding pastoral care and counselling in the context of global capitalism and identity in these times of change. Then, to clarify this relationship between identity, capitalistic society and pastoral care and counselling, I discuss three "identity traps." Finally, I discuss how this reflection sheds light on current challenges for pastoral care and counseling.

The crisis in the notion of identity

The song "iDentity," by the Dutch pianist and singer-songwriter Maurits Fondse, shows in a very creative way the identity issue in this time of change:

I blog and I write, I twitter and type, I google and Skype, I join the hype, I mail and I chat, it's my digital community.
iPod and iMac, iPhone and I check, MySpace and MyHyve, my Second Life, I'm a happy cat in my multi-personality.
I wonder and search and feed the urge to find the truth, am I on YouTube?
And am wondering still, is it me or is it me? I'm asking myself: what is my identity?

I RSS and do nothing less, I'm treating my tweets and feeding my feeds, where I'm making new friends, it's virtual humanity.

I pop and I surf, but don't have the nerve to go out on a date and now it's too late, so I google and chat, it's authorized insanity.
I don't have enough time, I'm running behind, right now I live a thousand lives so I blog and I hyve, is it really really me? And I'm asking myself: what is my identity? [1]

In his song, Fondse has wisely expressed some problems around the idea of identity. He surrenders to the contemporary demands that require from him a personal positioning about his personality. No one has ever had to say who one is, to show one's face, to introduce oneself to the world, with such frequency: blog, chat, email, Myspace, MyHyve, YouTube and Second Life. Fondse mentions the pain originated by such an identity based on appearance. "I am multiple". At the same time, Fondse is not worried about the conflict between the inner-self and the outer-self. No! Fondse notes that what the individual sees as a self image is not strong enough to work as self recognition. It is not going to take the subject any further from recognizing that the effort to have certain looks does not allow him/her to be fully oneself. At the most, it might help oneself realize that the effort to have certain looks does not mean he/she can live up to that appearance.

Fondse states that "iDentity" is a song he wrote "as a comment on the modern age with the rise of Internet. Who are [we] online and who are we offline?"[2] The composer expresses feelings that arise from the lack of identity consistency, from a weak identity and from the inability of recognising oneself in one another – in a real world.

"Identity on sale" – The offering of a capitalistic religious identity

Let us analyse another case in which some of the issues concerning identity are raised – a group identity.

The *Igreja Universal do Reino de Deus* ("Universal Church of the Kingdom of God") is a Brazilian church. But according to its own declarations, this church is now in over 170 countries.[3] Some years ago, I carried out a research project on this religious phenomenon.[4] The following story conveys an important aspect of how that religious group operates.

[1] M. Fondse has made his song accessible through a video on YouTube: https:// https://youtu.be/ww9ARO0b_k0 (accessed July 14, 2015). The lyrics as rendered here are transcribed from the video.

[2] This comment can be found on Fondse's personal web page, available at http://mauritsfondsemusicmatters.blogspot.com.br/2008_02_01_archive.html (accessed July 14, 2015).

[3] It is difficult to verify the figures, but obviously the church is rapidly spreading around the world. In 2006, it stated to be in 90 countries.

[4] Cf. Mary Rute Gomes Esperandio, "Igreja Universal do Reino de Deus: um remédio para curar os sofrimentos produzidos pelo capitalismo contemporâneo?", in *Via Teológica, 15: Vol II*, Curitiba: Faculdade Teológica Batista do Paraná, 2007.

It was Monday. I was standing in front of a Universal Church of the Kingdom of God (UCKG) temple in downtown Porto Alegre, Southern Brazil, waiting for the SIPCC group when they went to Brazil in 2006. A horror scene unfolded before my eyes: a woman in shabby clothes, probably a homeless beggar, was violently thrown out of the temple. She fell down on the pavement while a church security guard kicked her in the stomach and grabbed a plastic bottle of water from her hands. He opened it and poured out the content onto the street, throwing the empty bottle at her while she screamed and rolled on the ground in pain. Probably she had taken the bottle of water from somebody in the temple. Some people got angry watching the scene and called the police. Inside the temple about five thousand people were taking part in a so-called "Meeting (or Congress) for Businessmen."

If the scene itself generates horror because of its unprovoked violence, cruelty and "boldness" involved, the horror increased when a woman, a member of the church, approached me, vigorously defending that act of violence. She argued that "it was a demon who tried to ruin the meeting. But he has been thrown out of the temple and will not disturb us anymore!" To make sure that her explanation was right, she added: "Now, after this spectacle [involving the police, reporters and many people assembled outside the meeting], the demon is sleeping quietly." She was referring to the fact that the beggar, assaulted a while ago, was now calm, lying still on the ground with her eyes closed.

While that was happening, I saw a beautiful woman, neatly dressed, entering the church. She was the owner of a successful bakery established on the west side of the city. I had interviewed her six months before. She told me about how her life had been changed by this church. Extremely depressed, on the brink of committing suicide, she found herself deeply in debt and regularly attended Afro-Brazilian religious ceremonies. One night, when she was planning to commit suicide, she watched one of the UCKG TV programs and followed exactly what the bishop said to do. She put a glass of water on top of the TV set and, after a prayer blessing the glass of water, she drank it. For the first time after a month with very little sleep, she could finally sleep all night long. From that day on, she began attending the meetings, especially taking part in what the church calls "sacrifice campaigns," and now she feels happy to testify to her financial and emotional success, which she understands as a direct result of obeying all that the bishop said to do on TV. In short, sacrifice campaigns means: give much money to God (to the church) and God will give you back more than double in return.

Cf. also Mary Rute Gomes Esperandio, *Narcisismo e Sacrifício – Modo de subjetivação e religiosidade contemporânea*, doctoral thesis, São Leopoldo: Escola Superior de Teologia/Instituto Ecumênic de Pós-Graduação, 2006.

These stories about the UCKG are powerful. Regarding the first one, Yvan Droz, a Swiss ethnologist, makes similar remarks describing the way the UCKG treats the poor in Kenya. He says: "Beggars and tramps are excluded from the services. They must not bother the audience with their appearance or constant requests for alms... Nevertheless, poor people, like beggars or homeless children, are fed by the church... They are not abandoned. But they can't be on their own since their proper place is outside the walls of the temple."[5] Therefore, the ones who stay outside are those who can't be mirrors for the others. The second story serves as an example both of the fragility and the strength of what the UCKG system requires to put an end to suffering: make a sacrifice, which is a form of investment in oneself that will render profit. The successful and happy person is the one who can make an offering as sacrifice.

What is the relation between the conflict of identity presented by Fondse and the religious phenomenon called UCKG? Fondse shows the pain of not knowing who we are, of not being what we look like, to be paradoxically connected to the world and yet feeling alone. Actually, Fondse pictures the emptiness of the contemporary being. If the notion of identity refers back to the idea of consistency, permanence, acknowledgment, identification and belonging, all those elements seem to be fragile and not enough to shape the contemporary identity, as described by Fondse. By way of some contrast, the UCKG offers a certain kind of identity to the individual who is in suffering.

In the context of globalized capitalism and ongoing change, building one's identity has several possibilities. Such multiplicity can be simultaneously rich or debilitating. We are therefore led to suspect that the problem around the concept of identity does not rely on a more precise definition. The problem is, in fact, linked to the identity reference itself, especially in terms of stability, balance and permanence. We could name this problem as one of "identity traps." And that is where some of the challenges for the practice of pastoral care and counseling are found.

Some kinds of identity traps

There are several kinds of identity traps. Here I will discuss only three that, from my point of view, demand careful attention in pastoral care.

[5] Yvan Droz, "A Igreja Universal no Quênia", in Ari Pedro Oro, André Corten and Jean-Pierre Dozon (eds.), *Igreja Universal do Reino de Deus: os novos conquistadores da fé*, São Paulo: Paulinas, 2003, 119.

The identity trap of believing in the existence of an *ideal* identity

The process of building oneself – an identity – is basically related to relationships. There is no identity if not through those processes. Among others, two basic elements of the process are identification and acknowledgement. The feeling of being and existing is dependent on the identification experiences of recognizing ourselves in one another and begins with our early experiences in life. The feeling of "myself-in-the-world" arises from the mother-child-environment experiences. However, nowadays family relations are weakened and not seen as a safe, stable place of identification and recognition, so this need is fulfilled by the eyes of the other – any other – who offers a minimum mirror-like awareness, which allows the individual to identify and recognize itself. It is therefore a flat identification, which only confirms the individual as similar to the character images he recognizes in its official map, defined by the socio-economic-cultural environment.

This "personal identity" that is based on identity relations and recognition seeks identification "bonds" of belonging as well. A personal identity is not built separately from social identity. The feeling of belonging, along with the processes of identification and recognition, are forces that give consistency to the shape of existential territory that is called "identity" or "subjectivity," two words referring to our way of being in the world, which is built somewhere in time and as time passes by. As Donald Winnicott states, "a human being is a time-sample of human nature."[6] Still, there is a difference between the notion of subjectivity and identity: identity refers to the more visible, identifiable and stable form of subjectivity. It is related to a side of subjectivity that can be captured by the law, rules, and moral standards and, at the same time, allows individuals to be distinguished from each other. Identity indicates some regularity, predictability and permanence. On the other hand, the idea of subjectivity, such as developed by Deleuze,[7] Foucault,[8] and Guattari & Rolnik,[9] relates to the process of constitution of a being that is in permanent production and in constant change.

An existential territory – a subjectivity – is nothing more than a production of power relations, power games and knowledge production, which altogether creates a certain subjective character that arises in the social field. In this sense you can see that each historical age produces certain

---

[6] Donald D. Winnicott, *Human Nature*, Philadelphia: Brunner/Mazel, 1988, 11.
[7] Gilles Deleuze, *Foucault*, São Paulo: Brasiliense, 1998; Gilles Deleuze, *Conversações*, Rio de Janeiro: 34-Publisher, 1998.
[8] Michel Foucault, *Tecnologyas del Yo*, Barcelona: Paydós Ibérica, 1996; Michel Foucault, *Microfísica do Poder*, São Paulo: Graal, 1979.
[9] Felix Guattari and Suely Rolnik, *Micropolítica - Cartografias do Desejo*, 5th ed., Petrópolis: Vozes, 1999.

types of subjectivity to substantiate their system. The production of "flexible subjectivities" in globalized capitalism, open to the frequent changes in the open market, is a good example of it. These continuous changes caused by new universes, which are produced in a very short time, trigger a feeling of extreme fragility, vulnerability, and fear of "falling apart" in contemporary subjectivity. In this context, the belief in a stabilized, predictable and permanent identity is revealed as a trap, for at least two reasons. The belief in the identity reference interprets the destabilization of subjectivity as an evil power which destroys the subjective territory. So it is necessary to "anesthetise" subjectivity in order not to allow the process of dismantling the established identity territory. It is necessary to neutralize the identity territory against the feeling of destabilization. However, in doing so, the possibility to create other ways of existence is killed, since it is ignored that the forces that form new territories are mainly creative. The process of reorganization of a new territory, which may mean a new way of existence, is mixed with the loss of an identity assumed as ideal. Such a loss is interpreted as a psychological death. Thus, the process of creating a new territory is stopped due to an identity reference, even without a proper evaluation of the new possibilities that might be created with the destabilization of subjectivity. Therefore, the *a priori* "ideal identity reference" (stable, predictable, permanent) not only is an illusion. It might be a trap that can prevent the movements of creation and expansion of life.

The identity trap of consumption of *ready-to-wear* identity

The times of continuous and seemingly endless change characterized by cultural and economic globalization and by technological achievements, put us face to face with a reality that tests our identity references. There are so many identity models spread worldwide that make us feel threatened. This "identity trap" is originated when - by feeling the destabilization everywhere – in our subjectivity we decide for certain models of *ready-to-wear* identities. In this trap, we are not taking into account that destabilization is an opportunity to reorganize the existential territory. We are not making a thoughtful replacement of one identity for another. Rather, the old form is discarded without careful thought and substituted with a new one, which in turn will be substituted by another one in a short period of time, and so on. The standard identities are offered "according to each orbit of the market, ready to be consumed... and not linked to the geographical, national and cultural context."[10] The supply of standard identities to be consumed

[10] Suely Rolnik, "Toxicômanos de identidade: Subjetividade em Tempos de Globalização", in D. Lins (ed.), *Cultura e Subjetividade. Saberes Nômades*, Campinas: Papirus, 1997, 19.

(ready-to-wear identities) are an attractive strategy to cope with the contemporary feelings of emptiness and lack of meaning and purpose. Thus, it comes up as a "solution" to the subjectivity which, facing changes happening at an unprecedented speed, does not have enough time to create a new consistent subjective territory, since the subjectivity has to "give room" to a new territory produced by the capitalism and so on. Not by chance, a significant number of people with strong features of a borderline way of being have come to therapy and even to pastoral counseling with severe difficulty to maintain a minimum of meaningful bonds.

The identity trap of *capitalistic standard* identity: prosperity, success, happiness and well-being

Contemporary subjectivity is exposed to a process of identification with the images of the world broadcasted by the media and mass culture that fight for the instauration of values that will direct the choices of the customers.[11] The proliferation of these images spreads some imperatives lived in a paradoxical way: as an order to be obeyed and a way of obtaining pleasure. For example: "be successful!," "be happy!," "be healthy!," and, above all: "be flexible!" These imperatives give the map of happiness and point toward the way of living (how to eat, dress, live, love), the manner of obtaining success (continuous education, profitable work, individual performance able to beat the competitors, etc.) the way to be healthy (measures of the ideal body,[12] fitness, and diet, such as consumption of "light" products), etc.

Desire turns toward the world of products and profit, and it is seduced by offerings of consumption of the objects and worlds that transmit the promise of pleasure and the illusion of "belonging." These worlds express post-Fordist values and its imperatives for searching for success, prosperity and a perfect happy-and-healthy-body. However, other kinds of suffering follow these worlds that promise happiness. The effects of producing these ideals, as well as the offerings to "correct" or "increase" such images, generate pathologies, for example, depression, anxiety, anorexia, bulimia, different compulsions (for food, for buying things, etc.), panic disorders, and drug addictions.

Here we can understand the success of UCKG. They believe that through the technique of sacrifice they can reach prosperity, success and happiness.

---

[11] Maurizio Lazzarato, *As Revoluções do Capitalismo*, Rio de Janeiro: Civilização Brasileira, 2006, 101-102.

[12] The book organized (edited) by Mirian Goldenberg, *Nu e Vestido: Dez Antropólogos Revelam a Cultura do Corpo Carioca*, Rio de Janeiro: Record, 2002, shows that, in 2001, approximately 400,000 plastic surgeries were done in Brazil.

Challenges for pastoral care and counseling

One of the greatest challenges to pastoral care and counseling nowadays is helping to detect the strategies that constrain the process of creation, and to make visible the pitfalls that imprison subjectivity, causing pain and several pathologies. Therefore, pastoral counselors need to be aware of such strategies (or traps): the strategy of believing in the existence of a stable, predictable and permanent identity; the strategies of some "ready-to-wear identity" offered by the market (such as figures of success, richness and happiness); also, the strategies produced by the capitalistic standard of identity that produces a narcissistic identity (the one who only takes care of the self). If identity is subservient to the market, it is up to all of us to set life free from its chains.

How can we promote healing in times when pathologies of identities are produced? How can we promote healing and care in times when the necessity of identification is replaced by the search for identity bonds, in other words, when "belonging" and looking (appearance) become more important than "being?"

The practice of pastoral care and counseling in times of change has to face the challenge of promoting care, the challenge of healing subjectivity from the dominant mode of identity. In this sense, the fable of Hyginus might be an inspiration for our work as pastoral caregivers.

> When Cura was crossing a certain river, she saw some clayey mud. She took it up thoughtfully and began to fashion a man. While she was pondering on what she had done, Jove [Jupiter] came up; Cura asked him to give the image life, and Jove readily grant this. When Cura wanted to give it her name, Jove forbade, and said that his name should be given it. But while they were disputing about the name, Tellus [Earth] arose and said that it should have her name, since she had given her own body. They took Saturn for judge; he seems to have decided for them: Jove, since you gave him life, take his soul after death; since Tellus offered her body, let her receive his body; since Cura first fashioned him, let her posses him as long as he lives, but since there is controversy about his name, let him be called homo [human being], since he seems to be made from humus [earth].[13]

"Cura" (care/cure) was the one who shaped the "homo" (the human being). To solve the "identity conflict" of the name and identification of the human being, Saturn stated the belonging of the "Being" to the "Care." The fable shows that our existence as human beings is essentially dependent on care. Beyond an identity that care can give to oneself, only care can sustain the existence and transformation of the human being in the life journey.

---

[13] Gaius Julius Hyginus, "fabula CCXX", in Mary Grant (transl. and ed.), *The Myths of Hyginus*, Lawrence: University of Kansas Press, 1960.

Interfaith Pastoral Counseling: A Wisdom Model *

Daniel S. Schipani
Argentina, 2008

The unfolding process of globalization[1] together with the manifestations of post-modernity[2] are key factors that inform the social context of pastoral care practices in our time. The growing presence of a plurality of faith

* Lecture presented at the 20th International Seminar on Intercultural Pastoral Care and Counselling, 2008, in Bratislava, Slovakia. A German translation was published in *Interkulturelle Seelsorge und Beratung, 15*, 2009, 17-24.

[1] The globalization process under way includes political, economic, technological, and cultural dimensions. Interconnected systems of communication, transportation, and political organization tend to weave our world together into a single global locality. Indeed, globalization is restructuring the ways we live in diverse areas such as sexuality, family life, and the socialization of youth. See Anthony Giddens, *Runaway World: How Globalization is Reshaping Our Lives,* New York: Routledge, 2000. For a comprehensive introduction to the subject of globalization, see David Held, Anthony McGrew, David Goldblatt and Jonathan Perraton, *Global Transformations: Politics, Economics, and Culture*, Cambridge, U.K.: Polity Press, 1999. We agree with authors such as Robert J. Schreiter that "globalization" is the broad category to use in describing the signs of the times, "postmodernity" needing to be viewed within such a larger conceptual framework. See, for instance, Schreiter's *The New Catholicity: Theology Between the Global and the Local*, Maryknoll: Orbis Books, 1997, especially chapter 1.

[2] We are working with a straightforward account of postmodernity: a pluralist society in which not only are many theories and worldviews tolerated and accepted but there is also a profound suspicion of grand theories and theologies, of systems which make claims to truth (which are viewed as inadequate to reality and coercive). As an ideology, *postmodernism* celebrates the pluralism and fragmentation of so-called postmodern societies as a condition in which "true freedom" is possible. Further, postmodernists typically highlight alternative ways of knowing, restate the human value of emotions and feelings, wonder and mystery, and appreciate the experience of a "second naivete" (with an emphasis on the significance of living in the master stories as stories rather than as factual historical accounts). For an overview of the different sources and expressions of postmodernism, and an evaluation from a Christian perspective, see Stanley J. Grenz, *A Primer on Postmodernism*, Grand Rapids: Eerdmans, 1996.

expressions (religious as well as non-religious)[3] in our culture is indeed a major dimension of the social reality. Christian pastoral care specialists, both as practitioners and as pastoral theologians, need to work within, and reflect upon such reality in the light of normative claims of the Christian faith tradition (e.g. convictions about Jesus Christ, the church, the Bible, the Holy Spirit, and the Reign of God). Actually, pastoral caregivers have always had to engage in interfaith communication even if they have not always reflected critically and constructively on such phenomenon in a systematic way.[4] Some of them, however, have taken advantage of the contributions of *intercultural* study to pastoral care and counseling, which offers an opportunity for further exploration of *interfaith* pastoral caregiving as a structurally analogous experience.[5]

The questions that this lecture addresses concern the effective practice of *therapeutic*[6] *communication* that becomes "good news" (i.e. gospel) of

---

[3] We adopt the understanding of *faith* as a human universal that may or may not find expression in terms of a specific religious tradition and content (beliefs and rituals). It is the understanding articulated by James W. Fowler in his classic work: *Stages of Faith: The Psychology of Human Development and the Quest for Meaning*, San Francisco: Harper & Row, 1981. See also his *Weaving the New Creation: Stages of Faith and the Public Church*, San Francisco: Harper, 1991; *Faithful Change: The Personal and Public Challenges of Postmodern Life*, Nashville: Abingdon Press, 1996; and *Becoming Adult, Becoming Christian*, rev. ed., San Francisco: Jossey-Bass, 2000.

[4] An exception is the collection of essays in Robert G. Anderson and Mary A. Fukuyama (eds.), *Ministry in the Spiritual and Cultural Diversity of Health Care: Increasing the Competency of Chaplains*, New York: The Haworth Pastoral Press, 2004. See also Sue Wintz and Earl P. Cooper, *Learning Module Cultural and Spiritual Sensitivity: A Quick Guide to Cultures and Spiritual Traditions*, 2000, available at www. professionalchaplains.org. These valuable resources, however, do not include a systematic consideration of theological foundations and perspectives for interfaith spiritual care; further, they do not address the epistemological and methodological issues involved in the interplay between the human sciences and theology, which is essential for an adequate understanding and an effective practice of interfaith caregiving from a Christian perspective.

[5] During the last two decades a number of books addressing the challenges of intercultural caregiving have been published, especially in the areas of counseling and psychotherapy. Recent research connects issues of cross-cultural communication and spirituality, as documented, for example, in Mary A. Fukuyama and Todd D. Sevig, *Integrating Spirituality into Multicultural Counseling*, Thousand Oaks CA: Sage, 1999. On the one hand, *interfaith* spiritual caregiving can be viewed and practiced as a special form of *intercultural* caregiving, as caregivers and care receivers share meaning and values. On the other hand, the former presents unique features pertaining not only to the specific content of the verbal and non-verbal interactions between caregiver and care receiver but, especially, to the norms that guide and help to evaluate the very quality and effectiveness of those interactions.

[6] "Therapeutic" is here used with the twofold denotation of *ministerial* (from *therapeutes*, one who attends or serves, ministers) as well as *clinical* (literally, at the bed side). Simply put, then, *therapeutic communication* denotes the kind of verbal

hope and healing in pastoral care settings, and in pastoral counseling especially. It is our thesis that Christian pastoral caregivers can engage effectively and consistently in the practice of therapeutic communication in interfaith situations as a special way of *caring Christianly*.[7] Such practice may necessitate the transformation of Christian religious and theological language while remaining focused on the communication of good news for care-receivers regardless of their religious affiliation, the nature of their faith, broadly speaking (including, for instance, religious and non-religious humanism) and the overall quality of their spirituality.[8]

A wisdom model for pastoral counseling

For the past several years I have sought to serve with a nonmedical model of pastoral counseling, both in the congregation and in the medical setting of a community health center where I volunteer. In my view, pastoral counseling can be best understood as a specialized form of care giving ministry, centering on spiritual wisdom rather than mental health as its ground metaphor.[9] In pastoral counseling, *human emergence*[10] is uniquely

---

and nonverbal interaction experienced by the care-receiver as deeply caring in the senses of nurturing, supporting, guiding, reconciling and healing.

[7] By "caring Christianly" we mean the kind of spiritual caregiving that stems from three interrelated dimensions of the Christian faith: a particular vision of reality and the good life; a disposition to care as a form of love of neighbor (especially the care-seeking "stranger") inspired by Jesus Christ; and a certain sense of vocation to serve in partnership with the Spirit of God. These dimensions of the Christian faith define the caregivers' identity and ministry.

[8] The term "spirituality" is meant here as the overarching construct, connoting a fundamental human potential as well as need for meaning and value and the disposition for relationship with a transcendent power. "Faith" is used by us as denoting developmentally patterned ways of being "spiritual" in terms of Fowler's contribution.

[9] See Daniel S. Schipani, *The Way of Wisdom in Pastoral Counseling*, Elkhart IN: Institute of Mennonite Studies, 2003.

[10] The expression "human emergence" in this context denotes a process of humanization viewed primarily in theological perspective. It is about becoming "more human" in terms of (our understanding of) God's gift and promise of authentic freedom and wholeness; further, it connotes human becoming according to the wider ethical-political and eschatological framework biblically symbolized as the reign of God, that is, the normative commonwealth of love, peace, and justice. Hence the process of "emerging" involves the kinds of formation and transformation in people's lives that is associated with *Christomorphic* moral and spiritual growth. Therefore, human emergence must not be merely equated with psychological notions of development and maturation, even though connections with "natural" human development and with psychological understandings of human

sponsored through a distinctive way of walking with others – individuals, couples, family members, or small groups – as they face life's challenges and struggles. The overall goal, simply stated, is that they may live more wisely in the light of God.[11] My practice is aimed fundamentally, although not exclusively, at awakening, nurturing, and developing counselees' moral and spiritual intelligence. Simply put, moral and spiritual intelligence is about how to live well, especially in the face of conflict, crisis, difficult decision making, disorientation, trauma, suffering and loss.[12] Therefore, this ministry may be viewed as one dimension of the larger work of caring toward health and wellness.

This lecture presents such an understanding of pastoral counseling as a ministry of the church. It illustrates the contours of a new paradigm for the field of pastoral care and the discipline of pastoral theology, one that is centered on wisdom in the light of God. I will discuss a case from my counseling practice and, in relation to that case, offer a systematic discussion of the key components of the wisdom model.[13] I have chosen to discuss my work with a "non-Christian" counselee because both in counseling practices and in hospital chaplaincies, Christian pastoral caregivers must learn to care well for increasing numbers of "other-than-Christian" care seekers. I assume that we are called to care not only *Christianly*, as already indicated, but *pastorally* as well as. The pastoral nature of our work is determined, first of all, by our pastoral identity, including some form of ministerial accountability to the church regardless of the setting within which pastoral counseling is practiced. Second, our care is pastoral to the extent that we consistently work with a pastoral-theological frame of reference.[14]

---

flourishing must be adequately established in the theory and practice of pastoral counseling.

[11] This characterization is thoroughly explicated in Schipani, *The Way of Wisdom*, 91–114.

[12] The notion of *moral intelligence* is sometimes used as a present-day equivalent to *practical wisdom* (*phronesis,* which in Aristotle's ethical writings meant the intelligence or wisdom of the good person, closely associated with virtue and good character). My use of moral intelligence includes a holistic consideration of virtue and character in spiritually grounded and theologically defined moral formation. Further, I use the term *spiritual intelligence* specifically in reference to *wisdom in the light of God,* which necessarily includes and transforms moral intelligence.

[13] The following illustration is based on a real pastoral counseling situation. I have changed several pieces of information, however, in order to preserve confidentiality.

[14] For a systematic discussion of such a frame of reference, see Daniel S. Schipani, "The Pastoral-theological Nature of Pastoral Counseling", in Daniel S. Schipani (ed.), *Mennonite Perspectives on Pastoral Counseling*, Elkhart IN: Institute of Mennonite Studies, 2007, 7-29.

Case illustration

Annelies was a single woman, thirty-seven years of age, who had recently become chief executive officer of a major company. During the year prior to the counseling she had begun to wonder whether she should discontinue a close friendship with her former boyfriend, thirty-nine-year old Matt. Matt had married somebody else and become the father of two children, but had been separated from his wife for a couple of years. From time to time, Annelies had entertained the idea of reuniting with Matt. She recognized, however that, even though they could have much fun together, they were two very different people and not really compatible as a couple. For several weeks before pastoral counseling started, Annelies had had what she called "strange dreams" involving angels trying to communicate something to her. Her need to understand what was going on in her life and a deeply-felt desire to resolve her existential crisis became the occasion for counseling. She was referred to me by a mutual acquaintance.

Annelies had been raised in a Catholic family but she considered herself a non-religious person with deep spiritual sensitivities. From time to time she had enjoyed practicing diverse expressions of Eastern spirituality and "New Age"-like activities aimed at holistic cleansing, enlightenment, enhanced appreciation of beauty, and the freedom to create and to love.

In the first pastoral counseling session, while sharing her life story, Annelies confided that during the time she was originally involved with Matt she had had an abortion, about eight years earlier. Now at thirty-seven she deeply regretted the decision, which Matt had encouraged, and felt sorry about it. She indicated that she was sure that the child would have been a girl and, in fact, started to call "her" Naomi (the actual name of a dear, close relative). After clarifying mutual expectations, we agreed to meet for a short-term pastoral counseling process.

Annelies received as a hopeful sign my observation that the name "Naomi" means "pleasant." She also realized that we would need to revisit painful memories and to find ways to deal constructively with her sense of loss and guilt. I encouraged her to welcome her dreams and, as much as possible, write down their content so that, by considering them together in the counseling setting, we might be able to find meaning and a sense of direction. We also agreed that angels may symbolize "messengers" as well as "guardian spirits."

In addition to the attempt to reconcile and integrate unconscious material by attending to her dreams, Annelies found it especially helpful to engage her imagination in the manner of writing letters to "Naomi" and sharing them with me, including the possible response that she might have received from her child. As a therapeutic method, that activity became a fruitful way of processing both her grief and her guilt. It also made it possible for her to begin to visualize a way forward opened by a unique experience of forgiveness. No longer inhibited by the power of a buried secret, she decided to tell her mother and siblings about the abortion for the first time as well as about her work in therapy. Not surprisingly, she began to experience new freedom from bondage to the past as well as a sense of hope.

From the beginning I encouraged Annelies to consider her experience of loss and distress both as an emotional trauma and also as a spiritual struggle. At one point I told her that I always pray that I may be the best possible conversation partner in counseling, and I also pray for the counselees whether they know it or not. She indicated appreciation for my praying in her behalf. Interestingly, by the end of the counseling process Annelies had come to perceive me not only as a guide and as witness to her ongoing healing process but as a messenger (or "angel") as well.

The wisdom model of pastoral counseling that I have developed has four interrelated components, which are: (1) a four-dimensional view of reality and knowing; (2) interdisciplinary assessment and agenda; (3) complementary goals for care-seekers and caregiver, and (4) an overarching purpose and fundamental approach. I believe that this model is especially useful interfaith situations, as I will try to demonstrate in the remainder of this lecture.

A four-dimensional view

As a bright, energetic, socially popular and fun-loving woman, Annelies had been enjoying life surrounded by many friends and co-workers. She had accomplished much, yet she had begun to experience increased restlessness associated in part with her complex relationship with Matt, her long-time former companion, and the demands and opportunities of a successful professional career. Annelies was actually entering a new chapter in her life that presented serious challenges, including a changing sense of identity and conflicting desires regarding sexuality and the possibility of motherhood, as well as an increasing wish somehow to "get settled" in life. Her distress and disorientation involved several dimensions of her self and her lived world. Therefore, pastoral counseling would need to address a number of biological, emotional, and relational issues.

Our model, however, calls for an analytic framework and counseling strategy larger than the two dimensions – *the self* and *the lived world* – implied in the previous paragraph. We must also include two existential-spiritual dimensions – *the Void* and *the Holy*, as James E. Loder describes them. Loder writes that "[b]eing human entails environment, selfhood, the possibility of not being, and the possibility of new being. All four dimensions are essential, and none of them can be ignored without decisive loss to our understanding of what is essentially human."[15] These dimensions were also part of Annelies's experience and potential for healing and growth. The faces of the Void, the implicit threat of nonbeing, was experienced with existential anxiety connected with a deeply felt sense of loss – the loss of the opportunity to give birth to a child. Her choice to have an abortion, which she now regretted, was accompanied by the lingering effects of suppressed grief. Another face of the Void for Annelies was the fear that she might not be able ever to love and be loved again. That multidimensional threat had to be confronted in the counseling setting as I sought to guide her through a process by which she might experience the gifts of grace and freedom. Annelies's distress might thus be transformed into a new experience of light and love – that is, a negation of the negation – resulting in some degree of growth into "new being" or "being more." Her spiritual sensitivities and wholehearted search for reorientation and renewal were, of course, indispensable resources which elicited hope.

I seek to address the existential-spiritual dimensions in all counseling situations. I believe it is essential to evaluate those situations four-dimensionally, along the lines proposed by Loder. We must not only consider transactions between self and lived world, which is the limited horizon normally addressed in other forms of counseling and psychotherapy.[16] We must also work within a larger framework that includes the threat of nonbeing—the Void—and the possibility and invitation to new being—the Holy. Further, we must view and use the setting and the process of pastoral counseling as a Christian ministry of care according to the four dimensions (for example, by concretely honoring our partnership with the Spirit in our ministry practice).

---

[15] I allude here to James Loder's notion of "the fourfold knowing event" – which involves the lived world, the self, the void, and the holy. See his *The Transforming Moment*, 2nd ed., Colorado Springs: Helmers & Howard, 1989, 69.

[16] Excluded from this generalization are counseling and psychotherapy that intentionally address spirituality issues and practices in a nonreductionistic manner. See P. Scott Richards and Allen E. Bergin, *A Spiritual Strategy for Counseling and Psychotherapy*, Washington, DC: American Psychological Association, 1997; and William R. Miller (ed.), *Integrating Spirituality into Treatment: Resources for Practitioners*, Washington, DC: American Psychological Association, 1999. These contributions address spirituality both as a subject matter in its own right (including, for example, issues of acceptance, forgiveness, and hope) and as a resource for therapeutic intervention (meditation and prayer, for example). For an explicitly Christian perspective, see Mark R. McMinn, *Psychology, Theology, and Spirituality in Christian Counseling*, Wheaton: Tyndale House Publishers, 1996.

Interdisciplinary perspectives and assessment

In light of this component of the wisdom model, Annelies and I agreed that we needed to address interrelated issues. We needed to address her sense of loss and related guilt and depression, while keeping in mind systemic dynamics related to her family background as well as her current interpersonal, social and professional situation. Specifics of the pastoral counseling agenda that we identified included the following:

- Annelies's image of herself as a woman, in connection with her roles as a professional person, friend, and lover; this agenda included an understanding of the nature and the dynamics of her false self 17 nurtured by multiple superficial relationships, a number of sexual affairs, and professional overachievement.
- Relationships with significant people in her life, especially her former lovers, friends, and family, and the challenge of facing and dealing with suppressed anger, guilt feelings, and unresolved inner conflict.
- Appropriate identification of present needs as well as hopes, including her vocational sense of direction and projections concerning professional work.
- Availability of internal and external resources that would potentially contribute to the healing process.

In addition to these and related issues, the explicit pastoral-theological care approach that I brought to the counseling process elicited a number of concerns which can be illumined by a theological perspective, such as these:

- An appropriation of grace and care in connection with hurtful experiences in the past and inadequate processing and resolution, which might be characterized in terms of moral failure, and the possibility of transformation and healing.

---

[17] The notion of "false self" refers to a person's interaction with her world when it is determined more by the demands and expectations of others than by her own needs and desires. The concept comes from pediatrician and psychoanalyst Donald W. Winnicott and his study of the psychodynamics of early self-development (see *The Maturational Process and the Facilitating Environment*, Madison, CT: International Universities Press, 1965). As pastoral theologian Gordon Lynch helpfully notes, two significant implications stem from Winnicott's idea of the false self: "First, this concept indicates that attending to the needs of others can, for some involved in caring work, have a compulsive and pathological dimension to it. Second, Winnicott believed that individuals can recover more of their true selves in adult life through being in relationship with others who demonstrated reliability, attentiveness, responsiveness, recollection and durability. This highlights qualities which might usefully be embodied in pastoral relationships." G. Lynch, "False Self", in Wesley Carr (ed.), *The New Dictionary of Pastoral Studies*, Grand Rapids: Eerdmans, 2002, 124).

• Views of shame and guilt as well as acceptance, forgiveness, and reconciliation in the light of Annelies's own sense of moral integrity and responsibility, possibly connected in some way with a reconstructed memory of her early Christian views and practices.
• The meaning and function of Annelies's unique spirituality and its possible role in reshaping her life story, identity, and sense of life vocation.
• The overall potential for spiritual growth as the core of human flourishing to be uniquely experienced in a more wholesome life and in fashioning a better future.

The application of interdisciplinary perspectives and assessment is the second component of the wisdom model of pastoral counseling. We can state this guideline as follows: it is indispensable to identify the pertinent issues of the counseling agenda both from a psychological and a theological perspective, even as we work with an integrated understanding of those seeking care as well as the very setting and process of pastoral counseling. Therefore, we must affirm the integrity of the disciplines of psychology and theology. We must avoid reducing either to the terms of the other, even as we maximize the potential for complementarity between their unique contributions. At the same time, we must give priority to the pastoral and theological nature of our ministry work, including systematic reflection on the practice of pastoral counseling itself.[18] This priority is worth emphasizing, because of the ways theology addresses fundamental questions of life and thus distinctly informs the normative dimensions of pastoral counseling. What does it mean to live well in the light of God's reign and to seek wisdom in the midst of our life's challenges and struggles? What is the shape of human completion and wholeness? How do we understand and foster maturity, and how do we know which is the way forward in human emergence?[19] Theology is uniquely suited to address

---

[18] These three methodological and epistemological principles are viewed and explicated in detail by pastoral theologian Deborah van Deusen Hunsinger as the threefold "Chalcedonian pattern" applicable to the relationship between psychology and theology in pastoral counseling theory and practice. See Hunsinger's *Theology and Pastoral Counseling: A New Interdisciplinary Approach*, Grand Rapids: Eerdmans, 1995, especially chapter 3. See also by the same author "An Interdisciplinary Map for Christian Counselors: Theology and Psychology in Christian Counseling", in Mark R. McMinn and Timothy R. Phillips (eds.), *Care for the Soul: Exploring the Intersection of Psychology and Theology*, Downers Grove: InterVarsity Press, 2001, 218-240.

[19] These are questions explicitly addressed by, among others, the following: James W. Fowler, *Becoming Adult, Becoming Christian: Human Development and Christian Faith*, rev. ed., San Francisco: Jossey-Bass, 2000; James E. Loder, *The Logic of the Spirit: Human Development in Theological Perspective*, San Francisco: Jossey-Bass, 1998; and Neil Pembroke, *Moving Toward Spiritual Maturity: Psycho-*

such questions, always in creative conversation with the human sciences. By helping people like Annelies to make choices oriented to a more wholesome life, pastoral counseling can foster spiritual intelligence and moral and spiritual growth in wise living.

Complementary goals

I set for myself, and regularly review, goals that serve not only to provide overall orientation to my pastoral counseling ministry but also to evaluate that practice. These goals are indispensable to keep in mind as I remain accountable to the care-seekers, to colleagues with whom I work, and to the church I represent, which validates my ministry. Some of the general goals that apply to all kinds of counseling situations are:

- To welcome care-seekers in a safe and caring space where they can express themselves freely, clarify the nature of their challenges and struggles, make wise choices, and be empowered to move on.
- To faithfully represent the healing Christ and the church as a community of wisdom and healing, a role that includes the attempt to mediate grace in compassionate and generous ways.
- To become a temporary companion in people's journeys toward (re)orientation, transformation, reconciliation, and healing.
- To minister as a caregiving sage who practices counseling with clinical and therapeutic competence, especially by adequately employing the manifold resources provided by psychology and psychotherapy as a practical human science.

I needed to keep in focus these general goals as I tried to help Annelies in facing the crisis precipitated by her current existential disorientation and distress. At the same time, however, I also had to identify pastoral counseling objectives in light of her need for support and guidance. These specific objectives, which at the risk of oversimplification may also be considered desired outcomes of the counseling process, included the following:

- For Annelies to experience emotional relief through catharsis.
- For Annelies to begin to understand the nature of the crisis she was experiencing and to appreciate and integrate the reality of her pain and sense of loss and disorientation.
- For both Annelies and me to identify and activate available resources, both internal and external, in order to cope in healthy ways with the crisis and its ramifications.

---

logical, Contemplative, and Moral Challenges in Christian Living, New York: The Haworth Press, 2007.

- For both Annelies and me to help strengthen – emotionally and spiritually – her sense of personal identity and integrity.
- For both Annelies and me to develop a plan of action for her beyond the counseling setting.

I needed to apply therapeutic methods and resources commonly associated with the strategies of crisis, supportive, and narrative pastoral care and counseling.[20] Therefore, specific objectives for my caregiving endeavors with this counselee included the following:
- To be carefully hospitable to Annelies while keeping in mind that she had a spiritual and theological background, and a moral and ethical framework different from my own.
- To become a supportive pastoral presence and a source of emotional and spiritual comfort by listening responsively to Annelies, helping her find her voice, and making available resources from diverse sources (the human sciences, the Christian faith tradition and the local faith community) in order to sustain her process of painful recalling, lamenting, and grieving.
- To help Annelies clarify her own feelings and articulate her ways of understanding her experience of disorientation and loss in her own terms.
- To encourage Annelies to make healthy new choices in the face of the new realities in her life, and to guide her in reality testing in terms of her chosen path to restoration and healing.
- To sponsor Annelies' spiritual growth by exploring ways to nurture life-giving practices, both individual and communal, including new forms and disciplines such as meditation, journaling, and prayer.
- To encourage Annelies to reach out to other people who might extend responsible support and gentle accountability beyond our short-term pastoral counseling.
- To convey my openness to be available for further counseling for the next several days, while exploring where she could turn for caring support among her family and friends.

The third indispensable component of the wisdom model of pastoral counseling I work with consists in identifying and integrating two distinct sets of pastoral counseling goals. On the one hand, goals (in the sense of desired outcomes) must be selected from the perspective of the person seeking care, in consultation with the pastoral caregiver, as they emerge

[20] For descriptions and illustrations of supportive, crisis, and bereavement pastoral care and counseling, see Howard Clinebell, *Basic Types of Pastoral Care and Counseling*, Nashville: Abingdon Press, 1984, chapters 7, 8, and 9, respectively. Howard W. Stone, *Crisis Counseling*, rev. ed., Minneapolis: Fortress Press, 1993; and, especially, Christie Cozad Neuger, *Counseling Women: A Narrative, Pastoral Approach*, Minneapolis: Fortress Press, 2001.

from the counselee's felt needs, hopes, and resources. On the other hand, pastoral counselors must also seek clarity about goals for their work as they guide the counseling process. More importantly, Christian pastoral counselors must seek to honor their call to mediate divine grace and wisdom as representatives of the caring church and the healing Christ, regardless of the nature of the care seekers' spirituality and (religious or nonreligious) faith.[21] Their character must reflect their ongoing participation in faith communities attuned to the reign of God in the world[22] and their commitment to minister not only as competent clinicians or therapists but also as moral and spiritual guides.[23] In fact, these personal characteristics – call, character, competence, and commitment – along with explicit formal accountability to the church, are essential elements of counseling that is truly pastoral.

An overarching purpose and fundamental approach

Each pastoral counseling situation calls for specific objectives, however we may articulate them. Each situation also requires the application of pertinent strategies to reach those objectives. At the same time, it is also apparent that all pastoral counseling situations have much in common. I believe that those commonalities, which center on issues of overall purpose and fundamental process, the fourth component that point to wisdom in the light of God as a fitting, heart-of-the-matter metaphor for pastoral counseling.

Annelies had voluntarily entered a pastoral counseling relationship because she was experiencing disorientation and distress. In the course of our short-term counseling process, she was invited – implicitly rather than explicitly, to be sure – to become a wiser person in the light of God as we worked together in the face of the challenges and struggles she was encountering at this particular juncture in her life journey. The overarching

---

[21] See footnote no. 8 on the use of the term "spirituality".

[22] For an illuminating discussion of the relationship between the reign of God as ethical culture, the church as an ethical community, and the therapist as an ethical character, see Alvin C. Dueck, *Between Jerusalem and Athens: Ethical Perspectives on Culture, Religion, and Psychotherapy*, Grand Rapids: Baker Books, 1995.

[23] Rebekah L. Miles notes that good guides have distinctive knowledge and wisdom, and as practical pilgrims they are constantly training and preparing themselves for their art. Further, good guides are confident leaders who know their limits and temptations, know when they need help and are willing to seek advice, remember that others are free and responsible, teach others the lessons of pilgrimage and guidance, and develop excellent capacities for discernment. They not only know the rules but also know that the rules must sometimes be bent or even changed, and they remember the most important things – the shared destination and the source of power. Miles, *The Pastor as Moral Guide*, Minneapolis: Fortress Press, 1999, 6–7.

purpose of becoming wiser included three inseparable aspects of her search for relief and resolution. As pastoral counselor, I needed to keep in mind that each of these aspects integrates psychological as well as theological and spiritual perspectives on the self.

Growth in vision. First, the counseling experience was meant to help the counselee find new and better – more holistic – ways of knowing and understanding reality, including the dimensions of self, the lived or social world, the threatening Void and the gracious, embracing Holy. From a Christian formation viewpoint, Annelies needed to grow in her ways of seeing, so that she is increasingly able to perceive reality (especially herself and other people) with the eyes of God, metaphorically speaking. Such growth in vision would entail the practice and development of dispositions and behaviors such as heightened awareness, attentiveness, admiration and contemplation, critical thinking, creative imagination, and spiritual discernment.

Growth in virtue. Second, the counseling experience encouraged the care-seeker to discover more fulfilling and faithful ways of being and loving, with specific focus on her relationships with others – friends, family, and co-workers, especially – with the gracious Spirit, and with herself. In Christian formation terms, Annelies' heart needed to be increasingly conformed to the heart of Christ. Such growth in virtue entails an ongoing process of formation and transformation, shaping the inmost affections and passions, dispositions, and attitudes – habits of the heart – and defining the content of her moral and spiritual character. In short, in and through the counseling process, God was calling her to become a unique expression of human love.

Growth in vocation. Third, the counseling experience sought to empower Annelies to make sound choices and to invest fresh energies in relationships, work, leisure, spiritual nurture, and service, and to find ways to sustain those choices with integrity. She needed to find a freer and more hopeful orientation toward life, especially her social situation. Such growth in vocation may be viewed theologically as participating increasingly in the life of the Spirit in the world. For that counselee, it could open the possibility of a fruitful and joyful response to the invitation to collaborate with God in creative, liberating, sustaining, and renewing purpose and activity. As her ways of being and living became increasingly consistent with a wisdom understanding of divine purpose and activity, I anticipated that her life would receive the gifts of further meaning, value, hope, and courage.

In summary, the overarching purpose of pastoral counseling was to help Annelies to know how to live a more hopeful, moral, and wholesome life. In order to realize its potential as a ministry of care, pastoral counseling would need to awaken, nurture, and empower her moral and spiritual intelligence, as characterized above. Understood as wisdom in the light of God, spiritual intelligence transforms emotional and other forms of intelligence, whenever the latter have merely promoted adaptive or conforming aims and means of conventional and pragmatic wisdom in any given social and cultural milieu.

Though in each pastoral counseling situation we need to select diverse, appropriate counseling strategies and methods, nevertheless, our collaborative work in all cases must always involve the fundamental approach and pivotal practice of discernment as an essential aspect of pastoral counseling. Viewed from my perspective as pastoral counselor and theologian, a multidirectional critical conversation must always take place. The conversation includes the counselee's personal stories and hopes, located in family and sociocultural contexts; human science viewpoints, insights, and tools (especially from personality theory, psychodynamic and cognitive therapy, narrative and family systems theory and therapy); and theological, spiritual, and pastoral resources.[24] Stated in other terms, this hermeneutical activity of discernment leads us, first, to ascertain what a particular situation calls for; second, to search for alternatives and to develop a course of action; and third, to evaluate ongoing responses to the challenges and struggles the counselee is facing.

From a theological perspective, the setting and the process of pastoral counseling encompasses more than counselors and psychotherapists usually recognize (at least explicitly). The four-dimensional understanding of reality – and of knowing, in particular – determines the nature of the overall approach and the discerning activity we are discussing here. Counseling that is truly pastoral occurs not only in a safe therapeutic space but also in a sacred place where the presence and activity of the Spirit is acknowledged (at least by the pastoral counselor). Further, we seek to minister in partnership with the Spirit in the process of our endeavoring to know the real nature of the problems and the best ways creatively to confront and transform them.

Comprehensively viewed, therefore, the activity of discernment conditions the process (the *how* – approaches, methods, and techniques) as well as the content (the *what* – agenda, themes, and issues) of pastoral counsel-

[24] To say that a *critical* conversation took place means that the resources of the human sciences and theology, together with my personal and professional experience and expertise, were also subject to evaluation, correction, and improvement, even as they illuminated the counselee's life challenges and struggles and suggested ways to resolve them satisfactorily and wisely. In other words, the uniquely hermeneutical work characterizing the process of pastoral counseling that occurred in the counseling situation must be viewed dialectically. The implication, in this light, is that pastoral counseling is a way of doing practical theology, and must always be practiced as a dialectical-hermeneutical process.

ing in significant ways. Further, learning the very practice of discernment, especially as a collaborative, dialogical, and even prayerful endeavor, also becomes a distinct and overarching objective, a desired outcome for counselees in all cases. Indeed, an indicator of growth and progress for Annelies and countless other care receivers is their willingness and ability to engage in discernment. In other words, growth in wisdom always entails discerning and choosing wisely, as well as learning to act and to relate to other people wisely in a consistent manner. *Wisdom in the light of God* thus supplies the guiding principle and the master metaphor, because the way of wisdom thus understood and appropriated is a process of knowing how to live a better life in the midst of our existential and social circumstances.

That is what happened to Annelies. After we had completed the counseling process by mutual agreement, she wrote several e-mail messages to tell me about helpful conversations she had had with Matt and with key family members. She was also making good decisions in different areas of her life, even as she continued to heal. By Grace and Wisdom, the experience of interfaith counseling sustained with therapeutic love for a stranger with whom I partnered, had contributed to restoring her soul.

From the "Living Document" to the Living Web: Pastoral Care and Counseling Before New Challenges *

Ronaldo Sathler-Rosa
Brazil, 2010

Despite its rich and inclusive dynamic tradition, pastoral care and counseling, particularly in Protestant churches, has been overwhelmingly focused on the individual. This approach entails reductionism. Exclusively individual-based pastoral care misses the broader perspective which includes cultures, economic, and political aspects that shape individual ways of being on this side of heaven. *Vital networks*, social systems[1] as well as the *oikoumene* (*oikos*, house; the whole inhabited earth) that mold human life are left out. The individual "diagnosed" as healed has to live in a culturally sick atmosphere. This condition brings to the individual his/her former situation, that is, sickness. Human beings are themselves plus their cultural milieu.

Some Protestant and Catholic voices[2] have advocated for the extension of the many ways of doing pastoral care to other realms of cultures such as economic, political, and life sustenance. These aspects are factors of health, happiness, well being or the reverse. This broader perspective is largely justified from the best Christian traditions. For example, the historian

---

* Lecture presented at the 22nd International Seminar on Pastoral Care and Counselling, 2010, in Strasbourg, France. Published in *Intercultural Pastoral Care and Counselling, 16*, 2011, 116-122.

[1] Bonnie J. Miller-McLemore and Brita L. Gil-Auster (eds.), *Feminist and Womanist Pastoral Theology*, Nashville: Abingdon, 1999.

[2] See David W. Augsburger, *Pastoral Counseling Across Cultures*, Philadelphia: Westminster Press, 1986; Stephen Pattison, *A Critique of Pastoral Care*, London: SCM, 2000; Peter Selby, *Liberating God: Private Care and Public Struggle*, London: SPCK 1988; Michael Wilson, "Personal Care and Political Action", in *Contact, 87*, 1985, 12-22; Duncan Forrester, *Theology and Politics*, Oxford: Basil Blackwell 1988; Julio de Santa Ana, *Por las sendas del mundo caminando hacia el Reino*, San Jose: DEI 1987; Rubem Alves, "Pastoral Wholeness and Political Creativity: The Theology of Liberation and Pastoral Care", in *Pastoral Psychology, 26*, 1977, 124-136, among others.

Justo Gonzalez reminds us of the legacy of the Anglican theologian John Wesley: "Wesleyan doctrine of sanctification ... move us from any pseudo-private and individualistic holiness to a vocation to be faithful at the broader realms of social, political, and economic life."[3]

The way of doing pastoral care in the public dimension of life demands a theology and pastoral action aimed specifically at this field. The book *The public Church* written by Matin Marty[4] has been considered a hallmark in more recent discussions of the public mission of the Church. Engagement in *pastoral care of worlds*[5] requires that pastoral caregivers assume their task as one to be accomplished in the larger society, instead of reducing this task to the ecclesiastical field. Jürgen Moltmann and J. B. Metz[6] pointed out the widespread tendency towards privatization of faith and its consequence: the Church moves away from society by adopting an individualistic pietism instead of engaging in issues which seek policies to be implemented by political decisions. The traditional pastoral theologies and respective contemporary practices need new theoretical horizons. The well-used psychological and theological approaches to pastoral care and counseling have been challenged by the rising of *new historical subjects* – migrants, impoverished individuals, those who suffer discrimination for their sexual orientation, and many others. Metz[7] highlights *three crises and challenges in which this theological model* (named "post-idealist", by Metz) *seeks to adopt a position*: first, theology lacks its (apparently) *social innocence*. Instead of engagement with its own foundations, theology has to interact with societies in a non-hierarchical manner; second, there is no room anymore, if theology is to be all-inclusive, to disregard the emergence of the "new" players in history, such as migrants as well as others called "wanders" or "vagabonds" by the Polish sociologist Zygmunt Baumann[8]; third, we live in a *culturally polycentric world*; in addition to the theology of *option for the poor*, theology has to take into account the *option for others in their otherness*. From the perspective of my own social location I have identified three major problems in mainline theories and practices of pastoral care and

---

[3] Justo L. Gonzalez, *Wesley para a América Latina hoje*, São Bernardo do Campo: Editeo, 2003, 74.

[4] Martin E. Marty, *The Public Church: Mainline – Evangelical - Catholic*, New York: Crossroad 1981. Cf. *Teologia Publica* (Public Theology) by The Brazilian University of Vale dos Sinos.

[5] Cf. Larry Graham, *Care of Persons, Care of Worlds*, Nashville: Abingdon, 1992.

[6] J.B. Metz and J. Moltmann, *Faith and the Future*, Maryknoll NY: Orbis Books, 1995.

[7] Ibid., p. 50.

[8] Z. Baumann, *Postmodernity and its Discontents*, New York: New York University Press, 1997.

counseling – psychological reductionism, lack of theological anthropology, and political alienation.[9]

Psychological reductionism

In more recent times, the bonds between pastoral practices and theories with psychology go back to the end of nineteenth century and beginning of the twentieth century. This connection was strongly influenced by contemporary psychological studies regarding the nature of religious experience. This approximation was a decisive factor for broadening the field of studies on pastoral counseling and care. Pastors and teachers felt motivated to rely on psychology in order to have a better understanding of the *human soul.*[10] In the following period of time the so-called *modern movement of pastoral care and counseling* was heavily based on the psychological sciences. The preponderance of psychology to the detriment of other fields of knowledge does not allow for the accurate understanding of human problems resulting from cultural factors. For example, there are situations of suffering and deprivation which are consequences of social structures that favor social inequalities, conducive to violence and to the desperate search for a fair home, such as the majority of migrants. Of course, psychology can provide a better understanding of human personhood and behavior.[11] The inclusion of other social sciences such as cultural anthropology, political sciences, sociology, economics, besides others, enlarge the understanding of pastoral caregivers about the situation of those persons who look for pastoral care. Those sciences have the theoretical tools to cover aspects of human life which are not reached by psychology. Most

---

[9] Revised version of my article "Una aproximación critica de concepciones y practicas actuales de consejeria pastoral", in Hugo Santos (ed.), *Dimensiones del cuidado y asesoramiento pastoral*, Buenos Aires: Kairos, 2006; Cf. E.Y. Lartey, *In Living Colour: An Intercultural Approach to Pastoral Care and Counselling*, London and Herndon: Cassell, 1997.

[10] Major influential works were: Edwin D. Starbuck, *Psychology of Religion*, 1899; G.A. Coe, *Spiritual Life: Studies in the Science of Religion*, 1900; William James, *The Varieties of Religious Experience*, 1902; John S. Bonnell, *Pastoral Psychiatry*, 1938. Rollo May, *The Art of Counseling*, 1939, has been considered the first systematic study of counseling. Soon the well known books by the "pioneers" of the "modern movement of pastoral care and counseling" are published: Anton Boisen, *The Exploration of the Inner World*, 1936; Russell Dicks, *Pastoral Work and Pastoral Counseling*, 1944; Seward Hiltner, *Pastoral Counseling*, 1949; C. Wise, *Pastoral Counseling: Theory and Practice*, 1951, among others.

[11] In 1893, Henry Drummond stated that the study of the soul in health and disease ought to be as much an object of scientific study and training as the health and diseases of the body. See Wayne E. Oates (ed.), *An Introduction to Pastoral Counseling*, Nashville: Broadman Press, 1959, 15.

importantly, those fields of knowledge can work together in interdisciplinary mode aiming at a better comprehension of the human conditions. *Human beings are not only psychological or biological entities, human beings are social organisms* (Calvin and Lindzey). Furthermore, social and human sciences are auxiliary tools to help pastoral caregivers to avoid a kind of *transcendentalist spirituality* alienated from concrete, historical life conditions. Another aspect of psychological reductionism is that in large segments of pastoral counseling there is a tendency to focus on the past of individuals instead of his or her current and existential situation.[12] This past oriented approach has been emphasized in spite of the fact that the modern movement of pastoral care and counseling was heavily influenced by Carl Rogers and his *phenomenological perspective*, that is focused on the present of the individual life and his or her capabilities to grow, without neglecting the past.[13]

Lack of theological anthropology

The practice of pastoral care is rooted in the community of believers. Pastoral care is sustained and fed by the community of faith together with its continuing theological reflection. Theology provides a vivid and theoretical matrix which informs the practice of pastoral care and counseling. The relevance of theology both for the caregiver as well as for the careseeker comes from its own peculiarity. Clodovis Boff states that the relevance of "theology" goes beyond its literal meaning ("study of God").[14] Theology has an impact on human existence. From a Jewish-Christian perspective there is no "ulterior objective" for human life other than authentic happiness, identified with Love and Justice in God. Theology is an essential human instrument that helps human beings in the constant search for finding the radical meaning of existence. In addition, taking the perspective of practical theology, that is, to examine human existence from a theological standpoint, theology is not only a study of God. Rather, theology studies human processes towards the search for meaning. A pastoral-theological anthropology can provide a sound reference for the work of pastoral care and counseling. What is the *anthropos*? How are his/her life conditions shaped? How does he/she see the troubles and challenges of existence? Without neglecting contributions from psychological theories of human personality, theology can enlighten pastoral practices by offering a theoretical frame for a better understanding of humans and their life

---

[12] Cf. Pattison, *Critique of Pastoral Care.*

[13] Cf. Howard Clinebell, *Contemporary Growth Therapies*, Nashville: Abingdon, 1981, 117.

[14] Clodovis Boff, *Teoria do Método Teológico*, Petrópolis: Vozes, 1998, 360.

limitations, from the tradition of Creation. Furthermore, the dialogue between theology and psychology ensures mutual broadening of both fields of study. Theological anthropology puts the complaints, the *case* of the individual under a centralizing and structuring perspective: the ultimate meaning of life is found in living by faith. The human decision to live by faith gives a realistic comprehension of human conditions, their limitations and sufferings, and a realistic hope for life.

Political alienation

The practice of pastoral care with individuals and families comes across with a barrier: the dominant model of pastoral care and counseling has been settled in order to solve individual problems at the sphere of primary relationships. That model meets a significant aspect to be dealt with by pastoral caregivers. However, this model has an omission: How to care with individuals whose crises and sufferings are rooted in external conditions such as those established by unfair political powers, ineffective laws or lacking of them; or even resulting from the *exuberant irrationality* of the worldwide financial circle? Individuals and families become passive victims without the means to change *the order of things*.

I want to argue that we need to integrate into our current practices of pastoral care another dimension of life: care for the world of politics and other social systems which interfere with human well being.

Contemporary socio-cultural movements stressing the right and the duty to exercise citizenship denote that the unavoidable political condition of women and men has been widely acknowledged. The political nature of human beings places us in connection with a web of relationships, responsibilities and mutual rights. In Brazil, the current voices advocating for an awareness and effective citizenship agency by people is a consequence of two factors: the widespread disbelief in professional politicians and the awareness that only the full participation of *social subjects* (individuals and society at large) will open up the path to remove historical obstacles against a better future.[15]

I want to introduce a few words about the connections between faith and politics. Faith is also an expression of the perennial human search for comprehending the conditions of existence. Also faith is a human attempt to find meaning and purposes in life. Faith does not express itself only through symbols and traditional religious practices. Faith is an invitation to examine values and ideals that nurture human life.[16] Therefore, faith as a

[15] Adapted and expanded from R. Sathler-Rosa, *O sagrado da política. A dimensão esquecida da prática cristã*, São Paulo: Fonte Editorial, 2010.
[16] Paul Tillich, *Dynamics of Faith*, New York: Harper and Row, 1957.

human attitude facing life brings about a fresh perspective about existence and its social and political dimensions.

The Brazilian Dominican Carlos Josaphat argues that good politics is a privileged field for exerting Christian faith as well as other kinds of religious commitment.[17] Josaphat outlines six elements that legitimate Christian action in politics:

First, there exists a correlation between authentic vision of politics and the authentic comprehension of Christian faith. However, Josaphat warns that the ecclesiastical utilization of politics and manipulation of religion are distorted forms, even of the corruption of two excellent realities, actualizing the unhappy proverb corruption "optimi pessima". Nothing is worse than corruption of the best. Politics is in itself the best that exists, the highest form to accomplish common wellness. Faith is the foundation and source of divine justice in us, anticipatory presence of everlasting life that elevate our personal and social existence as well.

Second, faith is the source of love and discernment, care for the common good, and the continuing search for ways of actualization. To the extent that politics express the efficient and constant search for the common good in society, human existence is a continuing challenge for committed women and men.

Third, the Gospel is the matrix where we can find appropriate models towards fulfilling the common good in different configurations and phases of the historical development of societies.

Fourth, one of the objectives of politics is to analyze and implement factors that sustain the well being of all people. These duties demand from politicians, as well as from citizens, the fundamental virtues of justice, prudence, and solidarity. Therefore, politics, especially community-based, is a privileged space based on love that moves people towards the dynamism of this love. This love is the source of all virtues that orient and develop human beings in all dimensions: individual, family, and political.

Fifth, the complexity of social life, the diversity of relational and personal aspirations, call for lucidity and courage to search for the common good, that is, love in its highest form.

Sixth, Josaphat highlights the main contemporary hindrances to be challenged by faith: corruption, ethical and religious ideology, alienating and demobilizing systems, globalization as considered to be the law of history. These obstacles corrode both the authenticity of faith as well as the human quality of politics. In addition, vulgarization, sentimentalist devotion, egotistic concerns, and market orientation corrode religion through electronic means of communication.

---

[17] C. Josaphat, "Política, espaço privilegiado para a prática da fé", in J.E. Pinheiro (ed.), *Resgatar a dignidade da politica*, São Paulo: Paulinas, 2006, 219-222.

Pastoral care culturally-oriented

From the best traditions of pastoral care roots we learn that pastoral caregivers have a commitment to care for individuals, families, communities of faith, society at large, environment, and strive for fair and balanced social interactions. Pastoral care connotes an understanding that people carry on everlasting aspirations (such as to be cared for, to be respected, to have a decent job, to enjoy life, to find a meaningful life...), in addition to an existing conjuncture needs. Pastoral care brings together the past, the present, and the future. And the future is building up from the present.

I want submit to the readers a brief agenda for pastoral caregivers, from my own limited "social location". This agenda is an attempt to catch the spirit of contemporary cultures. Also, the following considerations try to take into account the situation of new historical subjects who become visible in the face of rootless people around the world. My hope is that they can be helpful as we look to be faithful to both the foundations of pastoral action and to the instances of thought and worldview of our contemporary fellows.

1. Individuals, families and many groups seem be living in a "society without parents". The expression connotes without roots. There are many signs of destruction of human bonds. The widespread distrust of politicians; the rise of corruption; the despair of migrants; the inability of parents to cope with disturbing behavior of adolescents; wars and the impact of TV images of violence; lack of self-confidence to cope with common fragilities of human existence. These human conditions and many more, indicate that the traditional work of pastoral care of individuals and their social milieu is needed.

2. Existential issues are to be considered more important than doctrines. This does not mean that people do not need principles to guide ones' decisions and life orientation. However, daily life and down-to-earth issues become prominent. Besides, the inherited doctrines have been expanded from a variety of sources and from personal life situations.

3. The growing participation of church-members in small communities signals that the longing for settling down bonds that promote solidarity and personalization. As a matter of fact, small communities or groups have been part of the history of Christianity. These communities provide for an intimacy and atmosphere of trust which cannot be weaved in large churches.

4. The recent trend toward dialogue and integration between sciences and religious faith will continue growing and expanding the areas of cooperation. The contributions of psychological, sociological, anthropological sciences to the whole field of pastoral care and counseling are well known. In addition, sciences help the believers to set up a well-reasoned

understanding of the differences between what we *believe* and what we *know*.[18]

5. Pastoral care of the public dominium of the life web, that is, at political, environmental, economic, financial, as well as other, levels is a continuum of pastoral care of individuals. Individuals are not healed if society is sick. To care for the public is to advocate for the fullness of life. Even though pastors as individuals have the capacity to engage in this type of pastoral care, local communities, ecclesial bodies, ecumenical bodies and institutions could be better channels to voice pastoral care concerns. Pastoral care committed to strive for fullness of life develops methods and actions that lead to approval of legislations and public polity which work for the benefit of abundant life. This type of pastoral care is not aligned with the State, but uses its spiritual orientation to confront the unfair use of power. To conclude, it is my hope that pastoral caregivers are not only on the way to build up new practical and theoretical models. Rather, my hope is that we are following the steps of those people who are wandering through the deserts on their continuing search for *another world*, where life becomes abundant for all.

[18] See Karl Rahner, *Teologia e ciência*, São Paulo: Paulinas, 1971.

Cura Animarum, Cura Terrae and Eco-Spirituality: Towards an Aesthetics of Humility in an Eschatological Approach to Land, Nature and Environment *

Daniël J. Louw
South Africa, 2012

Abstract: The article advocates for a paradigm shift within the caring ministry of the church. *Cura animarum* should be supplemented by *cura terrae* and eco-spirituality. In order to do this, an eco- and terra-spirituality should become sensitive to the issues of exploitation, being lost, displaced, homeless, dislocated and poor. Environmental issues and the notion of land forces a practical theological ecclesiology to introduce an ethics of habitus as reflected in the New Testament's virtue of praÿs. Praÿs (humility) as an exposition of wisdom, also implies an inclusive aesthetics, which can help people to live in hope and to put stewardship for creation into practical actions of caring. Praÿs as habitus prevents a *cura terrae* from the exploitation of *dominium terrae*.

Introduction

Within the tradition of the Christian church, the praxis of Christian ministry was always connected to the healing dimension. *Cura animarum*[1] still remains the essential function of a practical theological ecclesiology. Although this assumption has always been pivotal to understanding the task and challenge of ministry, it is no longer clear exactly what the cure of human souls entails in a secularised, postmodern and global society.

In the caring and healing ministry of the reformed tradition the main emphasis was mostly on the conversion of the human soul with the focus on personal (individual) salvation, confession of sins and justification – the so-called kerygmatic approach which focused primarily on the proclama-

---

* Lecture presented at the 24th International Seminar on Intercultural Pastoral Care and Counselling, 2012, in Moshi, Tanzania; theme of the seminar: "Caring for Creation – Caring for People". Published in *Intercultural Pastoral Care and Counselling, 19*, 2012, 168-187.

[1] See J.T. McNeill, *A History of the Care of Souls*, New York: Harper & Row, 1951.

tion of the gospel. Thurneysen,[2] for example, argued that the caring ministry of the church should be viewed as an extension of the proclamation of the Word. The sanctification of life was to a large extent a function of Word-care and the sacraments through the piety of the individual. The extreme example of the kerygmatic model with its tendency of theological and spiritual reduction is J. Adams' separation of soteriology from creation and the experiential dimension of life. "The Bible's position is that all counsel that is not revelational (biblical), or based upon God's revelation, is satanic".[3] Adams' nouthetic counselling separates the doctrine of salvation from the doctrine of creation with sin as the basis of all human problems.[4]

In reaction to this directive and confrontational model, the client-centered model put more emphasis on the individual's inner frame of reference, taking seriously the person as a living human document.[5] Due to the influence of Rogers,[6] care gathers (educes) its knowledge from the so-called "client" by means of observation, perception, and empathy. This approach gave rise to the well-known phenomenological method of induction in non-directive counselling.

It was, inter alia, Heitink[7] who tried to introduce a bipolar principle[8] in both the caring ministry and theory formation for practical theology[9]. Within the tradition of Schleiermacher, the emphasis became action and the empirical field of experience.[10] Practical Theology therefore is becoming more and more an action science. The theological theory is mostly determined by an empirical orientation in order to mediate the Christian faith within the praxis of our modern and secularised society.[11] The focal point of a practical theological ecclesiology becomes the praxis of the church. Ecclesiology should therefore not focus on the essence of the church anymore (the ecclesial and clergical model) but on the function of the

[2] E. Thurneysen, *Die Lehre von der Seelsorge* [A Theology of Pastoral Care], 2nd ed., Zürich: Theologischer Verlag, 1957, 129.
[3] J.E. Adams, *More than Redemption*, Grand Rapids: Baker, 1979, 4.
[4] J.E. Adams, *Competent to Counsel*, 10th ed., Michigan: Baker, 1977, 45.
[5] See A.T. Boisen, *Problems in Religion and Life: A Manual for Pastors*, Nashville: Abingdon, s.a. [1946]
[6] C.R. Rogers, *Counselling and Psychotherapy*, Boston: Houghton Mifflin, 1942; C.R. Rogers, *Client-Centered Therapy*, Boston: Houghton Mifflin, 1951.
[7] G. Heitink, *Pastoraat als hulpverlening: Inleiding in de pastorale theologie en psychologie*, Kampen: Kok, 1977.
[8] See also F.G. Immink, *In God geloven. Een praktisch-theologische reconstructie*, Zoetermeer: Meinema, 2003, 20.
[9] J. Heitink, *Praktische Theologie. Geschiedenis-theorie-handelingsvelden*, Kampen: Kok, 1993.
[10] F. Schleiermacher, "Ueber die Einrichtung der Theologischen Fakultät (1810)", in G. Krause (ed.), *Praktische Theologie*, Darmstadt: Wiss. Buchges., 1972.
[11] Heitink, *Pastoraat*, 18.

church, i.e. the ministerial praxis with its emphasis on transformation.[12] Immink refers to an analysis of the religious praxis[13] with less focus on the ecclesiological praxis.

It is clear that the shift is towards social and life issues. Browning[14] refers to a period of social reconstruction which challenges a practical reason, practical wisdom (*phronēsis*). In terms of Tracy[15] a hermeneutics of the contemporary situation is the focal point of practical theology. The principal praxis criteria for practical theology are therefore criteria of transformation and the principal theoretical criteria are those of a theological ethics related to that praxis.[16] Praxis is therefore simply action, that is, as what one does or possibly or probably can do in concrete circumstances.

The implication of a praxis-model is that models of human transformation, the analysis of the public (social context) as well as the public claims[17] for reconstruction, as well as the principles of hermeneutics and correlation, became pivotal for a more ethical approach to a practical theological ecclesiology. Orthopraxis and social action[18] set the agenda for practical theology.

In the struggle for justice and the reconstruction of the social environment (social engineering) the question for an appropriate practical theology is the following: should practical theology imply more than merely action? Should the emphasis rather be on imagination and creativity as well? Ogletree[19] argues that for the action dimension, the central interest is in appropriateness. One seeks to discern what is right and proper to do in specific situations. But appropriateness is not simply a moral category. Ritual actions, for example, call for aesthetic judgements, as do attempts to produce works of art that articulate faith understandings in a nonverbal fashion.

In his very powerful book, *Christianity, Art and Transformation*, De Gruchy[20] advocates for aesthetic judgement in doing theology. He writes: "For some reason the connection between aesthetics and social ethics,

---

[12] J.A. Van der Ven, *Ecclesiologie in context*, Kampen: Kok., 1993, 10-11.
[13] Immink, *In God geloven*, 19.
[14] D.S. Browning, *A Fundamental Practical Theology: Descriptive and Strategic Proposals*, Minneapolis: Fortress Press, 1991, 4.
[15] D. Tracy, "The Foundations of Practical Theology", in D.S. Browning (ed.), *Practical Theology*, San Francisco: Harper & Row, 1983, 62.
[16] Ibid., 72.
[17] Ibid., 76-77.
[18] D.P. McCann, "Practical Theology and Social Action: Or What Can the 1980's Learn from the 1960's?", in Browning (ed.), *Practical Theology*, 111-115.
[19] T.W. Ogletree, "Dimensions of Practical Theology: Meaning, Action, Self", in Browning (ed.), *Practical Theology*, 91.
[20] J.W. De Gruchy, *Christianity, Art and Transformation: Theological Aesthetics in the Struggle for Justice*, Cambridge: Cambridge University Press, 2001, 138.

between beauty and social transformation, was not apparent to those of us who were engaged as theologians in the struggle against apartheid."[21]

The concern for aesthetics in practical theology was the main topic of discussion at the meeting of the International Academy for Practical Theology (IAPT) in Quebec, 1999. F. Schweitzer refers to creativity, imagination and criticism as the expressive dimension in practical theology.[22] Despite of Schweitzer's criticism that Farley's argument for theology as *habitus* (*habitus* as the true perspective for practical theology) is too narrow and should be supplemented by a critical theory of praxis,[23] I want to elaborate on Schweitzer's plea for a critical hermeneutics of culture.[24] Schweitzer refers to the following fourth sub-movement: a hermeneutics of renewal and completion which aims at restoring and reforming human expressivity, which helps people not only to express their deepest quest for human dignity and meaning. It is my conviction that such a movement can help a practical theology to start to dream – to reshape the social and living environment and to transform "land" into a place of hope and enjoyment.

Hypothesis

My basic hypothesis is that a practical theological ecclesiology should be guided in theory formation by an eco-spirituality and an understanding of care wherein the traditional understanding of *cura animarum* should be supplemented by a *cura terrae*. The latter should not reduce "praxis" to merely matters of "practical concern". It should include matters of *habitus*, being, cultural paradigms and aesthetics as well. In this regard the art of hope can play a decisive role in the transformation of "culture". With culture is meant: *colo* – the way and mode in which human beings transform the environment, earth and land (creation) into a hospitable place of peaceful co-existence (home), cohabitation.

Actually the whole of the cosmos should be a habitat and place for stewardship. Processes for the transformation of land and the conservation of nature include not merely structural transformation, but a transformation of attitude and aptitude as well. *Habitus* (disposition) is indeed a very powerful act of the human "soul" itself.[25] For this one needs practical

---

[21] Ibid., 2.

[22] F. Schweitzer, "Creativity, Imagination and Criticism: The Expressive Dimension in Practical Theology", in P. Ballard and P. Couture (eds.), *Creativity, Imagination and Criticism: The Expressive Dimension in Practical Theology*, Cardiff: Cardiff Academic Press, 2001, 3-15.

[23] Ibid., 13.

[24] Ibid., 14.

[25] E. Fairley, "Theology and Practice Outside the Clerical Paradigm", in Browning (ed.), *Practical Theology*, 23.

reason (wisdom)[26] as related to the aesthetics of hope: the act of dreaming as anticipation of a better (beautiful) environmental future.

Paradigm shift: from ethics to aesthetics

The aesthetics of hope includes art. In this regard, beauty becomes an ethical quality. Therefore, in his most remarkable book, *On Beauty*, Umberto Eco[27] advocates very strongly for the rediscovery of the sublime in nature. To recognize the sublime in nature is inter alia to become aware of the deformation of nature in terms of ugliness, formlessness, terror and exploitation. Beauty then demands justice. "For example, in answer to a question on the criterion for appraising beauty, the Delphic Oracle replied: 'The most beautiful is the most just.' Even in the golden age of Greek art, beauty was always associated with other values, like 'moderation', 'harmony' and 'symmetry.'" [28]

In the words of De Gruchy, art has to do with that awakening that aesthetic existence becomes possible and transformation begins to take place.[29] Thus the following thesis: *practical concern* should be supplemented by *practical art*. Practical art then as the skill through which we beautify the place of land and the space of creation via the mode of *praÿs* – the creative power of humility (the *habitus* of eschatology) and the creative energy of hope. In practical art the endeavour is to beautify life and to rediscover the beauty of creation, thus the importance of the notion of a cosmological aesthetics.

Practical art then as related to the creative energy of hope, becomes structural "transformation": "the term (transformation) is an open-ended, multi-layered process, at once social and personal, that is energised by hope yet rooted in the struggles of the present."[30]

Creation within a practical theological ecclesiology

With a practical theological ecclesiology is meant:

(a) The art of interpretation – faith seeking understanding. To understand God within the realm of creation and land (*fides quaerens intellectum*);

(b) The art of communication – faith verbalising the beauty of God's fulfilled Word-promises (*fides quaerens verbum*);

---

[26] Browning, *Fundamental Practical Theology*.
[27] U. Eco, *On Beauty: A History of a Western Idea*, London: Secker & Warburg, 2004, 281.
[28] Ibid., 37.
[29] De Gruchy, *Christianity*, 8.
[30] Ibid., 3.

(c) The art of doing / acting – faith seeking appropriate actions of conservation, change, transformation and liberation (*fides quaerens actum*);

(d) The art of hope and creative imagination – faith seeking modes of realistic anticipation of a just society and a place for at-homeness (land as "Heimat") (*fides quaerens spem*).[31]

In all of the praxis-models for practical theology the emphasis are mostly on social transformation, political actions, practical concerns, contextual and ethical issues. However, creation and very specifically the use of land and the conservation of nature in itself receive little attention.

In order to reflect on creation as a theological issue, as well as its implication for human dispositions (*habitus*) (anthropology) and creative actions (hope), the paper will be divided into the following three sections:

(1) Receiving creation in hope – towards a practical *theology* of land and nature;

(2) Living and caring for creation in hope – towards an eco-spirituality of *cura terrae*;

(3) The beautification of creation in hope – towards an aesthetics of *habitus* (*praÿs*).

Receiving creation in hope – towards a practical theology of land [32]

The issue of land is in most cases more a matter for the agenda of politicians, economists and ecologists, than for theologians. "It is likely that conventional Christianity has wanted always to talk about Yahweh and neglect land. And conversely, secular humanism wants always to talk only of land and never of Yahweh."[33]

Land as territory: the preservation of life and promotion of peace

If one really wants to take up the issue of land as a point on the agenda of practical theology, the first thing to realise is that land in the Old Testament is immediately connected to the preservation of life and the notion of *shalom*. Land incorporates the whole of the creation as a space for life. The land is a vivid issue and refers to more than merely soil. It is part and parcel of the whole system of human life. For example, land issues were never separated from the familial paradigm. The reason for this was that the

[31] In this article I want to concentrate mostly on practical theology as *fides quaerens spem*.

[32] Land should be read as an inclusive concept. It includes the whole of the cosmos, creation, nature and environment.

[33] W. Brueggemann, *The Land*, Philadelphia: Fortress Press, 1977, 52.

preservation of life aimed to prevent exploitation and poverty; it should promote a dignified way of humane living and fosters peace.

Shalom in Israel was not an abstract or merely "spiritual" issue. *Shalom* corresponds with quality of life. "To restore *shalom* meant to preserve life by apportioning land."[34] Land was therefore a place for peaceful living and an exposition of human dignity. In the prophetic tradition the principles of *shalom* and hospitality have been maintained (see the story of Naboth's vineyard, 1 Kings 21). "God sends a prophetic word when life has been violated, when inheritance/land has been alienated, and when hospitality has been replaced by egoistic concern for self".[35] This Naboth incident explains the prophet's preoccupation with economic exploitation as an illustration of what the preservation of life and the promotion of peace entail. Territory, and therefore land, was constituted by three decisive theological indicators: promise, gift and grace (election).[36]

Land as a political, social, economic and national entity was therefore embedded in Israel's understanding of territory as part of creation, the earth. Land becomes an epitome for "Lebensraum", a space for human living, governed by the principles of justice, hospitality and integrity (Ps 137:16-18).

An ethics of land: on the boundary between promise and possession

Land in Israel was restricted to a sort of boundary situation. It functioned between the reality of Word (promise) and memory (remembrance). Possession of land was contingent in Israel on God's promise and leading (Gen 12:1-3, 7).[37] Landholding for Israel was based on God's promises – not on aboriginal claims nor on military power; it (land) is inheritance and rest (Deut 12:9) granted by God's grace.

The implication of the promise-principle is that God alone is the owner and human existence is properly existence as "strangers and sojourners" (Lev 25:23).[38] Therefore, a practical theology of land which wants to foster and promote a *cura terrae*, should understand the following inherent theological structure: land – God's grace – hospitality – *homo viator* – future. The reason for this structure is because land in all its dimensions – promise, conquest, shared possession, use and abuse, loss and recovery –

[34] W. Janzen, *Old Testament Ethics: A Paradigmatic Approach*, Louisville: Westminister/John Knox Press, 1994, 42.
[35] Ibid., 156.
[36] H.D. Preuss, *Theologie des Alten Testaments, Vol. 1: JHWHS erwählendes und verpflichtendes Handeln*, Stuttgart: Kohlhammer, 1991, 132: "Das Land wurde zur geschichtlichen Gabe des erwählenden Gottes an das erwählte Volk."
[37] Janzen, *Old Testament Ethics*, 42.
[38] Ibid.; see also Preuss, *Theologie*, 144.

was fundamentally for Israel a theological entity.[39] Land was a divine gift, defining the possessor as a sojourner. The possession of land manifested in an attitude of hospitality and humility. These became the norms how to "manage" and to "use" land. "Trusting in God's grace however, humans can live securely in that impermanent status, knowing that the hospitality of God alone offers the real secure home."[40] What Israel possessed was due to God's election of and promise to Abraham (see Deut 7:7, 8:17, 9:5). Land was therefore a metaphor for dependency (Israel) and God's dependability.[41]

The ethical principle at stake here is that ethical living is not active self-assertion, but trusting acceptance of God's "hospitality". Possession is the outcome of hospitality not of a basic right which can be claimed. Very specifically the hospitality principle focused on poverty and exploitation and has been seen as the extension of life to those for whose lives one is not held responsible through kinship obligations. It also focused on the stranger (Gen 24: 29) and transcended in-group selfishness. Hospitality could therefore cause sacrifice and suffering (Ruth 2:14-16; Deut 24:19-22). Individual property rights emanated from Israel's historical land-gift tradition.[42]

A spirituality of land: stewardship and qualitative relationships

The theological principle of promise as well as the ethical principles of inheritance (land as a gift of God) and hospitality (sharing in order to prevent poverty) corresponds with a deeper meaning. Land was a metaphor for a spirituality which reflects the quality of the relationship with things (economic relationships) as well as with people (social relationships). The land issue in Israel was always connected to the presence of God. Things and therefore the environment as well as the earth, should be stewarded (*cura terrae*); human beings should be cared for (*cura animarum*), i.e. the healing through qualitative relationships determined by *shalom* (peace) and hospitality. *Shalom*, hospitality and the land-gift tradition were intrinsically spiritual issues; "...the prophetic message did neither stem from a general concern for human rights, nor from an advancing ethical sensitivity. It was not even a merely economic issue. It was deeply spiritual."[43] The land issue impacted directly onto the covenantal relationship with God. Economic exploitation was a moral evil which should be condemned on the wide basis

---

[39] C.J.H. Wright, *Living as the People of God: The Relevance of Old Testament Ethics*, Leicester: Inter-Varsity Press, 1983, 50.
[40] Janzen, *Old Testament Ethics*, 42.
[41] Wright, *Living as the People of God*, 52.
[42] Ibid., 54.
[43] Ibid., 56.

of common humanity and an ethic of stewardship.[44] It was the belief that God owns the land and demands accountability in the use of it from his "tenants", that generates the literal "earthiness" of Old Testament ethics.[45]

Land was a sort of "spiritual thermometer".[46] It was an indication of the spiritual temperature in the economic sphere, revealing the equality of the relationship with God as well as the social shape of life in correspondence to the status of Israel as God's redeemed people.

Due to the "spiritual dimension," a mere phenomenology of land does not suffice. Although W. Brueggemann[47] opts for a phenomenological perspective on what land has meant to the people of Israel (land is a physical source of fertility and life; a place for the gathering of the hopes of the covenant people and a vibrant theological symbol), an eschatological interpretation cannot be avoided. Land in Israel remained an apocalyptic concern. One should also use and manage the land in hope which is articulated against land in possession. This hope is for a land transformed and renewed as a dwelling place for all of the nations of the earth. Land cannot be separated from the messianic yearning for a new Israel and a new Jerusalem: "Behold I will create new heavens and a new earth...I will create Jerusalem to be a delight and its people a joy...they will build houses and dwell in them; they will plant vineyards and eat their fruit" (see Isaiah 65:17-25).

A spirituality of land connects with the traditional African view of land. Within an African spirituality, land is a spiritual space and place. It belongs to the spiritual realm and the transcendent reality of ancestors. Land is also a relational issue as related to the living community. Land therefore has a sacred character; it constitutes a centre for the way of life and is viewed in many Christian circles in Africa as the basis of a God-given self-respect and creativity.[48]

Conclusion

A practical theology of land opens up in our discussion of land issues, a sensitivity for exploitation, being lost, displaced, homeless, dislocated and poor. Within the yearning in contemporary society for possession, control, management and exploitation – land opens up a new understanding and hermeneutics of belongingness and sharing.

---

[44] Ibid., 57.

[45] Ibid., 59.

[46] Ibid., 59.

[47] Brueggemann, *Land*, xii.

[48] See M. Guma and L. Milton, *An African Challenge to the Church in the 21st Century*, Cape Town: The Methodist Press, 1997; K.Th. August, *Landform and Traditional Society: The Impact on the Church*, unpublished paper, Faculty of Theology, Stellenbosch University, 2004.

- Land forces a practical theological ecclesiology to introduce an ethics of habitus as displayed in wisdom (a true discernment pertaining life issues and the fostering of human dignity) and hospitality.
- Land reframes our understanding of power. Power becomes related to the quality of relationships and should be accompanied by the virtues of hospitality and humility (see the third part of the article).
- Land as place is more than merely territory and possession. It introduces in economics the ethics of fair/just distribution and hospitable sharing. Place becomes a historical setting referring to the happenstances of life events. It is an indication of a human space for life and neighbourly livelihood. Land and place are becoming settings where covenantal vows are exchanged, promises been made and ethical demands are being issued. Place and land become a declaration that our humanness cannot be found in escape, detachment, absence of commitment and undefined freedom.
- Land places limitations on our human freedom. It demarcates freedom as hospitality. It becomes a fundamental theological critique on the economics of an affluent society (land as place for entertainment and exploitation) and the central temptation of coveting.

In order to safeguard these theological principles and guidelines for a practical theological ecclesiology of land, our fundamental theological understanding of our being human (the soulfulness of *cura animarum*) should be reframed – thus the issue of an eco-spirituality in a practical theological ecclesiology.

Living and caring creation in hope – towards an eco-spirituality in ecological thinking and "green nurturing"

The land issue challenges the dimension of ecological caring within practical theology. Pastoral care as a sub-discipline within practical theology is responsible for healing, growth and change. Besides the traditional functions of healing, guiding, sustaining and reconciling, the link between land and stewardship presupposes the function of nurturing and poses the following question to care and healing: should pastoral care concentrate mainly on *cura animarum* or should it be elaborated and extended to *cura terrae* in order to include issues related to land, creation, environment and ecology in the ministry of the church? Is the healing of the land and the ecology part and parcel of pastoral care? If it is indeed the case, what are the theological implications of a *cura terrae* on our understanding of the relationship between God and creation and our understanding of our human identity?

Clinebell's holistic approach: the nurturing of the ecological environment

The relationship between a pastoral theology and creation is not new. Clinebell's growth model attempts to incorporate Aristotle's view of the cosmos. It operates with the assumption: "In all living things there is an inherent striving toward fulfilling their possibilities. Every acorn has a 'need' to become an oak."[49] His growth model is linked to a holistic interpretation of spirituality: The spiritual dimension of our lives consists of the ways in which we satisfy seven interrelated spiritual needs: the need for a viable philosophy of life, for creative values, for a relationship with a loving God, for developing our higher self, for a sense of trustful belonging in the universe, for renewing moments of transcendence and for a caring community that nurtures spiritual growth.[50]

Clinebell's description of spirituality is important. He argues for the need to accept "human wholeness" as a starting point for a reflection on the character of pastoral care. The intention of growth counselling is to disclose and to utilize ("potentializing") the internal healing present in all forms of life (enabling healing and empowerment). In pastoral care, his concern is for human beings as well as creation. He therefore advocates a qualitative understanding of growth, rather than a quantitative one. Unbridled growth can destroy the earth. By qualitative he means: "personal, relational, and transpersonalspiritual growth." [51] This means that ecology may be incorporated into pastoral care. Clinebell argues that two ethical principles should be used when applying his growth model to ecology. "These must be a human wholeness ethic which commits our energies to maximizing the growth of persons and an ecological ethic which motivates us to work to make the whole ecosystem a place of growth." [52] The overarching goal of all pastoral ministry is to liberate, empower, and nurture wholeness centred in the Spirit.[53] Ecology plays a vital role in his understanding of wholeness, i.e.: "Deepening one's relationship with nature and the biosphere." [54]

Clinebell sees liberation as a broad concept, which encompasses life in all its fullness. "It (liberation) is life in all its fullness – to increasing caring and competence, and creative living." [55] Pastoral care's task is thus to free

[49] H.J Clinebell, *Growth Counseling: Hope-Centered Methods of Actualizing Human Wholeness*, Nashville: Abingdon, 1979, 45.
[50] Ibid., 106.
[51] Ibid., 45.
[52] Ibid., 44.
[53] H.J. Clinebell, *Basic Types of Pastoral Care and Counseling: Resources for the Ministry of Healing and Growth*, Nashville: Abingdon, 1984, 26.
[54] Ibid., 31.
[55] Ibid., 30.

nature from humankind's dominance and exploitation. "The fourth dimension of pastoral care and counseling is liberating our relationship with the biosphere by increasing our ecological awareness, communion and caring."[56] Healing in pastoral care therefore implies: developing and cherishing a nurturing interaction with our great mother – Mother Nature.[57]

In an article, "Salvation as healing and humanization", De Gruchy[58] advocates for a rediscovery of a holistic paradigm in theology, based on the biblical term, *shalom*. Therapy and healing include the physical and natural dimensions. The biblical sense of corporate responsibility is extended to the creation as a whole, and therefore demands husbandry of the earth and its resources. Thus, human well-being, or *shalom*, is about not only the physical and psychic (including spiritual) health of the individual, but with the health of the social and political order, and the vital balance of nature.[59] Healing cannot be separated in a dualistic way from nature. At stake in healing is our humanity, and humanity and creation are inseparable concepts. "Health is that which enables us to be fully human in relation to ourselves, our society and our environment." [60]

From soteriological reduction to pneumatological and ecological thinking: God in creation (panentheism)

Clearly, the relation between God and creation should be interpreted from a metaphorical perspective. McFague's model is helpful here. She sees the whole world as the body of God.[61] She does not assume that creation gives us a direct description of God, but employs an as-if mode of theologizing.[62] The description of the world as the body of God, describes the immanence of God in terms of his identification with the cosmos. McFague calls this panentheism: "... that is, it is a view of the God-world relationship in which all things have their origin in God and nothing exists outside God, though this does not mean that God is reduced to things."[63] God has an empa-

---

[56] Ibid., 32.

[57] For the relationship between God and creation and the role of the spirit (pneumatology) see J.J. Rebel, *Pastoraat in pneumatologisch perspektief: Een theologische verantwoording vanuit het denken van A A. van Ruler*, Kampen: Kok Rebel, 1981, 44; A.A. van Ruler, *De vervulling van de wet*, 2nd ed., Nijkerk: Callenbach, 1974, 47-55.

[58] J. De Gruchy, "Salvation as Healing and Humanization", in T.A. Hart and D.P. Thimell (eds.), *Christ in Our Place: The Humanity of God in Christ for the Reconciliation of the World*, Exeter: Paternoster, 1989, 32-48; see p. 38.

[59] Ibid., 40.

[60] Ibid., 43.

[61] S. McFague, *Models of God*, Philadelphia: Fortress, 1987, 69.

[62] Ibid., 70.

[63] Ibid., 72.

thetic, intimate and sympathetic knowledge of the world which implies that "the action of God in the world is similarly interior and caring".[64]

McFague's model should not be regarded as an ontological model which assesses concepts in terms of matter. Her metaphorical model maintains both the transcendence and the immanence of God for an organic understanding of the cosmos. "We are not describing God as having a body or being embodied; we are suggesting that what is bedrock for the universe – matter, that of which everything that is, is made – might be, in fact perhaps ought to be applied to God as well."[65] This panentheistic stance does not exclude the transcendence of God. "The transcendence of God then is the pre-eminent or primary Spirit of the universe."[66] Metaphorical theology views God as "the inspirited body of the entire universe, the animating, living Spirit that produces, guides and saves all that is."[67]

McFague's model has value because it awakens us to a revised sacramental approach. "It is the basis for a revived sacramentalism, that is, a perception of the divine as visible, as present, palpably present in our world."[68] It also challenges theology to rethink its stance regarding ecology. Sin also acquires a new extra meaning: it becomes the refusal to nurture creation. "To sin is not to refuse loyalty to the Liege Lord but to refuse to take responsibility for nurturing, loving, and befriending the body and all its parts".[69]

When God is regarded merely as a monarch or king, this could easily lead to a most aggressive model, to a violent approach and, inevitably, to the exploitation of the earth. But, the model of the world, as the body of God, enhances a holistic approach. It enables (and empowers) theology to abdicate from a hierarchical, to a more empathetic model regarding ecology. The beauty of the world and its ability to sustain the vast multitude of species it supports is not there for the taking. The world is a body that must be carefully tended, that must be nurtured, protected, guided, loved and befriended both as valuable in itself – for like us, it is an expression of God – and as necessary to the continuation of life.[70] It has emerged gradually from our discussion that the relationship between God and creation is closely associated with our God images. The question facing theology is whether we depart from an antithetical model, or whether we use a hermeneutical model to interpret the presence of God in creation.

---

[64] Ibid., 73.
[65] S. McFague, *The Body of God: An Ecological Theology*, London: SCM, 1993, 19.
[66] Ibid., 20.
[67] Ibid.
[68] McFague, *Models of God*, 77
[69] Ibid.
[70] Ibid.

We could isolate God from creation in order to safeguard his transcendence. But this runs the risk of selling out creation and delivering it to evil powers. The alternative would be to argue for God *and* creation. This parallel approach does not solve our problem. The challenge is thus to rethink the notion, God in creation, without necessarily falling prey to pantheism. For Moltmann, the challenge is to rediscover God in creation.[71] This view – which has also been called panentheistic (in contrast to pantheistic) – requires us to bring reverence for the life of every living thing into the adoration of God. And this means expanding the worship and service of God to include service for God's creation. Moltmann believes that a trinitarian model opens up new avenues for reflection on the relationship between God and creation. This is the fundamental idea behind a nonhierarchical, decentralized, confederate theology. In terms of pneumatology, Moltmann argues for an ecological doctrine of creation.[72]

An ecological doctrine of creation implies a new kind of thinking about God. Moltmann says: "The centre of this thinking is no longer the distinction between God and the world. The centre is the recognition of the presence of God in the world and the presence of the world in God."[73] The Old Testament distinguished between God and creation in order to safeguard Israel from worshipping nature and to prevent incorporation of fertility cults in their worship. The intention was not a metaphysical separation between God and creation. A causality approach, in terms of causes, should also be abandoned. If the Creator is present in his creation by virtue of the Spirit, then his relationship to creation should be viewed rather as a web of unilateral, reciprocal and multilateral relationships.

In this network of relationships, "making," "preserving," "maintaining" and "perfecting" are certainly the great one-sided relationships; but "indwelling," "sympathizing," "participating," "accompanying," "enduring," "delighting" and "glorifying" are relationships of mutuality which describe a cosmic community of living between God the Spirit and all his created things.[74]

The exposition of Moltmann's model for an ecological theology alters the notion from "God and creation" to "God in creation". The latter is an important point of departure, in order to combat the prevailing crisis of domination. Antithetical categories should therefore be exchanged for more sympathetic categories.

---

[71] J. Moltmann, *God in Creation: A New Theology of Creation and the Spirit of God*, Minneapolis: Fortress, 1993, xi-xii.
[72] Ibid., 2-19.
[73] Ibid., 13.
[74] Ibid., 14.

In his book on creation, Link reveals how the commission to subject the earth has been misunderstood (*Dominium terrae*).[75] This has led to the exploitation of the earth. Genesis 1:28 was not written to promote technological progress and scientific achievement. Humankind was created to present God in creation and to nurture it. Whenever we separate dominion from our responsibility to God, exploitation and destructive power emerge.[76] According to Link, creation is our home to be enjoyed, not the scrap-yard for our technological trash.

Brueggemann supports the notion of creation as a well-structured network of integrated relations.[77] The Psalms of creation reflect orientation and indicate that the cosmos is an ordered entity. "These psalms in various ways are expressions of creation faith. They affirm that the world is a well-ordered, reliable, and life-giving system, because God has ordained it that way and continues to preside effectively over the process." Creation is not a chaotic mass, but an image and sign. Gilkey describes God's creation as a sign of His glory:[78] In this context, image is taken to mean a sign, symbol or sacrament of the divine, disclosing through itself the divine glory. By image, then, I will mean that nature manifests or reveals certain unmistakable signs of the divine, namely power, life, order and redemptive unity bestowed on it by God. In conclusion, when a discipline of creation is developed for pastoral theology, the notion "God in creation" should be interpreted hermeneutically and pneumatologically, not ontologically. This is the difference between pantheism and panentheism. In panentheism, creation becomes a metaphor for the *shalom*, which is an intrinsic part of God's involvement in creation. Creation, when used as a metaphor for "home," challenges humans to husbandry of the earth. Caring and preserving the earth becomes the main objective of this husbandry. "So human mastery over the earth is intended to resemble the cultivating and protective work of a gardener. Nothing is said about predatory exploitation".[79] God's immanence refers to God's sympathetic identification with creation. The notion of creation, as the body of God, lays the foundation for an ecological theology. The earth (and therefore land as well) is regarded in terms of a sacramental understanding: life is seen as a symbol of God's presence and glory. Pastoral care becomes doxology when seen from the perspective of the sanctification of the earth: the playful nurturing and abundant enjoyment of creation.

---

[75] C. Link, *Schöpfung: Schöpfungstheologie angesichts der Herausforderungen des 20. Jahrhunderts*, Gütersloh: Gütersloher Verlagshaus, 1991, 391.
[76] Ibid., 397.
[77] W. Brueggemann, *The Message of the Psalms*, Minneapolis: Augsburg, 1984, 26.
[78] L. Gilkey, "Nature as the Image of God: Signs of the Sacred", in *Theology Today, 51:1*, 1994, 127-141, see p. 127.
[79] Moltmann, *God in Creation*, 30.

Cura terrae as a spiritual endeavour

The attempt to curb the ecological crisis by formulating a new understanding of pastoral care's nurturing function, presupposes a rejection of the reductionist approach of classical physics. In contrast to the reductionist approach, which isolates parts from the whole and thinks in terms of fractions and particles, ecological thinking reasons in terms of systems thinking.

For our purposes the most important feature of the science of ecology is its fundamental assumption about the natural world. The ecological view is that living creatures in any given environment are interdependent and have to be understood as a whole.[80] Two options may be considered in an attempt to combat the ecological crisis. Firstly, "technocentrism." This means managing the crisis by technical means, thus obtaining efficient control. Secondly, "ecocentrism." This approach operates with sensitivity and respect for all forms of life on earth. The latter may also be called a "green spirituality".[81] It represents the philosophy of the interconnectedness of ecosystems. McDaniel coins the term "ecological spirituality," indicating hope for a better earth.[82] It reflects on the relationship between God's immanence and the interconnectedness of all forms of life on earth.

The important question is whether such a holistic and ecological thinking represents the scriptural creation narrative. An exegetical approach should bear in mind that the Biblical writers were not aware of a "green spirituality." The Old Testament was written from the perspective of humans enjoying creation in the presence of God. "The earth is the Lord's, and everything in it, the world, and all who live in it" (Ps 24). Humans inherited the earth and should accept ownership. Obedience to the laws of God should lead to a nurturing attitude. "Then the land will yield its fruit, and you will eat your fill and live there in safety" (Lev 25:18-19).

Management of the earth is an art and culture. "Skills and technology of all kinds may be admirable, but the tyrannical or greedy use of human power over nature is a failure deriving from human sin – not from God's intention in creation."[83] The notion of a "green theology" and the perspective of a "green Christian faith" should be assessed in terms of a cosmic understanding of God's presence and Christ's work of redemption. In this regard, theologians appeal strongly to the Old Testament.

---

[80] L. Osborn, *Guardians of Creation: Nature in Theology and the Christian Life*, Leister: Apollos, 1993, 13.
[81] Ibid., 46.
[82] J.B. McDaniel, *Earth, Sky, Gods and Mortals: Developing an Ecological Spirituality*, Mystic: Twenty-third publications, 1992, 182-185.
[83] J.A. Baker, "Biblical Views of Nature", in C. Birch et al. (eds.), *Liberating Life: Contemporary Approaches to Ecological Theology*, New York: Maryknoll, 1990, 19.

A new, green economics is slowly emerging which embraces many Old Testament principles concerning economic life, such as the need to restrain the accumulation of wealth, to achieve justice through a "bias to the poor" in public policy, and to focus upon stewardship rather than ownership.[84]

McDonagh argues along the same lines. He tries to avoid a mechanistic interpretation of God and attempts to move towards a more sympathetic understanding of God's involvement in creation.[85] He calls this "the greening of the church." An ecological theology should consider the close association between Christ and the cosmos (Rom 8:18-25). Christology; and cosmology should not be separated. Such an approach opens up the possibility of an eco-spirituality. "Christian eco-spirituality attempts to integrate redemption-centered and creation-centered spiritualities by focusing on the new creation inaugurated by Christ in his redemptive incarnation, passion and resurrection."[86] Van Leeuwen attempts to combine resurrection with cosmology:[87] "If Christ in his death, wiped out evil and death, in his resurrection he vindicated the goodness of creation, its renewal and transformation; into a new creation."[88]

"Greening the church" does not mean that salvation is a soteriological issue which is applicable solely to human beings. Salvation also has universal and cosmic implications. In his book *God Is Green*, Bradley refers to the cosmic Christ as the link between the material and spiritual world.[89] The notion of Christ as a universal and cosmic saviour is also conveyed by the use of the Greek phrase *ta panta* (all things) (Eph 1:10).

Those who advocate for the "greening" of pastoral care also imply that pastoral care should not be separated from the diaconic and priestly function of our involvement in the cosmos. In *Christozentrische Diakonie*, Philippi recommends that the congregation should be a caring and serving fellowship.[90] Dominion should be abolished. In its place should be a diaconic expression of Christ's caring presence in the cosmos.[91] Christ transforms our *via gloriae* into a *via crucis* (the diaconic mode).

The diaconic mode of service should be an integral part of pastoral care. The care of souls should be expanded to the care of creation. If this

---

[84] T. Cooper, *Green Christianity: Caring for the Whole Creation*, London: Spire, 1990, 101.

[85] S. McDonagh, *The Greening of the Church*, New York: Orbis, 1990, 124.

[86] C. Cummings, *Eco-Spirituality: Toward a Reverent Life*, Mahwah/New York: Paulist, 1991, 106.

[87] R.C. van Leeuwen, "Christ's Resurrection and the Creation's Vindication", in *The Environment and the Christian*, ed. C.B. De Witt, Grand Rapids: Baker, 1991, 65-70.

[88] Ibid., 61.

[89] I. Bradley, *God Is Green*, London: Darton, Longman & Todd, 1990, 82.

[90] P. Philippi, *Christozentrische Diakonie*, Stuttgart: Evangelisches Verl., 1963, 81.

[91] Ibid., 100-101.

hypothesis is true, then the pastor should accept a stewardship which serves creation. "Grace is not just for us, but it is a gift for all life. Perhaps what best describes this relationship is the term servant priest; carrying with it both the notion of authority and service."[92] "Green spirituality" in pastoral care implies stewardship. The sole objective of this stewardship is to reveal the *shalom* of creation and to exercise husbandry. This is expressed in the pastor's priestly service.

A priest is a mediator and mediation is an essential part of our human vocation to have dominion over creation. By responsibly caring for and enjoying our environment, we represent, we make concrete, God's loving enjoyment of his creation. As priests of creation, we are called to symbolize and express at a personal level the unity of creation in praise of God.[93]

Clobus calls this priestly stewardship a "vice-gerent/khalifa," because "magnanimity is called for in us as caretakers of a creation, which does not derive its value from our estimation of it."[94] We can broaden the notion of "God in creation" when practical theology is related to the dynamics of a practical theological aesthetics. R. Bohren is convinced that through the contribution of aesthetics in practical theology, God becomes "beautiful".[95] When people discover unity with nature and meaning in creation, it arouses amazement and wonder. Art could be viewed as culture's attempt to restore order in creation. Through art man cooperates with God, in an attempt to care for creation. We may conclude from this that caring includes an ecological nurturing of creation. Caring for creation is not only an ethical issue, but also includes aesthetics. Care and playful enjoyment go hand in hand when not only the interconnectedness of creation is discovered, but also the interconnectedness with our natural environment as well.

"Greening the church" implies that ecology in pastoral care is the priestly art of sanctifying the earth. In eco- spirituality our humanity and healing is at stake, not exploitation and destruction.

The beautification of creation in hope – towards an aesthetics of habitus (praÿs)

We now come to the question: what is the implication of *cura terrae* for our human attitude and disposition within an ecology of land? What becomes evident is that the greening of the church and eco-spirituality within a

[92] M. Palmer, "The Ecological Crisis and Creation Theology", in V. Brümmer (ed.), *Interpreting the Universe as Creation*, Kampen: Kok Pharos, 1991, 141.
[93] Osborn, *Guardians*, 147.
[94] R. Clobus, *Environmental Care: A Possible Way to Restore God's Image to the Earth*, Eldoret, Kenya: AMECA Gaba, 1992, 45.
[95] R. Bohren, *Dass Gott schön werde: Praktische Theologie als theologische Ästhetik*, München: Kaiser Verlag, 1975, 90-95.

practical theological ecclesiology of land implies a totally different mode of being – a totally new state of being and transformed mind-set.

The dynamics of land, i.e. the boundary-situation between promise (inheritance) and stewardship (possession as sharing) guided by the undergirding principle of hospitality (ethos) presupposes a very specific anthropology. In terms of the fulfilment of the messianic dream and within the dynamic, theological connection between land and eschatology, a very specific mode of being surfaces in the New Testament. According to Matthew 5:5, as part of the beatitudes, meekness or humility could be viewed as a very specific disposition (aesthetic skill) which is needed in order to care for the land and the earth. "Blessed are the meek, for they will inherit the earth." In the light of Matthew 5:5 it should therefore be argued that in order to dream the land in hope, meekness and humility represents a sort of aesthetics of the soul which can beautify the earth and put stewardship into practice (the ethical principle).

The word for humility or meekness, *praÿs*, originally refers to love in terms of being considerate and gentle. The etymology implies mild friendliness and the creation of friendship. It presupposes (together with *epieikēs*), a thoughtful attitude in legal relationship which was prepared to mitigate the rigours of justice in contrast to the attitude which demands that rights, including one's own, which should be upheld at all costs. *Praÿs* therefore represents the wise person who remains meek in the face of insults. It is opposed to unbridled anger, harshness, brutality and self-expression.[96]

What is of special significance for a theology of land is the fact that *praÿs* in the LXX is the translation of the *'anî* – the poor, afflicted, humble and suppressed. The *'ānāw* in the Old Testament were the poor in Israel without landed property.[97] They were wrongfully restricted, disinherited and deprived of the fullness which God willed. Hence they were often the victims of unscrupulous exploitation (Isa 32:7; Ps 37:14; Job 24:4). In a general sense *'anî* denotes the defenceless, those without rights, the oppressed, those who are cheated, exploited and cursed (cf. Pss 9 and 10).

The Old Testament makes a direct connection between God and the *'anî* (Exod 22:21-24; Deut 24:14f). Yahweh takes the part of the *'anî*. Since Yahweh is the God of those without rights (Pss 25:9, 149:4; 34:2), he hears and comforts those who find no mercy among their fellow men (Isa 29:19; Job 36:15).[98] There exists an interchange between the *'ānāw* who are materially poor and the spiritually poor, i.e. those who in deep need and

[96] See W. Bauder, "Humility, Meekness *(praÿs)*", in C. Brown (ed.), *Dictionary of New Testament Theology, Vol. 2*, Exeter: Paternoster Press, 1976, 256-259.
[97] Ibid., 257.
[98] Ibid.

difficulty humbly seek help from Yahweh alone (Ps 40:17, 18; 102:1; Isa 41:17).

In Zech 9:9 the *'anî* is a title of honour given to the messiah. As the messiah rides the animal used by the socially insignificant, his way leads to the poor and those deprived of their rights. This messianic undertone underlines the fact that the reference to *praÿtēs* as a mark of Christ's rule, cannot be interpreted without keeping the Old Testament in mind. In 2 Corinthians 10:1 Paul mentions *praÿtes* and *epieikeia* as characteristics of Jesus' attitude to human beings in his pastoral ministry, and holds such a disposition out as an example to the church. In Mathew 5:5 meekness and humbleness cannot be separated from the poor. The poor will inherit the new promised land. Land becomes a metaphor for both the material side of the blessing as well as the spiritual dimension of virtue and attitude. "Just as obedience and righteousness are, for the Deutoronomist, the conditions of entrance into the promised land, so humble obedience to the teaching contained in the Beatitudes is the condition of entering the new land of God's kingdom."[99] "Meekness leads to turf. Not powerful grasping but trusting receiving."[100] When the New Testament advocates for *praÿtēs*, it connects attitude with wisdom and the new condition of the Christian. It is linked to the work of the Holy Spirit (Gal 5:23; see also Jas 3:17) and an indication of a spiritual disposition which should bring about justice, peace and healing.

Conclusion

1) *Praÿtēs* / *praÿs* connects the spirituality of land and environment to the reality of a very specific disposition, i.e. the disposition of hospitality and friendship as expressed in humility. This kind of humility presupposes the sacrifice of exchange. The disposition of humility implies identification with the desperate situation and position of the poor – the people deprived from land, rights and possession. This practice of sensitivity and identification is the first step in the direction towards a meaningful beautification of creation (land).

2) A practical theological ecclesiology of land and environment refers to the practice of *habitus* or wisdom in which the divine and messianic focal point sets requirements of obedience and hospitable sharing. "Theologia practica is simply the *habitus* viewed as to its end";[101] it enhances the quality of life.

---

[99] Ibid., 258.

[100] Brueggemann, *Land*, 176.

[101] Fairley, "Theology and Practice", 27.

3) The *habitus* of *praÿs* should be understood from the perspective of an eschatological hermeneutics. The implication is that stewardship, the greening of the church and the caring for, and healing of land (*cura terrae*), is a pneumatological concern. It implies "panentheism" as an awareness of the indwelling presence of God within creation, the earth. Land becomes a metaphor for God's eschatological acts for healing, peace and renewal. An eschatological hermeneutics, accompanied by the *habitus* of *praÿs* should become concrete and visible in acts of reconstruction, i.e. redistribution and restitution[102] of land in order to address the problem of poverty. Poverty then as the result of economic violence, the abuse of power, materialistic and ecological exploitation and the threat of egoistic coveting.

4) The hope generated by a spirituality of land and environment operates between the promises of God for a better, qualitative life (*promissio* as linked to acts of trusting and aesthetical beautification) and the ethical issue of justice (*promissio* as linked to acts of sharing and redistributing wealth).

5) A spirituality of land and environment that creates a vivid hope for the greening of life is not a pie in the sky. Hope presupposes the dynamics of imaginative anticipation and expectation. It portrays a better future due to the creativity and imagination of an aesthetics of hospitality: creating a home and a sense of belongingness for the homeless and the poor.

6) Land distribution and the transformation of agricultural structures and laws, for example in South Africa, should address three things: (a) the egoistic attitude of landowners (possessiveness); (b) land as place and its interconnectedness to sustainable development and livelihood (poverty); (c) the materialistic ethics of a global and market-driven economy (exploitation).

7) A practical theological ecclesiology should (a) promote a *habitus* of sharing and hospitality; (b) foster an eco-spirituality within the demands of a holistic and systemic understanding of healing. *Cura animarum* should therefore be supplemented by *cura terrae*; (c) A practical theological ecclesiology should develop a mentality of *praÿs* which implies the exchange of position – to sympathise with the poor. This exchange further implies the sacrifice of shifting one's position from the perspective of the privileged to the perspective of the oppressed. (A practical theology from

[102] Poverty alleviation and land restitution cannot be separated from one another. The important questions here are: do we see land rights as being primarily a *conceptual* matter and ask *what* they are, a *possessionary* matter and ask *whose* they are, or a *relational* matter and ask *who* they are? See D.S. Gillan, "Who are Land Rights? The Crisis of Interpretation in Land Restitution", in D.S. Gillan (ed.), *Church, Land and Poverty*, Braamfontein/Johannesburg: Progress Press, 1998, 105-136; see p. 108.

below). This position presupposes an attitude of hospitality (sharing) and the act of admonition: voicing the voiceless and confronting the powerful.

With a practical theology of below[103] is meant that land becomes a relational issue. It is referring to people and community. What is then becoming important are issues of sharing, sustainability and life. The implication is to move beyond the capitalist market approach which regulates itself on the basis of private property and contracts to a "common good approach".[104] Production of goods is then supplemented by personal development, entrepreneurial ownership, economic safeguarding of employees and the principle of participatory (codecision) rights. It implies: "macroeconomic planning from the perspective of life and common good…" [105]

The hope offered in a practical theological ecclesiology of *cura terrae* implies the aesthetics of creative hospitality, as well as the ethics of sharing as an emanation of the dynamics within the eschatological bipolarity of promise (trust) and sharing (gift). Within this eschatological paradigm, *praÿs* (humility) has the meaning of a total identification with the vulnerability of the poor, the homeless, the exploited and oppressed people. The *habitus* of *praÿs* is a practical theological and ecclesiological critique on the power structures of *dominium terrae*.[106]

---

[103] "Below" implies a "bottom-up" approach. "Only if people take economic, political and cultural action at the local and small-scale regional levels can the property system and the industry based on it ultimately be reorganized in the interest of all people and of life as a whole." U. Duchrow and F.J. Hinkelammert, *Property for People, not for Profit: Alternatives to the Global Tyranny of Capital*, London/NewYork: Zed Books, 2004, 200.

[104] See Binswanger in Duchrow and Hinkelammert, *Property for People*, 179.

[105] Ibid., 181.

[106] In the Roman empire there was a distinction between possession (*possesio*) and property (*dominium* or *proprietas*). Possession refers to the actual having of a thing. Property, by contrast, designates a comprehensive right to a thing. Property as *dominium* refers to ownership as the right to use and abuse/consume/destroy. See Duchrow and Hinkelammert, *Property for People*, 12. *Dominium* therefore refers to the absoluteness of property. The latter is directly related to the issue of poverty (ibid., 5-28).

Part B

Interculturality and Concrete Settings:

Voices from Different Contexts

Pastoral Counselling in Asian Contexts *

Robert Solomon
Singapore, 1995

Asian context or Asian contexts?

Asia is a large continent stretching from Afghanistan (if one excludes the Middle East) to the far reaches of the Siberian region in eastern Russia. There are at least 26 countries in this region. If the Middle-east is included, the number increases to some 45 countries. More than 60% of the world's population live in Asia. The continent expresses a rich diversity of cultures, languages, lands, religions, lifestyles, and economies. In this sense, I cannot adequately represent Asia. What I present cannot fully capture the diversity and vastness of the Asian contexts. Nevertheless, I am an Asian, living and working in Asia, and therefore my paper, though limited by my particular context, will attempt to discuss some aspects of my own as well as other Asian contexts to the best of my knowledge and experience.

My own context

I live in Singapore which is one of the smallest nations in Asia. It is an Island state measuring some 25 miles in length and 15 miles across, with a population of 2.7 million people. The island is part of the Southeast Asian region, comprising countries such as Malaysia, Indonesia, the Philippines, Brunei, Thailand, Cambodia, Laos, Myanmar, and Vietnam. This part of the world is a rapidly growing region economically though there are also many serious problems.

Singapore is a multi-ethnic, multi-cultural, and multi-religious nation. It has four official languages and has Chinese, Malay and Indian, and Eurasian communities in addition to other minority groups. It is thus an interesting

---

* Paper presented at the 9th International Seminar on Intercultural Pastoral Care and Counselling, 1995, in Mülheim/Ruhr, Germany, published in *Intercultural Pastoral Care and Counselling, 1*, 1996, 22-25.

"melting pot" of different cultures and peoples. In that sense, I am exposed to some aspects of the rich diversity in Asia.

I teach in a theological college as well as serving as an associate pastor in a Tamil Methodist church which has both English and Tamil services. My teaching ministry extends to several churches and Christian organisations in Singapore and to some in the region. I also have opportunities to do pastoral counselling with church members, seminary students, pastors, and others referred to me.

In this paper, I will raise some issues which I have found to be important. They represent my own experience and reflection.

Culture and religion

When Asia is mentioned, culture is one major consideration that immediately comes to mind. I use the phrase "culture and religion" because in the Asian contexts, culture and religion are generally closely related. The ancient religions of Asia have shaped Asian cultures for centuries. The pastoral care-giver and the pastoral counsellor (who generally is trained with Western models and methods since the modern pastoral counselling movement has largely developed in the West) thus have to be particularly aware of cultural realities and issues when working in the Asian contexts.

Culture has to do with beliefs, values, customs, and institutions.[1] While we recognize certain aspects of culture which seem universal, there are also particularities regarding the above dimensions in any given culture which affect the way pastoral counselling is conceived and practised.

Beliefs have to do with how reality is perceived. They help to shape worldviews which are hermeneutic sieves through which experiences are interpreted and assessed. If in a culture there is a strong belief in spirits, then that becomes an important part of the world view which therefore has to be taken into consideration by the pastoral counsellor.

Values have to do with what we value. Cultures may have different values though there may also be similarities across cultures. Our values affect the way we pursue certain things or goals, and determine how we react when we are unable to fulfil our goals or when we lose what we value. Pastoral counselling cannot be done effectively without due recognition of cultural values.

Customs have to do with how we do things. Cultures develop ways of doing things both at individual as well as communal levels. In a sense, customs determine what is normal or abnormal. What is customary is

[1] See Lausanne Committee for World Evanglization (ed.), *The Willowbank Report: Report of a Consultation on Gospel and Culture (Lausanne Occasional Paper, No. 2)*, Wheaton, IL, 1978, 7.

normal. But what is customary in the West may not be so in the East. How then do we determine whether a particular act or experience is healthy or not? What norms do we use? These are questions with which a pastoral care giver struggles in the Asian contexts, as many of the texts on pastoral counselling come from the West and may need to be re-interpreted and modified in the light of Asian cultures.

Institutions represent how a particular culture has organized itself. Cultures may vary in terms of the presence or absence, strength and weakness, relative importance and other aspects of institutions. Examples of institutions are family, courts, churches, schools, village councils etc.

Let's take a look at culture and pastoral counselling by considering some issues which I have found to be relevant in the region I come from.

The supernatural

In Indonesia, "belief in God" is the first of five national values (*pancasila*). Several Asian countries have state religions, especially Islam. Religion is thus important in the Asian contexts. Sociologists such as John Clammer have noted that in Singapore and other Asian countries, with modernisation one has not seen a parallel secularisation process as has been seen in Western countries.[2] In fact, with modernisation has come a resurgence of Asian religions. In Singapore, for example, the fastest growing religion is Buddhism.[3]

What is of particular importance in the Asian contexts in terms of counselling is what Paul Hiebert has called the "excluded middle zone".[4] This "middle zone" represents beliefs in the existence of spirits, demons, ghosts, and how they influence or affect us. It exists between beliefs concerning heaven and our experience of empirical earthly life. In many Asian contexts, including the developed countries such as Japan, the "middle zone" is alive and important.[5]

In my own experience, I repeatedly encounter counsellees who believe in spirits and demons, and wonder whether their problems are caused by these entities. This motivated me to write my doctoral dissertation on pastoral responses to demon possession in Singapore.[6] How should I respond as a

---

[2] John Clammer, *Sociology of Singapore Religion,* Singapore: Chopmen Publishers, 1991, chapters 5 and 6.

[3] Eddie C. Y. Kuo and Tong Chee Kiong, *Religion in Singapore,* Singapore: Ministry of Community Development, 1995.

[4] Paul Hiebert, "The Flaw of the Excluded Middle", in *Missiology: An International Review, 10:1,* 1982, 35-47.

[5] See e.g. Winston Davis, *Dojo: Magic and Exorcism in Modern Japan*, Stanford: Stanford University Press, 1980.

[6] Robert Solomon, *Living in Two Worlds: Pastoral Responses to Possession in Singapore*, Frankfurt am Main: Peter Lang, 1994.

pastoral care giver? I should not dismiss the "middle zone" lest I create, in my case, a "split level Christianity" with people seeking help from pastors as well as from *bomohs* (shaman healers).[7] On the other hand, I have the benefit of being exposed to a multiplicity of perspectives and I can reframe problems for people. Reality and truth become important issues in counselling.

Family and filial piety

The family remains a resilient institution in Asia though in many places it is experiencing serious challenges arising from the modernisation, urbanisation, and economisation of life. The family unit (whether extended or nuclear) is an important consideration for pastoral counsellors in Asia. On one hand, the family is an important aspect of well-being and pathology of people. On the other hand, the Asian family is generally wary of seeking professional counselling which uses models of family therapy developed in the West. Family counselling has been traditionally done by the larger extended family though in many urban places in Asia, the extended family is threatened. In these places, the church, for example, can be the new extended family and pastoral care can be done using more traditional paradigms.

One related issue is filial piety, especially in Chinese cultures. It is an important virtue and is expressed in various forms of ancestor worship (or ancestor veneration, as some would say). In my own ecclesial context, this has remained a big issue. Should Christians continue the practice of ancestor worship? Is this a cultural custom or is it a religious rite?[8] From a more psychological perspective, is filial piety a way of retaining the power structures of traditional society? Parents, especially the father, are to be honoured. What has filial piety got to do with the common experience of the "distant father" and sometimes the abusive father?

Recently, there was a seminar in Singapore in which some retired people shared from their experiences under Japanese occupation during the Second World War. One historian, a friend of mine, suggested that one of the reasons why the Japanese seem to be having great difficulty in apologising for the atrocities during the war was possibly filial piety.

Besides the above issues, the family in Asia is going through rapid changes, much faster than those in the West. Ten major changes in the Asian family have been noted in a well-known work on the family in Asia. These include egalitarian family relations, greater individualism and

---

[7] See Rodney Henry, *Filipino Split World: A Challenge to the Church*, Manila: OMF, 1986.

[8] See Bong Rin Ro (ed.), *Christian Alternatives to Ancestral Practices*, Taiwan: Asia Theological Association, 1985.

independence, marital disruption, urbanisation, and so on.[9] Pastoral counselling has to note these stresses and challenges to family life. In Singapore, the government as well as major institutions are taking an active role in developing family values and life.

Shame

David Augsburger has noted that Asian cultures are shame oriented cultures.[10] While that may be too much of a generalisation, I think it is still true to say that shame plays an important role in Asian cultures. Shame has tended to be seen in a negative way, and often as inferior to guilt. I like to see shame in a more positive light. Healthy shame is discretionary shame. It does allow for the well being of individuals and societies through the process of shared goals and values.

At the same time, however, shame can also cripple someone by preventing him or her to move on in life. A deep sense of shame can be motivation enough for a suicide attempt. This is especially the case in Japanese society. The pastoral counsellor must approach facts with a sensitivity to the counsellees' shame. "Losing face" is a disaster in Asian cultures. In counselling I have found the need to be sensitive to the importance of "keeping face" and "losing face" while helping people to find solutions to their problems. In the process I am also aware of my own "face" and have found avenues of personal growth through the experience of cultural relevance as well as countercultural stances. I am also exploring my possibilities as a pastoral caregiver in a region which has many cultural practices involving masks and shadow-play, through the concepts of a "demonology of masks" and a "theology of the face"[11].

Smooth interpersonal relationships (SIR)

When I was studying in the Philippines, I was introduced to the concept of SIR which is a key value in Filipino culture. Facts and justice are secondary to the primary value of interpersonal harmony. In Chinese culture, too, social harmony, group consensus rather than confrontation are highly appreciated values. One of the national values in Singapore is decision making through consensus rather than contention or confrontational

---

[9] Man Singh Das and Panos D. Bardis (eds.), *The Family in Asia*, Boston/Sydney/London: George Allen & Unwin, 1978, 419.

[10] David Augsburger, *Pastoral Counseling Across Cultures*, Philadelphia: Westminster Press, 1986, chapter 4.

[11] See Christopher Nugent, *Masks of Satan: The Demonic in History*, London: Sheed and Ward, 1983, 2, where these phrases are found.

means.[12] Pastoral counselling in conflict situations will have to bear this cultural ethos in mind.

An Asian psychology / Asian psychologies

William Wundt, the father of modern psychology, saw psychology based on two traditions: the natural sciences and the social sciences traditions. From the latter arose cultural psychology or indigenous psychology (*Völkerpsychologie*), which Wundt predicted would be the more important kind of psychology in the future.[13] In the Asian contexts, attempts have been made to develop such indigenous psychologies such as in India[14] and other countries.

This is an important process since it addresses important questions. For example, in Filipino culture, the concepts of *hiya* (shame), *pakikisama* (yielding to the leader or the majority), and *utang na loob* (gratitude) are all based on the core cultural value of *kapwa* (shared identity with others)[15]. A mature Filipino person is one who shares his or her identity with others. The most mature person is one who belongs, not one who is independent. Many Western psychologies are based on views of maturity linked with growing independence. The implication is that what is seen as healthy behaviour in one culture (say, in California) may be seen as unhealthy in another (say, China).

The global village

The discussion on cultural particularities must also be balanced with the trend of universal cultural patterns created by the media and technology. Many parts of Asia are open to modernity and the mass media originating in the West. The result is what Japanese writer Kenichi Ohmae terms the "californianisation of taste" with the phenomenon of common cultural icons in many different contexts: Nike shoes, Levi's Jeans, Windows 95, Mr. Bean, Michael Jackson, coke etc.[16] In fact, it may be true that teenagers across cultures may be more similar to each other as to their own elders. In this sense, I feel that what is written in one culture may increasingly have currency value and relevance in many other cultures.

---

[12] Jon S. T. Quah (ed.), *In Search of Singapore's National Values*, Singapore: The Institute of Policy Studies, Times Academic Press, 1990, chapter 7.

[13] See Uichol Kim and John W. Berry (eds.), *Indigenous Psychologies: Research and Experience in Cultural Context*, Newbury Park, London, New Delhi: SAGE, 1993.

[14] See e.g. D. Sinha, *Psychology in a Third World Country: The Indian Experience*, New Delhi: SAGE, 1986.

[15] As noted by Virgilio G. Enriquez, "Developing a Filipino Psychology", in Kim and Berry (eds.), *Indigenous Psychologies*.

[16] Kenichi Ohmae, *The End of the Nation State: The Rise of Regional Economies*, New York: Free Press, 1995, 28ff.

I live in the midst of these phenomena where there is a resurgence of traditional cultures but also a growing similarity of popular cultures with other cultures, largely because of new subcultures being promoted by the mass media as well as being created by new technologies e.g. the Internet, karaoke etc. We all seem to be riding the same waves of information these days.

The social-economic context

Discussions on Asia inevitably also deal with the social contexts. Here again, there is a wide variety. Life span in Japan is 81 years, while it is only 50 years in Bangladesh. In Japan, the infant mortality rate is 5 per thousand live births while it is 118 per thousand live births in Bangladesh. The GDP in Singapore is twenty times that in Pakistan.[17]

Economic tigers and dragons

I live in a region where economies are growing rapidly. There is a growing economisation of life. The economy has become the major paradigm of life in several Asian nations. How does this affect people? One obvious sign is the increasing stresses of life due to the rapid changes and pace of life. People work longer hours, are fatigued and stressed out, and have little time for relationships and for family life. Social pathologies are on the rise in many Asian countries. Family breakdown, drug addiction, suicide, violence and prostitution are some of such signs.

Another question is how the social environment defines and shapes the self. In these economically vibrant societies, the self is increasingly seen as efficient worker and increasingly wealthy consumer. Christopher Lasch has written about the "minimal self" as the product of a marketplace paradigm.[18] He is right, and I believe that as a pastoral counsellor, I am faced with evaluating such definitions of self in the light of what I understand to be human dignity and personhood through theological anthropology. The marketplace may be forcing people to be functioning as efficient but hollow selves. The challenge for pastoral caregiving is obvious.

Poverty and injustice

Many sections of Asian society are also marked with poverty and injustice, whether it is a village in Bihar or a kampong in Kalimantan. In our college,

---

[17] These figures are obtained from *The Economist Book of Vital World Statistics*, London: Hutchinson, 1990.

[18] Christopher Lasch, *The Minimal Self: Psychic Survival in Troubled Times*, New York: W. W. Norton, 1985.

we have some students from Nagaland, a politically restricted area in India. Last year, two of these students had to return home because of the death of loved ones through malaria and dysentery epidemics.[19] The health care system is poorly managed. Through corruption, supplies are diverted into the black market and the money is pocketed. How does the pastoral counsellor function in such situations? Where corruption is strife, how does one guide? What advice can be given? In a "corrupto-metre" study,[20] six of the ten most corrupt nations are Asian.

How can pastoral care be given to people suffering from poverty? Are Western models of pastoral counselling sufficient? Pastoral care in such situations has to take a more communal approach, since the problem is usually systemic in nature, and a social relief, social action, or development kind of approach.

Pastoral care as prophetic

Whether in a rapidly developing economy or a poor nation, the pastoral counsellor may often have to challenge the social assumptions or inertia. The role of the pastoral counsellor may be to go beyond helping the person to merely cope with the situation. If that is all the pastoral caregiver does, he or she is no more than a servant of the unhealthy or unjust system. The caregiver may have to challenge the social system itself which produces such social pathologies and dehumanises people either through consumerism or poverty.

Doing pastoral care and counselling in Asia

Before I conclude, I wish to mention two other issues briefly.

Models and training

Working in Asia I search for relevant home-grown models of counselling and care giving. There are some interesting models. One example is the "quiet therapy" model in Japan. Morita psychotherapy is a case in point.[21] It uses Japanese ideas and methods together with Western concepts to develop an indigenous model of therapy. The therapy involves putting a person in a simple room to be alone without the usual sensory stimuli and

---

[19] See Robert Solomon, "Epidemics in Nagaland", in *Newsletter of the International Pastoral Care Network for Social Responsibility*, Spring-Summer 1995, 16-17.
[20] Reported in *The Straits Times*, Singapore, 26 August 1995.
[21] See David K. Reynolds, *The Quiet Therapies: Japanese Pathways to Personal Growth*, Honolulu: The University Press of Hawaii, 1980, especially chapter 2.

activities. The patient discovers his or her own addictions, and also gratitude to significant people.

The interesting thing I have discovered is the close relationship between psychology and spirituality in traditional Asian societies. In the light of modern Western exploration of the interface between spirituality and psychology, it must be noted that this has been going on for centuries in the Asian contexts. The "quiet therapies" are a modern version of this process.

Any model must take into consideration the way how problems, the helper, and the helping process are perceived. In Asian contexts, these are shaped by culture and social factors as discussed above. Many problems are given a supernatural angle. The helper is seen as wise rather than as an expert. The helping process is strongly directive in many places. These facts must be remembered in developing culturally relevant models of pastoral counselling.

One interesting phenomenon in the West is the growing popularity of alternative medicine and a growing disenchantment with Western medicine. In the Singapore scene, Western modern medicine co-exists with traditional Chinese medicine. Would there be a growing popularity of traditional ways of caring and helping at the expense of modern professional counselling (cf. with Western modern medicine)?[22]

Networks

Modern pastoral counselling came to Asia when Carl Rogers visited Japan in 1952. The first pastoral counselling course was conducted at the Union Theological Seminary in Tokyo. Paul Johnson visited Japan in 1964 and started the CPE movement in Asia. In 1966, one of the pioneer counselling centres, the Churches Counselling Centre was started in Singapore. In 1981, the journal Bokkai Shinri (Pastoral Psychology) was launched.

Since then, the Asian Congress on Pastoral Care and Counselling was organized in Manila (1982), Tokyo (1984), New Delhi (1986), Manila (1989), and Bali (1993).[23] The sixth Congress will be held in Seoul in 1997. Recently a Christian Counselling Conference in Asia was held in Singapore with more than 800 people attending. Representatives from several Asian countries were present.

---

[22] See e.g. Sudhir Kakar, *Shamans, Mystics and Doctors: A Psychological Inquiry into India and its Healing Traditions*, Delhi: Oxford University Press, 1982, for an interesting account of how various traditional healing traditions co-exist with modern medical and psychological healing establishments.

[23] The above facts are described and more information can be found in Robert Solomon, "Pastoral Care and Counselling", in *A Dictionary of Asian Christianity*, ed. Scott W. Sunquist, Grand Rapids: Eerdmans, 2001.

There is a need for more work to be done in thinking about pastoral counselling in the Asian contexts. I would like to see more Asian contributions in terms of theory-building, writing, training, and leadership.

Conclusion

I have recorded impressions and thoughts on some issues which I think are important, based on my own reflection and experience. I live in an exciting region though it also has many dangers and difficulties. As a pastoral care giver, I am reminded daily to live and minister as a wise-fool, wounded healer, servant-guru, and powerless miracle worker in a rapidly changing context where good and evil, order and chaos, and life and death exist side by side.

Death and the Maiden:

The Complexity of Trauma and Ways of Healing – A Challenge for Pastoral Care and Counseling [*]

Ursula Riedel-Pfäfflin / Archie Smith, Jr.
Germany / USA, 1995

"Who are my mother and my brother?
Whoever does the will of God is my brother, and sister, and mother"
(Mark 3:33,35)

Introduction

The field of pastoral care and counseling is undergoing a shift in emphasis. It is moving from a focus on the private lives of individuals and the ego to a focus on the social, political and the ecological systems that determine individual and corporate life.[1] The shift from the person to broader challenges brings up the question of how does the teacher of pastoral care prepare the student to address complex issues without loosing sight of the individual, or self? What resources do teachers of pastoral care use to help illuminate the interplay between the personal, social-political, economic and ecological contexts? Feminist and liberation theologians have emphasized in their work that the personal is embedded in political contexts, hence, the political is personal and the personal is political. The question of the case study becomes important because the case study helps to determine what is to be explored, what are the relevant questions, and how we think about pastoral care issues. In this article we select, as our case study, the drama *Death and the Maiden*.[2] We reflect upon the interpersonal issues

---

[*] Lecture presented at the at the 9th International Seminar on Intercultural Pastoral Care and Counselling, 1995, in Mülheim/Ruhr, Germany, published in *Intercultural Pastoral Care and Counselling, 1*, 1996, 13-17.

[1] A few book titles signal this emphasis: Larry Kent Graham, *Care of Persons, Care of Worlds: A Psychosystems Approach to Pastoral Care and Counseling*, Nashville: Abingdon Press, 1992; George Furniss, *The Social Context of Pastoral Care: Defining the Life Situation*, Louisville, KY: Westminster John Knox Press, 1994.

[2] Ariel Dorfmann, *Death and the Maiden*, New York: Penguin Books, 1991. Citations from page 59.

of trauma and healing within a political context. From this focus we derive implications for teaching systemic thinking in pastoral care. Systemic thinking is a way of looking at the contexts in which behavior occurs and tracking the reciprocal connections between individuals as well as noting the changes that occur within individuals. We believe that the drama, *Death and The Maiden*, provides an opportunity to demonstrate systemic thinking in pastoral care by focusing on systemic violence. It also provides a challenge to pastoral care especially where it (pastoral care) has been defined primarily in individual terms and as a professional relationship between a help seeker and a help giver. We pursue the question of how to create relationships of safety, holding, trust and connections while acknowledging and finding value in differences.

In order to address this question we look at *Death and the Maiden*, a drama written by the Chilean author, Ariel Dorfmann. The context is the unstable political situation in Chile after fall of the dictatorship of General Augusto Pinochet. There are three characters in the play, Paulina Salas, her husband Gerardo Escobar, and Dr. Roberto Miranda. The drama unfolds in the main room of Paulina and Gerardo's home. There the history of violence which permeates every aspect of Chilean society now determines the interaction between the three characters and meaning in their personal lives. The drama shows how long standing patterns of injustice and violation create long-term trauma and irreparable hurt which can become an integral part of everyday life.

The story

Paulina Salas, around forty years old, had worked with her husband, Gerardo Escobar, around forty-five years old, for political change. One evening she is informed by TV that he was announced head of a committee commissioned to investigate the events of torture during the dictatorship of General Augusto Pinochet. Contingency wills it that he is hindered to return home by a thundershower and then finds help by a doctor who accompanies him back home. His way of talking, quoting Nietzsche, and his manner of behaving makes Paulina suspicious. Then she remembers the trauma situation. In her home is the man, Dr. Roberto Miranda, around fifty years old, whom she believes is the one who betrayed and violated her in the worst possible way. She was abducted and tortured because the Pinochet regime wanted the name of her husband. She was made naked, violated and tortured with electroshocks. After the torture, Dr. Roberto Miranda came to attend to her. He promised to help. Instead, he raped her repeatedly, using her as an object of his own will. She was humiliated and hurt even more than by the electroshocks. Dr. Roberto Miranda played the famous string quartet by Schubert, one of her favorite pieces of music: Death and the Maiden.

Paulina did not confess. When she returned to her husband, she found him in bed with another woman. She is now faced with her torturer and the husband who betrayed her, all in one room. She is absolutely clear and decided on what she needs in order to begin healing. To be healed is her sense of self-respect, self-agency, and spiritual wholeness. She needed a confession about the truth of what had happened. She needed an acknowledgement of her perception and her suffering by those who inflicted it on her. This is exactly what both men in the drama are not willing to give. By using all her wits, strengths, determination, and a gun, she attempts to get what is crucial to restore her inner and outer sense of identity. The confession she receives from Dr. Miranda contains some of the following statements:

"I raped you many times. Fourteen times. I played music. I wanted to soothe you. I was good at first. I fought it hard. No one was so good at fighting as I. I was the last one to have a taste.

No one died. I made it easier on them. That's how it started. They needed a doctor. My brother was in the Secret Service. He told me: Make sure nobody dies. You saw it yourself. You told me you are dirty and I washed you clean. The others said: You are going to refuse fresh meat, are you? And I was starting to like it. They laid people out on the table. They flashed on the light. People lying totally helpless, and I didn't have to be nice and I didn't have to seduce them. I didn't even have to take care of them. I had all the power. I could make them do or say whatever I wanted. I was lost in morbid curiosity. How much can this woman take? More than the other one? Howls her sex? Does her sex dry up when you put the current through her? Can she have an orgasm under those circumstances? O God, I liked being naked. I liked to let my pants down. I liked you knowing what I was going to do. There was bright light. You could not see me. I owned you I owned all of you. I could hurt you and I could fuck you and you could not tell me not to. I loved it. I was sorry that it ended. Very sorry that it ended."

Paulina was the maiden who died. True, she survived physically. But her soul, mind, hopes, trust, and the meaning of her life were killed. Even so, she was not broken by the torture. What Pauline needed was the truth from Dr. Miranda, her suspected torturer.

Significance of the story

The drama leaves open the question of whether or not Dr. Miranda's confession is real or contrived. Death and the Maiden is about systemic violence and its consequences for everyday life. It deals with the long-term effects of torture and violence on human beings. The drama is mythical and historical in that the themes it deals with are timeless and actual. The fact that violence surrounds us, trauma is complex and the need for healing is everywhere makes this drama systemic, mythical and immediately relevant.

We remember that Paulina sacrificed herself in order to protect her husband, and that her husband, Geraldo betrayed her. How can healing occur in the relationship between Paulina and Geraldo – that is to say, how can trust be restored? The way Gerardo Escobar can become the real partner of Paulina Salas is to bond with and trust her as she pursues her suspicion about her torturer. Trust becomes a first step to hearing her. He must hold, help and protect her as she did him during the time of her interrogation. He must not be afraid to hear and face the truth of her story which is also a part of his own. Once, Paulina experiences his courage to chose her side and acknowledge her pain, she can let go of her murderous rage. Both Paulina and Gerardo can begin a new phase of grieving and of working through their pain. The same possibility exists for Dr. Roberto Miranda, to the degree that he can confess his complicity in the collective and personal violence, acknowledge his responsibility, repent, and make restoration.

Death and the Maiden is a symbolic story. It is one of the key narratives of the present situation in many countries of the world. In October of 1994, we participated in the leadership of an International conference for pastoral counselors, held for the first time in the capital of the Czech Republic, Prague.[3] The theme of the conference, Changing Values, indicated the struggles which post-conflict societies are facing, especially the post socialist countries of Eastern Europe.

We listened to the report of two participants from Papua New Guinea, Biul Kirokim and his interpreter, George Euling. Their village was recently 'discovered' by international mining companies. Their natural resources of trees and land were razed. Their air and water ways polluted, their customs and traditional way of life irreparably destroyed. New diseases and forms of illness occurred for which they had no remedy. They had to learn to rely on Western medicines, which they could not afford. People became depressed, developed psychological illnesses that were unknown. Their culture was humiliated. An entire people were violated, their land raped, their food source poisoned. Theirs is a trauma of unknown magnitude, and they search for ways to heal. What needs to be confronted? Who must do the work? Who needs to tell this story? Who needs to hear it? How can relationships of safety, holding, trust and connections be made in order for victims and perpetrators to be healed? And, how do we enable our students

[3] 8th Intercultural Seminar on Pastoral Care and Counselling, 18-23 September 1994, Prague, Czech Republic.

to make these connections in ways that empower them to be effective pastoral care givers and learners in situations such as these?

One of the presenters, Dr. Jan Urban, a former Czech dissident offered an answer to these questions. A culture of humiliation and shaming develops where there is personal and systemic violation of the dignity of persons and the effects of trauma are widespread. A culture of humiliation and shaming develops when people are not given space to openly process their experience of trauma after the acute stages of conflict have passed. A culture of humiliation and shaming develops further when public policy promotes amnesia rather than remembering. Public and private amnesia can be as dangerous as the traumatization itself. Jan Urban mentioned *Death and the Maiden* as one of the most important plays which addresses severe trauma and processes of recovery. This drama was not admitted to be staged in The Czech Theatre even though its content deals exactly with the experiences that thousands of people have had in the past forty years during and after the war. In this way, public policy promotes amnesia when people are not allowed to publicly acknowledge the violence done to them and find appropriate ways to transform their lives. If people do not want to hear or be reminded, then how can they be prepared for the consequences?

Ways of working with the story in pastoral care education

The challenge for pastoral care here is in the whole movement of hearing the painful story of victims, and moving perpetrators through the processes of recognition, confession, repentance and restoration. The events of the drama could happen anywhere. They occur everywhere. But efforts to acknowledge such events may be resisted. Herein lies a partial challenge for pastoral care and counseling, namely to make known the subtle connections between personal suffering and public events, especially when people do not want to hear or know. Pastoral counselors may be in an uncommon position to do systemic thinking and reveal the connections between public events, psychic trauma, interpersonal relations and spiritual direction.

From these ideas we draw the following implications for teaching systemic thinking. The drama, Death and the Maiden will serve as guide.

First, the teacher or trainer may invite the students to read the drama and reflect upon its meaning for them.

Then teacher may lead the students in a discussion by asking, 'what is the problem?' Rather than to assume that the definition of the problem at hand is known or shared, it is important to ask 'what is the problem?' Just as there are different ways of seeing and knowing, there will be different understandings and conflicting definitions of the problem. The different ways of seeing and knowing may later provide alternative approaches to the problematic situation. Hence, it is important to ask what is the problem and uncover the different ways of seeing, and entering the problematic situation.

Next, the teacher can invite the students to do some background reading about the Chilean situation. Students are encouraged to identify new questions stimulated by the reading of historical documents and gain perspective on the political context and the authors point of view. Students can link these new questions with their previous questions about the definition of the problem.

Given what they now know, the students may work in small groups to develop a scenario of the situation which they will role play. Class members are invited to think about the definition of the situation implied in the particular scenario and how the definition of the situation determines the motives and interaction between the characters and possibilities for healing.

Role play this situation and think about it from the perspective of each of the individuals in it. After several role play situations are presented, the students are invited to think about the context as a whole. The overall purpose is to enable students to see multiple levels of interaction and meaning, and thereby identify alternative approaches and resources for healing. Some resources may already be available in the interaction system and wider society. Other resources need to be created in order to help transform painful situations.

During this process, another challenge for the teacher and trainer of pastoral care and counseling is to create space and time safe enough to address the pain, shame, anxiety, rage or denial connected to life stories of traumatization. There may be students or trainees who have been abused themselves and need protection for their own deep emotions, memories or present experiences. Also, the teacher and trainer need a place where they can take care of their own well being. Therefore, teaching and training which address violence and traumatization need special care given to the process in order to deal with the emotional involvement of all participants. The development of ritual elements may be helpful because ritualized beginnings and endings help to establish safe boundaries for the time and space need to process the emotions raised by the role play. Rituals can consist of small sentences like "I hear you, sister, or brother" by the whole group after a woman or man has shared her or his feelings. Rituals can include symbols like a bowl of water for cleansing and refreshing. A stone can be circled in order to contain pain or rage which then may be washed away by water. Rituals are most helpful when they are developed and agreed upon by the participants themselves. This is especially important in intercultural[4] settings where symbols have a different meaning for participants from diverse ethnic and spiritual traditions.

---

[4] By "intercultural" we mean a setting in which a member of one ethnic group facilitates a process or therapeutic intervention that empowers a member of another

Challenges for pastoral care and counseling

We draw further implications of this drama for systemic thinking and as challenge for pastoral care. Where justice has been long denied and the effects of traumas remain hidden, there will surface a need to deal openly with the trauma and right the wrongs. There will also be strenuous efforts on the part of perpetrators to deny wrong doings, and to disavow any knowledge of it. New identities may be created to cover up the violence.[5] Others may unwittingly become an accomplice in the cover-up. Death and the Maiden revealed how a dictatorship created complex public relationships, determined the quality of private lives, and effected an inner sense of self. These interwoven issues (complex external event, private lives, and inner sense of self), in various ways, are manifest through all three of the characters in the drama. Death and the Maiden is about a real life everyday situation, in that it deals with the long-term effects of betrayal torture and violence on human beings. This drama was written in a world marked by differences, unilateral use of power, changing gender roles, and increased violence. It forces the questions of how do we relate to those who have hurt us irreparably or whom we hurt? What knowledges need to be unmasked? What information needs to surface? Who is to do this work? Faced with such questions, and in such a context, can we create relationships of safety, holding, trust while such work is done? Can connections be made and sustained while acknowledging differences in ways of seeing and knowing?

Another important challenge was named by Jan Urban: the churches have access to social and political power by being able to speak up publicly. Traumatized persons, as the drama of Paulina's life demonstrates, need the naming of the atrocity that happened. One of the main problems for Paulina is that even in her own perception she is not certain if her identification of the perpetrator is right. Is Roberto Miranda the one who did the torturing? Not being reinforced in her perception by her husband and facing the denial of the perpetrator are among the most difficult experiences for her. Not being listened to and believed in telling the truth, is one of the worst experiences for girls or boys when they give signs to adults of being abused. For the speakers of the people in Papua New Guinea, one of the problems they face is the disavowal of the impact of Western econo-

---

ethnic group to make beneficial decisions. See Jafar Kareem and Roland Littlewood (eds.), *Intercultural Therapy: Themes, Interpretations and Practice*, Oxford: Blackwell Scientific Publications, 1992, 11.

[5] The North American Theologian James Poling has addressed the strong tendency of male perpetrators very well in his book *The Abuse of Power*, Nashville: Abingdon Press, 1991, in which he portrays two of his cases in his own work with victims and perpetrators of domestic violence. He also discusses the theological impact of the abuse of power in regard to the image of God and concepts of Christology.

my's destruction done to their ecological and social-spiritual system. Companies have produced films which are meant to demonstrate the environmental care of these Western companies based on scientific research whereas the knowledge of the inhabitants is neither heard nor acknowledged in the world's public.

To invite women and men as speakers and representatives of communities that continue to be exploited and traumatized is one step the intercultural pastoral counseling movement has provided. But even here questions such as, 'How did you learn English' and 'What kind of food do you eat' were addressed to Biul Kirokim of Papa New Guinea. Trainers and teachers of counselling from Europe demonstrated a profound lack of knowledge and interpathy because their questions failed to respond to his life threatening situation.[6] There was disappointment and anger about our own limitations amongst some participants of the conference. We became aware of how much we have yet to learn in order to develop models of intercultural counseling in which mutuality of learning and teaching are developed, hurt and anger can be worked through.

Pastoral counselors work between and within the realm of the personal and the political. We listen to personal and political stories like Paulina's when we work with refugees and victims of violence from all parts of the world, including the stranger from afar or the neighbor next door. It is a demanding challenge for a pastoral counselor to listen to stories of torture and respond appropriately to the counselee's or trainee's experiences of violation, dreams and flashbacks. We are challenged to help them to express their rage and ambivalence, and struggle with shame and isolation. Given this challenge, it is easy for the counsellor to feel overwhelmed by this complex reality, to feel helpless, discouraged, incompetent and burned out. We might identify strongly with the victim and condemn the perpetrator so that hopelessness or anger seem overwhelming. We might also recognize that there are many issues that we have not yet addressed adequately in our own lives. For example, our response to the amount of abuse of especially women and children, our own racism, our participation in the structural violence of exploitation of non-white societies by white western culture and economy may escape our awareness.

In the work with traumatized women, children and men it is important, not only to establish safety and reliable connections but also to make transparent the counselor's support of the victim. Counselors may show support of a traumatized victim and increase their understanding of the

---

[6] David Augsburger has defined a difference between sympathy, empathy and interpathy: "In interpathy, the process of knowing and 'feeling with' requires that one temporarily believe what the other believes, see as the other sees, value what the other values." See David W. Augsburger, *Pastoral Counseling Across Cultures*, Philadelphia, PA: The Westminster Press, 1986, 31.

victim's situation by acting as an advocate. The counselor may do this by helping a rape victim, for example, to gather a support network and by being present at a court hearing. In that way counselors not only show support for the counselee, but can enlarge their understanding of the legal process, and the counselee's personal and political situation. As the problem of traumatization is mainly one of losing the power of decision, the basic sense of self-agency and trust in self, other and world, it is crucial to address the meaning of life in the process of healing.[7] For example, once the counselor gains an enlarged picture of the counselee's situation, there is greater opportunity to help the counselee find new ways of understanding what happened and enable new connections.

It is here that we meet a further special challenge for pastoral counseling. Contemporary models of pastoral care and counseling continues to be under the influence of western psychology at the expense of engaging in critical reflection on ethical traditions as a source of meaning making. Traditional pastoral care used ethical traditions, Bible, theology, reason and experience as its basis. But with few exceptions, these sources have been neglected. Some of the questions that arise as theological challenges are: How do we use our traditions to address the confrontation with present day evil, violence and the traumatization of thousands of women, children and men. How do we do this theologically and spiritually? Where do we locate our own sources of meaning in our lives in the midst of such violence? What do biblical symbols like "the freedom to which Christ has liberated us" and "do the will of God", "brothers and sisters" mean to us? How do we listen to the voices expressed by women and men of diverse religious traditions? They question the androcentric metaphors and paradigms in which the Christian message of healing and restoration has been cast. Those who suffer point to the need for new interpretations that make sense of their experiences and offer hope for everyone. How do we communicate our own moral resources and committed actions in ways that respect the otherness of the other and at the same time, create safe space for steps towards healing and creativity? How can we teach others in a way that makes it a learning experience empowering for all participants?

Perspectives

Death and the Maiden moved both of us deeply. We identified with the victim's rage and uncompromising desire for revenge, to balance the scale

---

[7] Stuart Turner in his article on "Therapeutic Approaches Survivors of Torture" states: "Only if the therapist or group has developed some coherent understanding of the social and political context in which they are working, can they really start to address the ideological needs of their clients." In Kareem and Littlewood (eds.), *Intercultural Therapy*, 167.

of justice; to make the perpetrators pay-in-full. Why should they be let off? It brought up memories of our own pains, wishes to be acknowledged in our experience of abandonment, rejection and devaluation. But the drama must also permit us to identify with those situations where we have oppressed, violated or figured into the trauma of others. To recognize this more complex level of trauma can lead to denial or to healing. It can release energies of hope when emerging narratives are enlarged and incorporate both our idealized selves as well as our shameful self. A more complex understanding of trauma can offer metaphors of transformation that enable us to connect the violence that is within with the brutal, systemic violence that comes from without. Both may be denied. Both possibilities present us with opportunities to re-envision the meaning of care in a world of increased violence, where political change and upheaval are creating new forms of trauma and affiliations. Ours is a changing world, pushed by global developments, technological innovations, and uneven growth with deeper divisions between the wealthy and the poor. We are challenged to raise anew the question: Who is my mother, my sister and my brother? We have much to learn from the question and the answers, especially in contexts of worldwide economic and social change. Pastoral caregivers are further challenged to fashion creative responses to violence; to see and make the connections between personal suffering and political activity – especially where long standing patterns of injustice and violation contribute to long-term trauma and irreparable hurt.

There is a prophetic dimension to this challenge. It is to make known the subtle connections between personal suffering and public events, especially where people do not want to hear or be reminded of their past. Pastoral caregivers are challenged to find or create a role in situations where people who refuse to heed warning signs, will nevertheless, be unable to escape the consequences of their refusals. This is analogous to the young smoker who ignores the warning signs and refuses to stop. Such a person may soon be faced with the consequences of lung cancer and early death. She and he may never acknowledge their contribution to all the others affected by their behavior. We are challenged to find courage and skill to confront the perpetrators denial of violations, and find compassion sufficient to enable them to take responsibility for the consequences of their actions. This means that pastoral caregivers will be challenged to hear painful stories and learn to move perpetrators through the processes of recognition, confession, repentance, and restoration. And what about forgiveness? How do we deal with the perpetrators confession and repentance? Are there deeds so horrendous that forgiveness is impossible? In the process we too must learn to recognize our limitations, and the complex levels of trauma that incorporate both our idealized and shameful selves.

Pastoral Caregiving Within the Fragmentations of African Urban Life:

Creating Community and a Sense of Belongingness

Daisy N. Nwachuku
Nigeria, 1999

"*And the Lord God said, it is not good that man should be alone; I will make him a helpmeet for him*" (Gen. 2:18). Wholesome life implies caring and sharing together. From the biblical perspective, God's intention is that human life be shared in community of people and nations, beginning with the nuclear family as the smallest unit. Community life is inclusive. All living things live in families, colonies and communities.

The compositional dimensions of community are conceptually and empirically independent; i.e. communities can be found displaying all sorts of combinations. Due to the dynamics of community life, it can take on different kinds of characteristics. Within a metropolis, it is possible to find a highly sophisticated middle-class group with well-developed family coherence. In more poor communities, family relationships could be more complicated. Thus, the compositional variables are many and it is difficult to find completely homogeneous communities. One should therefore reckon with diversity and many forms of deviation from community norms.

This paper has a dual-focus. On the one hand, it seeks to understand modern cities as a context within which human life are frequently disposed to severe forms of fragmentation. On the other hand, there is a deep concern regarding the impact of the church on the predicament of families exposed to many influences stemming from fundamental changes within the social environment. What then is the impact of the church's pastoral care and counselling on the predicament of family life; very specifically, on the fragmentation of family life in the cities within the African context.

The search for community life in the intercultural context of city life through pastoral care, should be based on the following ecclesiological premise: the *koinonia* of the fellowship of believers as enfleshed in the unity and spiritual dynamics of the following theological principle: "our oneness in the Body of Christ." The Apostle Paul writes: "*Endeavouring to keep the unity of the Spirit in the bond of peace. There is one body and one*

Spirit, even as ye are called in one hope of your calling; One Lord, one faith, one baptism, one God and Father of all, who is above all, and through all, and in you all." (Ephesians 4:3-6) In this sense, we, being one Body, are called into the unity of God's community. Within a biblical perspective, one major characteristic of the community of believers is that we all share the same hope of our calling into eternal life. By experiencing salvation, through personal faith in Jesus Christ, we all partake in this eschatological reality.

Theoretical background

From a sociological concept, Parelius and Parelius[1] define communities as 'socially meaningful territories'. Within the context of this operational definition, it is implied that a community can contain a wide variety of interdependent institutions and social groups. Communities can be young or old. For example, a typical community might include a number of businesses, churches, service clubs, schools, young people, as well as old-timers who have lived within the confines of that territory all their life.

From a psychosocial context, a community offers to its inhabitants a kind of cultural particularity; it defines boundaries and their unique characteristics. In this sense, inhabitants and local groups often develop strong emotional attachments to the areas in which they live. Often, such sentimental feelings lead to a kind of community coherence and thinking, believing and behaving. This kind of cohesive particularity can lead to the impression that one group is better than the other. This local particularity creates a consensus of we-belonging. The implication is that a community often wants to defend itself against encroachment in a given metropolitan area or in a given rural setting. Community coherence is then structured along the lines of social hierarchy of prestige among communities.

Studies by Gerald Suttles[2] in the United States of America, revealed another very important variable in understanding the concept of community life. This is the variable of social cohesion. The cohesion of a community in this sense refers to the strength of its normative or moral order, and the degree of consensus on basic values and rules of behaviour that exists among residents. That is to say, a community is uniquely itself by its nature of homogeneity or heterogeneity of the population in terms of social rank, ethnicity, and life style.[3]

---

[1] A.P. Parelius and R.J. Parelius, *The Sociology of Education*, New Jersey: Prentice-Hall, 1978, 330.

[2] G.D. Suttle, *The Social Order of the Slum*, Chicago: University of Chicago Press, 1968.

[3] Cf. Parelius and Parelius, *Sociology of Education.*

There is yet a third concept of meaning to be explored. This is the concept of independence as emphasized by social ecologists. Studies by Donald Bogue[4], reported that the degree to which the community is self-sufficient and self-governing, containing all the basic institutions and resources necessary for the residents to maintain themselves, indefinitely determines a community. Although it is impossible to maintain total independence in contemporary urban African communities, in terms of economic, political, entertainment, medical care, police protection, general securities and other matters, yet, the issue of self-sufficiency is centrally a very important factor of consideration.

In summary, understanding the concept of communities within the context of this research involves three related variables: (a) social composition (i.e. rank, ethnicity and familial life style); (b) social cohesion and (c) independence.

African theological background

The spirituality of community life

In African theology, the Supreme Deity (God in heaven) rules over every community. He does this together with several other smaller deities (gods). Each of these deities is charged to supervise over an activity in the community e. g. fertility, harvest, fishing, healing etc. Among these gods, there is one named 'god of the land' (*ala*), governing the territorial space of each community. Its shrine represents the major altar of the land. Its priest is the chief priest of the land and people. The priest leads them in worship and purification rites. Thus, a community comes under the surveillance of the god of their land and is closely connected to ancestors as agents of life.

It is difficult to maintain the interplay between the spiritual realm and community life. The spiritual fragmentation of city life is then symbolized in non-ownership of the city. The concept 'land in the city' becomes confused and cannot be connected to one, specific deity, since urban dwellers come from several lands. By implication, the city as 'land' has not one major *altar*, or focal point, but several *imported altars.* The notion of one chief priest, becomes impossible, thus, but the development of priests for various cultures; priests for both foreign and indigenous religions.

Community life in African thinking: ancestral lineage

The African sense of community life was and still is that of being *his brother's keeper.* Theologically, psychologically and socially, the African *was*

[4] D.J. Bogue, "The Structure of the Metropolitan Community", in A.G. Theodorsen (ed.), *Studies in Human Ecology*, Evanston: Row, Peterson and Co., 1961, 524-533.

and is, because his brother was and is. Due to patriarchalism, family life is determined by the *male link*. The latter is framed by hierarchy and theory reinforces the African spirituality of ancestral lineage and worship. For example, in African thinking the mind-set is framed and structured by the following networking: *He is the son of his father, who was the son of his own father. Therefore, he lives because his father lived.*

The African community life is deeply embedded and rooted back to ancestral linkage. A Human being is primarily a member of a community whose smallest unit is not the nuclear family, but the *extended family*.[5] A male lives not in a house all by himself, his wife and children, but within *a compound of houses* as connected to his kindred of the same ancestral lineage. The kinsmen affinity extols the male child preference around which, in most cases, a compound can exist. The male child lives for the advancement of the kinsmen *(Umunna)*. He succeeds for them and makes them proud. Likewise, his failure brings them communal shame. The worldview is thus communitarian and this kind of patriarchal networking includes a 'troop of ancestors at the background'.

In summary, the African is a community-based person.[6] Extreme individualism, which extols western narcissism, capitalistic competitiveness and rivalry, was despised in the eyes of the elderly African.

But what is the situation now within the melting pot of interculturality and the fragmentation of city life? This dilemma creates a kind of *schizophrenic image* of current, urban life within an African context.

The umbilical cord theory of African community-based life

Nwachuku[7] noted that in contemporary Africa there is still the element of a kind of 'community mystery' built around the placenta of a newly born baby in the rural communities and villages. When a baby is born into the compound, the umbilical cord is cut. When this falls off the placenta, the waste cord is ritualistically buried at the base of a symbolic family tree. This gives a rite of passage and perpetually identifies the individual as a member of the larger family, comprising the ancestral clan. The *fetus' helplessness* experiences the collective protection as first experience of communal love. The umbilical cord tie serves as symbol of membership to the body of kinsmen (the *Umunna)*. The ritual thus introduces indelible concepts of belonging and acceptance. Thereafter, the child has a claim on the clan lineage and its inheritance. These in turn, produce a sense of connection,

[5] J.M. Mpolo and D.N. Nwachuku, *Pastoral Care and Counselling in Africa Today. Vol. 1*, Frankfurt a.M.: Peter Lang, 1991.

[6] E. Lartey, D.N. Nwachuku and K.W. Kasonga, *The Church and Healing: Echoes from Africa. Vol. 2*, Frankfurt a.M.: Peter Lang, 1994.

[7] D.N. Nwachuku, *Pastoral Care and Counselling Across Frontiers: An African Perspective*, Jos: Kenova Educational Publishers, 1995.

orientation, and rooted acceptance of the individuality of the member, and the sensitivity of his existence. Today, city born children do not experience anymore this community rite of entry. In its place there is the naming and christening ceremony.

Christian rituals, for example, have, gradually replaced ancestral worship, and its connection to the spirituality of the African community life, by the biblical understanding of baptism, confirmation and women dedication after childbirth. Thus the following intriguing questions: how can the city church emerge as a symbol of coherence and unifying principle within the fragmentation of city life? Can the church be viewed as a kind of substitute? How can the new symbols of community life and care in the church be transferred to, for example, a city born child or an adult urban dweller? Does the spirituality, offered by the church, provide enough coherence and identity to urban dwellers and member in order to replace the old symbols?

The interplay between 'spirituality of community life' and 'African theology': past and present

In the context of the ethnic, social composition of community life and its connection to ethnic kindred (the *Umunna)*, the latter provides a kin communal feeling; it induces the social cohesion. This also goes hand in glove with the notion of being independent from other communities around, very specifically in their political, economic and security services. Thus, the evolvement of a perpetually strong, collaborative partnership between the kinsmen. This was sealed in the rural village at events like the ancestral worship, and the sealing with blood sacrifices during cultic rituals, purificatory rites and ritual worships. It was used to celebrate births, weddings, deaths, festivals of seasons, harvests and victories, during moonlight stories and dances. The degree of kin togetherness was evident in the ritual and practice of men drinking wine together from one drinking horn at assemblies and household gatherings. Women cooked within the compound and children ate together. Suspicion and fear of witchcraft was minimal.

The living was sensitive to the cries of one another while the dead watched in surveillance of the living. It was one community, compiled by both the living and the dead (who were yet alive, despite of the reality of death). Life together was encompasses both the living and worship practices. The worldview was and still is cosmological. Theology was natural and practically emphasized in living a good life for yourself and your brother. The evil man, the witch and wizard *(Onye nsi)* was known and punished. The thief was killed and the rebellious son disowned.[8]

---

[8] D.N. Nwachuku, "Cultural and Psycho-Social Roots of Violence Against Women and Children in Selected African Milieux", in M. Cordner (ed.), *Pastoral Theology's*

One is tempted at present to believe that all was or is well with the idyllic characteristic of the rural village community existence. Although there are still remnants of the African understanding of community life in, for example Nigeria, one must admit that there is a gradual degradation of human life, even in rural, village communities. The mythical image of rural atmosphere and the all-embracing involvement of community life, leave one with the following dilemma: why the continuous rural migration to urban cities, which offer an insensitive social life in contrast? The fragmentation of life due to poverty, neo-slavery, illiteracy, underdevelopment and unemployment, seem to vex the mind of a growing new generation that could no longer contain the rural life. Despite urban challenges, rural population chooses to flee to the cities.

The urban question

Sule[9] describes urban attributes as seducing rural migrants to flock the cities because of the glamour of electricity, pipe-born water, better housing facilities and promises of higher income, for better life.

Defining urbanization, Wirth[10] noted that the concept carries with it the assumption of size, density and heterogeneity. These attributes produce such a wealth of stimuli on the inhabitants of cities, that they become indicators for a 'better life'. They either develop protective responses by making their social contracts more formal than informal, more particular than general, more secondary than primary, or more critical than natural. Consequently, this led to a growing specialization of roles, or where controls failed, led to a state of anomie, as well as to a state of social disorganization, vices, depravity and misery as are found in modern urban centres.

This aspect of urban social environment has attracted not only the attention of social ecologists, but also that of pastoral care givers and counsellors. The evidence of fragmented human life has underscored the conceptualization of the relationship between cities and community life.

The African concept of urban life and communities

The concept of communal life still permeates the rural communities as part of basic African philosophies of life, despite traces of disintegration.

---

and Pastoral Psychology's Contributions to Helping Heal a Violent World, Surakarta Indonesia: Dabara Publ., 1996.

[9] R.O. Sule, *Urban Development Planning in Nigeria*, Calabar: University of Calabar Press, 1994, 3.

[10] L. Wirth, "Urbanism as a Way of Life", in *American Journal of Sociology, 44*, 1938, 1-24.

African spirituality even transcends the western concept of urbanization despite signs of kindred disintegration. In this sense, urban dwellers in Nigerian and African cities still carry the idea of kindred togetherness into city life. Thus, urban dwelling congregates along parallel lines of ethnicity, local government areas, regional, state and village groupings. When any new city migrant arrives, he or she looks for a house near his people.

Nigerian cities therefore polarize in enclaves dominated naturally by major clan, ethnic, tribe and national lines, e.g. *Ibo quarters, Housa quarters, Yoruba quarters, Efik quarters* etc. The groupings in urban settings thus follow ethnic lines. Naturally, the boundaries expand beyond ethnic lines to embrace state boundaries in cities, outside the state. Outside Nigeria, the tribal boundaries yet expand to include all Nigerians, no matter the state or tribe.

The sense of affinity strives to maintain certain symbols of togetherness in the cities by certain social activities such as:

- Building a civic hall of meeting known by their name e.g. Ibo Hall, Yoruba Hall etc.
- Institutionalizing ethnic unions and making membership almost mandatory for everybody from that particular village or group e.g. Ibo Union, Yoruba Union, etc.
- The assemblies serve as both support and censor to monitor good behaviour, progress or failure, as well as show support and solidarity in weddings, burials or emergency needs.
- Yearly during Christmas festivals, which serve as holidays for Africans, over 80 % of urban dwellers in their urban-based unions, return to their village communities to organize community development building projects in liaison with the rural unions. That is to say, ethnicity and kindred have not yet been drastically fragmented in Africa by urbanization.

However, city fragmentation of human life to an African takes a different dimension from that of the Western World. The issues of fragmentation in African cities are greatly evident in terms of poverty, slum dwelling, overcrowding, diseases, hunger, begging, homelessness, unemployment, illiteracy, and low standard of living, widened gaps between the rich and the poor, and marginalization of majority masses. Generally, it also shows consequences of the national debt burden on the poor masses of the citizens, and these are debts incurred by the government to urbanize and industrialize for the comfort and leisure of the rich and the governance.

African theology and pastoral care must address these issues in recreating African urban life.

It is, therefore, evident that both development and fragmentation are neither Western nor African. Life fragmentation is a human factor. Although Western modernity has affected African community life in the urban societies faster than would have occurred in indigenous settings, yet it cannot be argued that urbanization is purely Western. For example, the Yorubas of Nigeria had always been urban dwellers, yet with very strong communal ethnic orientation wherever they are located, whether in the past or the present.

The fragmentation dilemma and our African stories

It has been argued in the preceding discussion that, primarily, fragmentation is a human factor enhanced by city structures and social environment. Somehow, the African is still unaware of the changing, social environment and its impact on human identities. Therefore, we Africans struggle to live in the reality of the fragmentation dilemma and city schizophrenia. Caught in social transition, we still live in the daily schizophrenia of being African and Western, rural and urban, elite and illiterate, rich and poor, sophisticated and simple, informed and ignorant, independent and dependent, religious adherent and syncretistic, Christian and idolater. Our daily struggles with fragmented life are reflected in the brief stories below. All names are imaginary but real life stories.

Ahmed Ali: Ahmed, a professing Moslem youth, went to Lagos to write the Federal Government College Common Entrance Examination. He arrived at the famous city of Lagos excitedly, being his first time. But his joy was soon gone, when he observed several lunatics along the road. Why are they so mad here, he asked? He soon discovered that many Lagosians face disorganized life; people break down in health due to the fast pace of big city life. Why is this so in Lagos? Why is everybody moving so fast, even cars? To Ahmed, these are questions without answers. His dreams and excitements about Lagos soon die off, and he starts to face extreme nostalgia of his rural hamlet in the village. He longs earnestly to go home for fear of running mad, too. In fact, the people he saw were not all lunatics, but normal people, homeless and living under the bridges and flyover structures. Everybody ran and rushed to take a bus or taxi. In short, life was maddening in itself. Lagos looked more like the biblical city of Gadarenes with many possessed by demons of legion. Young Ahmed did not want to run mad soon. So he resolved to return to his village.

Franca Joe: Miss Franca Joe was born and bred at Abuja, the Federal Capital of Nigeria by Christian middle class Nigerians. She had never visited the village and relatives. Rather, she spends her holidays overseas. Once, her father was pressurized by his kinsmen to bring his children home to know their roots. During one Christmas season, Franca's parents took them "home" (to the village). At lunch, some relatives, who were present when meal was served, were invited to share with them. Franca was shocked at the ease and joy with which the two visitors gladly dipped their hands together into the meal, served for her father and drank from the same cup, sharing childhood stories and jokes in reminiscence of the "good old days". Franca was disappointed at the regular invasion of their privacy. Relatives moved straight into the bedroom to greet and share their joy at seeing them. She longed to go back soon, in order to escape from everybody's eyes and intrusion. "Here", she said, "everybody wants to know what you are doing. There is a lot of intrusion", she complained. She hated the idea completely and was glad to get back to the city life, where she could be "herself".

Bob and Uncle Mike: Mr. Robert had been sent overseas for further studies. His Uncle Mike financed him. On graduating, Bob decided to reside in New York. After several years, Mr. Mike specifically invited his nephew Bob, for a family meeting. When Bob arrived in Nigeria, his first shock was over Uncle Mike's slum dwelling in the ghetto. He, his wife, five children and four relatives were living in two rooms. Bob would neither sit down and eat, nor drink any substance. Mike felt very much humiliated and rejected.

Furthermore, Bob proposed that the family meeting be held in his hotel room. Mike and the rest of the family members felt further insulted. The family elders turned down Bob's offer with vows and curses, swearing never to be involved with him as a family member anymore. After few days, Bob flew back to New York. Since then, there had been a total breakdown in communication between Bob and his uncle Mike and the family elders. Kinsmen were shocked at Bob's behaviour towards his uncle Mike who financed his education.

All our African stories points to the following conclusion: African life in modern times is severely fragmented. However, the fragmentation of life means different things to different people within their specific context of village and city life.

Creating caring communities

Suggestions for congregations

Due to faith in Jesus Christ and the gospel of salvation, God is still rendered as the creator, giver and sustainer of life. Believers need no other help of ancestors or any other symbols. This knowledge is fundamental to the African convert because many Africans who go to church still practice syncretism.

Pastoral care givers should strengthen believers in Africa to see beyond the immediate ethnic community. They should discover and see the church as one big family. They should equip the believers with practical strategies, in a dialogical community model. They should strife and work together towards the realisation of hope.

Meaningful worship and bible studies should be self-understood. There should be interpretation of the worship process and messages to the local languages where English is used as medium of communication. Anybody in the community should be able to participate in one language or the other in a community church.[11]

Care counsellors could mobilise the local congregation to bring hope, love and practical help to the community, together with proclaiming the gospel, in personal contact through door-to-door evangelism within neighbourhood. Care efforts must be backed up with active follow-up projects resulting in visible outreaches to the needs of people. This strategy creates friendship, love and support with a semblance of a sense of intimate belongingness.

Each local congregation should have a baseline data bank on the disabled in the community. Congregations should creatively reach out to meet needs of local communities. The help needed includes advocacy in government policies and social welfare services.

Church members are encouraged to invite, on regular basis, families or couples from the same local congregation into their homes to share a meal. This helps to break down the cold walls of impersonal relationship found in city churches.

In all African Churches there are lively men, women and youth fellowships, sharply demarcated by differences. More joint fellowships across the board will bring people closer and minimise the gender biases, gaps and differences.

The church should spearhead development projects and poverty alleviation programmes, encouraging combined efforts such as community tree planting, farm plantations, cottage industries, animal farm projects, poultry etc.

Suggestions for working with youth

Churches in Africa have not yet recognised the importance of recreational facilities, especially for the youth as part of their services to be rendered. Church-based clubs such as sports teams, music, drama, art, educational and several other types of clubs, will provide a very reliable support body to the Christian youth. They will also provide good peer role models for the city adolescent, exposed to several confusing models.

The African Church and city life face serious and increasing problems due to the generation gap. It could be helpful to initiate seminars where

---

[11] See Nwachuku, *Pastoral Care and Counselling Across Frontiers.*

parents and youth meet in regular dialogues, regarding life skills management. A space must be created where they can share concerns over interactional conflicts. This forum will help, in a steady manner, to bridge the generation gap that keeps many of the neighbourhood youth outside the church.

In Africa, vocational and employment development seminars, should receive top priority among youth due to the high rate of unemployment, mass retrenchment and ill prepared retirements. The Church caregivers need to give regular seminars and workshops in this area. This is an area where the state government has been very silent.

Suggestions for working in neighbourhoods

The situation of portable water is one of the most life devastating factors in African cities. Every urban church should provide and service borehole water in her premises. Clean water, purchased at regular period of supply from the church, will be a great hope of restoration to her community. In African rural villages, the local streams provide rallying points of recreation with children singing and swimming together in water games. These lost good images of a shared life would be restored, if the borehole water point at the church is initiated and maintained as an on-going, essential service of care for the people in the community.

Caring believers should find out the interest and needs of the neighbourhood and run seminars on them. The church should initiate regular open seminars and workshops to inform, as well as, create awareness on needs of the hour. They should also aim at recapturing lost and decaying moral values of community life.

From time to time, the church could organise a people's open forum where the neighbourhood adults meet to evaluate the development progress of the entire community, dialoguing over point in time issues of general concern (e.g. crime rate and securities) and initiating further ideas and action for communal good. This concept of open forums recaptures and recreates the lost village kin's meetings. Neighbours are encouraged to have a personal contact and face to face dialogue with one another.

Generally, in the process of counsellors reaching out to create and recreate communities within the city population, the strategies also recapture re-orientation to love, helping attitude and unity of spirit, which are lost in the impersonal nature of city life. Through newly created care and support communities, new neighbourhoods of inter-tribal and intra-group friendliness emerge across frontiers. Likewise, a new sense of openness, trust, sensitivity, consideration and connectedness is generated towards bridging the gap between the rich and the poor which is very evident in city churches and neighbourhood.

Conclusion: 'water of life' to quench a city thirst

Who would give a cup of cold water to quench the thirst of a nameless African city woman whose life has became so fragmented in the big cities of Lagos, Kaduna, Port-Harcourt, Aba and Abuja? The biblical counterpart of so many marginalised and fragmented city women, is to my mind the Samaritan woman in the gospel of John. She had become both nameless and faceless in trying to cope with battered life in the city. At the point of the biblical story, her face and her name (the Samaritan Woman) were worthless. There are many "Women of Samaria" today in our African cities, many "men sick with palsy", and many "Gerasene demoniacs moving about with legions".

Both they and their cities are fragmented and disconnected from community reality. They need healing and a sense of belongingness in order to become human again. Christian African spirituality should strive to encourage a practical, daily theologising for community care and the restoration of lives, broken by our cities, broken by poverty, hunger, corruption, oppression, the abandoning of street children, wars, and diseases. The church in Africa must theologise about care and counselling strategies, namely how to deliver life and to quench the thirst of so many lonely and neglected city dwellers. But such theologising must, at the same time, also seek to quench the thirst of the community where the well is situated. This is the model of the Good Shepherd. He healed both the spiritual and physical thirst of the woman and also healed her city. All Samaria came to see the Lord themselves. We Africans, together with our sisters and brethren in the West, must seek to see the Lord through the eyes of His loving care.

The Christian community should act as connecting points like in the narrative of the Samarian woman. People should be reconnected to the fellowship of believers (the *koinonia* and *diakonia* of the church as the body of Christ). Spiritual wholeness implies the following: "*And he showed me a pure river of water of life, clear as crystal, proceeding out of the throne of God and of the lamb. And the Spirit and the bride say, Come. And let him that heareth say, come. And let him that is athirst Come. And whosoever will, let him take the water of life freely*." (Revelation 22:1 & 17)

Cultural Diversity in Sickness and Healing:

The Domain of Caring in South African Traditional Cultures [1]

Edwina D. Ward
South Africa, 2005

Understanding the meaning of sickness and healing in the South African context is necessary for pastoral counsellors to work successfully in an environment where the society is multicultural. Being a person dedicated to ministry does not automatically free us of our underlying biases. Understanding and attitudinal changes are required.

The current HIV/AIDS pandemic in South Africa calls for many pastoral carers and counsellors to undergo training and to offer their services to those infected and affected. This is an opportunity to bridge the gap between Western and African understandings of sickness and healing. Instead of blaming and denigrating the other, we are challenged to look at why we are afraid to be tested, and why we are denying that all South Africans are HIV positive (for when one member of the family is sick, the whole family is sick).

The stigma of being HIV-positive is underlined by the Church, who blames it a result of the sin of sex, and is emphasised by society, who sees it as the problem of the poor. Yet it is all South Africans who are challenged not to remain silent any longer, but to care for all who are suffering from HIV/AIDS. Those who do not have the HI virus are often lacking an understanding of the infected person's fear of stigmatization, ostracization, and condemnation. Scripture calls us to care for and love our neighbour. Those trained in pastoral care and counselling are challenged to empower others to cope with personal crises and to make positive changes in their lifestyles.

Many Western counsellors consider themselves to be lacking understanding of the African comprehension of sickness and healing. In this article I will address the concerns of cross-cultural experiences that most

---

[1] Paper presented at the International Seminar on Intercultural Pastoral Care and Counselling, 2005, in Düsseldorf-Kaiserswerth, Germany. Published in *Intercultural Pastoral Care and Counselling, 13*, 2006, 43-46.

pastoral counsellors and Church workers experience when working in a climate of cultural diversity. A growing concern for multicultural organisations, both in the Church and in the business world, is that of dealing better with stereotyped prejudices and underlying biases.[2] The need for tolerance, a better understanding of cultural differences, and empathy is seen as a key factor in groups that wish to continue in the global village.

African worldview

A person's perception of the world is basically his or her worldview. People have a way of accepting their culture as the best and right way of doing and looking at things. You look at the world from your ethnic centre – we are all ethnocentric. The way we understand our world is the frame from which we view our world. Because I live in KwaZulu-Natal, I will discuss the worldview of the Zulu, which is essentially religious. It is not necessary to teach the Zulu how to pray but rather to focus on expanding the wonder and mystery of a gracious Divinity for those in our care. Nearly all Zulus come from a religious background and when they encounter difficulties, they pray about them. When they come to a Christian pastoral counsellor to talk about these difficulties, we can but guide them to deepen their understanding of God as loving Father and Mother.[3]

As Westerners, we have a tendency to pray from "our heads" and give God a time slot and a space slot, whereas the Zulu African experiences God with and through the senses and prays only when there is an immediate need or when something happened which is significant or presents a crisis. A Zulu is more likely to pray for what has happened than what will happen. For Africans time is both past and present; for Westerners time is in the future. When a person dies in Africa, they are said to have joined their ancestors, so there is a sense of their lives being controlled by those who have gone before them. The past is present through tradition, and the ancestors belong to a time that is past and this is part of the worldview of the Zulu.

Different mindsets of the Zulu and the Westerner

Our mindsets are very different in character. As Westerners we analyse, categorise and relate ideas to reality to see if they work. Whereas the Zulu prefers to experience the situation and lets it surround him or her and then lets it rest. If the experience is uncomfortable, only then will assistance be sought from the ancestors, the community, or the Church leaders. This

[2] Mary D'Arcy, "The Challenge of Diversity", in *Horizon, Vol.15 No.1*, 1989, 3.
[3] M. O'Reilly, "Cross-Cultural Religious Formation: Human Development", in *Human Development, Vol. 11 No. 1*, 1990, 34.

gives insight to the fact that Zulu thought is basically a relational thinking. Anything of significance is seen as something personal and of the community. Many Africans see Westerners as knowing too much and feeling too little. Gestures are important in the Zulu culture and often stories are acted out so that their full impact may be realised by the listeners. We need to understand that being different is not a negative but a potential enrichment. People often think that if you are different you are 'better than, or worse than' me.

The problem of language

We tend to forget that most of our African Zulu clients are not working in their native language. We speak English too fast, use expressions and idioms which are unfamiliar, and fail to grasp that besides a different vocabulary each language has its own internal logic. In Zululand if one is to ask a person how far she or he has travelled to the clinic, the response may well be, 'five rand away'. The distance is measured in terms of taxi fares rather than in kilometres. If as a white African I make no attempt to pick up the local expressions I will never fully communicate with my clients. It seems that although this is Africa, the Africans have to adjust far more than the Westerners do. There is a natural resistance to looking at diversity. We perceive differences as barriers; in fact research shows that persons usually are suspicious of others who differ from themselves. I believe that the pandemic of HIV/AIDS is bringing together all the people of South Africa in their efforts to fight a common evil. We are caring for each other, counselling each other, comforting and consoling each other.[4]

Cross-cultural adjustment

There is more to enculturation than learning a new language. There are non-verbal behaviours, new values and unfamiliar customs. These can be around the use of relationships, food, time and hospitality. As we prepare ourselves to work across cultures we gradually become at home and more adjusted in the new culture. Slowly I have come to accept that Zulu people do not speak up loudly and audibly to me and this is in respect of my standing as a counsellor and a lecturer who is mature in age. I have realised that the Zulu men often speak with their hands over their mouths and this demonstrates that they are feeling unsure of communicating to me in a foreign language. The behavioural patterns differ and many physical postures and gestures have different nuances.

---

[4] E. Ward, "Enabling Lay Pastoral Care and Counselling of People Living with AIDS: Clinical Pastoral Education as a Training Ground", in *Bulletin for Contextual Theology in Africa*, 7, 2000.

Eye Contact: For a Zulu it is almost impossible to in my eye when in counselling. Many young Africans feel that it is disrespectful to look elders in the eye when talking to them. We may easily misinterpret this as a sign that they feel guilty about something.

Space: In a counselling session I would prefer to sit a certain distance away from my client, but here in KwaZulu-Natal I have come to realise that the acceptable distance between us is far closer than in many other cultures. When we keep the Western distance, we may be misinterpreted by Africans as not wanting to associate with them.

Hospitality: The Zulu people value hospitality highly. When visiting, the visitors are treated as guests and given food and drink, long before the purpose of the visit is made known. When counselling a person in distress, the Zulu person likes to discuss all kind of things before the actual concern is raised. This is tiresome to the Westerner and yet I have realised that this 'warming up' gives both parties an opportunity to asses each other and to come to trust the other.

Taboos: There are so many taboos in the Zulu culture. The greatest of these is the mentioning of the words HIV/AIDS. In a hospital, where I supervise a Clinical Pastoral Education (CPE) programme, almost 75% of patients are HIV positive. When reading the verbatim reports of the participants, I am totally surprised that only 20% acknowledge the presence of HIV and AIDS. Most of the patients are "sick" and that is the extent of the disclosure of the illness. It is almost impossible to get a patient to discuss his or her impending death for fear of bringing down the anger of the ancestors. This talk about the future is not seen as a preparation for death, but a bringing down of bad fortune on the living.

I would advocate that we as counsellors spend more time in struggling to see people as individuals and not as types. That we learn to be more empathetic and to strive to stand in someone else's shoes and look at the world from their point of view. When we find ourselves in a struggle with someone of a different culture, race, or generation, pull back and try to search for the underlying values that cause the person to act or react in a different way. No one who has not experienced the stigmatization and the loneliness of having HIV/AIDS will ever comprehend the fear of dying outside of the favour of one's family, community or Church community.

Community verses individualism

Westerners tend to feel that counselling and problems are best worked out on a one-to-one basis. In my experience this is not the best approach with Africans. The Zulu people like to resolve issues in a community meeting where everyone has the opportunity to speak. In my own experiences of being in the Communicable Diseases Clinic (CDC) I am shocked at the lack of privacy and confidentiality when a person is found to be HIV positive. There are at least eight people who are privy to this information before the patient leaves the hospital, nurses, the doctor, the counsellor etc. If treatment is to continue, the sufferer is bound to make his or her status known to a member of the family. This is to control the taking of medicine on a regular basis. This is the one time in the life of a Zulu that he or she does not want to share with the community for fear of being ostracised.

This brings us to the understanding of sickness and healing amongst the African people in South Africa. We now look at culture texts: We need to look at culture as a meaning system made up of signs and codes which transmit messages through culture texts.[5] As pastoral counsellors working in a multicultural environment we experience our very being called into question. "You can turn back on the challenge and stay in your ethnocentric parochialism or you can open yourself to the process of struggle and change. You know that you will never be the same person again... Let us struggle to go beyond what we know and understand in order to be enriched and gifted by what we don't understand in those that are different to us".[6] Looking at culture as a meaning system which is made up of signs and codes which transmit messages through culture texts introduces us to the semiotic approach to culture.[7] This involves some clear understanding of signs and symbols in the other person's culture. A simple sign points to something else, for example, a stop sign tells us clearly to stop the car at a certain point in the road. Whereas a symbol points to something more, for example, water as a symbol of baptism, cleansing, ritual purification, wealth for the crops and pleasing the ancestors.

Both signs and symbols have power for the people of a culture. Often ritual has power to make a boy into a man, a non-believer into a Christian believer. How do we as counsellors read and understand culture texts? To grasp the meaning of sickness and healing in the African Zulu context, we as Westerners must locate the signs with the message conveyed. The semiotic domain is the drawing together of culture texts which are linked to a theme of healing and sickness.

The domain of caring in sickness and healing

In this section I would like to present the semiotic domains of sickness and health in three cultural paradigms.[8] These are the Western culture, African

[5] St. Bate, *Human Life is Cultural*, Pietermaritzburg: Cluster Publications, 2002, 46.
[6] D'Arcy, "The Challenge of Diversity", 7.
[7] Bate, *Human Life is Cultural*, 46.
[8] Dr. Stuart Bate, OMI, a professor at St. Augustine's College in Johannesburg, has recently written extensively on these areas. I acknowledge an unpublished paper of his as a resource in this area. Cf. also: St. Bate, *The Inculturation of Christian Healing in the South African Context*, New York: Edwin Mellen, 1999.

traditional culture and African Initiated Churches culture. All three have an effect on different groupings' understanding of sickness and health. Through this analysis we see differing comprehensions of sickness and health and healing, as well as looking at their commonality. Pastoral counselling in South Africa needs to recognise that this multicultural society operates through cultural borrowing, and counsellors should be open to accepting that cultural diversity is a *gift*.

Western culture

In the Western understanding of sickness and healing the language we use includes culture texts like diagnosis of the disease, cure, medicine, surgery. There are further codes like clinical testing of medicines, clinical diagnosis and mechanisms of sickness and healing. If a person is sick the first step is to visit a doctor for a diagnosis of the sickness. This is achieved by looking at the symptoms, analysing them, using scientific methods and finally arriving at a clinical diagnosis. If an organ of the body is 'sick' then the patient may undergo medical intervention, surgical intervention, or counselling if the sickness has an underlying pathology. Needless to say, there is still a certain stigma in receiving counselling from a psychologist or pastoral counsellor.

Sickness in the African traditional culture

Sickness is seen as a need for restoration in relationships. Restoring life is a human process which includes physical health and inter-relational harmony, giving a balance between body, mind and soul. In the Zulu culture text sickness is usually attributed to inter-relational causes. These non-harmonious relationships may be caused by the ancestors, spirits, witchcraft or other people. The Zulu people consult the *inyanga* (herbalist) or the *sangoma* (traditional healer) for a remedy which usually includes the slaughtering or sacrifice of animals to appease the angered ancestors.

Healing in African Initiated Churches

These churches have developed culture texts from other cultural sources. They believe that some forms of sickness can be cured by certain medicines. These would include stomach pains, pain in limbs, headaches, tension points and diarrhoea or constipation. They emphasise the importance of dreams as a means of communication from the ancestors or spirits. Many a Zulu person has expressed fear at a certain dream which in counselling exploration has been unravelled as a person's guilt or a sense of impending doom. They place great importance on the support coming from the group or community. If the community or family disapprove of a certain marriage union for example, there is little hope that the marriage will ever be successful. There would be too many members of the family on the side of the groom and the bride who would not wish the couple well for their future. This sector of the African church believes strongly in the role of touch, laying on of hands, music, dance in the healing process. These churches which emphasise healing are presently growing in huge numbers in South Africa.

It would seem as if the mainline churches would do well to recover their rituals of prayers for healing, laying on of hands, invoking the power of the Holy Spirit and blessing with Holy water. We have these rituals within the church, but do not emphasise them in the process of healing. Each of the mainline churches would do well to re-introduce healing services and all-night vigils. In this crucial time where so many are dying of AIDS, the church has the ability to bring comfort to her believers.

The notion of life

Life is central to the experience of the family community.[9] Life is health, being well, and harmony with people and the world. This harmony includes family members, neighbours, and the world. Life is health and peace. A person who is not in peace with his or her surroundings will become sick. When a person is sick, the question for the counsellor is 'who is the cause of this sickness' or 'what relationship is out of balance'? To restore health and bring healing would mean to restore the relationship. Often the counsellor will have to accept the cultural diversity and listen to the story of the ancestor who has been offended.

Life is not an individual affair, but made up of communal relationships. The Zulu believe that 'a person is a person through other people' (*umuntu ungumuntu ngabantu*). This clearly shows that 'someone' is to blame when things go wrong, not 'something'. For the Zulu person, his world can become infected and this problem arises out of the fact that the environment may have a quality of evil as a result of human and spirit activity. This is then seen as the cause of suffering. Examples of this can include death, funerals, and terminal sickness such as HIV/AIDS.

All sickness has a cause. What a pastoral counsellor has to do with the client is to determine the cause of the sickness. An ordinary sickness will be treated through herbs. More serious sickness is usually the result of an ill relationship. If there is friction in relationships (with the living or with the dead) then peace must be restored for healing to take place. A diviner is usually called in to pin-point the responsible person. A person who causes social friction is considered to be one who breaks moral standards of living.

[9] L. Magesa, *African Religion: The Moral Traditions of Abundant Life*, New York: Orbis, 1997.

If their fault is confessed the sickness can be healed with ritual appeasement to follow.

The notion of healing

Medicine can be used in healing both as *imithi* (medicinal) or symbolically. If used symbolically, they can imitate the evil they are fighting, for example: a thorn will protect a person from being stabbed. Colours are used to symbolise fertility (red) or strength (white), and certain roots which resemble a male can be given to women in order for them to produce a male baby.

To be a human being is to be a cultural person, and human life is cultural. Sickness and healing serve to indicate right and wrong relationships within the community of the living and the dead. The pastoral counsellor who works in a multicultural environment is challenged in many ways to understand that culture is complex and multi-layered. It is a combination of family and ethnic roots that shape our values, assumptions, opinions, self-image and that consciously or unconsciously govern our behaviour. It is the frame of reference that gives meaning to our environment and helps us to interact appropriately. Successful pastoral counselling and integration of Western and African values comes from using cultural diversity as a resource rather than a liability.

Becoming truly empathetic and stepping in the shoes of the other for a while and seeing the world from another point of view will prevent some of the prejudices and stereotypical thinking so apparent in our South African society. The Christian commitment is not to have token groups, but truly to become multicultural groups. The figures of HIV/AIDS are still climbing and we as counsellors have to learn new ways of caring for those who are infected and affected.

Explorations into Reconciliation:

The Corrymeela-Community in Northern Ireland *

David Stevens
United Kingdom, 2008

2005 marked the 60th anniversary of the bombing of Dresden – a terrible story of death and destruction. 2005 was also the 40th anniversary of the foundation of Corrymeela. What is the connection? The answer is a person. Ray Davey, the founder of Corrymeela was a prisoner of war just outside the city. He records this in his diary for the 20th March 1945 when he returned to the city for the first time after the bombing:

> Today I went down into Dresden and saw all for myself. All the buildings I had come to know so well are now at best shells and mostly rubble. I felt strangely uncomfortable walking around the sorrows of this once beautiful city. In some of the streets it was like climbing on the Giant's Causeway. Places that had been the hub of human activity and action are now still and few people pass by. I don't think one could find a habitable building in some ten square miles in the central area. I "climbed" round to the remains of the Dom Kirche, a month ago probably the most beautiful church in the city. Now it is but a mass of ugly masonry, with the statue of Martin Luther, legless, lying face down in the street, blown 10-15 yards from its pedestal.

It was out of this experience of seeing the depths of what human beings can do to each other that Ray Davey's vision of reconciliation was born and he has devoted his life to it. He founded a Christian community and a place of meeting and encounter, not just for people from Northern Ireland, but from all over the world.

This vision was tested in the crucible of Northern Ireland from 1969 on and was made concrete in Corrymeela's go-between work between Protestant and Catholic, Unionist and Nationalist. But it is a vision with a universal relevance and it is at the heart of Christian faith; speaking of

---

* Paper presented at the 20th International Seminar on Intercultural Pastoral Care and Counselling, 2008, in Bratislava, Slovakia. A German translation was published in *Interkulturelle Seelsorge und Beratung, 15*, 2009, 67-74.

remade humanity, of renewed and redeemed relationships and identities, of restored community, of suffering vulnerability, of self-emptying love that makes space for others. All of this in the context of a fragmented world – our world – where hatred, enmity, violence and antagonised differences are common.

Reconciliation faces the reality of pain and death and destruction and makes visible, new life. It breaks down walls of antagonised division and offers a new world. That is what Easter is about.

The point of intersection

Christ is at the point of intersection between humanity and God and at this point of intersection there is a supreme act of self-giving love. I want to explore this idea of reconciliation work as being at a point of intersection and I will do it first through the story of another community of reconciliation in Northern Ireland – the Cornerstone Community.

When the Cornerstone Community came into being twenty years ago, the choice of place to live was deliberate. The house is at the intersection of two communities in West Belfast, two communities then at war. Violence was rampant, people lived with grief, pain, fear and mistrust. A wall was being built to keep us apart. Cornerstone hoped to show there was another way of living. For the place of intersection is also the meeting point, and the function of a cornerstone is to unite the two intersecting parts, making both one (cf Eph 2:20-22).

Twenty years on, we are still at the point of intersection. The physical wall is higher, but many encounters have taken place at the meeting point. We celebrate the fact that the Community house has been a place of welcome where people have met across many divides. We celebrate the way our own lives have been enriched by encounters with visitors from across the world, each one a gift. We celebrate the generosity of the many volunteers who have come to us over the years, bringing their gifts of energy, enthusiasm, caring, practical faith. We celebrate republican ex-prisoners meeting with groups of English church people and tackling difficult questions together, and we celebrate people from different political persuasions using the house as a place to thrash out new political possibilities as part of the peace process. Above all, we celebrate our belief that Jesus Christ is himself the cornerstone.

Cornerstone's point of intersection was at a point of physical intersection between two opposing communities in West Belfast. Corrymeela's was the need for change in Northern Ireland in the 1960s, with a background of Ray Davey's experiences in the Second World War. But a point of intersection could be anything or anywhere where there are tension points. Where are the hurting places? Where are the silences? It could be around gays, battered women, race relations, anything. So find your point of intersection.

And finding your point of intersection involves attentiveness to what is going on. It is not a form of cleverness. Maybe it is a form of seeing out of the corner of the eye, the lucidity to see the shadow of the victim. It is a form of creativity. We desperately need this sort of 'knowledge'.

In the post September 11 world, if we are to break the deadly cycle of escalating violence – of strike and counter-strike, of atrocity and enraged reaction – we must start by paying attention to what everybody is saying, even our enemies and there are real enemies here, and be sincerely ready to let it change us; to get beyond rhetoric, decode the imagery, and hear the subtext of rage, grief, fear, pain, hatred and despair.

A place of uncomfortableness

Reconciliation work is not some soft, comfortable option, as I hope I have made clear. A recent report into the concept in Northern Ireland suggests one reason why. Let me quote:

> Reconciliation… is seen as a deep and sometimes threatening process. Respondents chose not to use the term in their daily work because they feared it would scare some people off. In some cases this might have been associated with the perceived religious overtones, but in others it was because reconciliation was understood as somewhere 'coming together' and thus some process of social and political transformation.

And, of course, the respondents in this research are profoundly right. Reconciliation is not about something comfortable, warm and fuzzy; it is about social and political transformation. We might add spiritual transformation. And this, of course, is totally biblical.

Jesus was profoundly threatening to his society and he was forced out of it onto a cross. A picture of gentle Jesus meek and mild is simply wrong, the gospels are riven by conflict and violence from beginning to end, and show our incapacity to live with truth, shalom and right relations.

So this sort of work can bring us and the people we work with, into a place of profound uncomfortableness. There is a sense in which reconciliation work is leading people out of their comfort zones into discomfort with the hope that we come to a fuller humanity – both for ourselves and for others. So one of the challenges is: How do we get people into the room? We have to think about how we engage with people about different issues. Often we have to build up relationships of trust before we can explore divisive issues.

Specific learnings

Now I want to move to some more specific Corrymeela learnings which I hope will be useful to your situation.

The importance of vision

Corrymeela began with a vision of Ray Davey, of Christian community and reconciliation which took the form of a centre and a community in 1965. One of Ray's key themes was the idea of the 'Open Village' which he expressed at the opening on 30 October 1965.

> We hope that Corrymeela will come to be known as 'the Open Village', open to all people of good will who are willing to meet each other, to learn from each other and work together for the good of all. Open also for all sorts of new ventures and experiments in fellowship, study and worship. Open to all sorts of people; from industry, the professions, agriculture and commerce.

This vision expressed a commitment to encounter, interaction and positive relationships between all sorts and conditions of people. The vision was global as well as local. It was not just about community relations in Northern Ireland. It was about a totality of relationships. The vision put an emphasis on openness and hospitality. Hospitality and reconciliation are linked. In the words of Henri Nouwen "Hospitality is about offering people space where change can take place". And we have tried to live out that vision.

The importance of place

Place is important. Corrymeela is in an incredibly beautiful place. The backdrop of the new Coventry Cathedral is the old cathedral destroyed by bombing in 1940. The new emerges out of the brokenness of the old and every week day at noon the Coventry Litany of Reconciliation is said. The Iona Community's work for justice and peace has a physical context in the rebuilding of an Abbey. There is a resonance of place. There is a healing power of place, there is a healing power of beauty. Places can speak profoundly of transcendence.

Reconciliation is a practice not a theory

Ray Davey was a person who enabled young people to take significant responsibility and provided a context for incredible learning (learning by doing). Ray and other important individuals in Corrymeela's history provided key models and conversation partners for learning about reconciliation. They taught the practice of reconciliation. It is not enough to 'know' (ideologically, theologically, intellectually) about reconciliation. We need places where people can experience trust and reconciliation. We need people who can 'model' reconciliation; we need people of character who embody the peacemaking virtues. Thus encounter and relationships are central. It is only in encounter and relationships that words like trust, reconciliation and forgiveness become real.

The early experience in the work camps, which helped to reconstruct the site at Ballycastle, (and later in the family weeks which brought families from the most troubled areas of Belfast and elsewhere, often on a cross-community basis) was about reconciliation as doing things together. It also created a strong context of community building and learning. And the Corrymeela Community, through being a group of diverse people committed to and involved in reconciliation, created a context for learning – both structured and unstructured – about reconciliation. This has continued all through our history. It has had implications directly for the work of Corrymeela but Corrymeela members, staff and long-term volunteers have carried their learning throughout Northern Irish society and beyond. Many Corrymeela members (nearly 400 in 40 years), former long-term volunteers (upwards of 300 since the early 1970s) and staff are active in a whole variety of reconciliation and community relations activities, and some have created their own training agencies in community relations and conflict transformation issues.

A range of different programme models

Initially we had hoped that by bringing people together in an environment where they could live, talk, work and play together, that the experience could help break down the barriers of ignorance that separated them. It was not that this was unsuccessful but we soon realised that more was required – we needed to develop and support new ways of meeting. At the beginning we had also used the time-honoured conference model. This revolved round the speaker or speakers who had come to impart specialist knowledge and skills. It was basically a teaching model.

We began to realise that while this was useful and had its place other models were required. We moved to models that began with the participants, where they were and their life experiences. Greater emphasis was put on people sharing their experiences and developing relationships between participants. We used games and activities that could lead to honest conversations and robust meetings. We have sought to develop resources and modes of practice around understanding politics, history, identity and other sectarian issues. We widely used a seed group model where a diverse group of people (particularly young adults) worked together over a number of weekends. Each weekend had a particular theme, for example family relationships, the meaning of faith, sexuality and relationships, the Troubles, diversity. This model has a strong emphasis on personal development.

Safe space

We developed the understanding that it was not just the bringing people together that was important but also that the context within which the contact happened was crucial. The way we set up our initial group processes and allowed the programme to evolve was key to achieving the outcomes that the groups hoped for. We referred to this as the 'creating of safe space'. It was providing such a space where difficult stories and experiences could be raised and shared that took our programmes into a new level of encounter.

The phrase 'safe space' is an easy phrase to use and is both simple and quite complex at the same time. It includes something as simple as a smile for and the recognition of, the stranger arriving at the Centre. It involves giving a direct welcome and ensuring that the unit in which they are staying is warm, welcoming and friendly. It involves setting a contract with the group based on our hopes, fears, expectations and limitations. Above all, it allows, through evolution of the sense of safe space, for people's stories and questions about one another to emerge. In a safe space people can be vulnerable and vulnerability also creates safe space. Safe spaces are also places where the difficult and uncomfortable emotions can be 'held'. Safe spaces are not just neutral spaces – spaces have character and are distinctive.

The telling of stories

We have learnt the importance of people telling their stories. We are 'storied' people, we understand ourselves and what has happened to us and our communities in and through stories. We can decide how we want to tell our story – it is always possible to tell it another way. You cannot tell a story without someone listening to you and you have to tailor the story to reach the other person. What happens when you tell your story in the presence of someone from the 'opposing' community? How do you tell a story that starts a conversation? What happens to you when you listen to their story? Does your story alter? Do you alter? It is always possible to tell it another way and that the 'other' finds a different place in it. It is always possible to hear the other person's story in a different way. And stories can be added to. And there can be a different ending. Story telling and memory can ultimately be a means of reconciliation as we struggle to hear and speak truthfully to each other.

Creative and adventure learning

To support the process of sharing stories whilst also trying to create a sense of community, we had always used different activities. We had a well established set of recreation resources, arts and crafts and we, occasionally, used drama, beach walks and forest walks to provide variety. However, for the most part, these activities were used to fill the 'spaces' when we weren't 'working'. The 'real' work, in the late seventies and early eighties, was in the meeting, the discussion and in the talk. By the early nineties, we began to understand the limitations of talk or discussion.

Often, when we evaluated the group's experience we would regularly find that the group would name the creative learning and recreational activities as having been the most important part of it. Many of the young people and some of the adult groups had little or no experience in and/or comfort with engaging with each other through words. What was done in group settings and how it was done, was much more important than what was said or how clever the use of words might have been. In light of this experience, we began to think more creatively about these activities. Large elements of what had previously been termed 'recreation', were transformed in both content and use to become what we now know as 'adventure learning'. We developed an exciting and diverse range of activities that could be used on or off site. These activities are used to help build groups in terms of the communication, risk taking, problem solving, gender differences and physical support of one another. These activities have become increasingly adapted and designed to create experiences which allow group members to enter new relationships with one another at many different levels.

Our Creative Learning work (art, drama, puppetry, etc) developed in essentially the same way. Our recreational use of arts and crafts had always been well appreciated but the new thinking allowed us to translate and transform many of these activities into discrete activities, which could equally be used to help build and enhance both group processes and the individual experience. Involvement in the arts engages the whole person, 'speaking from the heart' and using his or her creativity and emotions. It can reach our hopes, dreams, aspirations, fears and pain. This can lead to learning and insights that can pave the way for personal and relational change.

The importance of celebration

Because this is often hard work and emotionally draining work we have learnt the importance of celebrating together. One of the biblical images of reconciliation is the messianic banquet. There are times to celebrate our being together, in all our diversity. We bring our gifts to the party.

Not doing things to people

Reconciliation work is about not doing things to other people – making them more tolerant, open, etc. This is a mutual exploration or at least an exploration that I too have gone on. We cannot expect other people to cross boundaries and go on journeys of exploration that involve the 'other' if we have not done so in some way too. One of the big problems that occurs time after time in reconciliation work is that we discover that it is the workers (the custodians of young people or school children) who are often a major barrier to useful work. They cannot cope themselves with issues of diversity or whatever, so how can we expect the groups they work with to do so?

The learning from the people we have met along the way

We have been profoundly influenced by people we have met along the way over the last 40 years. I have only time to mention two – particularly chosen because they illuminate issues to do with reconciliation.

The first was a Dutch man, *Roel Kaptein*. Roel started with a person's questions; these questions could be personal, religious, social or political. He illuminated these questions by the use of pictorial models and by the use of theory derived from the French thinker René Girard. Thus many people learnt about the importance of imitation, rivalry and scapegoating. They were able to see reconciliation in new ways: as undermining exclusionary behaviour and expulsive mechanisms; of (re-)incorporating the vulnerable and scapegoats; and challenging the things which alienate and separate us. Many people were able to see the gospel in a new way. They also learnt about the importance of sticking with their/our questions. 'Head' and 'heart' knowledge was also brought together. Reconciliation was about us, not other people out there. It was not a 'theory' or abstract knowledge.

The second is the work of *Frank Wright*. Frank Wright, who was a Corrymeela member and a political scientist, brilliantly analysed societies where two groups with different national allegiances and identities shared the same territory. He called these societies ethnic frontier societies and Northern Ireland is obviously one such. Ethnic frontier societies are contested spaces characterised by histories of antagonism and lack of trust. In such societies

- There is a lack of ease in the presence of those who are different from 'us'. In a context where suspicions about the intentions of the 'others' abound, a lack of real knowledge about the others breeds speculation, and speculation breeds fear. These fears merely demonise the other, reinforcing separate identities and stereotypes.
- Separate and exclusive identities are insisted upon but there is often insecurity about identity – the 'other' in the same space challenges and problematizes our identity. People proclaim their identity stridently but there is often insecurity underneath.

• There is a deep insecurity about the outcomes of talking about division in a society where relationships between people from different traditions and structures in which people feel safe together are so fragile;
• There is a 'cultural common sense' that supports separation, avoidance and politeness rather than taking risks together about working through issues that touch on core divisions.

Reconciliation work involves the creation of 'space' for open meetings across divisions. It concerns the growth of trust and relationships in order that the difficult and sensitive issues associated with an ethnic frontier society around politics, human rights, equality, education, cultural identity, the economy, social development and law & order can be worked through rather than around. It involves meeting each other across divisions in different ways so as to undermine previous separate certainties. Such possibilities of meeting can often be fragile and hostage to the wider atmosphere of inter-communal fear and violence that may be threatening or occurring. The people who are involved are usually 'exceptions'.

In Corrymeela we were always clear that a stable political settlement was vital for cross-community trust building; without a stable political settlement the work was always at risk. We were also aware that without a certain amount of trust you couldn't have a stable political settlement. Therefore, from our earliest days we ran political conferences and members were involved in political parties.

One of the first conferences was at Easter 1966 and it had the then Prime Minister of Northern Ireland Terence O'Neill speaking. Outside was a certain cleric protesting about sell-out to the enemies of Ulster. This figure was the Rev Ian Paisley – the embodiment of Ulster says No. Some of you may have seen a picture at the end of March 2007 of Ian Paisley sitting down with the Leader of Sinn Fein, the epitome of all he opposed and announcing an agreement which led to the sharing of power between Unionists and Republicans on May 8. Ian Paisley became First Minister. The outsider became insider. The man who always said no said yes.

Ray Davey in the 1960s recognised that something had to change in Northern Ireland. He knew that there that to be new imaginations, new conversations, new meetings and new journeyings. Paisley resisted new imaginations, new conversations, new meetings and new journeyings – and it's now over. There is a sense that Ray Davey was a prophet, and we can see reconciliation work – which may start at the margin and look small and irrelevant – as prophetic activity. That brings us back to the importance of vision, and we may only know about the authenticity of that vision decades later.

We also had conversations with paramilitaries at a time when few wanted to talk to them, encouraging them to become constructively involved in politics and community building. We have learnt that it is important not to write people off as incorrigible 'baddies', no matter what they have done – and this is not to trivialise evil or say wrong does not matter.

Conclusion

In the Northern Ireland painter Colin Middleton's Jacob Wrestling with the Angel (1948) Jacob's raised right hand is big and strong – symbolising the struggle with God. But there is also a delicate, fragile butterfly, signifying the angel/God figure. The butterfly symbolises resurrection and transformation. And transformation does not come without struggle, conflict and pain. In Middleton's picture Jacob's face is anguished and sad. And there are two 'sides' to his coat, one in bright positive colours and the other in dark colours, representing suffering.

Ray Davey, past the destruction of Dresden, saw Easter fitting into "the realness of things, its tragedy, despair and sorrow" but "also climbing up the other side into life and victory over death". These words pull us into the reality of God's reconciling activity and call us, like Ray Davey, to mend brokenness where we find it. And remember the butterfly.

Islamic Care for the Victims of War in Bosnia *

Emina Čorbo-Mešić
Bosnia / Germany, 2013

Personal remarks

The theme, care and counselling or general help for the needy, bothers me and is going with me because of my own Bosnian background from my childhood days. My parents are from East Bosnia, an area that was the scene of repeated brutal attacks on Muslims over the last hundred years. Today this is part of the Republika Srpska, and an area that has suffered the most casualties in the war. I myself was born and raised in Stuttgart, but from childhood, I always heard horrible stories from my grandmother about how they were persecuted by the Serbs in the first and Second World War. Her mother and many relatives were killed in a bestial manner and that just because they were Muslims. In the Bosnian war my grandmother lost her husband and a son. Countless aunts and cousins from paternal and maternal sides were arrested and raped in camps. Some of the husbands were murdered. My parents have tried in various ways to help the relatives, as far as possible.

This war has affected me greatly. The fact that Muslims in Bosnia-Herzegovina were persecuted and killed for their faith, aroused in me a thirst for knowledge, to engage myself even more into my own beliefs and my heritage. Ultimately, those were the reasons why I decided to wear a headscarf. I realized that I was lucky that my parents had come to Germany to work here, because the story seems to repeat itself now to the fourth and fifth generation.

From this background there grew in me the desire to share these matters with people of other faiths and people in general. Until today I am concerned about the question how people can be capable of such cruel things,

* Paper presented at the 25th International Seminar on Intercultural Pastoral Care and Counselling, 2013, in Mainz, Germany. The German version was published in E. Begic, H. Weiß and G. Wenz (eds.), *Barmherzigkeit. Zur sozialen Verantwortung islamischer Seelsorge*, Neukirchen-Vluyn: Neukirchener Verlag 2014, 2014, 89-98.

as were happening in the Bosnian war and still occur elsewhere. How can it be that the story of evil be repeated so often at the same place? And how can you learn to trust people of other faiths, and try to build bridges? I started to engage even more with the inter-religious dialogue and saw it as an important task, so to remind people to remember the war, that victims are not forgotten.

Before I refer specifically to the systematic rape of women during the genocide in the Bosnian War 1992 until 1995, I would like to introduce some important aspects of Islam on living and social action at the beginning of my presentation. And since the effects of such traumatic violence accompany the victims for lifetime, I would like to introduce two organizations that have set themselves primarily the target to help these women medically and psychosocially.

Life and social action in Islam

Life is regarded in Islam as the highest good, which must be protected and preserved. The Qur'an states: "Whoever kills a person, it is as if you had killed all mankind, and whoever saves the life of a human who has saved all mankind." (Al Qur'an 5:35)

From the core of the self-understanding of Islam you can derive the main guiding principles for both, your own life and for living together in a community. The most important task of every devout Muslim is the effort to achieve peace with himself, with his fellow men and his environment, and to be at peace with God according of God's commandments. You should meet the evil with positive attitudes (Al Qur'an 23:96). This reflects the word "Islam": The call to just action is a priority.

On the day of the last judgment each person is accountable of what he has made of his life and how he dealt with his fellow humans and his environment. The day of the last judgment is also the time of absolute justice, which gives hope to those who are in misery.

The relationship to his fellow man reflects the relationship with God. Thus, true religion should always lead to active social behaviour in society. God's mercy encompasses all things (Al Qur'an 7:156), but those who help people are helped by God.[1] The following saying of the Prophet Muhammad shows the high priority of caring for others in Islam:

> Verily, Allah, the Exalted and Glorious, would say on the Day of Resurrection: O son of Adam, I was sick but you did not visit Me. He would say: O my Lord; how

---

[1] Riyad us-Salihin, Hadith No. 233, available at http://islamische-datenbank.de/option,com_riyad/action,viewhadith/chap_nr,27/min,10/show,10/ (accessed 3 August 2015).

could I visit Thee whereas Thou art the Lord of the worlds? Thereupon He would say: Didn't you know that such and such servant of Mine was sick but you did not visit him and were you not aware of this that if you had visited him, you would have found Me by him? O son of Adam, I asked food from you but you did not feed Me. He would say: My Lord, how could I feed Thee whereas Thou art the Lord of the worlds? He said: Didn't you know that such and such servant of Mine asked food from you but you did not feed him, and were you not aware that if you had fed him you would have found him by My side? (The Lord would again say:) O son of Adam, I asked drink from you but you did not provide Me. He would say: My Lord, how could I provide Thee whereas Thou art the Lord of the worlds? Thereupon He would say: Such and such of servant of Mine asked you for a drink but you did not provide him, and had you provided him drink you would have found him near Me.[2]

The family plays a major role in Islam and forms the nucleus of society. The woman and the man are equal in the Qur'an. They are described as protectors of one another (Al Qur'an 9:71). Furthermore, they are referred to as "twin creatures", which complement each other in differences and in perfection. The marriage is viewed as a sign of God in the Qur'an and should be the basis of love and mercy, and provides the fulfilment of human needs and serves as a protecting frame (Al Qur'an 30:21). Only having this background it can be understood, that the core of the deliberate systematic rape was, to destroy the Muslim population and what the devastating effects they have had.

Systematic rape as a means of ethnical cleansing

Of the former 4.4 million inhabitants of Bosnia-Herzegovina hardly a family is not affected by the war. According to the report of "Research and Documentation Center" (DRC), a non-governmental organization founded in 2004 in Sarajevo, this war had between 100,000 and 110,000 deaths, half of them civilians and over 80 % Bosnians. The real figure is considered to be much higher, partly because entire families were killed.[3] There are still 15,000 people who are missing and new mass graves are found. The massacre in the UN-protected zone of Srebrenica, where in 1995 more than 8,000 men and boys were killed, was only the completion of a number of many massacres between 1992 and 1995. The goal was the

[2] Sahih Muslim, transl. Abdul Hamid Siddiqui, Book 32 (*Kitab Al-Birr was-Salat-I-wa'l-Adab*) No. 6232, available at http://www.usc.edu/org/cmje/religious-texts/hadith/muslim/032-smt.php (accessed 3 August 2015).

[3] Cf. e.g. Dzenana Halimovic, "Bosnian Researcher Counts War Dead, and Faces Threats for his Methods", in *Radio Free Europe / Radio Liberty*, 11 Nov. 2008, available at http://www.rferl.org/content/Bosnian_Researcher_Counts_The_Dead_And_Faces_Threats_For_His_Objectivity/1350799.html (accessed 3 August 2015).

large-scale ethnic cleansing of Bosnia-Herzegovina from the Muslim population. Places such as Bratunac (3,604 deaths), Zvornik (4,127 deaths), Vlasenica (2,934 deaths) or Foca (2,805 deaths) are standing for the epitome of the genocide in the Bosnian war.[4]

Very early in the Bosnian war there have been reports of systematic rape as a weapon of war. It is not the first war in which mainly women became victims of sexual violence, but it is the first war that has brought into the recognition the issue and removed the taboo to keep down the issue. In addition to various human rights organizations the UN Security experts appointed by the Commission (Final Report of the United Nations Commission of Experts, 1994) has documented, too, the systematic rape of women in war in October 1992. An estimated 20,000 women fell victim to this systematic rape. The real figure is estimated at up to 50,000. It will most probably not be possible to give exact figures about abused women during the genocide in Bosnia-Herzegovina, as many women were killed or prefer not to talk about what happened with them.[5]

Mostly Serbian soldiers have killed the women. But similar crimes have been committed also by Croatian soldiers in Muslim-Croatian areas. The strategy of the Serbian army was often in a similar manner: First, the towns and villages were bombarded with bombs and grenades to spread fear. Then paramilitary soldiers raided the population that from there on had been exposed to looting, rapes and murders.

After the women and children were separated from the men, they were imprisoned in concentration camps where they were subjected to continuous torture and humiliation. Often they were used as human shields. The age played no role. Girls of 10 years were not spared as older women at the age of 80 years. Often, the women were raped by several men at once and permanently. Many women committed suicide or asked their tormentors to kill them. These crimes were directed against the dignity of Muslim women because of their religious identity.

Both the official political leaders of Serbs, as well as the actual perpetrators were known to the victims. Most of them were neighbours, friends or bridal witnesses who raped and killed. They knew everything about their moral and cultural values, their religious beliefs and their psycho-social environment in which they lived. They also knew the consequences of such a rape in women's lives and also to their family members and to the society as a whole. The aim of this strategy was to destroy the Muslim society and minimize the fertility of families. The women were "injured in their gender

[4] Michael Martens, "Das bosnische Totenbuch", in *Frankfurter Allgemeine Zeitung*, 22 June 2007, available at http://www.faz.net/aktuell/politik/ausland/kriegsopfer-das-bosnische-totenbuch-1437993.html (accessed 3 August 2015).

[5] Cf. *Sexualisierte Kriegsgewalt und ihre Folgen*, ed. Medica Mondiale e.V., Frankfurt a.M.: Mabuse Verlag, 2004, 43-44.

identity"[6] and they were attacked and their role in society vehemently. This had the strong weakening of Muslim society and result in the decline of the population.

Consequences of rape

Many women were imprisoned intentionally in camps for such a long time so that abortion was no longer possible. Some women kept their children, others gave them for adoption. The aim of the systematic rape in addition to the systematic executions was to reduce the number of Muslims on the Balkans, not just for a short term, but for a long term. Many young women and girls did not survive these rapes, and if so, they are often physically and mentally not able to marry or are able to think about having children at all. The social environment is affected by these cruel acts. Very often the women were raped in the presence of their husbands, children or other family members. Some women have been abandoned by their husbands; others do not even know about it. For women who have not been abandoned by their husbands, the family provides an important psycho-social support in the overcoming the trauma.

In addition to the many physical injuries, the psychological consequences of rape are usually much more severe. According to studies by Harry Feldmann, 98 % of the women feel at the moment of the rape "a sense of desperate helplessness".[7] In the long term, about 85 % of the victims develop "sexual defense, phobias, and 72 % change their external life style". Many women suffer from depression and anxiety as well as long-term insomnia. Many of the women are not able to go to a job and take care for themselves.

Breaking the silence

The film "Grbavica"

For a long time the systematic rape was a taboo and no one wanted to speak publicly about it. And no one was talking about the fate of unwanted children who were born after rape. The film *Grbavica*, which won the "Golden Bear" 2006 in Berlin, led to a significant rethinking and to improving the legal status of the victims. The director Jasmila Zbanic watched as teenager women who were taken away in buses and brought back in a

---

[6] Cf. Ingeborg Joachim, in *Sexualisierte Kriegsgewalt*, 57.

[7] Harry Feldmann, *Vergewaltigung und ihre psychischen Folgen: Ein Beitrag zur posttraumatischen Belastungsreaktion*, Stuttgart: Ferdinand Enke Verlag, 1992, 27.

terrible state. These experiences motivated the young woman to make a film on this subject.[8]

The film tells of a woman who was a victim of such rape at war, and lives with her daughter in Sarajevo. One day it happens that the daughter learns the truth about her origins, which leads to a new beginning of their relationship. This film moved many people – and has thus has become a means for them to be aware of the suffering of these women and to work for them. Two examples for that:

The therapy centre Medica Mondiale

Within four months, the women's therapy centre Medica Mondiale was launched in Zenica by the gynecologist Monika Hauser in 1993. The centre focuses on "the traumatisation of women as specific human rights violation through sexual violence in war".[9] The aim of Medica Mondiale was from the beginning to provide for the affected women a safe space where they can receive medical and psychosocial care. This was of vital importance for the victims, as they otherwise had no chance to receive help. The organization serves for over 30,000 women and girls, and operates in eight other countries. Up to 985 women and 727 children could be materially assisted by mother-to-child care. From the beginning, the centre worked with Bosnian female doctors, psychologists and social workers. It was organized locally and the entire staff was educated for a sensitive treatment of the affected women. In 2008, Dr. Monika Hauser received the Right Livelihood Award, the so-called alternative Nobel Prize, "for her tireless commitment to working with women who have experienced the most horrific sexual violence in some of the most dangerous countries in the world, and campaigning for them to receive social recognition and compensation."[10]

Medica Mondiale is committed as an advocate for women as victims by addressing the public rape as a weapon of war, breaking the taboo. The centre has developed methods and concepts that take the "political and social conditions" into account in addition to the individual suffering. The women are viewed not only as victims but as "survivors who have managed, despite the traumatic experiences, to give meaning to their lives." Medica Mondiale tries to support the women so that they improve their long-term life situation through their own engagement. For example, the centre offered 600 women the opportunity to be trained as a hairdresser, seamstress or knitter with machines. In addition, English and computer courses

---

[8] Cf. Chantal Louis, *Monika Hauser: Eine Ärztin im Einsatz für kriegstraumatisierte Frauen*, Zürich: rüffer & rub, 2010, 19; cf. also the interview with Jasmila Zbanic, available at http://www.coop99.at/grbavica_website/ (accessed 3 August 2015).

[9] *Sexualisierte Kriegsgewalt*, 9

[10] The Right Livelihood Award, http://www.rightlivelihood.org/hauser.html (accessed 3 August 2015).

were offered. Only through this help it has been possible for many women to be able to think of an independent future.

Even after the twentieth anniversary, the work in Bosnia has not become easier. Although the Medica centre in Zenica cooperates with more ministries and state organizations than before, it suffers from scarcity of funds. Medica Mondiale is the only centre that cares holistically for the raped women, but it is not easy to convince the state, who has scarce resources, that these women require a tremendous support even 20 years after the war. Since the foreign donations are greatly reduced, in 2007 two of the three project houses had to be closed, although every year hundreds of women come to the Medica Mondiale centre.

Some women only find the courage to speak about their suffering now, others meet their rapists on the street or during the process. Therefore for many women it is impossible to return to their hometowns. Women, who have an unplanned pregnancy, are confronted during their whole life with the rape and need special assistance – and also do their children.

The association "Zene zrtve – Rata" ("Women: Victims of War")

Bakira Hasecic, 55, and her underage daughters were raped and tortured by Serb soldiers in Visegrad. Her sister did not survive the rape. The perpetrators were neighbours and close friends, with whom they had lived together peacefully before the war.[11] She herself had learned in her childhood from her father that Serbian soldiers had a similar number of Muslims in Visegrad killed in World War II, but she could hardly believe these facts. She asked the perpetrators to kill her, as many women have done. But they did not. She says: after that she had sworn to defend herself.

When she lived in freedom again, she tried to come to terms with her trauma by talking. Her goal was to fight to ensure that the perpetrators receive appropriate punishment for their deeds. In 2003 she founded the organization "Women: Victims of War", after she had seen with some other women in Visegrad, that the rapists and murderers remained in good positions and were still free. The women began to look for witnesses and gathered important information about the crimes. Thanks to their commitment Milan Lukic, the "butcher from Visegrad", was brought to the tribunal of war crimes in The Hague in the year 2000, after the rapes previously were not even mentioned in the indictment. Lukic burned in a house 70 women, children and elderly people who were captured there.

Another problem is also that the police of Republika Srpska (Serb Republic) to the present war have not arrested other criminals of the war. Any debt is denied and the perpetrators enjoy a high reputation and are hailed as

[11] Erich Rathfelder, "Die Unversöhnliche", in *taz – die tageszeitung*, 25 July 2008, available at http://www.taz.de/1/ archiv/.de/ (accessed 31 August 2013).

heroes. The tireless struggle of these women for justice had the result that Lukic was also accused of rape and that ten more murderers and rapists were arrested.

On 24 May 2013 Bakira Hasecic has organized a commemorative event in Foca, 3,000 people threw roses into the river Drina in memory of the victims. Several times she was arrested by the Serbian police because of their prejudice. A board to commemorate the victims was destroyed by the ruling Karadzic-SDS party, instead they erected a monument for Serbian soldiers and Russian mercenaries who have also murdered and raped in the war.

The association has 1,550 members, among them 220 men.[12] Among the women are 10 Orthodox, 41 Catholic and 1,499 Muslims. 54 women gave birth to children from the rapes. Among the men are two Catholic and 218 Muslims. The association is funded by donations and occasional support of the Government of Canton Sarajevo, without that the work would not be possible.

The objectives of the association "Women: Victims of War"

The main tasks and objectives of the association are the research, collection and documentation of information and data on all aspects of the suffering of women during the war in Bosnia and Herzegovina. This is done to keep the memory of the victims. Furthermore, the legal and moral support of women during legal processes is of the utmost importance. In addition, there are many other tasks that I would like to explain in our discussion.

The association is also supported by the Islamic Community of Bosnia-Herzegovina, which has led to a greater opening of the Islamic communities to this topic. In a meeting with the former Grand Mufti of the Islamic Community of Bosnia and Herzegovina and President of the Bosniak Congress (Reisu-l-ulema), Dr. Mustafa Cerić, Mrs. Bakira Hasecic explained the problems with which the association and the women have to fight: the rights of women who have been the victims of this war because they have been raped and often have to live at the poverty level without anybody.[13] She also complained about the fact that the association does not receive sufficient support as a non-governmental organization, considering its commitment on the path to truth and justice and the expenditures of the association. Bakira Hasecic emphasized that they fought for three years for the "Law of Protection of Civilian Victims of the Bosnian war", which

---

[12] http://www.zena-zrtva-rata.ba/ (accessed 25 August 2013).

[13] See the report "Reis-l-ulema primio Bakiru Hasecic", publ. by The Islamic Community in Bosnia and Herzegovina, 29 November 2007, available at http://www.rijaset.ba/index.php?option=com_content&view=article&id=2364:reisu-l-ulema-primio-bakiru-hase-podrcka-udrurenju-rena-rrtva-rata&catid=40:minine-vijesti/ (accessed 3 August 2015).

officially was enforced on September 1, 2006, but in reality is not put into power anywhere. This is the first post-war country where women, who ware raped, have obtained a similar legal status like war veterans. Raped women and men have the right to receive a payment of about 514 Mark, equivalent to 250 Euros. The former Grand Mufti of the Islamic Community of Bosnia and Herzegovina and President of the World Bosniak Congress (Reisu-l-ulema), Dr. Mustafa Cerić, praised the courage and strength of women of this association on their way to justice. He appealed to those who have responsibility and are able to help the victims, to do so, and that he himself is committed to do everything in his power, to help these women.

From an Islamic perspective, the entire community is invited to support victims in their efforts to find a way to a normal life. This is part of their responsibility to their fellow humans. If you have managed to read through a testimony of a raped woman in Bosnia, you will understand that these women deserve high respect for their courage and strength to make such a testimony or to go public in court. And so I end my presentation with a statement of Bakira Hasecic:

> We have the right of truth and justice, and are the perpetrators of just punishment. Women as victims of war are most important witnesses. All remind us that those people, who have committed war crimes of any kind, live in this society. These women show new courage every day by bearing witness in statements and public appearances. Our truth is our reality in which we live, sleep and wake up. It is a lesson that should be learned from each one of us, so that such a thing never happens again. [14]

[14] Bakira Hasecic in an interview with Bedrudin Gusic, posted 19 November 2011, available at http://bedrudingusic.wordpress.com/2011/11/19/bakira-hasecic-predsjednica-udruzenja-„zena-zrtva-rata-iz-sarajeva-bakira-hasecic-predsjednica-udruzenja-„zena-zrtva-rata-iz-sarajeva/ (accessed 3 August 2015), my translation.

Diversity Management in European Healthcare Organizations:

The Catholic Chaplain as Advocate *

Dominiek Lootens
Belgium, 2014

In 2011 *Zorgnet Vlaanderen*[1] released an important ethical recommendation on 'Proper care in ethnic-cultural diversity'. In this document, they examine how caregivers can provide care in an ethically responsible manner to clients with a diverse ethnic-cultural background. Although this recommendation focuses on the treatment of patients and residents, it likewise pays attention to an employee policy that aims at diversity.[2]

The development of such an employee policy requires a strategic management that connects with the specific identity of the healthcare organization.[3] Structural and cultural change and the provision of diversity training are included in that strategy.[4] Developing such a strategy will not be possible without the cooperation of the employees. Research has demon-

---

* Paper presented at the 26th International Seminar on Intercultural Pastoral Care and Counselling, 2014, at Mennorode, Netherlands. An earlier Dutch version of this article was published in Caritas Vlaanderen (ed.), *Jaarverslag 2013*, Brussels, 2014, 86-99. I wish to thank the group of Flemish Catholic chaplains and colleagues who have discussed this text with me: Steven Cappellen, Heidi De Clercq, Koen De Fruyt, Paul Eylenbosch, Lucia Goubert, Dik Madder, Jan Michels, Rony Timmermans, Ingrid Van den Akker, Anne Vandenhoeck, Ilse Van Gorp, Lieve Van Malderen, Frederique Vanneuville, Liselotte Vanooteghem and Filip Witdouck

[1] Zorgnet Vlaanderen is an employers' organization uniting more than 500 private social profit organizations situated in the Flemish part of Belgium: hospitals, care provisions for elderly and organizations providing mental health care. Taken together, these organizations employ more than 80.000 employees.

[2] Zorgnet Vlaanderen, *Ethisch advies 15: Goede zorg bij etnisch-culturele diversiteit*, Brussels, 2011, 33-35.

[3] L. van Braeckel, "Tijd voor diversiteit: Zorgsector zoekt allochtoon zoekt werk", in *Weliswaar, 112*, June-July 2013, 4-7.

[4] D. Marrill-Sands, E. Holvino and J. Cumming, *Working with Diversity: A Framework for Action, Working Paper 24,* Boston: Center for Gender in Organizations, Simmons School of Management, 2000, 65-71.

strated that it is important that policy can rely on sufficient advocates.[5] These social change agents can be found at every level of the organization. In this article we assume that the Catholic chaplain can be one of those advocates.[6]

The text consists of three parts. In the first part we clarify what we mean when we speak of the Catholic chaplain as advocate. Next we give a broad definition of diversity. We do so from critical perspectives. We distinguish nine possible forms of diversity, which includes ethnic-cultural and religious diversity. Finally we provide an ideal type overview of possible motifs that policymakers and HR managers can make use of when they select and hire candidate employees from social minorities. These motifs influence the range of action of Catholic chaplains and other advocates.

The second part offers a Catholic-inspired ethical frame of reference for policymakers, Catholic chaplains and other advocates. For them this can serve as a foundation and source of inspiration for working on diversity in the context of their own healthcare organizations.

In the third part we offer a few practical points of consideration for Catholic chaplains. These can also be useful for policymakers and other advocates. They deal with self-knowledge, supporting and learning with employees from the social majority and from social minorities and stimulating structural and cultural change from below. We then bring this article to a close with a brief conclusion.

The Catholic chaplain as advocate

For some time, the Catholic chaplaincy in Europe is in full swing. There is talk of deepening: Catholic chaplains make use of professional reference frameworks that have been tested in practice. In addition there is also talk of broadening. Catholic chaplains assume responsibility on different levels: in relation to patients, residents and their relatives, in relation to employees, in relation to (the policy of) the healthcare organization, and in relation to the wider society. Finally the Catholic chaplaincy has also

---

[5] M. Chesler, A. Lewis and J. Crowfoot, *Challenging Racism in Higher Education: Promoting Justice*, Lanham: Rowman & Littlefield, 2005, 191-192 and 295; M. Janssens, F. Chiapparino, N. Ferro, K. Hamde, N. Wåhlin, A. Nilsson, R.N. Landsberg and P. Zanoni, *Diversity in Organizations: Towards a Non-Essentialistic, Dynamic Approach. Position Paper of Research Task 1.1.*, SUS.DIV, 2005, 20.

[6] M. Threlfall-Holmes, "Exploring Models of Chaplaincy", in M. Threlfall-Holmes and M. Newitt (eds.), *Being a Chaplain*, London: SPCK, 2011, 124; B. J. McClure, "Women, Professional Work, and Diversity: Pastoral Theology in the Midst of Globalization", in J. Stevenson-Moessner and T. Snorton (eds.), *Women Out of Order: Risking Change and Creating Care in a Multicultural World*, Minneapolis: Fortress Press, 2010, 270-289.

become more pragmatic. Catholic chaplains must see to it that they go about their work in a manner that is sufficiently efficient and effective.[7]

One of the tasks that Catholic chaplains fulfil is supporting employees.[8] They can take on that support from various perspectives:[9]

a) Catholic chaplains can offer support from a spiritual perspective, when for instance an employee would like to reflect on existential questions.

b) In addition Catholic chaplains can also act from a pastoral-psychological perspective, when for example an employee needs counselling in a crisis experience.

c) Catholic chaplains can also take up their task towards employees from a societal or organizational perspective. To support a co-worker in one's efforts at an ecologically sustainable work context can be an example thereof.[10]

Although the three perspectives mentioned are distinct, in practice they often are intertwined. Supporting employees regarding diversity is linked more profoundly to the last perspective.

From their frame of reference Catholic chaplains can choose to be advocates on the level of diversity within their organization. Policy can also explicitly assign them the task to be one of the advocates. As advocates, Catholic chaplains can react against expressed or subtle forms of discrimination in the work environment, support and stimulate employees on this theme, and work together as much as possible with other advocates and with policy. Catholic chaplains in European healthcare organizations are well-suited for this because they avail of the necessary social skills and because they can move freely on all levels within the organization.[11]

---

[7] Caritas Vlaanderen, *Pastoraal advies: Spiritualiteit en pastorale zorg in een christelijk geïnspireerd woonzorgcentrum*, Brussels, 2014, 15; Zorgnet Vlaanderen, *Pastoraal advies 1, Pastorale zorg in christelijk geïnspireerde ziekenhuizen*, Brussels, 2008, 5-7.

[8] Caritas Vlaanderen, *Spiritualiteit*, 17-18; K.J. Flannely G.F. Handzo, A.J. Weaver and W.J. Smith, "A National Survey of Health Care: Administrator's Views on the Importance of Various Chaplain Roles", in *The Journal of Pastoral Care & Counseling, Vol. 59 Nos. 1-2*, 2005, 87-96.

[9] D. Nauer, "De pastor als profeet?!", in D. Lootens (red.), *Ontsluitende zorg: De toekomst van het pastorale beroep*, Antwerpen: Halewijn, 2011, 42-59; D. Nauer, "Profetisch-kritisch handelen vanuit het perspectief van de pastorale zorg", in A. Dillen et al. (reds.), *De moed om te spreken en te handelen: Profetisch pastoraat*, Antwerpen: Halewijn, 2009, 132-172; D. Nauer, *Seelsorge: Sorge um die Seele*, 2nd ed., Stuttgart: Kohlhammer, 2010, 150-227.

[10] D. Lootens, "MVO als kernstrategie voor zorg- en welzijnsorganisaties", in D. Lootens (red.), *Mensgericht sociaal ondernemen*, Antwerpen: Garant, 2014, 27-47.

[11] C. Leget, "De rol van de pastor in multidisciplinaire spirituele zorg", in Lootens (red.), *Ontsluitende zorg*, 34; Zorgnet Vlaanderen, *Pastoraal advies 2: Competentieprofiel pastores*, Brussel, 2011.

At the same time, however, the question arises whether Catholic chaplains avail of sufficient possibilities to do this. Since they are few in number they themselves form a numerical minority within the healthcare organization. Just like employees from social minorities they can be confronted with structural and cultural barriers.[12] They belong to a double culture: that of Christian faith and the Catholic tradition, and that of the services in which they work.[13] That double identity sees to it that they themselves are challenged to acquire an integrated place. Nonetheless, until recently Catholic chaplains took a privileged place within European healthcare organizations.[14]

Diversity in organizations

Diversity can include a number of factors. It has been argued from critical perspectives to treat diversity within organizations from the point of view of social minorities: women, gays and lesbians, ethnic-cultural and religious minorities, people with learning difficulties, senior citizens over 50, low-skilled workers, single parents and persons in poverty.[15] By opting for critical perspectives in this article we concur with the critique on the classic approach to diversity.[16]

Firstly, in critical perspectives it is emphasised that the characteristics ascribed to social minorities are a social construct. In a classic approach on diversity unchangeable characteristics are often attributed to social minori-

[12] F. Norwood, "The Ambivalent Chaplain: Negotiating Structural and Ideological Difference on the Margins of Modern-Day Medicine", in *Medical Anthropology, 25*, 2006, 1-29.

[13] C. Leget, "De rol van de pastor", 30-31.

[14] S. Gilliat-Ray, M.M. Ali and S. Pattison, *Understanding Muslim Chaplaincy*, Farnham: Ashgate, 2013, 167-189; bell hooks, *Feminist Theory: From Margin to Center*, 2nd ed., Brooklyn, NY: South End, 2000, 45-47; B.J. McClure, *Moving Beyond Individualism in Pastoral Care and Counseling*, Eugene, OR: Wipf & Stock, 2010, 256; L. Schlosser, "Christian Privilege: Breaking the Sacred Taboo", in *Journal of Multicultural Counseling and Development, 31*, 2003, 44-51; T. Seifert, "Understanding Christian Privilege: Managing the Tension of Spiritual Plurality", in *About Campus*, May-June 2007, 10-17.

[15] K. van Laer, M. Verbruggen and M. Janssens, *Diversiteit in loopbanen. Over (on)gelijke kansen op de arbeidsmarkt*, Leuwen: Acco, 2011.

[16] M. Janssens and P. Zanoni, "Diversities for Many Services: Theorizing Diversity (Management) in Service Companies", in *Human Relations, Vol. 58 No. 3*, 2005, 313-314; P. Prasad, K.J. Pringle and A.M. Konrad, "Examining the Contours of Workplace Diversity: Concepts, Contexts and Challenges", in A.M. Konrad et al. (eds.), *Handbook of Workplace Diversity*, London: Sage, 2006, 1-22; P. Zanoni, M. Janssens, Y. Benschop and S. Nkomo, "Guest Editorial: Unpacking Diversity, Grasping Inequality: Rethinking Difference Through Critical Perspectives", in *Organization, Vol. 17 No. 9*, 2010, 9-29.

ties. By doing so, as social minorities they would be distinguished in an essential manner from the social majority. In principle critical perspectives proceed from the notion that social minorities can also be looked at differently. An organization with a well-developed diversity policy can consequently exert influence on how employees from the social majority look at social minorities.

Secondly, it has been pointed out that the individuals concerned are often not sufficiently taken into account in the development of a diversity policy. Social minorities are usually approached as a group, without sufficiently figuring out how those concerned consider their status as minority. The danger exists that their own strength and professionalism are thereby much relegated to the background.[17]

Thirdly, it has been emphasised that social minorities often have to deal with a combination of social identities. For instance, one can think of a low-skilled employee with a migrant background. As a result, it is not evident for policy and for the advocates to put themselves in the shoes of such individuals in their specific work experiences.

Fourthly, diversity also has to do with contextual hindrances and barriers. The manner in which an organization functions is often perceived by the social majority as neutral towards diversity. Whether an employee attains one's rights or not, seems to depend only on his or her personal efforts. And yet in practice mention is often made of structural and cultural barriers that make it extra difficult for social minorities to take part in an equal manner in the life of the organization.

Policy on diversity in organizations

For some time, European healthcare organizations have been challenged to implement actively an employee policy on the level of diversity.[18] That development is likewise the result of initiatives from the political field, of the increase in diversity among clients, and of the influence of interest groups. Policymakers and HR managers can have one or more motifs to employ candidates from social minorities. As an ideal type, four motifs can be distinguished.[19]

---

[17] M. Janssens and P. Zanoni, "Deconstructing Difference: The Rhetoric of Human Resource Manager's Diversity Discourses", in *Organization Studies, 25*, 2003, 55-74; P. Zanoni and M. Janssens, "Minority Employees Engaging with (Diversity) Management: An Analysis of Control, Agency, and Micro-Emancipation", in *Journal of Management Studies, 44*, 2007, 1371-1397.

[18] L. van Braeckel, "Tijd voor diversiteit", 4-7; A. Klarsfeld (ed.), *International Handbook on Diversity Management at Work: Country Perspectives on Diversity and Equal Treatment*, Cheltenham: Edward Elgar, 2010.

[19] M. Alvesson and Y.D. Billing, *Understanding Gender and Organizations*, 2nd ed., London: Sage, 2009, 164-187; R.J. Ely and D. Meyerson, "Theories of Gender in

Ethics

Difference			Equality
	Alternative values	Equal opportunity	
	Special Contribution	Meritocracy	

Efficiency

Meritocracy

A first motif can be described as meritocracy. Here the emphasis lies on efficiency and equality. A shortage in the labour market can be a reason for recruiting candidates from social minorities. Since insufficient employees are found in the normal recruitment circuits, new channels will have to be tapped. The intention is to ensure sufficient personnel, to increase the efficiency of service. The recruitment criterion applied is that employees from social minorities should possess the same competencies as those from the existing majority.

The advantage of this approach is that employees from minorities are addressed as to their professionalism. The disadvantage is that in the recruitment of these employees only the perspective of the healthcare organization is taken into account. When they do not fully meet the required profile, they are likely to fall by the wayside. In a meritocracy motif, one can choose to remedy this by offering professional training or by means of mentoring. Nonetheless, in the one-sided use of this motif it seems that social minorities are to be found in the lower echelons of the organization.

Organizations: A New Approach to Organizational Analysis and Change", in B.M. Staw and R.I. Sutton (eds.), *Research in Organizational Behavior*, New York: JAI Press, 2000, 103-152; D.A. Thomas and R.J. Ely, "Making Differences Matter: A New Paradigm for Managing Diversity", in R.J. Ely et al. (eds.), *Reader in Gender, Work and Organization*, Malden, MA: Blackwell, 2003, 362-377; P. Zanoni, A. Nilsson, M. Janssens and N. Wåhlin, "Towards Sustainable Diversity in Organizations: Lessons from Good Diversity Management Practices", in M. Janssens et al. (eds.), *The Sustainability of Cultural Diversity, Nations, Cities and Organizations*, Cheltenham: Edward Elgar, 2010, 261-280.

Special contribution
In the second motif emphasis is put on the special contribution that employees from minorities can deliver. The starting point here is difference and efficiency. Since the client base is becoming more diverse it is advisable that the personnel base also becomes varied. Employees from minorities possess specific competencies whereby they can be given special tasks: for instance as mediator or as interpreter. From the motif of special contribution, policymakers can choose to organize specific training on diversity.

The advantage of this approach is that the uniqueness of employees from social minorities becomes acknowledged explicitly. A disadvantage can be that the professionalism they share with other employees is pushed more to the background. Their professional conduct is thus appreciated insufficiently. The danger exists that they are strongly expected to concentrate mainly on specific target groups. Thus they cannot exert enough influence on the development of core activities and the decision-making within the service.

Equal opportunity
The third motif is political and ethical in nature. The emphasis lies on a policy of equal opportunity. The service assumes that in the past too few employees from social minorities were recruited. They react positively to the incentives given by the government on the matter. They want to achieve a more equitable balance in the personnel base. They thus adapt, for example, the recruitment procedure so that it corresponds more to the needs of applicants from minorities. The service then actively seeks out candidates from social minorities. For instance, they work together with interest groups or they appeal to the network of employees from minorities.

The advantage of this approach is that one actively does away with a number of structural obstacles. The disadvantage is that this manner of working can evoke resistance amongst the employees from the existing majority. Employees from minorities appear to be unfairly advantaged. They are seen mainly as representatives of a certain minority group and not as equal professionals. The stereotypes that belong to a certain group are hereby confirmed.

Alternative values
A last motif puts the emphasis on both ethical principles as well as on the acknowledgement of difference. The starting point with this approach is that the recruitment of employees from social minorities can lead to a broadening of the range and a renewal of the current practice of work. A one-sided instrumental and bureaucratic development of the core activities is hereby fundamentally questioned. One strives for an in-depth cultural

change from the bottom up, whereby everyone's contribution is counted. One wants to arrive at a creative and sustainable learning environment that responds to the complexity of the demand on care and support.

The advantage of this approach is that the choice for recruiting employees from minorities is placed within a broader project of organizational change that is value-orientated. In the range, they want to create space for experimentation and renewal. Just like all other collaborators, employees from minorities can deliver a specific contribution here. The disadvantage of this approach is that it is not evident to take along the entire organization in this. It is not easy to maintain the orientation towards a sustainable cultural change all throughout. Moreover, the danger exists that insufficient attention is paid to the structural obstacles that nonetheless confront employees from social minorities.

Policy on diversity and the Catholic chaplain as advocate

When Catholic chaplains want to act efficiently as advocates on diversity, it makes sense that they have a sufficient view on the motifs used by the healthcare organization's management and HR in their policy on diversity. The Catholic chaplains' room for manoeuver will differ depending on the motifs. With the meritocracy motif, the chance is slight that Catholic chaplains will be addressed as advocates by the management. After all in this perspective the emphasis lies in the efficient input of technical competencies and in instrumental merits. In the motifs on special contribution and equal opportunity, the chance is greater that Catholic chaplains are given the task to act as one of the advocates on diversity. In the motif on alternative values, management will most likely explicitly request Catholic chaplains and other advocates to collaborate on a value-orientated organizational change from the bottom up.

A Catholic-inspired ethical frame of reference

When employees and policymakers want to act responsibly on the level of diversity, it is necessary and meaningful that they appeal to an ethical frame of reference. In what follows, we distinguish ten substantive criteria that can be found in Catholic Social Thought.[20] This Catholic-inspired frame of reference offers an ethical foundation upon which one can build on diversity within the context of one's own healthcare organization. Policymakers, Catholic chaplains and other advocates can find inspiration therein.

---

[20] D.G. Groody, *Globalization, Spirituality and Justice*, Maryknoll, NY: Orbis, 2012, 91-121; F. Kammer, *Doing Faithjustice: An Introduction to Catholic Social Thought*, New York: Paulist, 2004, 126-128.

The dignity of the person
The dignity of the person has its religious foundation in the presence of God in every human being. From an ethical standpoint, this means that policymakers, Catholic chaplains and other advocates are invited to uphold in their own work contexts for the dignity of other people, regardless their gender, sexual orientation, ethnic-cultural and religious backgrounds, physical and mental capabilities, age, training, family circumstances and class.

Life as a gift
In Catholic Social Thought, the sanctity of human life is a central theme. Concretely, this implies the task in society to resist situations and practices that form a threat to the giftedness of life. Examples of societal threats are inhumane living conditions, environmental pollution, racism, sexism, abuse of children and women, poverty and unjust working conditions.

God's liberating deeds
The uniqueness of God becomes manifest in the acts and deeds of Jesus of Nazareth. Herein lies the conviction that God loves every human being unconditionally. In following Jesus, Catholic chaplains, other advocates and policymakers can stand up in their work contexts for compassion and social justice.

Freedom as right and responsibility
The human person is created as a free being. Ethically speaking, this means that the person is challenged to deal with that freedom responsibly. Policymakers, Catholic chaplains and other advocates can see it as their task within their own work contexts to support others in their endeavours for freedom and responsibility.

Preferential option for the poor
The preferential option for the poor is a central theme in Catholic Social Thought. Catholic chaplains, other advocates and policymakers can consider themselves thus challenged to stand by those who are marginalised by society and its structures, and to collaborate with them on achieving liberation and integral human development.

Human interconnectedness
The solidarity between people forms a central value. This is not a vague sympathy with the suffering and injustice of others. It is about a concrete commitment in the awareness that every person is responsible for other persons. Here one speaks of a worldwide interconnectedness that surpasses generations. With the Biblical view on peace and social justice as a source of

inspiration, policymakers, Catholic chaplains and other advocates can consider themselves challenged in their own work contexts to deal with conflicts non-violently.[21]

Analysis of social reality

To act ethically does not only begin from a spontaneous indignation. Acting responsibly occurs within a serious analysis of the social context where one finds oneself. One hereby avoids giving simple answers to complex questions.

A more humane societal plan

Society does not evolve in an arbitrary direction. What counts as a central criterion in the evaluation of societal developments is more humanity. From this one can question oneself when it turns out within one's own work context that emphasis is laid one-sidedly on power, control or profitability.[22]

The involvement of all people in developing the social order

Upholding social justice cannot be entrusted only to specialists, among whom are politicians, labour unions, managers or interest groups. This is about a commonly shared responsibility. The principle of subsidiarity counts here. This means that all those involved are challenged within their own work contexts to lay down the steps in that regard.[23]

Ecological responsibility

Upholding solidarity in society does not take place detached from an involvement with the natural environment. Globally, it is often the weakest who are confronted the most with the effects of human activity on the environment and the climate. Healthcare organizations are themselves likewise challenged to implement an ecologically sustainable policy.[24] Standing up for humans and for the environment in one's own work context can go hand in hand.

Catholic Social Thought offers to policymakers, Catholic chaplains and other advocates a Catholic inspired ethical frame of reference. Within their

---

[21] J. Van den Berghe, "Geweldloze communicatie in pastorale contexten", in A. Dillen and D. Pollefeyt (red.), *Ga nu allen in vrede! Omgaan met macht en conflicten in pastorale contexten*, Leuven: Davidsfonds, Pax Christi Vlaanderen, 2010, 55-67.

[22] Zorgnet Vlaanderen, *Together We Care: Ziekenhuizen als schakels in een keten van zorg*, Leuven: Acco, 2013, 26-27.

[23] Kammer, *Doing Faithjustice*, 229-230.

[24] Lootens, "MVO als kernstrategie", 27-47.

organization context they are invited to weigh out and legitimate their own commitment and choices in dialogue with that framework.

Practical focus points

In what follows, we shall enumerate a number of concrete focus points that Catholic chaplains can take up in practice when they fulfil the role of advocate on diversity.[25] Which focus points they shall concretely tackle will depend among others on the possibilities that are offered to them from the context wherein they work. These are focus points that can likewise be relevant to other advocates and policymakers.

Self-knowledge

• Identifying your different social identities (majority and/or minority), acknowledging their mutual interaction, the manner in which those identities change in the course of your life and can acquire another meaning depending on the context.[26]
• Critically reflecting on your own role in relation to power, privilege and discrimination in your daily life, and arriving at a concrete undertanding on the matter.
• Reading and studying on the theme of diversity, whereby your insight can grow on themes like power, privilege, discrimination, solidarity and social change.[27]
• Consciously reflecting on and recognising the personal and professional challenges that are part of acting as advocate.[28]

---

[25] D.J. Goodman, *Promoting Diversity and Social Justice: Educating People from Privileged Groups*, 2nd ed., New York: Routledge, 2011; D. Meyerson, *Rocking the Boat: How to Make Change Without Making Trouble*, Boston, MA: Harvard Business Press, 2008; D. Meyerson, "Radical Change, the Quiet Way", in *Harvard Business Review*, October 2001, 92-100; D. Meyerson and M. Scully, "Tempered Radicalism and the Politics of Ambivalence and Change", in *Organization Science, Vol. 6 No. 5*, 1995, 585-600; R. Reason and E.M. Broido, "Issues and Strategies for Social Justice Allies (and the Student Affairs Professionals Who Hope to Encourage Them)", in R.D. Reason et al. (eds.), *Developing Social Justice Allies*, (*New Directions for Student Services, 110*), San Francisco: Wiley, 2005, 81-89.
[26] R. Ely, "The Role of Dominant Identity and Experience in Organizational Work on Diversity, in Jackson", in S.E. Jackson and M.N. Ruderman (eds.), *Diversity in Work Teams: Research Paradigms for a Changing Workplace*, Washington, DC: American Psychological Association, 1995, 161-186; Meyerson, *Rocking the Boat*, 19-33 and 155-164.
[27] Bell hooks, *Writing Beyond Race: Living Theory and Practice*, New York: Routledge, 2013, 160-164; hooks, *Feminist Theory*, 32-33 and 108-116; A.G. Johnson, *Privilege, Power and Difference*, 2nd ed., New York: Mc-Craw-Hill, 2006.

• Reflecting on your own competencies. Perhaps you are familiar with organising trainings, but you have less experience in policy negotiations. Perhaps you have much experience in counselling employees and less in reacting directly on discriminatory comments. Being familiar with and developing your own competencies help in contributing effectively to social change as advocate.[29]
• Being capable of clarifying why you are taking up this role. What motivates you? How does this work relate to your values and faith?[30]
• Clarifying what the taking up of this role as advocate gives you.[31] Being aware that your work as Catholic chaplain shall increase in quality when discrimination in your work context decreases can help you persevere in moments of difficulty.
• Avoiding impulsive actions out of guilt or shame, in favour of actions that are based on reflection and cooperation.

Actions

Supporting and learning with employees from the social majority
• Integrating your role as advocate in all your daily contacts. Diversity is not only a theme during specific training moments, but is equally pertinent for instance during interdisciplinary briefings.[32]
• Reacting as such to discriminatory comments and behaviours so that the other can learn from them and not be embarrassed or put on show.[33]
• Developing skills in dealing with stereotype and defensive reactions of employees from the social majority.[34]
• Building up a relationship of trust with employees from the social majority by committing oneself to a personal and professional cooperation in the long term.
• Inviting employees from the social majority to take up along with you the role of advocate.

Supporting and learning with employees from social minorities
• Listening. Not supposing that you are an expert. No matter how long you have already been an advocate, continuing to learn with employees from social minorities.

---

[28] Meyerson, *Rocking the Boat*, 141-155; Meyerson and Scully, "Tempered Radicalism", 588-594.
[29] Goodman, *Promoting Diversity*, 157-165 and 170-177.
[30] Ibid., 121-156.
[31] Ibid., 101-120.
[32] Meyerson, "Radical Change", 96-97.
[33] Meyerson, *Rocking the Boat*, 57-76.
[34] Goodman, *Promoting Diversity*, 165-170; Meyerson, *Rocking the Boat*, 41-43 and 152-153.

• Approaching employees from social minorities as individuals and professionals, and not merely as representatives of groups with a diverse background.[35]
• Making your contacts at work more diverse. Choosing consciously to cooperate with employees from social minorities.
• Accepting that conflicts may arise between you as advocate and employees from social minorities and being prepared to learn from them.[36]
• Making small, attainable and constructive steps that promote inclusion in the workplace, together with employees from social minorities.[37]

Stimulating structural and cultural change from the bottom up
• Encouraging recruitment and mentoring of employees from social minorities.[38]
• Making a plea for organising training with employees on diversity.[39]
• Making a plea to have the competencies on the area of diversity is part of performance measurements and evaluations.
• Reflecting along with other advocates and policymakers on 'neutral' procedures, practices and rules. Analysing in how far social minorities are being disadvantaged structurally, for instance with respect to recruitment or promotion. Stimulating obtaining advice on this matter from interest groups and organizations.[40]
• Keeping contact with organizations outside your service that are committed to social minorities.
• Dealing with decision-making bodies wisely. Being aware that from your position as Catholic chaplain you can exert a constructive influence on policymakers.[41]
• Studying and influencing the culture of your healthcare organization. There is need for a culture of creativity and cooperation in order to grow and learn.[42]

---

[35] Hooks, *Feminist Theory*, 58-61.
[36] R.J. Ely, D.E. Meyerson and M.N. Davidson, "Rethinking Political Correctness", in *Harvard Business Review*, September 2006, 1-8; hooks, *Writing Beyond Race*, 143-152; hooks, *Feminist Theory*, 64-67.
[37] Meyerson, *Rocking the Boat*, 101-138.
[38] B.R. Ragins, "Diversity, Power and Mentorship in Organizations: A Cultural, Structural and Behavioral Perspective", in M.M. Chemers, S. Ostkamp and M.A. Costanzo (eds.), *Diversity in Organizations: New Perspectives for a Changing Workplace*, Thousand Oaks, CA: Sage, 1995, 91-132.
[39] Goodman, *Promoting Diversity*, 178-195.
[40] For an overview of Flemish Organizations, see Zorgnet Vlaanderen, *Ethisch advies 15: Goede zorg bij etnisch-culturele diversiteit*, 36-37.
[41] Meyerson, *Rocking the Boat*, 77-100.
[42] Meyerson, *Rocking the Boat*, xxi-xxiv.

• Being aware that organizational change from the bottom up occurs slowly. In spite of that, not being deterred from acting.[43]

Conclusion

In European healthcare organizations it is part and parcel of the task of Catholic chaplains to support employees. Acting as advocate on diversity is a meaningful and concrete embodiment of that support. The service's policy can assign this task to Catholic chaplains, among others. Taking up this role takes place in cooperation with other advocates. Catholic chaplains as well as policy and other advocates can find inspiration in a Catholic-inspired ethical frame of reference. Catholic chaplains invite employees from the social majority to act as advocates as well. Together with employees from social minorities, they work professionally, constructively and uninterruptedly at achieving an inclusive workplace.

[43] Meyerson, "Radical Change", 100.

Part C

Interreligious Reflections and Dialogues on Pastoral Caregiving

The Ethics and Practice of Caring in Islam: A Sufi Perspective *

Jalaluddin Rakhmat
Indonesia, 2002

My dear heart,
never think you are better than others.
Listen to their sorrows with compassion.
If you want peace, don't harbor bad thoughts,
do not gossip and
don't teach what you do not know.

(Jalaluddin Rumi)

Abou Ben Adhem (may his tribe increase!)
Awoke one night from a deep dream of peace,
And saw, within the moonlight of the room,
Making it rich and like a lily in bloom,
An angel writing in a book of gold.
Exceeding peace had made Ben Adhem bold,
And to the Presence in the room he said,
"What writest thou?" The vision raised his head,
And, with a look made all of sweet accord,
Answered, "The names of those who love the Lord."
"And is mine one?" Said Abou. "Nay, not so,"
Replied the angel. Abou spoke more low,
But cheerily still, and said, "I pray thee, then,
write me as one who loves his fellow-men."

The angel wrote and vanished. The next night
He came again with a great wakening light,
And showed the names whom love of God had blessed,
And Lo! Ben Adhem's name led all the rest.

(James Leigh Hunt)

---

* Paper presented at the 16th International Seminar on Intercultural Pastoral Care and Counselling, 2002, in Basel, Switzerland. Published in German translation in H. Weiß, K. Federschmidt and K. Temme (eds.), *Ethik und Praxis des Helfens in verschiedenen Religionen*, Neukirchen-Vluyn: Neukirchener, 2005, 125-145.

To care for them is to care for Me

Abou ben Adhem, whom Leigh Hunt describes beautifully in her poetry, is a Sufi, probably born in today Afghanistan. He is quite unknown, when compared to another great saint of Afghanistan, Jalaluddin Balkhi (a.k.a Rumi). Both of them, however, put emphasis on the love of God as the essence of religiosity. To all of us, Rumi sings the following song:

> Let us fall in love again
> and scatter gold dust all over the world.
> Let us become a new spring
> and feel the breeze drift in the heavens' scent.
> Let us dress the earth in green,
> and like the sap of a young tree
> Let the grace from within sustain us.
> Let us carve gems out of our stony hearts
> And let them light our path to love.
> The glance of love is crystal clear
> and we are blessed by its light. [1]

Both Ben Adhem and Rumi believe that you cannot love God without loving your fellow men. They just reiterate what God says to His servants in the day of Resurrection, as reported by the Prophet Muhammad:

> On the day of Judgment, God calles upon his servants. He says to one of them, "I was hungry, but you did not feed me." He says to the others, "I was thirsty, but you did not give Me to drink." He says to another of his servants, "I was ill, but you did not visit Me." When the servants asked Him about these, He replies to them, "Verily, so-and-so was hungry; if you had fed him, you would have found Me with him. So-and-so was ill; if you had visited him, you would have found Me with him. So-and-so was thirsty; if you had give him to drink, you would have found Me with him."[2]

When a novice joins a Sufi order, the *sheikhs* (mentors) subject him to spiritual discipline for three years. He can be admitted to the Path only if he fulfills all the requirements of this discipline. The first year is devoted to service of the people, the second year to service of God, and the third year to watching over his own heart. You cannot do service to God, if you cannot give service to people. To worship God is to care.

Abul Said Abul Khayr is remembered as the Sufi who established the first Sufi order. When one of his disciples mentions before him a saint who

---

[1] Azima Malita Colin and Maryam Mafi, *Rumi: Hidden Music*, London: HarperCollins Publisher, 2001, 117.

[2] Ibn Arabi, another great sufi who claims that his religion is that of love, frequently mentions this hadith in his *Futuhat al-Makkiyyah.* See W. Graham, *Divine Word and Prophetic Word in Early Islam*, The Hague: Mouton, 1977, 179-180.

can walk on the water, he replies, "Since time immemorial, frogs have been able to do that." When he further mentions a saint who can fly, he retorts: "A gnat can do better." The disciple inquires what the best sign of saintliness is. He answers, "The best way of getting closer to God is to do the best service to mankind, to bring happiness into their hearts."

Perhaps, for its emphasis on love, Sufism has been considered as having a very close affinity with Christianity. Tor Andrae, once a Lutheran Bishop of Linköping, reveals the dominant position Jesus occupies in the pronouncements and ideas of the Sufis[3]. They learn from Jesus not only the asceticism he practices but also his care for the soul. However, it is interesting to note that the Sufis refer to Christ as well as Moses, when showing their followers the path of love. Here is one of the stories narrated by a *sheikh*:

The Children of Israel once said to Moses, "O Moses, we want to invite our Lord to a meal. Speak to God so that He may accept our invitation!" Moses angrily replied, "Don't you know that God is beyond the need for food?" But when Moses ascended Mount Sinai, God said to him, "Why did you not inform me of the invitation? My servants have invited me; tell them I shall come to their feast on Friday evening."

Moses told the people, and everyone began making great preparations for days. On Friday evening, an old man arrived, weary from a long journey. "I am so hungry," he said to Moses. "Please give me something to eat." Moses said, "Be patient. The Lord of all Worlds is coming. Take this jug and fetch some water. You can also help serve." The old man brought water and again asked for food, but no one would feed him before the Lord arrived. It got later and later, and finally, everyone began criticizing Moses for misleading them.

Moses climbed Mount Sinai and said, "My Lord, I have been put to shame before everyone because You did not come as You promise You would." God replied, "I did come. I actually approached you yourself, but when I told you I was hungry, you sent Me to fetch water. I asked again but was sent away to serve. Neither you nor your people were able to welcome Me with honor." "My Lord, an old man came and asked me for food. But he was a mere mortal."

"I was together with that servant of Mine. To honor him would have been to honor Me. To serve him would have been to serve Me. All the heavens are too small to contain Me, but not the hearts of My servants. I neither eat nor drink, yet to honor my servants is to honor Me. To care for them is to care for Me." [4]

Everyone is entitled to another's care

To care for our fellow humans, to help people, is not confined to a certain group of people. It is incumbent to every Muslim, regardless of sex, age, tribe, and social status. A Moslem is obliged by Allah and His Prophet to

---

[3] Tor Andrae, *The Garden of Myrtles*, New York: Univ. of New York Press, 1987.
[4] James Fadiman and Roger Frager, *Essential Sufism*, New Jersey: Castle Books, 1997, 221.

treat people in need kindly. As every Moslem believes that Allah is also the God of all religions, to care has been commanded in the previous religions:

> Thus we made an agreement with the children of Israel: "You shall serve God Alone, and treat your parents kindly, and (also) near relatives, orphans and the needy, and say kind things to (other) people, and keep up prayer, and pay the welfare tax"; then you turned away and except for the few of you, you avoided doing anything. (Al-Qur'an 2:83)
>
> Worship God (Alone) and do not associate anything with Him. Show kindness to both (your) parents and with near relatives, orphans, the needy, the neighbor who is related (to you) as well as the neighbor who is a stranger, and your companion by your side and the wayfarer, and anyone else under your control. God does not love someone who is conceited, boastful, nor those who are tight-fisted and order (other) people to be stingy, and hide anything that God has given them out of His bounty. We have reserved humiliating torment for disbelievers who spend their wealth to be seen by other people and yet neither believe in God nor the Last Day. Anyone who has Satan for an intimate has such an evil soul mate! What does it matter for them whether they believe in God and the Last Day and spend something from what God has supplied them with? God is Aware of them. (Al-Qur'an 4:36-39)
>
> Virtue does not mean for you to turn your faces towards the East and West, but virtue means one should believe in God (Alone), the Last Day, angels, the Book and prophets; and no matter how he loves it, to give his wealth away to near relatives, orphans, the needy, the wayfarer and beggars, and towards freeing captives; and to keep up prayer and pay the welfare tax; and those who keep their word whenever they promise anything; and are patient under suffering and hardship and in time of violence. Those are the ones who act loyal, and they perform their duty. (Al-Qur'an 2:177)
>
> Believers, whether men or women, must (act as) friends to one another; they should command decency and forbid wickedness, keep up prayer, and pay welfare tax as well as obey God and His messenger. Those God will grant mercy to; God is powerful, Wise! God has promised believers, whether they are men or women, gardens through which rivers flow to live in forever, and goodly dwellings in the gardens of Eden. Yet approval by God is greatest; that will be the supreme Achievement! (Al-Qur'an 9:71-72)
>
> Render your close relative his due as well as the pauper and the wayfarer. Yet, do not squander (your money) extravagantly; spendthrifts are the devils' brethren, and Satan has always been ungrateful toward his lord. Yet if you have to avoid them, seeking some mercy which you may expect from your lord, still speak a courteous to them. Do not keep your hand gripping at your throat nor stretch it out as far as it will reach, lest you sit back blamed worthy, destitute. (Al-Qur'an 17:26-29)

To act as friends to one another is a mutual duty. You have to care for them; and they are entitled to your care. By the prophet's injunction, to care becomes the rights – *huquq*. The Prophet is reported as saying:

> Every Moslem is entitled to seven things from another: respect for his dignity, love for him in his heart, equal exchange in his wealth, his backbiting prohibited, his

sickness visited, his funeral performed, and saying nothing about him but good after his death. (Bihar al-Anwar 47:222)

In another tradition, the Prophet says:

A Moslem is entitled to six: when you see him, you greet him; when he invites you, you answers him; when he asks for counsels, you counsel him; when he sneezes, you praise Allah for him; when he is sick, you visit him; when he dies, you escort him to his final resting place. (Kanz al-'Ummal 24771)

To care is, in short, to bring happiness into the people's hearts. In one of the traditions, a very impressive account on the Day of Resurrection is narrated:

When a believer arises from his grave (on the day of Judgment), another person will arise from the same place. He will tell him: Do not worry. Be delighted with divine reward and bliss. Then, he will go with him comforting on his way. When passing by a terrible thing, he will say: This one is not for you. When passing by a good thing, he will say: This one is for you. He will go along with him giving solace to him in time of fear, continuously comforting him with that he loves. When standing before Allah, he will tell him: Be delighted, for Allah has sent you to Paradise. The believer will ask him: Who are you? May Allah shower you with His Mercy. You were comforting me when I got up from my grave. You made a good company and gave me glad tidings from my Lord. And he will answer: I was the happiness you brought into the hearts of your brothers and sisters in your previous world. I was created thereof to console you and to free you from fear. (*Bihar al-Anwar* 7:197)

To seek for care is recommended

Since everyone is entitled to another's care, he/she is advised to seek for counsel in his/her distress, especially from the adept. The Qur'an mentions "*hakam*", translated arbiter, and derived from the same root as "*hakim*" meaning wise man, sage. *Hakam* must be consulted to help solve family problems:

If you fear a split between a man and his wife, send for an arbiter from his family and an arbiter from her family. If both want to be reconciled, God will arrange things between them. God is Aware, informed. (Al-Qur'an 5:36)

In terms of Sufism, one is advised to find a teacher, a guide, a *murshid*. The murshid is the living representation of the Prophet. He carries on the prophetic mission:

We have merely sent you as a mercy for (everybody in) the Universe. (Al-Qur'an 21:107)

Allah says with respect to the purpose of sending His Messenger:

Those who follow the Messenger, the Unlettered Prophet whom they will find written down for them in the Torah and the Gospel. He commands them to be descent and forbid them dishonor. He permits them wholesome things and prohibits them evil things and relieves them of their burdens and the shackles which have lain upon them those who believe in him, reveal him, and support him, and follow the light which was sent down with him; those will be successful. Say: "Mankind, for all of you I am but a messenger from God (Alone), who holds control over Heaven and Earth. There is no deity except Him; He gives life and brings death. Believe in God and His messenger, the Unlettered Prophet who himself believes in God (Alone) and his words: Follow him so you may be guided. (Al-Qur'an 7: 157-158)

Being an heir of the Prophet, a counselor in Islam must follow the Messenger, "commanding them to be descent and forbidding them dishonor; permitting them wholesome things and prohibiting them evil things and relieving them of their burdens and the shackles which have lain upon them." In modern terms, he must help his disciple to solve his problems, to improve his health, and to grow a spiritual growth. I will discuss the duties of a teacher, when talking about the ethics of caring in Islam. But, let me first describe in brief the Islamic worldview.

The Islamic worldview

View of the relationships between God and human beings.

God can be conceived as He is in Himself (the Essence) and as we relate to Him (the Divinity). In terms of His Essence, He is incomparable indefinable, indescribable, unimaginable. He is beyond any human comprehension. God is therefore transcendent. This is the dimension of His Majesty. In this respect, a Muslim must not describe God in anyway.

Say: God is Unique! God is the Source (for everything); He has not fathered anyone nor was He fathered, and there is nothing comparable to Him! (Al-Qur'an 112: 1-4).

In terms of His Divinity, God has a certain similarity with His creatures. We cannot understand His Essence but we can comprehend His Attributes. With respect to His Essence, we have to do *tanzîh*; and with respect to His Divinity, we have to do *tashbîh*. *Tanzîh* means not to compare God to anything. *Tashbîh* means to be similar with God in all His Attributes.

Tanzîh derives from the root *n.z.h.*, which means to be far away from, to be untouched by, to be free from. Hence *tanzîh* means to declare or to affirm that something is far away or free from something else. In other words, *tanzîh* is to declare that Gods transcends any attribute or quality possessed by His creatures. *Tashbîh* derives from the root *sh.b.h.*, which means to be similar or comparable. It signifies declaring or affirming that something is similar to something else; to compare, to liken. Hence *tashbîh* is to maintain that a certain similarity can be found between God and creation.

Human beings are related to God in His Dual Dimensions. When related to His Essence, His Majesty, a human is a servant (*'abd*). When related to His Divinity, His Beauty, a human is a vicegerent (*khalifa*) or a representative. "The vicegerent of the King represents the King by making use of His prerogatives. It is understood that the vicegerent has already submitted to the King. No king appoints a rebel as his representative. Once having submitted, the servant is given a robe of honor. The robe comes from the king, and the vicegerent wears it in his name... If we look at the vicegerent in relation to the king, what distinguishes him or her from other servants is nearness to the king. God relates with this servants predominately in terms of the names of mercy and beauty.

From *tanzîh* point of view, God is far off. This relationship results in fear, awe, and submission. From *tashbîh* perspective, God is near, close by. This relationship brings out love. "Distance and incomparability (relationship of servant hood) demand awe. While nearness and similarity (relationship of representativeness) demand intimacy. Intimacy is togetherness in union, and this is achieved through love... "He Loves them and they love Him" (Al-Qur'an 5: 54). This dual relationship is expressed in the opening chapter of the Qur'an, Al-Fatiha, which is recited in each cycle of the daily prayers: "*Thee Alone we serve and Thee Alone we ask for help*" (Al-Qur'an 1: 4). Service is the attribute of the servant who obeys the command of the King. Asking for help is the attribute of the supplicant who goes to the Kings door and seeks entrance into His Court.

View of human nature

A human live in three different level of existence. He/she belongs to three different world: *nafs* (bodily, physical), *fikr* (mental, psychological), and *ruh* (spiritual). Shaykh Hakim Moinuddin Chisti describes them[5]:

In Arabic, *nafs* is the word for the body and its appetites. *Nafs* means all of the demands of the body – for food, for warmth, for fame and fortune (all of these include emotional needs or drives). One or more of these physical dimensions can mark out all physical diseases. The word *nafs* has many meanings; breath, animal life, soul, self, a person, essence, and more. In Sufism, the progression of the soul is described by considering the evolution of the *nafs*, which manifests in human behavior as one's entire character, personality, and behavior. The *nafsî am-marâ* is the commanding

[5] Hakim Moinuddin, *The Book of Sufi Healing*, New York: Inner Traditions International, 1985.

soul, which creates inordinate appetites. This is the condition of the *nafs* referred to when one occupies the station of egotism (*maqâm an-nafs*). The behaviors recommended in the Qur'an (*shari'at*) are meant to control and subdue these inordinate appetites, leading the *nafs* to a more refined status. The soul that has been entirely purified is called *nafsî kull*, meaning "universal soul," which unites with Allah in the final stage of Sufism. However, even at the latest stages of Sufi practice, one cannot assume oneself immune to the blemishes of the soul.

The second aspect of our existence is the mind world, or let us say the emotional and mental world. The mind is not entirely separate from the physical body, but is part of and intimately connected with physical functioning. Moods and feelings that originate in the mind *frequently* have an effect on the body –emotions such as anger, fear, or extreme joy. When one or more of these is experienced, the blood pressure may rise or fall, the body sweats, and tears may come. Interestingly, some ailments or conditions that we have come to regard as purely emotional have their origin in physical unbalances. An example is severe anger. Psychologists would usually attribute this to a condition of the mind or emotions. But according to the Tibb system of the Persian physician Avicenna, severe anger is one of the body's most effective wave of dispelling excess moisture in the area of the heart. It is easily corrected with diet. The realm of the mental world is called *fikr* in Arabic. In essence, *fikr* means meditation or deep-thought process.

The third component of our existence is the soul, called the *rûh*. The *rûh* is that which exists after death, which marks the end of both physical and mental life.

The interaction of three realms (or the activation of the physical and mental realms by the soul realm) is carried out by means of the spirit. Many people use the words "spirit" and "soul" to mean the same thing, yet they are distinctly different and separate. The spirit is what activates the physical-level existence, including thought processes. The word for this spirit activator is *nafas*. It is activated at the point of the breath. The point of the lips where in-breath and out-breath unite is the link between life and death.

The Sufis consider that the breath of life exists and continues by that virtue of the *idhn*, or permission of God, the One Who has created us all. What we call the Creator – God, Allah, Yahweh, or whatever – does not matter. In His ultimately reality, God is one. He gives His permission for human life to exist in the first place, and as long as that permission remains, we may draw breath in and out. Regardless of which system of healing we may wish to apply, or how skilled the practitioner, even if all the healers of the world come together, they could not counteract the *idhn*. When the permission is withdrawn, there is no more breath; life ceases.

The center, or seat, of the soul's existence is the heart. With what do we associate heart and soul? Love, compassion, sympathy, mercy, and all of our religious sentiments. When someone dies, the grief of the survivors is felt in the heart. It is actually a physical pain. The heart aches. There is so much terminology in our language about these soul-related aspects of the heart. In addition, no one can deny that these feelings of love and compassion do exist. No one is without them

In Arabic, the heart is called *qalb*. The heart, according to the Sufis, is not just a physiological pump for dispersing blood about the body. It serves two more vital, interrelated functions. Firstly, the heart is the storehouse of divine attributes; and secondly, it is the seat of manufacture of the *nafas* – that life-activating force which enters with each breath, the breath that activates all physiological functions.

Thus, when the *idhn*, or permission of God, is drawn in, it goes immediately to the heart. In some manner, this *idhn* activates all of the divine attributes in various combinations, and these then are carried out into the body. The Qur'an informs that these divine attributes are approximately ninety-nine in number and are what Allah uses as the means of allowing the human to function and work on the created place of being.

View of life

The Qur'an describes life in three ways. First, life is pain, distress, suffering, tribulation: "*Certainly, We have created man to be in distress*" (Al-Qur'an 90:4). The Qur'an exegetes explain this verse:

> Yes, from the early moments of life, even as a foetus in the womb, Man passes through different, difficult stages with pain and toil until the time he is born, end even from then on; during his childhood, the period of his adolescence, and the most difficult times, his mature years, he is always faced with many kinds of trouble and misery. This is the nature of the present world. Those who have other expectations, about this world, other than that there is pain and toil, here, is wrong. The lives of the prophets and saints of Allah who have been the best of all creatures, have been full of diverse difficulties and painful situations. When the world has been like this for them, then, the status of others is clear.
>
> We may see some people or some societies, which have no apparent trouble and seem to live in ease. It is either because of our insufficient information about them, and when we approach them and study their outwardly comfortable lives, we see the depth of their pain and suffering; or their comfortable situation exists for a short time or in an exceptional period, but however, it does not change the general law of the world. [6]

[6] Somaiyah Berrigan (ed.), *An Enlightening Commentary into the Light of The Holy Qur'an*, Isfahan: Ali Library, 2000, 2:38.

Second, life is a test: "*The One who created death and life, so He may test which of you is finest in action.*" (Al-Qur'an 67;2)

We are brought to life in order to get tested, which of us does good deeds. Sometimes the test comes in tribulation: we shall test you with a bit of fear and hunger, plus a shortage of wealth and souls and produce. Announce such to patient people who say, whenever misfortune strikes them: "*We belong to God and are returning to Him*" (2:155-156). However, sometimes, the test takes the form of wealth, health, and fortune: "*We split them up into nations (that exist) on earth. Some of them are honorable, some are otherwise. We have tested them with fine things and evil things so they might repent.*" (Al-Qur'an 7:168, cf. 21:35)

Third, worldly life is a sport, play, and pastime. "Know that worldly life is merely a sport and a pastime (involving) worldly show and competition among yourselves, as well as rivalry in wealth and children. It may be compared to showers where the plant life amazes the incredulous: then it withers away and you see it turning yellow; soon it will be just stubble. In the Hereafter there will be both severe torment and forgiveness as well as approval on the part of God. Worldly life means only enjoyment of illusion."

God, like a mother, sends His children to play in the field of life. Some are so much absorbed in their play that they forget to return, despite their repeated mothers' calls. Some play dirty things and fear their mothers' scold.

The ethics of caring in Islam

Both friends and a counselor who is a spiritual guide, as shown above, can provide caring in Islam. Let me start first with the ethics of brotherhood and close up with second, the ethics of spiritual guides as well as disciples:

Eight Duties of Brotherhood:

At the lowest level, give spontaneously from your surplus; at the middle level, treat your brother as an equal partner; at the highest level, prefer him to yourself.

Spontaneously provide for your brother's personal needs, giving them priority over your own. At the lowest level, attend plentifully when asked, with joy and cheerfulness, showing pleasure and gratitude; at the middle level, treat the person as an equal partner; at the higher level, prefer the other to yourself.

For your brother's sake, feign ignorance of his faults, even if you must lie to do so.

Express affection to your brother; ask agreeably about his circumstances; praise him, and convey the praises of others; defend him in his absence; instruct him as needed in worldly and spiritual matters. Take him to task if he does not act appropriately, but only in private. Avoid alienation by not pointing out faults that are known to your brother; instead, exercise compassion and point out only faults not known to him.

If someone errs in his duty as a brother, forgiveness and patience are always the proper course.

Pray for your brother, that he may have all he wishes for himself, his family, and his dependents, both during his life and after his death.

Show "steadfastness in love." Such love requires you to care for a brother's children after his death. Loyalty includes preventing a relationship from degenerating into one of humility; not agreeing to something contrary to religious principles; not listening to gossip about him; and not befriending his enemy.

Relieve your brother from discomfort and inconvenience. For example, do not ask him for services or require that he be polite. [7]

The characteristics of Spiritual Guides:

Abu Sa'id was asked, "Who is the spiritual guide who has attained to Truth, and who is the sincere disciple?" The sheikh replied, "The spiritual guide who has attained to Truth is he in whom at least ten characteristics are found, as proof of his authenticity:

First, he must have become a goal, to be able to have a disciple.

Second, he must have traveled the mystic path himself, to be able to show the way.

Third, he must have become refined and educated, to be able to be an educator.

Fourth, he must be generous and devoid of self-importance, so that he can sacrifice wealth on behalf of the disciple.

Fifth, he must have no hand in the disciple's wealth, so that he is not tempted to use it for himself.

Sixth, whenever he can give advice through a sign, he will not u se direct expression.

Seventh, whenever he can educate through kindness, he will not use violence and harshness.

Eighth, whatever he orders, he has first accomplished himself.

Ninth, whatever he forbids the disciple, he has abstained from himself.

Tenth, he will not abandon for the world's sake the disciple he accepts for the sake of God.

If the spiritual guide is like this and is adorned with these character traits, the disciple is bound to be sincere and a good traveler, for what appears in the disciple, is the quality of the spiritual guide made manifest in the disciple. [8]

As for the sincere disciple, the sheikh has said:

No less than the ten characteristics which I mention must be present in the sincere disciple, if he is to be worthy of discipleship:

First, he must be intelligent enough to understand the spiritual guide's indications.

---

[7] Fadiman and Frager, *Essential Sufism,* 139-140.

[8] Llewellyn Vaughan-Lee, *Sufism: The Transformation of the Heart,* California: The Golden Sufi Center, 1995, 131-133.

Second, he must be obedient in order to carry out the spiritual guide's command.
Third, he must be sharp of hearing to perceive what the spiritual guide says.
Fourth, he must have an enlightened heart in order to see the spiritual guide's greatness.
Fifth, he must be truthful, so that whatever he reports, he reports truthfully.
Sixth, he must be true to his word, so that whatever he says, he keeps his promise.
Seventh, he must be generous, so that whatever he has, he is able to give away.
Eighth, he must be discreet, so that he can keep a secret.
Ninth, he must be receptive to advice, so that he will accept the guide's admonition.
Tenth, he must be chivalrous in order to sacrifice his own dear life on the mystic path.
Having these character traits, the disciple will more easily accomplish his journey and more quickly reach the goal set for him on the mystic path by the spiritual guide.[9]

Al-Suhrawardi, in his classical treatise on *tasawwuf*[10], inserts one important characteristic of a good guide: confidentiality. A teacher must not violate the disciples' confidentiality. To the characteristics of good disciples, a very significant attitude must be added: sincerity in seeking, by having a complete trust in the teacher, regardless of his behavior. Vaughan-Lee describes this attitude by inserting a Hindu story:

It is the attitude that we bring to the teacher that opens the gates of grace. This is told in the story of a poor Indian woman who needed to visit her sick son. He lived on the other side of the river. But the river was in flood, and the ferryman would not take her across. On the rocky banks of the river, a holy Brahmin was performing a fire ceremony with the ritual incantations.

The poor woman approached him to ask for some divine charm to help her to cross the river. The Brahmin, not wishing to interrupt his sacred ceremony and thus have to repeat the complicated ritual, wanted to get rid of her as quickly as possible. "Just repeat 'Ram, Ram,' and you will cross the river," He told the old woman and returned to his incantations. Later, as the evening sun was setting, the Brahmin was still sitting beside the river, having finished the sacred ceremony. He was surprised to see the old woman again approaching him and was even more surprised by the look of joy and reverence on her face. She bowed before him and said, "Oh holy one, so great are your wondrous powers. Repeating 'Ram, Ram,' I walked across the river and was able to stay and comfort my son. Again repeating the sacred syllables I returned back across the river. I offer eternal thanks for your divine aid." The Brahmin looked at the old woman in astonishment and wonder. So great had been her belief in him that it had carried her across the flooded waters. He felt humbled before her and the power of her faith. [11]

---

[9] Ibid.
[10] *Kitab 'Awarif al-Ma'arif.* Beyrut: Dar al-Kitab al-'Arabiy, 1983, 425-422.
[11] Vaughan-Lee, *Sufism,* 135-136.

The practice of caring in Islam

Prayer

The Qur'an says: "You who believe, seek help through patience and prayer. God stands alongside the patience." (Al-Qur'an 2:153)

Injunctions for prayers are frequently repeated in the Qur'an. Prayers in Islam consist of two groups. First, *salat* or regular prayers conducted in a certain procedure. Some are obligatory and some are recommended. Salat is mostly recited in Arabic. During a certain part of the salat, a Moslem can and is urged to say his own prayer in his language. There are many kind of salats, performed for different purposes: request for help, protection, provisions, divine forgiveness, knowledge, best decision, and others. Second, general prayer, not conducted in a strict procedure. There are as well many kinds of prayers: confession, petition, thanksgiving, intercession, lamentation, request for forgiveness, blessing for the Prophet, expression of love (and longing) for God and others. Moslems help one another by saying their prayers for the benefit of one another. In night vigilant worship, a Moslem is required to pray for his brethren.

Repeating the name of God *(Zikr)*

The Qur'an says: "Truly in the remembrance of God hearts find rest." (Al-Qur'an 23:28) "And contain yourself patiently at the side of all who invokes their sustainer, mornings and evenings, seeking his face nor allow your eyes to go beyond them in search of the attractions of this world's life, and pay no attention to any whose heart we have made unaware of all remembrance of Us because he had always followed his own desires, abandoning all that is just and true." (Al-Qur'an 18:28)

By zikr, a Moslem repeats the names of God; therefore, trying to be absorbed in His names. Zikr is not only calming, healing, putting mind in order; but also transforming. Zikr can be done either individually or in assembly.

Sahl said to one of his disciple: "Try to say continuously for one day: 'Allah, Allah, Allah' and do the same the next day and the day after, until it becomes a habit." Then he told him to repeat it at night also, until it became so familiar that the disciple repeated it even during his sleep. Then Sahl said, "Do not consciously repeat the Names anymore, but let your whole faculties be engrossed in remembering Him." The disciple did this until he became absorbed in the Truth of God. One day, a piece of woods fell on his head and broke it. The drops of blood that dripped to the ground bore the legend: "Allah, Allah, Allah".[12]

[12] Ibid., 55-56.

Service (*Khidmat*)

The Prophet says: "God always helps a servant who helps his brothers."

Doing service to people is caring and curing. Service is a form of worship – and a powerful method of self-transformation. Most service that we offer is selfish; it is service for the sake of reward: money, price, or fame. By service, the Sufis mean service "for God's sake," without any thought of reward. This kind of service comes when we remember that we are a part of God's creation, and that by serving creation, we are serving our Creator – not for a heavenly reward, but out of love and gratitude. An old sheikh once said, "Service without love is like a beautiful corpse. The outer form is lovely, but it is lifeless." Service does not have to be great or dramatic:

Years ago, the mother of one of the Ottoman sultan was devoted to charity. She built mosques and a great hospital and had public wells dug in parts of Istanbul that were without water. One day, she went to watch the construction of the hospital she was having built and she saw an ant fall into the wet concrete of the foundation. She lifted the ant out of the concrete and set it on the ground.

Some years later she passed away. That night she appeared to a number of her friends in their dreams. She was radiant with joy and inner beauty. Her friend asked her if she had gone to Paradise because of all her wonderful charities, and she replied, "I am in Paradise, but it is not because of those charities, it is for the sake of an ant."

Examples from my practice of counseling

Case 1: death anxiety

I was invited to see a father in his dying chamber in the hospital. The doctor told him that he suffered a terminal illness. Within one week, he would lose consciousness and in the following week, he would die. He was recommended to collect his children and relatives and say good-bye to them. The news filled him with panic. He fell apart. He could neither eat nor drink. He was so frightened that he could not sleep.

I found myself in a room crowded with members of a grand family. The dying was lying motionless. I asked him as to what had been troubling him. In tears, he said:

I am nearly sixty. I feel I am not yet ready for death. I have many things to do. None of my daughters have been married. It is my responsibility to bring them to their wedding day. If I could send a petition to Him, I would ask Him to give me enough time, just to have them married.

Secondly, I don't know what will happen to my soul. I used to have works in Borneo. I learned that deep in the jungle of Borneo there stood a big tree. People believe that many souls have been lingering in the tree for hundred years. I do not want my soul to remain on this earth, roaming aimlessly. I want to know where my soul goes after my departure.

Thirdly, I have been used to a family get-together. I love being with them. You can see my wife, my kids, and my close relatives visit me every day and some stay with me overnight. Their presence brings comfort to me. Death will set us apart. I will be alone and lonely.

Finally, I have sinned and done only a few good deeds. To die means to get punishment that I might not be able to bear. The disease I am contracting now is hardly bearable, let alone the torments in the grave.

The patient, belonging to Javanese aristocracy and following Javanese mystical view, had only a very limited knowledge of Islamic eschatology. I started with the description of soul, which troubled him most.

They ask you about the soul. Say the soul is part of My Lord's command; You are given only little information about the soul. The first thing you have to do, with respect to the soul, is: Do not believe in what people say about souls. Believe in what God and His Messenger say about souls. As far as I can understand from the Qur'an and hadith (tradition of the prophet), all souls will return to Allah. None of them will be roaming on earth. That is why, a Moslem is recommended to say: "Indeed, we belong to Allah, and to Him we shall return".

Death is an outset of a new journey, a home coming trip. God is a Merciful Mother, who has sent Her children to this world. This world is our playground. She sets up for us rules of the game. When we came here, we were all pure and clean. But, having played a lot, we have become dirty, our nafs filthy, and our souls soiled. That is because we have broken the rules. Repeatedly, God calls us to return, to come home: "Follow the path of those who have returned to Me; To Me, you are returning, and with Me is your reckoning."

Since Allah is the Holiest, the Purest, you will be received with His Mercy, if you return clean and pure. There are two kinds of purification. One is done by yourself. You purify yourself. You repent by asking for His forgiveness. You can practice it now.

I taught him the following *istighfar,* supplication for repentance:

O Allah, indeed Your forgiveness is more to be hoped for than my deeds. Certainly Your Mercy is larger and more far-reaching than my sins. O Allah, if my mistakes, in the matter of Your Law, are big; Your pardon is far greater than my mistakes. O Allah, if I am not worthy of reaching Your Mercy; Your Mercy is most worthy of reaching me and embracing me, for Your Mercy envelops everything. Through Your kindness, O The Most Merciful.

I told him:

You can cleanse your soul by doing good deeds, such as caring for people. However, you may not be able to clean your soul completely. You are told you are running out of time. Through His Mercy, God purifies you with His holy hands. The Prophet says, "Every affliction that befalls on you cleanses you of your sins." You are suffering a disease that will purify you. So, accept His Mercy and submit totally to His Will. Regarding your unmarried daughters, leave them to the Merciful. He is the One Who always takes care of you.

As for your family that you will leave behind, they will be able to accompany you in your trip by sending their good deeds to you. Any time they do good deeds in remembrance of you, God will create a very good companion for you over there. Just be happy. You are lucky; you have such a good family.

Finally, don't forget that Allah is the Almighty. HE is the Most Powerful. Don't count on the doctor too much. Rely on HIM only.

Of course, I retold here the story in brief. What was really going on in that session was a lively discussion. I was surprised to find out that everybody seemed to learn a new belief. I closed up the session by asking everyone to say a prayer for the patient, while submitting ourselves totally to the Merciful. We also recited *salawat* (prayer for the intercession of the Prophet) together. I asked the patient to keep on reciting the two names of God: Ya Rahman, Ya Rahim – O the Most Merciful, O the Most Beneficent.

All was done in a hurry, because I was about to depart to the United States. Two months later, when I was home again, I was invited to attend a thanksgiving ceremony in the patient's house. A miracle happened. He did not lose consciousness on the expected day. On the contrary, he slowly recovered. Presently, he lives in Jakarta; although still under medical treatment.

Case 2: family conflict

Mrs. Fulanah is a daughter of a high-ranking official in the government. She was married to a big business man. Both were educated in business in the United States. Both managed to build a business empire of their own. In spite of their wealth and health, they did not make a happy couple. Her husband, too much absorbed in his enterprise, rarely returned home. Even if he did, he abused his wife, beating her in front of their children. Once when his business was broke, through the intercession of his wife, his father-in-law helped him out. It was a blessing in disguise. During that time, her husband got along with her quite well.

It did not last long, though. As his business was getting bigger, he was more distant from his wife and his children. The downpour of wealth brought out different responses from two of them. The husband was engrossed in the life style of jet-sets. He indulged himself in women, wine, and gambling. The wife turned to religion. She attended the religious study session I was conducting.

At was at this time that she came up to me for counseling. She consulted me whether it was good for her to ask for divorce. She wanted to avoid her abusing husband. However, she was thrown onto the horns of a dilemma. If she was divorced, she would tarnish the image of her father and hurt her mother. She said she respected her mother very much. She did not want her to know the turbulence that was striking her marriage. She always made believe that her marriage was OK and even happy. If she continued her relationship with her husband, she was afraid she could no longer bear the pain. She was worried about the consequences of the conflict on the children.

I did not recommend a certain decision. I left it to her. She can ask for divorce, and divorce is justified in certain cases. She can be patient. It was all her choice. Then, I quoted a hadith:

> A woman came up to the Prophet. She complained about her husband's body odor. She said she could not serve him well. She was afraid that God would punish her for her wrongdoing. The Prophet said, "You can ask for divorce by returning your dowry to him."

I followed by narrating a story quoted from the Qur'an. The Qur'an gives an example of the wife of the Pharaoh – Asiya bent Mazahem. She fought against the oppression of her husband, while strongly placed reliance on God. She bore all the pain for the sake of God. The Prophet mentions her name as one of the most honorable lady in the sight of God.

Another story was told in Sufi literature. A high minister of Khalifah Al-Mansur came across a beautiful young lady in the desert, while hunting. She stayed in an isolated tent far from human dwellings. He found her abused by her old and ugly husband. When the minister was wondering why she maintained the marriage, the lady said: "I have been granted a beautiful face, a healthy body, and a safe shelter. I am thankful to God for everything he has given me. According to the prophet, *shukr* – thankfulness – is half a faith. Another half is *sabr* – patience. Let me complete my faith by being patient."

The lady finally decided to protect her marriage. She considered her mission to bring her husband to the right path. I introduced her to the teachings of Sufism. She practiced regularly reciting certain prayers, remembering certain names of Allah in a certain procedure. She had quite frequent religious experiences. She felt she was reborn. She spent much money for charity. The lady has been making a lot of attempts to bring him closer to God. In his later age, it seems that her husband is beginning to respond to her invitation, quite slowly; as if God were still testing her patience.

Case 3: substance-induced anxiety disorder

Mrs. Tommy is a lady of about forty. She has been married for fifteen years. For years, they have lived happily in a quite stable family. She has two kids. Her husband has a good business; and she is a manager of a training firm. Then, one night she woke up drenched in sweat. Someone whispered persistently, "Kill your husband. Kill your children."

She was aware it was a delusion. Yet, she feared that one day she does kill them. Worry and fear, compounded with doubt, clearly indicates anxiety. She went to a psychiatrist, who inquired whether she had consumed a substance. She confirmed it, but she said she had used (abused) the drug long time before her marriage. And she used it very little, simply to get "in" with her peers. The doctor prescribed her a certain drug that she did not tell me.

The psychiatrist, being well known in the city, had very little time for discussion. She was disappointed. Many friends recommended her to consult traditional faith healers. She changed from one faith healer to another. The fear remained. Eventually, she came up to me. She added up another kind of fear to the prevailing one: fear of God's punishment. Every time she performed her regular prayer, she had an uneasy mind of not doing it properly. She fancied the procedure might be wrong. The drug could temporarily help her. She also learned from some faith healers that the illness might be induced by a jinn-genie. She asked for my help to get rid of the disturbing jinn.

I have got a friend in Jakarta, who is known as an expert in matters of jinn. He does not exorcise, but he can converse with the jinn in their language. He is a healer and to some extent, a counselor. By profession, he is a professor of Islamic studies in the State Islamic University in Jakarta. I sent her to him. She called me afterwards, saying that she doubted my friend's treatment. Since I had told her before that faith healers might lie to her, she hesitated to practice what he suggested her to do. I had also told her not to change doctors frequently. Stick to one of them. She obeyed. While given a medical treatment, she has been taught to recite a certain divine name continuously in a certain procedure. She has been learning to concentrate on the names of Allah and to get rid of evil thoughts. She has been listening to the Qur'an and contemplating its translation.

It is a habit for me to close up every season with prayer. Just before I departed here, she came to me. She said she felt better. She promised me to perform the zikr I recommended, while consulting my friend during my absence. We prayed together. I also promised her to include her in my prayers. The story is yet unfinished.

A Jewish Perspective on the Ethics of Care *

Elliot N. Dorff
USA 2005

The "lig" in the word "religion" comes from the same Latin root as does the word "ligament" which is connective tissue. The Latin root *ligare* means to tie, connect, or link. Religions, among other things, provide us with a broad picture of how we are and ought to be linked to our family, the members of our community, other human beings, the rest of the animate and inanimate world, and to the transcendent element of our experience, imaged in the Western religions as God. That is, religions give us a perspective on who we are, both as individuals and as members of a family and community, and who we should strive to be.

Secular philosophies, such as Western liberalism, existentialism, and Marxism, do that too, but they are usually created by individuals and often remain the views of individuals. They may be adopted by nations, as the United States adopted Western liberalism and China adopted communism, but that is a subsequent and accidental occurrence. Religions, on the other hand, usually begin within a community and remain linked to that community, the members of which try to live their lives in accordance with their religion's assertions, values, and hopes.

While the various religions of the world share some important values, they do not amount to one and the same view of life. That is easy to see in two ways. First of all, even in what is presumably a fundamental value of all faiths – the value of life – the various religions of the world interpret that very differently, with some forbidding all killing of people and others demanding that one kill others, if one must, in self-defense and still others, like the religion of ancient Rome, making war and the warrior an ideal. Some religions think that abortion is always a violation of the value of life,

---

* Published in German as "Kranke besuchen. Die Ethik des Helfens in der Krankenfürsorge aus jüdischer Sicht", in H. Weiß, K. Federschmidt and K. Temme (eds.), *Ethik und Praxis des Helfens in verschiedenen Religionen*, Neukirchen-Vluyn: Neukirchener, 2005, 100-116.

while others assert that abortion is permissible in some circumstances and actually required in others (e.g., to save the life or health of the woman), and still others leave it to the individual person's conscience. If religions differ on how to interpret and apply even as fundamental a value as preserving life, one can imagine that they differ even more on other values, such as the role and place of work, play, art, education, family, community, individual autonomy, and health care.

Another way to see that all religions are not one, is to compare how each one describes the ideal person and community. Is the ideal person one who marries, as in Judaism, or one who remains celibate and serves the church, as in Catholicism? Is the ideal person necessarily a man? How does the ideal person spend his or her time? What level of education does he or she attain? To what extent does the ideal person seek and hold power over others, and what kind of power is that? By asking such questions, it will quickly become obvious that even if religions share some values, they are not all alike, differing not only in some values but also in how they interpret and apply those values that they share.

This is important to keep in mind if we are to understand both the similarities and the differences in how the various religions of the world handle any topic, including the nature and provision of care. In another place,[1] I compare the ethics of the American secular ideal, Christianity, and Judaism, and so I will not do that here. Instead, I will simply describe a Jewish ethic of care and leave it to the reader to draw the appropriate comparisons to how other religions treat the same topics. I will begin with some underlying principles of a Jewish ethic of physical care, proceed to a discussion of spiritual needs and care, and then discuss one extended example of how a significant Jewish care practice illustrates these forms of care.

Jewish perspectives and values on health care

One basic principle of Jewish medical ethics, and Jewish ethics generally, is that God, as Creator of all, owns everything in the world, including our bodies.[2] That means that God appropriately makes demands regarding the

---

[1] Elliot N. Dorff, *To Do the Right and the Good: A Jewish Approach to Modern Social Ethics*, Philadelphia: Jewish Publication Society, 2002, Chapter One and Appendix B. See also Elliot N. Dorff, *Love Your Neighbor and Yourself: A Jewish Approach to Modern Personal Ethics*, Philadelphia: Jewish Publication Society, 2003, Chapter One and the Appendix.

[2] For further discussion of all of the fundamental principles that I am about to describe briefly, see Elliot N. Dorff, *Matters of Life and Death: A Jewish Approach to Modern Medical Ethics*, Philadelphia: Jewish Publication Society, 1998, Chapter Two. God's creation and ownership of all creation, including our bodies: Genesis

use of our world and our bodies, just as the owner of an apartment has the right to impose restrictions on the renter's use of it. The Jewish tradition has understood God's demands to include prohibitions against destruction or abuse of the body and positive requirements of proper diet, exercise, sleep, and hygiene to take reasonable care of it.[3]

While the Torah states that God inflicts illness, among other things, as punishment for sin and that God is our Healer,[4] those passages have *not* been interpreted in the Jewish tradition to prohibit medical care as an act of human presumptuousness. On the contrary, the Rabbis used other verses in the Torah to assert that we not only have the right, but the duty, to avail ourselves of medical care. Indeed, Jews are required (not just allowed) to violate all but three of the Torah's commandments if that is necessary to save a life.[5]

Along these same lines, a Jew, according to talmudic passages, may not live in a town lacking a physician,[6] for that would subject God's property to undue risk. Since the physician was seen as the medical expert, Jewish sources take a largely paternalistic view of the doctor-patient relationship: the patient must do what the doctor says. At the same time, however, the Talmud recognizes the right of patients to choose among several medically reasonable therapies,[7] and presumably patients had to know their doctors well enough to trust their advice sufficiently to follow it. Thus even if

---

14:19, 22 (where the Hebrew word for "Creator" [*koneh*] also means "Possessor", and where "heaven and earth" is a merism for those and everything in between); Exodus 20:11; Deuteronomy 10:14; cf. also Leviticus 25:23, 42, 55; Deuteronomy 4:35, 39; 32:6; Psalms 104:24.

[3] In the following notes, these abbreviations are used: M. = Mishnah, ed. by Rabbi Jehudah HaNasi about 200 CE; T. = Tosefta, about 200; J. = Jerusalem Talmud, about 400; B. = Babylonian Talmud, about 500; M.T. = Mishneh Torah by Maimonides, finished 1177; S.A. = Shulhan Arukh, finished about 1565 by Rabbi Moses Isserles.

The general principle that "endangering oneself is more stringently [prohibited] than the [explicit] prohibitions [of the law]" (*hamira sakkanta me'isurah*) is stated in B. *Hullin* 10a, and it is included without demur in the codes (e.g., S.A. *Orah Hayyim* 173:2; S.A. *Yoreh De'ah* 116:5, gloss). The Talmud and codes include many injunctions which apply that principle in practice, as, for example, the command not to go out alone at night (B. *Pesahim* 112b). For other examples of this, see: B. *Shabbat* 32a; B. *Bava Kamma* 15b, 80a, 91b. The laws articulating a positive duty to care for one's body are best summarized in M.T. *Laws of Ethics (Hilkhot De'ot)*, chs. 3-5, but, as usual, Maimonides derives these from many talmudic precedents.

[4] God inflicts illness for sins: Deuteronomy 28:59-61. God as our Healer: e.g., Exodus 15:26; Deuteronomy 32:39; Isaiah 19:22; 57:18-19; etc.

[5] B. *Yoma* 85a-b; B. *Sanhedrin* 74a-b; *Mekhilta* on Exodus 31:13.

[6] J. *Kiddushin* 66d; see also B. *Sanhedrin* 17b, where this requirement is applied only to "the students of the wise".

[7] B. *Bava Metzia* 85b.

Jewish law grants the physician the right to determine treatment, the patient must be brought into the process of deciding what to do, and the doctor-patient relationship must be one of mutual honor and trust.

Not only must the individual seek medical care; the physician and the community jointly have the duty to provide it. Thus the Talmud praises one physician for putting his collection box outside his office so that the sick could put into it what they could afford.[8] Ultimately, Joseph Caro, author of the *Shulhan Arukh*, an oft-quoted sixteenth-century code of Jewish law, states: "The Torah gave permission to the physician to heal; moreover, this is a religious precept and is included in the category of saving life, and if the physician withholds his services, it is considered as shedding blood."[9]

This ethic must have been quite powerful because it is not until the nineteenth century that a rabbi rules that the communal court should force physicians to give free services to the poor if they do not do so voluntarily.[10] Sometimes communities even gave physicians tax breaks in consideration for such services to the poor. Depending on unpaid health care, however, was not the norm, for, as the Talmud specifically states, "a physician who charges nothing is worth nothing."[11] The Talmud thus lists medical care among the requirements of any Jewish settlement, and it asserts that communal funds must be used for that purpose. Nahmanides understands this social obligation as an implication of "Love your neighbor as yourself" (Leviticus 19:18), for just as you want to be healed of your ailments, you must love your neighbor enough to make sure that he or she is healed too.[12]

Moreover, communal provision of health care for the poor must be understood against the background of broader Jewish commitments toward the indigent and unfortunate. Basic needs such as food, clothing, and shelter have been understood since biblical times as the obligation of the community to provide for its members, not as a matter of humanitarian charity or out of considerations of equal opportunity, as some religions and some modern theorists suggest, but as a requirement of justice (*tzedakah*)

---

[8] B. *Ta'anit* 21b.

[9] S.A. *Yoreh De'ah* 336:1.

[10] Rabbi Eliezer Fleckeles, *Teshuvah Meahavah*, III, on S.A. *Yoreh De'ah* 336.

[11] B. *Bava Kamma* 85a.

[12] That every Jewish community must have a physician: B. *Sanhedrin* 17b. The duty to heal and to expend the community's resources on this: B. *Bava Kamma* 85a; B. *Sanhedrin* 73a. Nahmanides' derivation of this from "Love your neighbor as yourself": *Kitvei Haramban*, ed. Bernard Chavel, Jerusalem: Mosad Harav Kook, 1963 [Hebrew]; this passage comes from Nahmanides' *Torat Ha'adam (The Instruction of Man), Sha'ar Sakkanah (Section on Danger)*, on B. *Bava Kamma*, Ch. 8, and it is cited by Joseph Caro in *Bet Yosef* (his commentary to the earlier law code, the *Tur*), *Yoreh De'ah* 336.

as Judaism defines it. Second-century Jewish sources describe a number of institutions to accomplish this, including the soup-kitchen and the communal charity fund, collected and distributed by some of the most respected people in the town. These were not just rules written into a code as an ideal; the historical record indicates that Jewish communities extended themselves to lengths far beyond those of other groups and, in many cases, even beyond the requirements of Jewish law itself.[13]

The sick enjoy priority over other indigent persons in their claim to private or public assistance. Thus Joseph Caro records the view that while contributions to erect a synagogue take precedence over ordinary forms of charity, even the synagogue's needs must give way to the requirements of the indigent sick. And the sick may not refuse such aid if they require it to get well.[14]

Attention to the specific needs of the individual is one instance Jewish law's insistence that the whole tenor of communal services be one that sustains the honor of all concerned. Attention to the patient's desires is another mark of such respect. In Jewish belief, this aspect of health care is absolutely critical, for it recognizes that the person being treated is not simply a machine needing fixing, as American medicine all too often has conceived of patients, but a person created in God's image.

Types of spirituality

People have not only bodies, but souls, and the Jewish tradition was keenly aware of the critical need to care as well as to cure. In order to understand this dimension of a Jewish ethic of care, it is important to spell out what we mean by spiritual life in the first place. People have many different things in mind when they refer to the "spiritual" side of life, but I would suggest that the various definitions generally fall into three categories: (1) one's inner thoughts and feelings; (2) one's moral state of being; and (3) a linkage with the transcendent.

Inner thoughts and feelings

Probably the most common thing people want to denote when they speak about the spiritual component of life is the non-physical parts of it – the elements, in other words, of their inner being, their "spirit", here used in contrast to their body. In this first sense of the term, people are referring to their thoughts, will and feelings – that is, the mental, conative, and emotional parts of their being. Moreover, because human beings are

---

[13] For classical sources and some historical examples of how Jews treated their poor, see my book *To Do the Right and the Good* (see footnote 1 above), Chapter Six.

[14] S.A. *Yoreh De'ah* 249:16; 255:2.

inherently social, a person's spirit is very much a function of his or her relations with others. All of these things affect the extent to which people feel at peace with themselves.

In this first sense, then, people seeking spiritual meaning are looking for a sense of wholeness and meaning, both within themselves and within their community. They want to feel that the various vicissitudes of life either make sense in the larger scheme of things in some way, or, if they do not, people want to feel that they nevertheless have the strength to cope with life somehow. This inner peace is not necessarily a sense of quietude, although it often is, at least in the end. It is rather a sense that one's life has meaning and purpose, and for some people that is consistent with a very active life with little time left for leisure activities. For people in need of care, this spiritual need can initially take the form of expressions of anger and frustration at their inability to overcome the limitations of their lives, whether those come from their bodies, their minds, their emotions, or their relationships with other people. They want to know that such feelings have not gone unnoticed by those near and dear to them, and they want such feelings to be validated by such people as appropriate or at least as understandable and tolerable. They also want their family and friends to support them in their feelings and in their attempts to deal with them. In this mode of spirituality, they do not want judgments from others and maybe not even suggestions; their overwhelming need is for a listening ear, an understanding presence, a friendly hand. They thus gain spiritual "comfort," even if they have not been able to resolve the problems that thrust them into turmoil in the first place.

Health care professionals accustomed to working toward clearly definable goals of physical recovery and function may find this all rather spooky and maybe even annoying, but it is important to remember the concept of human beings underlying this kind of spirituality. Human beings are not just machines that either accomplish their ends or break down; people do want to resolve their physical problems, but that is not all that matters to them People are also intellectual, conative, psychological, and emotional beings, who respond to what is happening in their lives with inner thoughts and feelings and need help in dealing with their responses. From a practical point of view, this makes people much less efficient than unemotional robots would be, but, on the other hand, it is also part of what makes us distinctly human. It is what makes individuals unique and interesting, what gives them verve, and what makes them who they are. Moreover, as we have learned increasingly over the years, this part of human beings is not separate and distinct from their physical components, but rather integrally integrated with their bodies such that those who would care for the latter must inevitably pay attention to the former as well.

Moral state of being

Another part of human spirituality is the moral side of life. A person's inner being is not only mental, psychological, and emotional, but moral as well. Therefore, people stricken with traumatic illness, and especially those facing impending death, will inevitably ask tough moral questions. So will couples facing infertility or the prospect of aborting a compromised fetus. The issue will not just be what they *can* do and what will be the consequences of the various things they can do; the issue will be what they *should* do. Moreover, that question will not be just an inquiry asking for practical advice, but a true quest for moral rectitude. They might ask, for example, "*May* I (not just can I) fill out a Durable Power of Attorney for Health Care? If so, what *may* I include in it? I want to know not just what the law allows or what I can get the nurse or doctor to do; I want to know what I *should* do because I want to die a good person. I may not have always succeeded in living out my moral commitments in my life, but I surely want to end my life 'with clean hands and a pure heart,' as the Psalmist says,[15] if I can possibly do so. I therefore want to talk about these moral quandaries with people who care for me and whom I respect." Similarly, young people facing infertility or the prospect of aborting a defective fetus want to know now only what they can do, but what they should do.

In making these moral decisions, religious beliefs become critical, *for concrete moral norms are rooted in the broad perspectives that religions provide*. That is, whether we should or should, may or may not, do a specific thing depends ultimately on how that decision fits into the larger scheme of life, our ultimate understanding of who we are and who we should strive to be. That is precisely what religions talk about, and so religious questions will commonly, if not inevitably, arise when such matters need to be decided.

Linkage with the transcendent

The intellectual/psychological/emotional and moral components of spiritual care, though, are ultimately linked to a person's wider understanding of the nature of human life, the world, and God. It is precisely when people face the trauma of catastrophic illness that they are the most likely to ask serious questions about such things, for the illness threatens all their normal ties to the world. Thus cancer patients may well raise these deeper spiritual questions, even if they never affirmed much religion in their lives before. The same is true for young couples facing infertility or the prospect of an abortion. They are likely to ask how this affects their image of

---

[15] Psalms 24:4.

themselves as a man or woman and as a couple as they come to terms with the fact that their dreams and most personal wishes may not come true – at least not in the uncomplicated way that they had imagined. Other events in life can also raise such ultimate questions, and the more philosophically inclined may think about them without needing prompting by such events; but certainly those needing medical, psychological, and spiritual counseling because of something that has questioned all of their usual assumptions of life will be interested in probing this aspect of our spiritual being.

Health care professionals normally avoid all of these issues for lack of both time and expertise. That unfortunately conveys to themselves and their patients that they are only interested in the aspect of the person that they have been trained to heal. That fragments the person and, in so doing, dehumanizes him or her. It makes the patient seem like a machine, with specialists dedicated to fixing this part or that part but nobody interested in the whole. Given managed care and the highly specialized nature of medical training in our time, that is understandable, but it is also unfortunate. Not only patients, but also doctors and nurses themselves will gain immensely from indicating to patients that they recognize the spiritual aspects of the care they need. Ultimately, doctors and nurses may not provide that care, but they should at least speak with the patient about it to indicate that they too are human, that they too understand that there are elements to the patient's humanity that are not captured by physical treatment but are critical for their care.

Health care professionals who engage in this kind of spiritual care will not only help their patients cope with their illness, but will simultaneously help themselves to find meaning in their profession and avoid burnout. One of the oncologists who worked with me on the Los Angeles Jewish Hospice Commission was an unusually optimistic, happy man. When I asked him how he could be that way when he dealt with brain tumors, most of which he could not cure, he told me that a long time ago he had concluded that even if he could not cure, he could care, and he could make sure that family members, social workers, clergy, and others would join him in that process. That, in fact, was what got him involved at a very early stage in hospice care. Unknowingly, he was reflecting the teaching of the *Zohar*, a thirteenth-century work of Jewish mysticism, which says, "If a physician cannot give his patient medicine for his body, he should [at least] make sure that medicine is given him for his soul."[16]

[16] *Zohar*, I, 229b.

Visiting the sick

I have discussed a Jewish perspective on most of the moral aspects of health care in my book, *Matters of Life and Death: A Jewish Approach to Modern Medical Ethics*. As a result, I have chosen to discuss here one concrete example of how the Jewish tradition shapes the other two aspects of spiritual care. That example is visiting the sick.

We do not gain a sense of wellbeing in all three of these aspects of spirituality solely by what we do ourselves, for other people affect us all immensely. In one of the earliest passages of the Bible (Genesis 2:18), we are told that "it is not good for a person to live alone," and, indeed, short of execution, the harshest form of punishment in prisons is solitary confinement. Conversely, "people who need people are luckiest people in the world" – to quote an old Jewish authority!

Illness, though, is isolating. The sick person cannot leave home or the hospital to meet people in the usual places of work and leisure; on the contrary, anyone who wants to see that person must make special arrangements to do that. Knowing the importance of human interaction and the difficulty of having it when one is sick, the Jewish tradition classifies visiting the sick (in Hebrew, *biqqur holim*) as one of God's commandments.

Visiting the sick is a requirement of every Jew (not just the rabbi, doctor, or nurse); and so at least as early as the fourteenth century and continuing today in many contemporary congregations of all denominations, synagogues have established Biqqur Holim societies, consisting of members who have taken it upon themselves to make sure that the sick people are visited, whether or not they also have family doing that.[17]

Visiting the ill, though, is often uncomfortable for both the sick person and the visitors. The ill feel not only the physical pains of their illness, but also the loss of self-esteem associated with diminished capacity. They do not know how to handle themselves in these new, strange circumstances. This awkwardness is coupled with embarrassment, for friends see them dressed in pajamas. Moreover, the ill often feel as if they are intruding on their friends' time and making them do something they really would prefer not to do.

These suspicions are frequently accurate. Friends and family feel annoyed and put-upon by this new duty. They may also feel ill at ease because they are not used to interacting with people in this diminished state, and they do not know what to say or do. This is compounded by their discom-

---

[17] Rabbi Nissim Gerondi (c. 1360) is the first to mention such societies, perhaps because in earlier times Jews lived in communities sufficiently small to insure that everyone would be visited even without such a formal structure to make sure that that happened. See *Encyclopedia Judaica, 14*, 1498.

fort with illness altogether: seeing a sick person starkly reminds them of their own vulnerability.

The Jewish tradition was keenly aware that recovery from illness involves the patients' minds and spirits as well as their bodies. The Talmud says this: "Rabbi Abba son of Rabbi Hanina said: He who visits an invalid takes away a sixtieth of his pain [or, in another version, a sixtieth of his illness]...When Rabbi Dimi came [from Palestine], he said: He who visits the sick causes him to live, while he who does not causes him to die. How does he cause this? ... He who visits the sick prays that he may live,...[while] he who does not visit the sick prays neither that he may live nor die."[18]

The Talmud here is asserting two aspects of the spiritual elements of recovery. On a social plane, those who visit the sick help, to shift the patient's focus from the pain and degradation of the illness to the joy of the company of friends and family. They thus take away part of the pain of the illness. Visitors also reassure the patient that family and friends are keenly interested in their recovery, and they remind the patient of life outside the sick room. They thereby re-enforce the patient's determination to overcome the illness altogether or at least as many of its effects as they can. Visitors are thus instrumental in motivating the patient to follow a medical regimen of healing, however tedious or painful it may be, and so, in the Talmud's alternate reading, they effectively take away part of the patient's illness itself.

Visitors affect the patient on a more religious plane as well. By praying for the patient, and by indicating that prayers are being offered in the synagogue on his or her behalf, visitors invoke the aid of God, the ultimate Healer. Jewish prayer is traditionally done in community, in part because Jewish sources maintain that communal prayer convinces God to grant a request more effectively than private prayer does.[19] Visitors' prayers and those recited in the synagogue on behalf of the patient thus throw the weight of the entire community behind the patient's own plea to God for recovery.

Visitors must pay attention to the physical needs of the sick. Thus the Talmud tells the following story: " Rabbi Helbo fell ill. Rabbi Kahana then went [to the house of study] and proclaimed, 'Rabbi Helbo is ill.' Nobody, however, visited him. Rabbi Kahana rebuked them [the disciples], saying, 'Did it ever happen that one of Rabbi Akiba's students fell ill, and the [rest of the] disciples did not visit him?' So Rabbi Akiba himself entered [Rabbi Helbo's house] to visit him, and because they swept and sprinkled the ground before him [that is, cleaned the house and put it in order], Rabbi

---

[18] B. *Nedarim* 39b-40a.

[19] B. *Berakhot* 6a; 7b-8a; J. *Berakhot* 5:1; cf. M.T. *Laws of Prayer* 8:1.

Helbo recovered. Rabbi Akiba then went forth and lectured: He who does not visit the sick is like one who sheds blood."[20]

Taking physical care of the sick can include not only cleaning house, but shopping for groceries, doing laundry, taking over carpool duties, and seeing to the other needs of the patient's children. Depending upon the circumstances, it can also include more direct physical interventions like taking the patient for a ride in a wheelchair (if medically permitted), feeding the patient (if necessary), and attending to the patient's other physical needs.

Mostly, though, visiting the sick involves talking with the patient, and that is what often causes the greatest degree of discomfort. Those who visit the sick often do not know what to say or do. Some would rather not hear about the patient's aches and pains, much less about a painful or dangerous procedure the patient just endured or is facing, because such talk makes them sad and engenders thoughts about their own vulnerability. The food served at the facility and the weather quickly lose their interest as topics of conversation. Since few of us are trained in effective visiting techniques, visitors soon feel frustrated in their desires to help and support the patient. All of these feelings deter people from visiting the sick any more than they feel they absolutely must.

The Jewish tradition has some practical advice for making such visits more pleasant and effective:[21]

(1) *Insuring that a visit is welcome*. Through consultation with the patient's family or friends, potential visitors should make sure that a visit would be neither embarrassing nor physically detrimental to the patient.[22]

---

[20] B. *Nedarim* 39b-40a.

[21] The primary places where the classical codes deal with this are in M.T. *Laws of Mourning*, chapter 14, and in S.A. *Yoreh De'ah* 335. Other sources in English on Jewish practices regarding visiting the sick include: Elliot N. Dorff, *Matters of Life and Death* (at footnote 2 above), chapter eleven; Isaac Klein, *A Guide to Jewish Religious Practice*, New York: Jewish Theological Seminary of America, 1979, 271-272; Pesach Krauss, *Why Me? Coping with Grief, Loss, and Change*, Toronto and New York: Bantam, 1988, esp. chapters 16 and 17, pp. 123-139; Tsvi G. Schur, *Illness and Crisis: Coping the Jewish Way*, New York: National Conference of Synagogue Youth/Union of Orthodox Jewish Congregations of America, 1987, esp. chapter 6, pp. 66-69; Abraham S. Abraham, *Medical Halachah for Everyone*, New York: Feldheim, 1980, chapter 35, pp. 135-138; and *Bikkur Holim*, New York: Women's League for Conservative Judaism, 1992.

[22] Thus Maimonides (M.T. *Laws of Mourning* 14:5) says this: "We visit neither those with bowel disease nor those with eye disease nor those with headaches, for visits are hard on them", either because the patient will be embarrassed by the disease, as in bowel trouble, or because a visit will add to the patient's pain and impede recovery, as in the cases of patients with eye trouble or frequent headaches, for

(2) *Timing the day of one's visit.* "As a matter of good manners", according to the Jerusalem Talmud,[23] only family and close friends should visit during the first two days of an illness, and others should wait until the third day. That restriction does not apply, however, to patients with acute, life-threatening illnesses.

(3) *Timing the hours of one's visit.* The hours of visitation must not interfere with the patient's medical treatment or unduly tax the patient's strength.[24] Hospitals have the right to restrict visiting hours to assure this. If the patient is helped by visits, though, they need not be limited to one per day.[25]

(4) *Positioning oneself to make the patient feel comfortable.* Visitors who stand accentuate the patient's incapacity in comparison to their able-bodied state. They also indicate that they do not plan to stay long. To avoid these feelings, visitors should sit at the same level as the patient's head so that their relative heights communicate equality and support.[26]

(5) *Attending to the patient's needs.* As discussed above, part of the point of visiting the sick is to learn how one can help the patient or the family cope with the illness. Since patients and their close family members are often reticent to ask for help, visitors need to offer it. They should suggest one or two specific things so that the patient or family members under-

---

whom speaking with visitors is, according to talmudic medicine (B. *Nedarim* 41a) physically and psychologically burdensome.

[23] J. *Pe'ah* 3:9. Other sources (e.g., *Bayit Hadash* on Tur 335; M.T. *Laws of Mourning* 14:5; S.A. *Yoreh De'ah* 335:1 and *Turei Zahav* there) tie this to the story in the Talmud (B. *Nedarim* 40a) of Rava, who, when he fell sick, asked that on the first day of the illness his servants not make it known, "lest his fortune be impaired" – that is, lest people talk about it generally and thus attract evil spirits. Relatives and close friends who commonly come into the house to visit would not arouse such spirits.

[24] Thus Maimonides (M.T. *Laws of Mourning* 14:5) says: "We do not visit the sick in the first or last three hours of the day because at those times the care givers are busy with the needs of the sick person." The Talmud (B. *Nedarim* 40a) and, following that, the *Shulhan Arukh (Yoreh De'ah* 335:4) give a less medical and more theological reason: During the first three hours of the day, the illness is generally less acute than it is later, and so visitors will not remember to offer prayers on behalf of the sick because they will not think it necessary. During the last three hours of the day, the illness may appear so serious that visitors will despair from offering prayers for the sick, thinking that prayer in such serious cases would inevitably be ineffective.

[25] M.T. *Laws of Mourning* 14:4: "People should visit many times during the day, and all who add to their visits are to be praised – as long as they do not burden the patient."

[26] M.T. *Laws of Mourning* 14:6; Tosafot on B. *Shabbat* 127a; S.A. *Yoreh De'ah* 335:3, gloss.

stand that the offer is serious and get a sense of the scope of what the visitor is willing to do.

(6) *Praying for and with the patient.* Jewish sources state that one fulfills the commandment of visiting the sick only if one prays with and for the patient for healing.[27] One should use the short, standard formula stated in the Talmud and codes – namely, "May the All-Present have mercy on you among the sick of Israel"[28] – and then add whatever one thinks appropriate and meaningful, whether in Hebrew or in English.[29] Many prayer books include suggested texts, often from the Book of Psalms.

(7) *Speaking with the patient.* Aside from praying for and with the patient, how do you fill the time? What do you talk about? Conversations normally flow out of joint activities, but patients cannot engage in the work or recreation that usually bring people together and get them talking. How, then, can they engage in meaningful and helpful conversation?

Some topics that should be raised are practical in nature. Specifically, if the patient has not previously filled out a will or a living will for health care, she or he should be asked to specify their wishes about how the disposition of their property and the course of medical treatment they prefer. Visitors, especially family members, can help them do that.

Most time spent with the patient, though, does lend itself to discussion of specific decisions or projects. How, then, should visitors fill the time of their visit? Jewish legal sources are silent about this, but Jewish theological concepts provide important clues. Every human being, according to the Torah, bears the dignity of being created in the image of God. The key to speaking with sick people, then, is to bolster that sense of worth.

Illness is inherently degrading: it incapacitates the person from doing what people of the patient's age normally do. Visitors must be especially on guard, then, to avoid infantilizing the patient, for talking down to the patient reinforces his or her sense of loss of power and honor. Visitors should rather engage the patient in conversations on the level and subjects of the patient's normal interests. That communicates that the visitor still cares about the patient's opinions, and it thus reinforces the patient's sense of normalcy and worth.

One of the most enlightening experiences of my early rabbinic career was giving a series of lectures on Jewish theology to residents of a Jewish nursing home. The

---

[27] Ramban (Nahmanides), *Torat Ha-Adam*, "Sha'ar Ha-Mehush"; S.A. *Yoreh De'ah* 335:4, gloss.

[28] B. *Shabbat* 12b; S.A. *Yoreh De'ah* 335:6.

[29] S.A. *Yoreh De'ah* 335:5. Hebrew and/or the vernacular may be used in the presence of the patient; presumably the visitor should decide that on the basis of his or her own abilities and the knowledge and sensitivities of the patient. In the synagogue, though, Jewish law states that the prayer for healing should be done in Hebrew.

group included former doctors, lawyers, teachers, and entrepreneurs. The residents themselves, all college graduates, had specifically asked for these classes, even though none of them had ever studied Jewish theology before, because, as the social worker told me, they were sick of playing Bingo! They had been intellectually active at earlier stages of their lives, and their physical illnesses now did not significantly change their intellectual interests or even their mental capacity – except that I had to speak just a little more slowly than I usually do. The social workers who arranged these lessons had also warned me not to be deterred by the fact that sometimes the students' eyes would close, for in older people closed eyes do not necessarily signal sleep. As the social workers predicted, some of the people who had their eyes closed through most of the class later asked me pointed questions about what I had said; they clearly were awake and listening. The students even read assignments in preparation for the class from specially prepared sheets with enlarged print. I wish my younger students were always as well prepared!

Visitors do not normally discuss Jewish theology, but this example will, I hope, make clear that conversations with patients should be challenging and should cover a wide variety of topics. The very normalcy of such discussions communicates that the illness has not diminished the visitor's respect for the patient's intelligence and humanity.

Finally, especially for people with long-term illnesses, the Jewish tradition has a vehicle to make continued visits interesting and meaningful for both patient and visitor. That is the *ethical will*. An ethical will, addressed to children, grandchildren, other family members, and friends, is a document in which the author articulates his or her most important experiences, values, thoughts, feelings, dreams, and hopes. The writer may be sick or healthy, young or old, but ethical wills are most commonly written by people in their fifties or beyond.

In times past, ethical wills were written, but now they can be taped or even videotaped. There are no requirements in Jewish law that govern such documents; in fact, most, whether written or oral, take the form of an extended, personal letter.

To create an ethical will, people need not be especially religious; piety and knowledge are not required for this. Moreover, they do not have to be unusually articulate. What may sound like the people for whom one's ethical will is intended will not hear platitudes to other people that way. Family and friends will read or hear it with a personal knowledge of the author in mind, and so they will understand the message even if it is not expressed very well. The point is not to create a literary masterpiece, but rather to write or tape an honest and straightforward expression of what the author feels. Some people create one ethical will for their entire family, others produce separate ethical wills addressed to specific individuals, and some do both.

Some of the topics commonly included in ethical wills include the following:

(1) The experiences most important to the author in her or his relationship(s) to the recipient(s).

(2) The values the author considers most critical to living a morally sensitive and worthy life, perhaps with some examples to help make the point clear and memorable.

(3) Reflections on the relationships of the recipients among each other, together with expressions of joy, concern, or hope.

(4) Specific desires the author has -- e.g., that the children care for each other, that they establish Jewish homes, that a surviving spouse remarry.

(5) An expression of Jewish commitment with examples of what Judaism has meant in the author's life.

(6) An account of the family history, including the author's own life story. This often takes up most of the will, and it is most worthwhile in giving children and grandchildren a sense of their roots. In particular, stories about the author's parents and grandparents provide a strong sense of rootedness to the surviving members of the family.

(7) Some proverb or saying the author finds especially meaningful.

(8) An expression of concern and love for the people receiving the ethical will.

Patients who know that they have a task to accomplish in leaving their children and (especially) their grandchildren a record of their experiences, values, thoughts, dreams, and hopes will redouble their efforts to live as long as they can so that they can complete this important project.[30] Ethical wills are also a boon for visitors. In providing a program and goal for visits, helping a patient complete an ethical will can transform visits from boring and uncomfortable encounters to be avoided to interesting and meaningful exchanges for all concerned.

Talking with a patient about a will, a durable power of attorney for health care, and an ethical will, coupled with the other forms of conversation and physical ministration mentioned above, makes visits to the sick a critical part of the person's chances for speedy recovery. No wonder, then, that the Rabbis understood visiting the sick as an activity we do in imitation of God: "'Follow the Lord your God' (Deuteronomy 13:5). What does this mean? Is it possible for a mortal to follow God's Presence? The verse means to teach us that we should follow the attributes of the Holy One, praised be He. As God clothed the naked, for it is written, 'And the Lord God made for Adam and for his wife coats of skin and clothed them'

[30] For some poignant examples of ethical wills, including many modern ones, see Jack Riemer and Nathaniel Stampfer (eds.), *Ethical Wills: A Modern Jewish Treasury*, New York: Schocken, 1983. For some suggestions for preparing an ethical will, see Jack Riemer and Nathaniel Stampfer (eds.), *So That Your Values Live on - Ethical Wills and How to Prepare Them*, Woodstock, VT: Jewish Lights Publishing, 1991.

(Genesis 3:21), so you should clothe the naked. The Holy One, blessed be He, visited the sick, for it is written [after the description of Abraham's circumcision], 'And the Lord appeared to him near the oaks of Mamre' (Genesis 18:1), so you should visit the sick. The Holy One, blessed be He, comforted those who mourned ... and so should you comfort mourners. The Holy One, blessed be He, buried the dead ... and so should you bury the dead.."[31]

Moreover, visiting the sick, as an act of both loyalty and kindness (*hesed*), is, according to the Rabbis, one of a small list of commandments that have no limit and that yield immediate fruit (to both the visitor and the patient) while the principle redounds to the benefit of those who do them in God's ultimate judgment in the World to Come.[32]

---

[31] B. *Sotah* 14a.

[32] B. *Shabbat* 127a. See also M. *Pe'ah* 1:1, where acts of loving kindness, such as visiting the sick, are described as deeds for which there is no prescribed measure since they are limitless in their benefit – although only, as the Rabbis said, when one is sensitive to the needs of the patient so that one's visit does not become a burden and a source of suffering (cf. B. *Nedarim* 40a). The first two passages cited above are included at the very beginning of the daily morning service; see, for example, *Siddur Sim Shalom: A Prayerbook for Shabbat, Festivals, and Weekdays*, New York: Rabbinical Assembly and United Synagogue of America, 1985, 8-9.

Pastoral Theological Reflections on Caregiving and Religious Pluralism *

Kathleen J. Greider
USA, 2010

In this essay, I take up the topic of what is required of religious caregivers to "open up" to persons of different faiths. Religious pluralism is a crucial focus for reflection on caregiving because of the obvious increase in recent years of interreligious encounter in everyday life and in the practices of caregiving. I explore this topic, first, by making explicit some of the challenges inherent in interreligious caregiving. This is an important first step in light of the risks of romanticism and simplification with regard to openness and interreligious care. In the remainder of the essay, from my religious location within Christianity, I offer pastoral theological reflections on caregiving in light of religious pluralism by means of two methods commonly employed in the field: selfreflexivity and reflection on a specific relationship of care.

Challenges of caregiving in interreligious relationships

The possibility of offering care in the context of religious pluralism presents immediate challenges. First, the topic is wonderfully and maddeningly ambiguous. For example, what qualifies us to be called "open"? Like the door to our home, shop, or church, the door to our minds and hearts can be wide open, or halfway open, or barely ajar, left open accidentally or intentionally. All these forms of openness suggest different degrees – and qualities – of openness. The ambiguity of openness can also be attributed to the fact that it is constituted by the best aspects of both our naiveté and our wariness – thus, the memorable phrase attributed to Jesus: "be wise as serpents and innocent as doves" (Mt. 10:16 NRSV). The spiritual demands of integrating wisdom and innocence on a daily and consistent basis tax the

---

* Modified version of a paper presented at the 22nd International Seminar on Intercultural Pastoral Care and Counselling, 2010, in Strasbourg, France. First published in *Intercultural Pastoral Care and Counselling, 16*, 2011, 106-115.

most spiritually mature persons. It is not difficult to think of well-meaning persons – others, ourselves – who actively cultivate openness and still hurt persons of religious identities different than our own. The harm done may be severe or slight. In either case, we are reminded that our openness brings us into relationship with the tender and tough religious sensibilities of others. Once our openness has brought us that far, navigating such a complex relationship requires knowledge and spiritual grace not gained through will or good intentions alone.

Closely related is a second challenge – that religion can be used to harm as well as to help is arguably the most profound dimension of the ambiguity of trying to relate religious pluralism and caregiving. As we affirm the possibilities of care in religious pluralism, we must just as faithfully and rigorously cultivate consciousness that even though we think we are using religion to help, we may harm. Again, the harm done may be severe or slight. In either case, the harm adds to centuries of violence and alienation between religious communities. Given the long history during which religions have been deformed by use of them to rationalize violence, we have accomplished only basic decency and the most obvious requirement of non-violence if we have managed to curb our physical violence. We must continue in our commitment to non-violence, ferreting out how our thoughtlessness, attitudes, and behaviors sometimes do violence in the communal, interpersonal, and psycho-spiritual dimensions of interreligious relationship.

A third challenge when considering what is required of religious caregivers to open up to people of other faiths relates to the diversity of opinion about what constitutes "care". The integrity of our inquiry into how we can be caregivers to persons of other faiths depends on honesty about the differences *within* religious traditions about how open we are required to be in order to be caring. Arguably the most acute questions relate to the truth, holiness, and transformative possibilities of diverse traditions. In Christianity, some Christians say that they can assess their religious tradition as superior to other religions and at the same time offer care that is experienced as such. Other Christians say that assessing one's religion as superior is inherently an uncaring stance toward persons of other religions, that the most profound care requires a non-judgmental stance that affirms the religious commitments of those to whom care is offered. My descriptions of these positions are somewhat caricatures, but they point to the extreme differences within Christianity regarding the interplay of religious difference and caregiving.

There is voluminous support in Christianity for both positions and many in between, and this fact leads to a fourth challenge: there is biblical support and theological exposition to support whatever opinion Christians hold relative to religious pluralism, so what shall we say is the basis for our positions? The different and often vehement positions we take relative to the value of religious pluralism seem to boil down not much to choice but the dynamism of our different life histories and the mystery of how any spiritual path is shaped. This being the case, caregiving in interreligious relationship is a challenging subject because it is very personal and often contentious. This is true not least among my people, Christians, since it so often leads to intractable and excruciating painful arguments that our religion is or is not superior to others. In my experience among Christians, the topic of this essay is more likely to lead to judgmentalism and division than to openness. What have we accomplished if our theology allows us to open up to one degree or another to people of other faiths, but not to people of our own faith with whom we are in disagreement?

Finally, a fifth challenge relates to methodology. The responsibility of being educated in the theories and methods of pastoral theology and care includes, among other things, the obligation to speak contextually and self-reflexively as well as for the purpose of care. On the one hand, practical theologians must aim to develop theology that arises from and speaks to the actual, specific, personal, chaotic, and compromised conditions of human living as we have experienced it. This honesty and particularity about the complexity of human experience includes self-reflexivity and a degree of transparency about our personal and social locations – our own experience of the actual, specific, personal, chaotic, and compromised conditions of human living. Academic, political, or civic engagement with religious pluralism can be conducted at the level of the abstract, generalized, or ideal. In contrast, pastoral theological engagement with religious pluralism must be grounded in the concrete, particular, and real. On the other hand, pastoral theologians are responsible to speak in ways that privilege the requirements and responsibilities of care. As religious caregivers, we are charged to care for the traditions of which we are representatives, but even more so for the people and communities we encounter in our work. Though we may not agree on what constitutes care for human beings, it is clear that the responsibilities of pastoral theologians and religious caregivers are somewhat different from, for example, those who are called to clarify doctrinal orthodoxy or preserve religious institutions.

Given these combined challenges, it is clear to me as a pastoral theologian and caregiver that this topic – so full of ambiguity, complexity, and danger – cannot be addressed appropriately as if it were an objective matter with generalizable options for response. Fortunately, methods in pastoral theology and care take just these conditions into account. We construct theology and shape our practices with full awareness of the necessity of particularized and partial reflections on the human condition, and with full confidence in the value and persuasive power of every human life. In the following sections, as a means of reflecting on how religious caregivers can open themselves to persons of others faiths, I will employ two widely endorsed methods in pastoral theology and care: self-reflexivity and reflection on a specific relationship of care

Reflections on caregiving and religious pluralism: the pastoral theological method of self-reflexivity

In my pastoral and personal experience, theologies that open religious caregivers to people of other faiths result from one's particular life narrative, especially one's spiritual path and formation. The degree and qualities of our openness to people of other faiths are partially a result of our own choices but arguably just as much a result of happenstance and our response to it – the synchronicity of the family and communities into which we are born, the religious culture we inherit, the teachers that cross our path, the interreligious relationships we build. As a pastoral theologian, I would not – because I cannot – tell you what theology will open you up to persons of other faiths. To put it theologically, we can say that it is finally a matter that each of us must work out within our own religious framework and within relationships with persons of other religions.

I can, however, through the method of self-reflexivity, offer reflection on some of what has happened in the synchronicity of my life narrative to open me up to people of other religions.[1] The field of pastoral theology and care places a high value of self-reflexivity in academic and professional discourse because, as a mode of transparency, it makes the personal bases and biases of our theological assertions more accessible to our readers. Therefore, I offer these reflections for the purpose of honesty about the subjectivity of my approach to religious pluralism and care. I do not presume that my choices, rationale, and beliefs are or should be your beliefs. I offer my selfreflexivity to you in the spirit of openness to religious pluralism.

For as long as I can remember, I have been seeking to comprehend, love, and respond to what I have come to call Divine Mystery – the mystery many people call G-d.[2] Relative to religious pluralism, it is crucial for me to remain mindful that though my search for the Divine Mystery began in

[1] I could offer reflections as well on what *is* happening, what continues to open me to other people of faith. However, given the limitations of space, I choose to focus on my youth and young adulthood, as these periods were most formative for me with regard to openness to religious pluralism and care.

[2] It is my custom to use the formulation "G-d" to refer to divinity, rather than spelling the word in its entirety. Following its use in Judaism, this incomplete spelling symbolizes the humility we are advised to practice when speaking of the divine and the incapacity of humans to know the divine completely.

Christian community, in the beginning, I did not choose Christianity, it was chosen for me. Christianity is the religion of my ancestors, as far back as I know, and so Christianity was chosen for me by my parents, and their parents before them, and so on. My Christian identity remains to this day partially an accident of birth. I was baptized into the Christian church as an infant. I was taught the Christian language – it became my first religious language, my native spiritual tongue. Through the Christian language, my whole being was shaped. Christian stories, ideas, values, and practices were primary in the ecology in which grew – it was like the air I breathed, the food I ate, the love in which, as a dependent vulnerable child, I had no choice but to trust. I grew to love the G-d and Jesus I was given.

Of course the Christian church can be likened to the vast geography of this planet and the diverse peoples that inhabit it. I was born and reared in the Evangelical United Brethren region of Christianity. The orthodox and pietistic beliefs of that denomination nourished and sustained me for my earliest years. But for reasons I cannot fully explain, very early I was filled with what for me were questions, though something gave me the impression that my elders experienced them as doubts. The only vivid memory I have of Sunday church school was of raising my hand to ask for an explanation of miracles and of the teacher who responded with a blank look and a painfully long silence before he could find words. By the time I was nine years of age, my question about one type of miracle was especially persistent: "exactly how did Jesus heal the sick?" I was disquieted by healing stories. I had been taught that the G-d I had been given is omnipotent, omniscient, and omnipresent. This conveyed that the G-d given to me was choosing not to heal my mother, who was seriously ill, and not getting better. Later I learned that some of the Christian leaders around my family, including our pastor, held the belief that her illness was a result of her insufficient faith. I was deeply troubled by this response, which struck me as dangerously self righteousness and a failure of respect and compassion, especially since I had no memory of their relating to us much at all. This very common struggle – to make sense of the co-existence of suffering, the hard-heartedness of religious people, and a powerful, loving G-d – was the first aspect of my life experience that began to open me up to other religious possibilities. I was also troubled at a young age by the call to evangelize others: I distinctly remember refusing to hand out religious literature on a city street corner because it seemed to me much like what was offered to my family – Christian judgment and a failure of respect and compassion, on the basis of no real relationship.

I had no significant exposure to religions other than Christianity until I was a college student. Through this exposure, I arrived at a second aspect of experience that continued to open me to people who belonged to other religions and to those of no religion at all. I learned about and met people living what my Christian community called "spirit-filled lives," even though they were not Christians. They were doing the good work that I had come to think was the fruit of a Christian life. But it was clear that people outside the Christian church had passion and commitment and brilliance and love to build the kingdom of G-d on earth, more so than some Christians I knew. Yet all I had been taught to that point was that these good people would be condemned by G-d, because they were not Christian. This second aspect of experience – the Christian church's assertion that people whose lives were marked with the holiness to which Christianity taught me to aspire would still be condemned – became a second arena in which I was left deeply troubled by what I could experience only as a lack of Christian humility and compassion.

In my early twenties these experiences brought me to a turning point in regard to my openness to people of other religions. I was faced with a choice that has been presented to many Christians: choose to believe that G-d condemns good people because they aren't Christian or find another way. This turning-point was both disconcerting and clear for me. It was clear that I would not, could not, surrender my love of G-d to Christian doctrine. In my own devotions I had come to know G-d to be endless love, disciplined mercy, and ultimate compassion. Also, this condemnation seemed ludicrous to me, since Jesus was not a Christian. It was disconcerting, though, because at the time I did not know if my refusal to join in the condemnation of people outside the Christian church meant that I was no longer a Christian. Not long after, I continued my search for Divine Mystery by going to theological school, where I learned that there were other Christians who were troubled by this and similar choices.

Finally, I will share beliefs that have evolved to be a foundation for the degree of openness and kind of care I am called to offer in light of religious pluralism. These beliefs have grown out of my encounter with the diversity within Christianity, with people of other religions, and with people who choose no religion. I grasp and practice these beliefs imperfectly, but they orient my life and I have found them fully trustworthy. I could make substantial arguments for each of these. Given the limits of space, however, I can only list them, though with some attention to their logical relation.

- Most fundamentally: That which is sacred and holy is a Divine Mystery never fully comprehended by human beings.
- My first loyalty is to this sacred and holy Divine mystery, as the origin of the gift of all life, and of my particular life. Therefore, my first loyalty is not to any particular religion, denomination, congregation, or human leader but to Divine Mystery.
- Because Divine Mystery passes all human understanding, to name it – whether as Divine Mystery, G-d, YHWH, Jehovah, Adonai, I AM WHO I AM – or to speak of it in any way is to risk arrogance. Therefore, humility

is the condition of my right to speak of it at all. And, to think or make definitive statements about Divine Mystery, as if we fully know the Divine Mystery, to think or speak in any way that forecloses on the possibility we are mistaken, is blasphemy.

- Divine Mystery is and has been present at all times and its power shared with the whole creation, including humanity. All creation, which includes all religions, has the potential to be a means by which Divine Mystery can be glimpsed and can be distorted. All humanity and all religions have used the power of Divine Mystery for evil and for good. No religion can fully contain or express the Divine Mystery.
- Human life has meaning and humans are saved from ultimate destruction by devotion to Divine Mystery, demonstrated through, as the Hebrew Bible puts it, the essentials of kindness, justice, and humility (Mic. 6:8). I cannot earn and or repay the gift of my life. I can, however, honor this gift by living with gratitude and by protecting the gift of life wherever it is found.
- Human life is at least as sacred as human institutions, such as religions, especially where human life is squandered through suffering and unnecessary violence.
- My primary teacher is the Jew and rabbi, Jesus of Nazareth. The Jewish life and teaching of Jesus was the primary inspiration for the formation of Christianity and, finally, for my eventual choice to affiliate myself with Christianity.
- The Christian Church is a human and limited expression of Christianity.
- The Divine Mystery has no arms or legs but those of humanity.[3] The Divine Mystery calls me into caregiving, to embody Divine Mystery as nearly as possible through responding to the suffering and joy of the creation, and seeking to curtail unnecessary violence.
- The biblical mandate to Christians to make disciples is best illuminated for me in the words of a Christian woman writer: "We convert, if we do at all, by being something irresistible, not by demanding something impossible." [4]

Reflections on caregiving and religious pluralism: the pastoral theological method of case study

I turn now to a second pastoral theological method as a means of responding to the question of what is required of us if we are to open up to people of other religions. Case study is one way to practice pastoral theological

[3] Dorothee Sölle, *Death by Bread Alone*, transl. David L. Scheidt, Philadelphia: Fortress, 1978, 98-99.

[4] May Sarton, *The House by the Sea*, New York: Norton, 1977, 57-58.

commitment to the capacity of any life situation, through our careful reflection on it, to be a source of wisdom, and perhaps of Divine Mystery. In this practice of close reflection on human experience, pastoral theologians and caregivers often choose narratives of actual people, perhaps people we meet in caregiving situations. However, we can also begin by reflecting on narratives that come from the human imagination. For our purposes, I have decided to use a story told on film as the basis of reflection. Since migration is a widespread contemporary phenomenon that has increased exponentially the amount of contact between persons of different religions, I have chosen to reflect on the film "*The Visitor*", in which migration plays a central role.[5] The film does not explicitly address religious pluralism. It nonetheless offers rich material for our reflection because it is a story about deeply significant themes in spirituality: vulnerability and mortality, loss and grief, meanings and values, and how encountering persons different from us can set in motion profound changes in all the participants' lives. I will begin, as this method always does, with careful description of the human situation being considered, avoiding any interpretive comments unless offered by the persons directly involved. After the description, I will comment on three dimensions of human experience evident in this narrative that seem to contribute to openness.

Description

Walter Vale is a middle-aged white male who lives and works somewhere outside New York City. For twenty years, he has been an economics professor at a college in a small town. But Walter has long ago become disillusioned with the academic life. He has taught the same class with the same syllabus for as many years as he can remember. He is supposedly writing a book, but progress stopped years ago. When we meet him, Walter is also in grief, suffering from the death of his wife a few months earlier. Because she was a concert pianist, he is trying to learn the piano and often spends his time listening to classical music. Walter seems like he is sleepwalking through his life, all his emotion deadened. When a student troubled with personal problems tries to submit a paper late, Walter turns away the paper and the student brusquely, without empathy, even though Walter knows all to well what it is like to be troubled. When Walter's dean requires that he go to New York City to present a paper for a colleague who is under medical restrictions, Walter tries to refuse. Soon we learn that Walter does not want to go to the city because, before her death, he and his wife shared an apartment there. Walter has not relinquished the apartment, but he has not been there for many months. The Dean insists.

---

[5] Michael London and Mary Jane Skalski (producers) and Tom McCarthy (director), *The Visitor* [Motion Picture], USA: Alliance Films, 2008.

When Walter arrives at the apartment, he discovers that a young couple, Tarek and Zainab, has been living there for two months, having fallen prey to a real estate scam. Walter is very startled but manages to tell them politely that they must leave. Walter sits on the couch, watching impassively as they pack their belongings and struggle with their bags as they depart. Moments after they leave, he finds a picture they have forgotten to pack, a picture of the two of them together, happy. Suddenly, Walter is hurriedly walking down the street, trying to find them so he can return their picture. Walter finds them and in their brief conversation realizes they have nowhere to go. Something causes him to reverse himself. Walter invites Tarek and Zainab back to his apartment to stay there until they can find other lodging. Tarek, like Walter's wife, is a musician, a drummer. The next day Walter comes back to the apartment and finds him practicing. Tarek invites Walter to join him in the drumming. Walter quickly refuses, but when Tarek persists, and offers to help him, Walter slowly sits and begins hesitantly tapping on a drum. Over the next few days, Tarek draws Walter into a world with rhythms different from any Walter had known before. He goes to hear Tarek's group play in a jazz club and joins Tarek in a drumming circle in the park. Walter hears Tarek's story of migration, of coming to the U.S. from Syria at a young age. With the encouragement of Tarek, Walter becomes a fairly good drummer. Just as noticeably, Walter becomes less isolated and shy, and smiles a bit more. A friendship seems to be developing between them.

One afternoon, Walter and Tarek are hurrying to catch a subway train. After paying for the ride, Tarek has trouble getting himself and his drum through the gate, so he jumps over the gate. The police, watching from nearby, use this as an excuse to detain and arrest Tarek, despite Walter's explanations and protests. Walter returns to the apartment and must tell Zainab that Tarek has been arrested. Though Walter is sure that Tarek will be released and everything will be okay, Zainab is terrified. They both are undocumented, she tells Walter: "It will not be okay."

Having been drawn into their lives, Walter is desperate to help them. He hires an immigration lawyer for Tarek. He visits Tarek at the detention center. When Tarek's mother, Mouna, arrives from Michigan, he hears the whole story of their migration – Mouna brought Tarek to the U.S. when he was very young to escape persecution in Syria; they both immigrated illegally in order to not to be sent back to the trouble in Syria; she and Tarek have lived in the U.S. for twenty years and she has worked hard for them to have a stable life and make many friends; like Tarek and Zainab, Mouna is undocumented.

Now Walter cares for Mouna, as well. He invites her to stay at the apartment. Since she cannot enter the deportation center where Tarek is being held because she has no legal papers, Walter takes her there and carries her letters to Tarek inside for her. Walter introduces Mouna and Zainab. Walter and Mouna, both widowed, also find companionship and tenderness together.

But all Walter's efforts for this family are like a drop in a bucket. Within days and without warning, Tarek is deported to Syria. Walter screams at the deportation officials, realizing that his citizenship gives him no power to affect the situation. Zainab is heartbroken and disappears out of fear the police will find her because of her connection to Tarek. To help Tarek, Mouna returns to Syria, unsure whether safety awaits her there and sadly aware that she will never be allowed back in the U.S. and is losing the life she had forged. Now, Walter is alone again, except that he has the drums left behind after Tarek deportation. The closing shot of the film is of Walter, now a street musician, playing the drums in the subway. Over the space of ten days, Walter's perspective has been profoundly altered.

Reflections on the narrative

In my view, the question of how to open up to people of other faiths is a question of spirituality at least as much as it is a question of doctrine. Genuine suffering and acute human need of lives created as part of the Divine Mystery can sometimes quite suddenly reveal the incompleteness of doctrine. Perhaps this is why a saying of the Dalai Lama – "My true religion is kindness." – is so often quoted. But kindness worthy of being called a true religion is not easily practiced. It requires spiritual resources and maturity and, even then, the spiritual demands of openness across borders are considerable. I am reminded of two friends who have participated in the New Sanctuary Movement by hosting in their home an undocumented woman, her husband, and their three children. They all lived together, two families under one roof, for eighteen months. Recently, one of the friends was talking about the cost of providing sanctuary to this family: she gave them sanctuary, she said, and thereby had lost her own sanctuary, the quiet refuge of her own home upon which she had previously depended for her spiritual life. Because of the spiritual demands of openness and caregiving in situations of religious pluralism, I am deliberately trying to avoid the most commonplace concepts used in such discussions: for example, inclusivity, respect, welcome, hospitality, empathy, compassion. These are essential elements of our caregiving, of course. However, given the continuing plague of disrespect, rejection, hard-heartedness, self-orientation, and other forms of unnecessary violence, they seem not to be adequate by themselves. So, very briefly, through reflection on *The Visitor*, I will draw attention to three less commonly addressed aspects of openness to persons of other faiths: our emptiness, our strangeness, and our childlikeness.

Our emptiness

Relative to our topic, a pivotal moment in the film comes when Walter reverses himself and invites Tarek and Zainab back to his home. What makes it possible for this to happen? When we meet Walter, he seems to be an empty man. The death of his wife seems to have been a psychospiritual tsunami, sweeping away not only his wife but also the rickety structures that comprised much of his life. Indeed, it seems perhaps this final assault has swept away all his life force. It is not that Walter is wallowing in his wounds. It is simply the case that his normal human grief has not run its course. He seeks comfort in the classical music she loved, but it does not fill him. When he tells Tarek and Zainab they must leave, he watches them from a distance, not unkindly but also in a disinterested, unmoved way. But when he finds the left-behind photo, the photo of them together and happy, he opens up a bit. He opens enough to try to find them to return the picture. Then, again engaged more closely into their situation, Walter invites them home.

This moment reminds us that our wounds can open us up. Henri Nouwen did us a good service by calling our attention to the wounded healer.[6] But we are in danger of misusing this concept. One way we misuse it is to continue to think of ourselves as healers, only now to think of ourselves as healers who are wounded. This is different than knowing that we are first and always wounded, able to "manage" our wounds and knowledgeable about healing perhaps, but not expert. I have always been sobered and helped by the well-known Buddhist koan about Nanin, a Japanese master during the Meiji era (1868-1912), who received a university professor who came to inquire about Zen. Nanin served tea. He poured his visitor's cup full, and then kept on pouring. The professor watched the overflow until he no longer could restrain himself. "It is overfull. No more will go in!" "Like this cup," Nan-in said, "you are full of your own opinions and speculations. How can I show you Zen unless you first empty your cup?"

Our strangeness

In our search for how to open ourselves to people of other faiths, another pivotal moment in the film comes when for the first time Walter reaches for the drum. This moment builds on the first moment – Walter can reach for the drum in part because of his emptiness. Before the death of his wife, Walter was full of the ordinary and typical. When we learn he has taught the same economics course for twenty years, this suggests that there were likely numerous things Walter did that were very routine and unsurprising. But with the loss of his wife, the very heart of his routine is gone and

[6] Henri J.M. Nouwen, *The Wounded Healer: Ministry in Contemporary Society*, New York: Doubleday, 1972.

strangeness takes over outside and inside Walter. When he hears Tarek's drumming, it seems it is a call to Walter's body, and he seems to be drawn by a magnetic force in the direction of this strangeness. But it is not Tarek's strangeness or the drum's strangeness that ultimately opens Walter. It is rather his willingness to risk encountering the strangeness in himself. When Tarek first invites him to play, we can see the inner struggle on Walter's face. Will I risk feeling uncomfortable? Will I allow myself to be vulnerable to this man I have just met, and allow him to be my teacher? Will I follow him out into his world, to jazz clubs and drumming circles in the park? Will I allow myself to feel not in charge, not knowledgeable, vulnerable?

As we reflect on migration and on how to open to people of other religions, we rightly give attention to the otherness of the migrant and the otherness of people of other religions. But their otherness is not the only or perhaps even the most difficult impediment to our openness. We can open ourselves to otherness only to the degree we can tolerate to encounter the strangeness in ourselves. Walter's blossoming happens not so much because he hospitably opens his home to Tarek, Zainab, and Mouna, but because once they are there, he allows himself to encounter the stranger in himself: we can imagine him asking himself, incredulously, "What am I doing living with strangers, drumming, making music in the streets?" Christians have heard Heb. 13:2 countless times – "Do not neglect to show hospitality to strangers, for by doing that some have entertained angels without knowing it." In my hearing, the text has usually been a call to be hospitable to the strangeness of others. However, there is no reason that it cannot be considered a call to open ourselves to the strangeness in ourselves, and perhaps find there some Divine Mystery. Of course another text puts it plainly: "You shall also love the stranger, for you were strangers in the land of Egypt" (Deut 10:19).

Our childlikeness

In our search for how to open to people of other faiths, a third pivotal moment comes when Walter is open enough to behave like a child. Again, this aspect builds on the previous ones: Walter, in his emptiness, is willing to try strangeness, and in this way, he finds in himself the fearlessness of the well-loved child. He is childlike when he plays the drums with Tarek and when he shyly joins the drumming circle in the park. And, when Tarek is suddenly deported, he is now open enough to throw a childlike tantrum. And with a teenager's sense of justice, Walter screams at the impassive immigration officers about Tarek's goodness and his life and the wrongness and unfairness of what has been done to his friend.

Since keeping ourselves closed to people of other religions is accomplished primarily through adult reasoning and strategies, our childlikeness will help us open up. If we can open up to our childlikeness, we will not be so discouraged if others in our tradition treat us like a naïve or misbehaving child for our openness to religious pluralism. If we can risk being childlike, we will be not only moved by the music of other religions, we will join in and try to learn the music loved by people of other religions. If we can give way to the child's need for love and fairness, we will be not only open to people of other faiths. We will be able sometimes to throw caution to the winds by demanding what in this world seems almost impossible: equity with our religious sisters and brothers and an end to killing in the name of religion.

Conclusion

The story of Walter, Tarek, Zainab, and Mouna is a reminder that it is not always clear who is visitor and who is host. It also is an encouragement that we can be gracious whether we are host or visitor, if we allow ourselves to be opened to our own emptiness, strangeness, and childlikeness. Similarly, all of us are migrants, traveling in the presence of Divine Mystery. Our openness to and caring for people of other faiths will depend ultimately on our openness to Divine Mystery, the otherness that matters most of all.

Faith Specific and Generic Chaplaincy: "Jewish Chaplain" or "Chaplain who Happens to be Jewish"? *

Indigo Jonah Raphael
United Kingdom, 2010

If you have watched the television series M*A*S*H, you will have encountered fictional character Father John Francis Patrick Mulcahy: US Army chaplain and spiritual advisor to the 4077th Mobile Army Surgical Hospital during the Korean War. Although a Roman Catholic priest, Father Mulcahy ministered to people of all faiths, reciting a Jewish prayer for a wounded soldier and presiding over a *bris* (circumcision) in the absence of a rabbi.

Some people have encountered chaplains within the military, healthcare contexts, prison services and higher education. For those, however, who have never met a chaplain in the flesh or vicariously on a television screen, chaplaincy may be an intangible, invisible concept.

Father Mulcahy clearly extends his care for people beyond the boundaries of his own faith. In spite of being fictional his actions challenge us, as chaplains, to consider to whom we minister and how we work with people. This article reflects on my chaplaincy within the United Kingdom, focusing on what informs it and touching on some of the challenges and achievements of denominational and generic chaplaincy.

---

* Written for *Handbuch Interreligiöse Seelsorge*, ed. H. Weiß, K. Federschmidt and K. Temme, Neukirchen-Vluyn: Neukirchener 2010, published there pp. 366-379 in German under the author's former name Melinda Michelson-Carr, republished now with minor revisions.

The author has requested this essay be published under his current name and his previous name also be included. He feels it important for individuals who have changed their names to be able to *make their own decisions, within each context*, whether or not they wish to include their previous name – rather than assumptions being made that it is acceptable to refer to someone else's previous name, without their consent.

Basic aspects of Jewish Chaplaincy

Rather than as a military chaplain like Father Mulcahy, my experience has been as a rabbi in faith communities and as a chaplain in various healthcare contexts. At the heart of my pastoral work is the uniqueness of people's life journeys: what experiences impact them and how they cope, what their needs are, who and what they value and where they find meaning. With a background in Progressive Judaism and as a Liberal Rabbi, my model of chaplaincy is deeply rooted within a context valuing diversity and inclusivity. This informs who I am and how I relate to and support people. I work both in denominational and generic ways. As "Jewish Chaplain" I support the Jewish community in all its enriching variety, whichever part of the community someone comes from. In certain contexts my remit has extended beyond faith specific, denominational chaplaincy as I see people of other faiths and those whose spirituality finds expression in sources other than religion.

Although my religious and spiritual framework is Judaism, the role of the chaplain necessitates meeting people in the place that *they* are spiritually, religiously, physically and emotionally. It is for this reason that chaplaincy has been termed a "ministry of noticing."[1] It is not possible to meet people in their model of the world and in their reality, in how they think and feel, without attentively and actively "noticing" where they find themselves.

To be a "ministry of noticing" which enables a sense of what illness means to people chaplains need to practice *tsimtsum*[2] or "contraction". Filling the space with ourselves allows little or no space for anyone or anything else. This makes a "ministry of noticing" impossible as our own agendas can become consuming for others as well as ourselves. Self-contraction and not filling the room with our presence allows space for others. It then becomes permissive for people to fill the space with themselves and their lives, expressing and sharing whatever they may choose.

We ought however not to neglect ourselves, as one of our most significant resources is who we are as people. We need to be aware of where we are in encountering others, what impacts and touches us and how we can best manage these experiences whilst being attentive and focusing on the person concerned.

In order to contextualise the situation in which a person may find him/herself/themselves healthcare chaplaincy material often refers to supporting people as a "patient-led" process. I struggle with the term

---

[1] J. Swinton, in M. Cobb, *The Hospital Chaplain's Handbook: A Guide For Good Practice*, Norfolk: Canterbury Press, 2005, page vii.

[2] According to Lurianic Kabbalah "tsimtsum" refers to God withdrawing or contracting in order to make space for creation to take place.

"patient" as at the root of the chaplaincy encounter is a person – the essence of who someone is. A depersonalising label fails to appreciate that a person is much more than the context in which he/she/they literally finds him/her/themselves.[3]

Rabbi Dayle Friedman[4] uses the model of Genesis 21:17[5] to reflect the notion that chaplaincy is "person" focused. We read that God hears the voice of Ishmael "*ba'asher hu sham*", "where he is" – exactly in the place that he is and in all that he encounters. God's listening presence is there with Ishmael, right where *he* is. This is about encountering a person within their place in the world, meeting them in *their* world. This enables us to reach an understanding of the unique ways in which ill health impacts individuals as well as those around them and what their needs are. Being ill may be an isolating experience, evoking a plethora of feelings around loss that can, at times, seem overwhelming. It can also be a process of reflection and/or re-evaluation, of saying and doing important things and a time of solace and peace.

Within Judaism *bikkur cholim,* or visiting the sick, is a religious duty as well as a meritorious act. After Abraham was circumcised in Genesis 17:26 the text tells us in Genesis 18:1 that "The [Eternal] appeared to him by the terebinths of Mamre..." Since the preceding verse refers to Abraham's circumcision the rabbis deduced that God "appeared to him", actually visited him, in his recuperation. As God visited the sick so too are we required to do so.[6] In visiting the sick one therefore imitates and models God's behaviour.[7] Friedman notes that the text reflects no dialogue between God and Abraham.[8] God's presence, perhaps more than any spoken words, seems to be of paramount importance.

---

[3] The term "patient" can be a poignant reminder to care givers that the person who they support within a hospital environment is vulnerable. See J. Goodrich & J. Cornwell, *Seeing The Person in the Patient*, London: The King's Fund, 2008, also available at http://www.kingsfund.org.uk/publications/seeing-person-patient (accessed 7 August 2015).
Also, in reference to "they" and "themselves": regarding the use of pronouns it is best to check with people what their preferred pronouns are. For a list of pronouns non-binary people may use, see http://nonbinary.org/wiki/Pronouns (accessed 7 August 2015).

[4] D. Friedman (ed.), *Jewish Pastoral Care: A Practical Handbook from Traditional & Contemporary Sources*, 2nd rev. ed., Vermont: Jewish Lights Publishing, 2005, xv & xxiv, footnote 10.

[5] "God heard the cry of the boy, and an angel of God called to Hagar from heaven and said to her, 'What troubles you, Hagar? Fear not, for God has heeded the cry of the boy *where he is*.'" Translation from *JPS Hebrew-English Tanakh*, 2nd edition, Philadelphia: The Jewish Publication Society, 2003, 38.

[6] Babylonian Talmud Sotah 14a.

[7] Genesis Rabbah 8:13.

[8] Friedman (ed.), *Jewish Pastoral Care*, 57-58.

According to Maimonides[9], visiting the sick although rabbinic in origin, is included in the Biblical precept "and you shall love your neighbour as yourself."[10] The obligation of *bikkur cholim*, visiting the sick, extends also to those who are not Jewish, as Ozarowski cites from the Babylonian Talmud (Gittin 61a): "[We] support non-Jewish poor along with the poor of Israel; we visit non-Jewish patients along with the sick of Israel; we bury the dead of non-Jews as we do the Jewish dead, all because of 'the ways of peace.'"[11]

Although *bikkur cholim* is an important obligation within Judaism and an integral part of the pastoral role of the rabbi, there is no Hebrew equivalent of the term "chaplain". Within some Jewish circles, the Hebrew term used for chaplaincy is *livui ruchani*, or "spiritual accompaniment".[12] The chaplain is therefore a *milaveh* (male) *or milavah* (female) *ruchani*, a person who accompanies someone spiritually. The root of the word livui is "lvh" which is found in Biblical and Rabbinic texts in reference to someone who "walks with" another. It is of interest that this Hebrew term encompasses a wider concept of "spiritual" rather than specific "religious" accompaniment.

Achievements and challenges for Chaplaincy in the UK

Within chaplaincy in the United Kingdom there has been a focus on the importance of recognizing "spiritual" and "religious" needs. In this multicultural, multi-faith society there has been a tangible "move away from 'organised' religious practice to an individual spiritual journey based on the patient's own knowledge and values."[13] This has led to a decline in people requiring religious care within healthcare contexts and "an increase in spiritual awareness... [which] require[s] the chaplaincy to support a wide range of potentially complex spiritual journeys which are not allied to any one faith community."[14]

Within healthcare contexts people's needs are to be respected whether they are specific religious needs or spiritual needs.[15] National Institute for

---

[9] Maimonides, Mishneh Torah: Laws of Mourning, Ch.14.

[10] Leviticus 19:18.

[11] J. Ozarowski, *To Walk In God's Ways: Jewish Pastoral Perspectives on Illness and Bereavement*, London: Jason Aronson Inc., 1995, 33.

[12] Friedman (ed.), *Jewish Pastoral Care*, xvii & xxiv, footnote 13.

[13] Yorkshire and the Humber NHS, Draft Document *Improving Healthcare Chaplaincy Services: A Guide for Commissioners*, Dec 2007, page 13.

[14] Ibid, page 5, "Executive Summary".

[15] Article 9 of the Human Rights Act (1998) refers to the "freedom of thought, conscience and religion", freedom to change religion or belief and "to manifest...

Clinical Excellence (NICE) Guidelines recognise that people's "beliefs can be religious, philosophical or broadly spiritual."[16] "Religious" refers to "the need to put into practice one's usual expression of spirituality"[17] which may mean the need to see a faith representative, to experience religious rituals and prayers and to attend a place of worship. "Spiritual" refers to "a concern with ultimate issues and ... a search for meaning" and may include existential questions.[18] We all have spiritual needs: that which gives purpose, meaning and hope to our lives and enables us to make sense of our lives. "Spiritual" healthcare therefore encompasses the needs of all human beings – those whose spirituality is found in religion as well as those whose spirituality is found in other sources. Cobb writes about an "individualistic model of spirituality" within healthcare.[19] This is about appreciating what is meaningful for each individual in order to support and "walk with" him/her/them.

Much has occurred in terms of Multi-Faith chaplaincy over the past fifteen years in the UK. Up until then there were hardly any world faiths represented in hospitals offering spiritual support other than Christian and Jewish chaplains. Today many chaplaincy teams have representatives of a variety of world faiths. A Multi-Faith Group for Healthcare Chaplaincy was launched in 2003 which is "seek[ing] to advance multi-faith chaplaincy in England and Wales" and includes representatives of 9 world faiths: Bahai, Buddhist, Christian, Hindu, Jain, Jewish, Muslim, Sikh and Zoroastrian.[20] Another major development is that some faith communities who have not had a tradition of chaplaincy have received support and training leading to people of good standing in their community being authorized as appropriate chaplains. It is to be celebrated that across the country chaplains are supporting a range of people in a variety of contexts.

In the National Health Service ("NHS"), however, healthcare chaplaincy is not a statutory, commissioned service as it is in the military, prisons and higher education. NHS chaplaincy is therefore a vulnerable service with local decisions made about how much and whether to spend on chaplaincy. There is also only policy *guidance* issued in regard to NHS chaplaincy. Members of Parliament have been involved in discussions about chaplaincy

---

religion or belief, in worship, teaching, practice and observance." Available at http://www. opsi.gov.uk/ACTS (accessed 6 August 2015).

[16] National Institute for Clinical Excellence, *Improving Supportive and Palliative Care for Adults with Cancer: The Manual*, London: March 2004, p. 95. Online available at http://www.nice.org.uk/guidance/csgsp (accessed 7 August 2015).

[17] Peter Speck, *Being There: Pastoral Care in Time of Illness*, London: SPCK, 1995, 31.

[18] Ibid, 30. See Speck also for Indications of Spiritual Distress, ibid, 33-37.

[19] Mark Cobb, *The Hospital Chaplain's Handbook: A Guide for Good Practice*, Norwich: Canterbury Press, 2005, 22.

[20] See http://www.mfghc.com (accessed 7 August 2015).

as there is now an All-Party Parliamentary Group on Chaplaincy in the NHS. We are awaiting their consideration of the evidence they have gleaned. If they recommend that chaplaincy in the NHS become a statutory service then every NHS authority would have to provide chaplaincy according to an individual's faith community and staff would be the key people to make referrals to chaplaincy teams. There would also be an agreed national framework of standards as well as performance criteria. Hospital Chaplaincy has never been a core standard in the NHS and it is interesting to consider what the implications for chaplaincy of a commissioned service might be.

Chaplaincy is being called on to reflect that it is a viable evidence-based service. For many people our work is an invisible and intangible concept and it is up to us to proactively meet the challenge of gathering evidence reflective of both the need for chaplaincy as well as our efficacy. The National Secular Society[21] commissioned a survey, through the Freedom of Information Act, of the costs spent on chaplaincy. They would far rather the NHS were not employing chaplains and the taxpayer not having to spend money on chaplaincy. Instead they would rather the NHS had local clergy responding to people's needs. What would this mean in terms of generic chaplaincy? While acknowledging people's religious needs this approach does not seem to recognize people's wider spiritual needs outside of a religious framework. As a chaplain doing both denominational and generic work, I certainly find myself at the bedside of people who define themselves as being secular, humanist, atheist or agnostic!

The model of local clergy is one used by many Roman Catholic communities where chaplains are appointed by the Church and have a contract of service with the NHS. Having local clergy paid for by their own community fulfil the daily role of the chaplain is fraught with potential problems: local clergy may have no expertise or experience within healthcare chaplaincy and being ordained does not necessarily imply that pastoral care is someone's strength. If local clergy are also ministering to the needs of a whole community they may not readily be available, as there may be competing needs. A part-time faith representative would be unable to provide the regularity and continuity of support and care that a person may need. Local clergy, who are called to visit occasionally, could find being part of an integrated holistic care team challenging. Faith communities may also have different standards, guidelines, expectations and codes of conduct regarding the role performed by local clergy, which could impact the quality of service and care provided. What would the model of local clergy being called upon to visit people of their own faith mean for people who are not members of a faith community who have spiritual needs which are

[21] See http://www.secularism.org.uk (accessed 7 August 2015).

not religious? Who would be accountable for the work of local clergy or responsible for addressing any of their actions?

In order to provide appropriate spiritual support for people, chaplains need access to relevant information. Previously chaplains were provided with a list of people's religions but in some Trusts this has changed. One of the challenges faced by chaplaincy in the United Kingdom arises out of the Data Protection Act (DPA) 1998 and the various interpretations practiced within Trusts. The DPA requires people handling information to comply with certain principles, giving people rights over their personal information. A person's religion is considered to be sensitive personal data. While other healthcare professionals do not require informed consent to have access to this information chaplains are not included within this category. They cannot take advantage of the exemption in Schedule 3 of the Act allowing, for medical purposes, sensitive personal information to be passed on without the need for explicit consent. The Information Commissioner does not consider "medical purposes" to include spiritual care nor are chaplains included as healthcare professionals. People therefore need to give explicit consent in order for this information to be passed on to chaplains. What message does this send regarding the professional standing of chaplains? Does this value integrated holistic care, inclusive of people's spiritual needs?

Excluding chaplains as healthcare professionals seems incongruent for, as Cobb points out, chaplains, like other healthcare professionals, are already subject to a duty of confidentiality which "is evident in the professional Code of Conduct, the contractual obligations of chaplains to their Trusts and the terms by which faith communities authorize chaplains."[22]

Each Trust has a Caldicott Guardian who is appointed to protect patient information and who interprets the DPA. In certain Trusts chaplains still have access to people's religious information, others deny any access and some allow access on a "need to know" basis. If this information requires explicit consent for it to be passed on to chaplains, then without the appropriate systems in place chaplains and visiting clergy have difficulty in identifying people who may need their support. National Health Service Trusts have interpreted the act differently and therefore the practical implications for chaplaincy vary. In some Trusts chaplains have access to no data and go on to wards, introducing themselves and their service, seeing whether people wish to give consent for a visit. Some Trusts ask at admission whether people would like their religion recorded and then need to gain explicit consent in order to pass this information on to the chaplaincy. Chaplaincies have also been informing people about the spiritual and religious support they can offer through leaflets and information

[22] Cobb, *Hospital Chaplain's Handbook*, 113.

packs. Faith communities have been informing people that if they want chaplaincy support whilst in hospital they will need to proactively ask for it themselves or inform someone in their community who can make a referral with their consent. In the case of people who are unable to give consent "disclosure may be justified on the grounds of necessity if it is clearly in the individual's interest and the disclosure is not contrary to the individual's known values and beliefs. The views of people close to the patient, especially close relatives, partners and carers, about what the patient is likely to see as beneficial must be taken into account."[23]

Providing for the day to day and occasional needs of any faith communities can be subject to practicalities: physical space, finance and any competing priorities within a healthcare context. The challenge is how best to support people while the practicalities of meeting those needs are being assessed or in cases where needs cannot be met.

Denominational Chaplaincy

As a "Jewish Chaplain" working denominationally with the Jewish community my role encompasses: identifying existing and anticipated communal and individual needs and seeking best possible and appropriate ways of providing for these. One cannot assume that all people of a particular faith and culture have the same beliefs, ways of expressing their faith or share the same values. It is important that I recognize that even though someone may describe themselves as coming from a specific part of the Jewish community (Ultra Orthodox, Orthodox, Masorti,[24] Progressive: Reform or Liberal), it is best not to make assumptions about what is meaningful or important to them and what their needs are but rather to check with the person concerned. If the person I am supporting asks me to contact a Rabbi on his/her/their behalf it is important that I find out whether he/she/they have their own rabbi and are a member of a particular community and which type of Rabbi he/she/they would be comfortable with: Ultra Orthodox /Orthodox/ Masorti/ Reform or Liberal Rabbi. I may also be supporting people who are Jewish by birth or culture but who are Agnostic or Atheist.

Individuals within the community may have specific religious needs some of which are: access to *Kosher*[25] food, a space in which to meet, eat and pray and Sabbath accommodation. When a loved one has died people

---

[23] Ibid., page 114-115.

[24] See http://www.masorti.org.uk/about-masorti/faqs.html (accessed 6 August 2015).

[25] Food that according to the Jewish dietary laws is "fit" for consumption.

may need somewhere to perform *Shmirah*[26], and if accepted by the coroner, being able to arrange an MRI as opposed to a Post Mortem. There are occasions when certain ritual needs within particular healthcare contexts cannot be met due to health and safety, for example, lighting Sabbath candles on a ward. As I write, the UK Home Office has described the current terrorist threat level as "severe" – that an attack is highly likely. One of my roles as Jewish chaplain is to compile resources that can be used by the community within the hospitals in case of a major incident. Resources include both people who can be available to offer support and appropriate ritual and prayer items.

As a chaplain it would be naïve of me not to recognize the impact my gender might have on parts of the community and within the interactions I have with people. This can be dependent on which part of the community people come from. Seeing a chaplain of a particular gender may feel comfortable and normative, whilst for others it may be a new experience and there may be issues around modesty making it inappropriate to have a female chaplain at a male bedside or vice versa.

I understand the impact my gender may have in terms of being able to offer people support and respect each individual's right to make a decision that feels comfortable. For certain individuals seeing someone with whom they have a pre-existing relationship, their own rabbi or community representative, is the norm and they may choose whether or not they also wish to see a chaplain.

With the challenges chaplains have in accessing information regarding people's religious affiliation the visibility of chaplaincy has become even more important. The presence of chaplains on wards creates awareness and reinforces their availability, enabling people to approach chaplains directly or through referrals from staff. Colleagues of other faiths are often visible due to the religious garb they wear. Many male Jewish chaplains wear a kippah, or head covering. As a female Jewish chaplain I often wore no overt Jewish symbols – unless I put on a kippah specifically to take a service or pray with someone. Within the Ultra Orthodox and Orthodox community it is not normative for a woman to wear a kippah and my doing so would risk alienating people. Therefore I was mindful about when to wear a kippah and when I might choose not to do so. Not wearing any constant visual clues meant that I had some invisibility: no one would know I was Jewish, nor that I was the Jewish Chaplain. Naturally this changed when introducing myself and/or building relationships with the people I was visiting and with staff. Since I re-affirmed my masculinity and now live as male, I have become increasingly aware of how this impacts my chaplaincy.

---

[26] "Watching" (literally: "Guarding") over the body of a loved one who has died.

My experience thus far as a male Jewish chaplain who has chosen to wear a *kippah* all the time is that I am often instantaneously recognized as Jewish because I am wearing an overt, visible traditionally male symbol. It is also clear to certain parts of the community that I am from another part of the community, as I do not currently (or yet) have *payes* (side locks) or wear traditional black attire and head covering. Although generally people acknowledge me as Jewish I had someone recently from the Ultra Orthodox community ask, in spite of the colourful *kippah* adorning my head, "are you Jewish?" That said something about this person's normality and point of reference – that I did not fit with what he feels a Jewish man, let alone a Jewish chaplain, should look like. After initial surprise I realized that I was not offended by the question, instead I could see it as providing a sacred opportunity – to share some of my identity with someone for whom this may be a new experience, beyond their normative point of reference and perhaps beyond their comfort zone. The late Rabbi Dr Louis Jacobs (*zichrono livrachah* – "may his memory be a blessing") wore a dog collar but I can foresee this evoking definite confusion!

When going to visit someone from the community, I often will not know from which part of the community they are from, unless they or someone else has told me. I may be able to see visual clues about the person however it is still important that, if able to do so, the person him/her/themselves can self define.

There is currently more conversation taking place around people's gender identities and whether a person identifies as: binary, transgender, genderqueer, non-binary, intersex, gender variant or a combination of some of these. We can be quick to assume what someone's gender identity is by visual clues, which can leave us with just that: an assumption, which may or may not have bearing on their own reality. It is for the individual him/her/themselves if they wish to share this with the chaplain. We need to be open to understanding how someone's gender identity may impact their relationship with religion, spirituality and health. Enabling people to self define can alleviate potential fantasies, allowing us as chaplains to have a sense of each person's own unique reality.

Issues around visibility may also impact the Jewish community regarding concerns and fear of Anti-Semitism. Within a healthcare context, having a room publicly designated as a "Jewish Room" can potentially increase feelings of vulnerability for some of those who may use it. If the room is not overtly labelled and visible to the public, then one is dependent on communal word of mouth outside of hospitals and on staff making people aware of the existence of such a room.

Generic Chaplaincy

Working generically as a "Chaplain who happens to be Jewish" means offering support to people who are of other faiths and those who are of no faith, identifying individual needs and seeking appropriate ways of providing for them.

> Over some months I got to know Jen[27] while she lived with cancer. She was articulate about where she found her meaning: as a Catholic she felt disconnected to the faith that had once been important to her. I told her that, if she wanted to, I knew a Catholic chaplain with whom she could meet. This did not seem possible for her. She knew I was Jewish and a Rabbi and felt I could identify with some of her spiritual journey and religious dilemmas. Talking to me placed her under no pressure to confront or resolve thoughts and feelings and yet it was clear that she desperately yearned to reconnect with her faith. When Jen became weak I reminded her of the Catholic chaplain and again said that he was a gentle, sensitive man. I asked whether she would like him to come with me to see her. She agreed and over cups of tea, we listened to how she was feeling. A rapport was building between her and my colleague. I asked whether she wanted us to pray with and for her. She did. After a few lines of Psalm 23 she joined in with both of us, tears streaming down her face. It was a deep moment as the three of us sat together. As we left her my colleague gave her a crucifix which she began to stroke gently and hold on to. Jen knew I would be willing to officiate at her funeral and my colleague and I spoke about jointly officiating. She died when I was on leave and he led her service. Jen had allowed me to be part of her journey and to support her in reconnecting with her faith. She had rediscovered a place for herself in it and had come home.

Some denominational chaplains do not wish to work generically with people of other faiths and those of no faith. Some cannot comprehend why one would want to do so, feel that people of faith are best served by chaplains of their own faith and wonder in any case what they could possibly bring either to those of other faiths or to those of no faith.

Denominational chaplains are considered inappropriate to offer spiritual care because they are representatives of faith and of faith communities. Pattison writes about his concern regarding Christian chaplains "Dumbing Down the Spirit"[28] in order to work generically. In "seeking to become being all things to all people"[29] and as "facilitators for the spiritualities of the world"[30] they will negate who they are, what they represent and downplay, abandon and diminish their faith risking their integrity and religious identity as Christians. Another concern Pattison has is that Christian chaplains working generically may misrepresent other faiths and

---

[27] In the interests of respecting confidentiality, this is not her real name.

[28] S. Pattison, "Dumbing Down the Spirit", in Helen Orchard (ed.), *Spirituality in Health Care Contexts*, London: Jessica Kingsley Publishers, 2001, 33-46.

[29] Ibid 39.

[30] Ibid 40.

therefore it is far better for each faith representative to be witness to its own faith.

From a personal perspective, asking why I would wish to do work generically is like asking me why I would wish to support another human being! In terms of what a chaplain can bring, in our "toolkits" we have our humanity and the skills enabling us to offer and give support: respect, openness, empathy, compassion, being present, listening and noticing. I accept that we each have unique resources and skills however there are many skills that we use in supporting people of our own faiths that serve us equally well in supporting other human beings.

It is an assumption that every person of faith is best served by a chaplain of the same faith. Often an immediate connection is both possible and important for people because of a shared faith however this relationship, like any, has various aspects that can affect it. As a Jew I would not want others to presume that just any Jewish chaplain would be acceptable to me. Given a choice between a Jewish chaplain with whom I felt no connection personally and/or theologically and a chaplain of another faith with whom I felt a connection, I know which one I'd choose to ask for a visit! Some people may feel too vulnerable having a chaplain of their own faith visit and not being part of someone's faith community may feel more comfortable and permissive in terms of discussing concerns and issues, as was the case when I first met Jen.

The risk of generic chaplains misrepresenting someone else's faith is only possible if one sets oneself up in the role of representing another faith. In working generically we need to learn about the needs of other communities of faith, as well as the individual's needs which can at times be the same or markedly different. In supporting someone generically my role is not to be everything and anything! Can Father Mulcahy abandon being who he is because he supports someone who is not Catholic? Can he be Rabbi Mulcahy one day and Imam Mulcahy the next, ending up as Pandit Malcahy on the weekend? Surely not! The good Father would be a candidate for a major identity crisis.

When I visit someone who is Christian I do not go as a Reverend, Priest or Vicar. That is not who I am. I am a Chaplain, a Jew and a Rabbi. Supporting people of other faiths and those of no faith I do so carrying all my skills, identities and integrity. I introduce myself as "part of the chaplaincy team... and I happen to be a Rabbi". This provides a framework reflecting that I cannot be all things to all people and maintains authenticity in terms of who I am rather than setting people up to expect or fantasize that I am something else. In generic chaplaincy I am not seeking to replace denominational chaplains or trying to be a chaplain of another faith.

The appearance of a chaplain can evoke conscious or unconscious fantasies. In sharing my identity as a Rabbi there sometimes followed a question or comment about women rabbis (which unsurprisingly I don't get as a male rabbi!) or being Jewish and I need to be aware of the projections and fantasies sharing this information can evoke so that it does not threaten to consume a conversation. Sometimes both people of faith and those of no faith assume that my role is to be "a dispenser of religious goodies"[31] with the goal of making them religious or more religious. The anxieties and guilt this can cause may lead to someone declining a visit or beginning a visit by the need to confess that they are "not religious at all" or "not *that* religious" or "non practicing". A young woman in the midst of experiencing mental illness eloquently asked: "Are you here because I am dying?" She wasn't but had articulated one of the fantasies many people think about. She'd assumed that my arrival must herald her impending death. And perhaps she may have felt like she was dying. Working with fantasies gives us insight into people's thoughts and feelings and an opportunity for people to understand that we are present to offer them support in *their* journeys, that we do not expect them to live our or anyone else's life and that we support people at whatever stage on their journey.

Brent[32] allowed me to be part of his journey. Religion was of no importance to him although it was to his wider family. He knew I was Jewish and a Rabbi. His initial hesitancy about what I might expect of him in terms of religion passed when he realized I did not have a specific agenda and focused on *his* journey. He began to speak about his life and the loss of what was no longer possible. He loved art and each week we talked about what he was creating. Art was a means of self-expression, giving Brent's day meaning and purpose. He was able to accomplish something tangible and experience the joy of working together with others. He made things to give people. Shaun McNiff notes that "whenever illness is associated with loss of soul the arts emerge spontaneously as remedies, soul medicine."[33] It was through art that Brent shared some of his world, hopes and fears and I got to know him on a deeper level.

Cobb mentions that there is transcendence in spirituality "going beyond the self, the body, the physical and the mortal… It… can convey a sense of being part of a greater whole, of connecting with something outside of oneself, or of becoming open to a greater reality that may be in the depths of one's being, with another person, with the world or with God. Common experiences of transcendence involve the awareness of an 'other' beyond the immediate and of losing oneself in its contemplation. Falling in love with another person, taking in a dramatic landscape, viewing beautiful work

[31] Speck, *Being There*, 31.
[32] In the interests of respecting confidentiality, this is not his real name.
[33] Shaun McNiff, *Art As Medicine: Creating a Therapy of the Imagination*, London: Shambhala Publications Inc., 1992, 1.

of art or listening to music can all be occasions for transcending our selves as well as the object of our consideration."[34]

As a person who has a faith that is important to me I could understand that Brent's art elevated him, made him feel connected to himself and others and transported him to a place he wanted and needed to be, providing him with meaning and strength. It took him out of himself, elevating him beyond his illness and was his source of coping. He took some of his art home, giving it to family and friends. I hope that through it his family have been able to find comfort and strength and that looking at it transports them to parts of Brent's world.

Working generically with the Jewish community

As a chaplain working denominationally with the Jewish community and generically with people of other faiths and those of no faith I am interested in the experiences colleagues of other faiths have had in supporting individuals from the Jewish community. I have spoken both with colleagues who work generically and with those who have been willing to work generically when specific situations have arisen.

Some colleagues have made faith specific referrals for families at their request to their own rabbi and/or to Jewish chaplains, spent time with family members who were doing *Shmirah* ("Watching"), helped with practicalities and said prayers. Certain colleagues had concerns about how they would be received as generic chaplains by the Jewish community. Most recognized that certain parts of the Jewish community were more receptive to support from a generic chaplain but this could also depend on the individuals concerned. Some chaplains said that in their experience the more Orthodox a Jewish person was the less receptive they seemed whilst another mentioned his experience with an Orthodox Jewish lady who had called him over and said to him "we all worship the same God". She had then asked him to say a prayer for her. My sense is that chaplaincy colleagues had offered support in terms of what felt theologically comfortable and congruent to them.

There are some Jewish families who have been on the receiving end of a few of my non-Jewish colleagues reciting a prayer... in Hebrew! It mattered that they had been sensitive to asking people how they could support them; checking in specific circumstances whether they would like a prayer said and being willing to respect whatever response came their way. There are people for whom a non-Jewish chaplain would be unacceptable in terms of their faith, expectations and integrity and would carry no appropriate authority.

---

[34] Mark Cobb, *The Dying Soul: Spiritual Care At The End Of Life*, Buckingham, England: Open University Press, 2009, 22.

Taking a "person led" approach to chaplaincy reminds us not to make assumptions. Wearing religious garments and symbols of another faith may impact people's comfort level in receiving support. For some Jews this would be an immediate barrier, precluding any connection whatsoever whilst others may be receptive to seeing what support the person behind these garments and symbols may bring.

In working generically with people of other faiths it is important to have resources that we can contact and refer to – both people and material that provide us with an understanding of the variety of religious needs. Having a faith calendar can help us to be aware of festivals, celebrations and commemorative days and what needs may arise for people and communities. With resources we need to be mindful that some may have been written for certain parts of the community and not be applicable, appropriate or inclusive to other parts. Cobb mentions that chaplains need to be culturally competent in order to provide appropriate religious and spiritual needs as "culture plays a critical role in the way people perceive illness, the beliefs they hold in respect to health and healing, their attitudes and expectations towards healthcare providers."[35]

Most importantly, in chaplaincy we ought not to try to be who we are not! Attempting to be someone else will surely take a toll on us, our ministry and/or on the person/s to whom we are offering support.

Jewish Chaplain or Chaplain who is Jewish?

Father Mulcahy's actions have encouraged me to think about whom I support and to whom I minister. In denominational work I represent a faith community. I am a "Jewish Chaplain" and my focus is the Jewish community and the individuals within it, whatever their spiritual needs.

As a generic chaplain my focus is on human beings of other faiths and those whose spirituality is found in other sources, outside of faith. Perhaps here I am a representative of a wider humanity! In working generically I am a "Chaplain who happens to be Jewish".

Both of these identities are about bringing an openness to accompany people on their journeys rather than bringing along any prescribed agenda. Being human and supporting people of faith and those of no faith does not provide me with a role conflict, nor does it diminish me as a Jew for my faith underpins who I am and how I work.

The skills we bring as denominational chaplains enhance our generic work. Coming from a faith tradition provides insight and an understanding of the role faith may play in people's lives: the meaning and nourishment it

---

[35] Cobb, *Hospital Chaplain's Handbook*, 87.

can provide, the challenges it can bring as well as existential questions people may be grappling with.

Fictional Father Mulcahy encourages us to reflect on our chaplaincy and on the journeys we are willing and prepared to make. I have met some incredible people who have allowed me to accompany them on their unique journeys. Being invited to walk alongside people, wherever they choose to go, is a privilege.

Mercy as Basis of Care and Counselling: A Jewish View *

Daniel A. Smith
United Kingdom, 2013

Mercy in psychotherapy

I look for the word "mercy" in the index of the books I have on psychoanalysis and psychotherapy. There are volumes of Freud, Jung, Winnicott, Klein and others. There is not one reference to the word "mercy" in all their indexes. Perhaps there is no mercy in psychotherapy? The word "love" does appear in many an index, but is often followed by the instruction to see under "Transference and Counter-transference." So it seems that even the feeling of love is not fundamental in its own right, but might be considered a symptom that provides useful information in formulating a diagnosis. However, this conclusion would be a caricature of psychotherapy. In fact, I think there is a great deal of care and concern in psychotherapy, but it is not often expressed in clear language.

Winnicott compared psychotherapy to childcare. He divided his cases into three categories that require different kinds of treatment.[1] *First* there are patients who operate as "whole persons" and whose difficulties are in the realms of interpersonal relationships. They can be treated by classical psycho-analytic techniques. *Second* there are patients in whom wholeness of personality is just beginning to be established, and they are dealing with the coming together of feelings of love and hate, and issues of dependence and independence. Here one task of the analyst is to survive the patient's love and hate without retaliation. *Third* there are patients whose analyses must deal with very early stages of emotional development. They lack psychic wholeness and are in danger of "falling apart". Here the treatment

---

* Lecture presented at the 25th International Seminar on Intercultural Pastoral Care and Counselling, 2013, in Mainz, Germany. German translation published in E. Begic, H. Weiß and G. Wenz (eds.), *Barmherzigkeit: Zur sozialen Verantwortung islamischer Seelsorge*, Neukirchener Verlag, 2014, 33-40.

[1] Donald W. Winnicott, *Through Paediatrics to Psycho-Analysis*, London: Hogarth Press, 1982, 278-280.

is more to do with "management" rather than analysis. The therapist "holds" the situation for the patient, and helps the patient contain their feelings. Winnicott even says, "Probably there are times when a psychotic patient needs physical holding, but eventually it will be understanding and empathy that will be necessary"[2]

Books on Pastoral Care and Counselling find it easier to speak of the counsellor's "understanding," "empathy" and "concern." I think these words are attempts to express the love and compassion that therapists have for their patients in clinical practice. Perhaps we can say that, in general, what is most healing for a client is the presence of an attentive caring person rather than the presence of textbook skills and theories. However we should not dismiss the need for therapeutic practice to be intelligent and informed.

Mercy in Judaism

I turn to my books on Judaism, and they are rich in references to the word "mercy." Whether dealing with biblical, rabbinic, or modern Judaism, many books refer to mercy, and some have whole chapters devoted to this subject. There are several different Biblical Hebrew words that are often translated by the word "mercy". I will focus on two frequently used words, namely "*Rachamim*," and "*Chesed*".

Mercy as *rachamim*

Rachamim is commonly translated as "mercy" or "compassion." It is often pointed out that this word is connected to the Hebrew word "rechem" which means "womb," and therefore has a connotation to a maternal love and concern. Yet *rachamim* is also paternal: "As a father has compassion (*rachem*) on his children So the Lord has compassion (*richam*) upon those that fear Him" (Psalm 103:13).[3]

In the synagogue morning service, when we open the Holy Ark to bring out our scroll of Torah, we sing to God and call Him "*Av Harachamim*" (Father of Mercies.). In rabbinic writings, God is very often called "Harachaman" which is usually translated as "The All-Merciful".

In the Book of Exodus, God graciously forgives the Israelites after the great sin of the Golden Calf. God proclaims His name or reputation in the

[2] Donald W. Winnicott, *The Maturational Processes and the Facilitating Environment*, London: Hogarth Press 1985, 240.

[3] Modern scholarship suggests that "*rachamim*" is connected to the "innards" or "guts" and the emotions felt there by both genders. See W. Gunther Plaut, *The Torah: A Modern Commentary*, rev. ed., New York: Union for Reform Judaism, 2005, 541.

following formula: "The Lord, The Lord God, merciful and gracious, longsuffering and abundant in mercy and truth. Keeping mercy for thousands, forgiving iniquity and transgression and sin" (Exodus 34: 6,7).

This declaration is traditionally called "The Thirteen Attributes of Mercy." The rabbis divided it into thirteen words or phrases that refer to different aspects of mercy. Rabbi Joseph Hertz gives some examples:[4]

"The Lord, The Lord." In Hebrew this is "*Adonay, Adonay*". This name is traditionally understood to disclose God's attribute of mercy. The rabbis explain the repetition of the name as meaning "I am the merciful God before a man commits a sin, and I am the same merciful and forgiving God after a man has sinned. Whatever change is to be worked must be done in the heart of the sinner; not in the nature of the Deity".

The word "merciful" means that God is compassionate," – full of affectionate sympathy for the sufferings and miseries of human frailty.

The word "gracious" means that God always shows helpful concern.

The phrase "keeping mercy" means that God is abundant in kindness beyond what we deserve.

As for the word "truth," Hertz notes that here and generally throughout scripture, the word for lovingkindness precedes the word for truth, as if to say "speak the truth by all means but be quite sure that you speak it *in love*."

The rabbis call on us to emulate these merciful ways of God. Abba Shaul taught "Just as God is gracious and merciful, so you should be gracious and merciful" (Mechilta, Shira 3). Rabbi Chama ben Chanina gives practical examples of how to emulate God's grace and mercy. "Just as God clothed the naked [Adam and Eve], so you shall clothe the naked. Just as God visited the sick [Abraham], so you shall visit the sick. Just as the God comforted the bereaved [Isaac], so you shall also comfort the bereaved. Just as God buried the dead [Moses], so you shall bury the dead" (Talmud Sotah 14a)

Mercy as *chesed*

The word "*chesed*" is commonly translated as "mercy" or as "lovingkindness". *Chesed* is an overflowing abundant love expressed by the giver that does not depend on the recipient's worthiness. Maimonides explains the meaning of *chesed* as an "excess in beneficence". He writes that Creation itself was an act of divine *chesed*. Maimonides follows the tradition of interpreting Psalm 89:3 as "The world is built upon lovingkindness (*chesed*)". (Maimonides, Guide to the Perplexed 3, 53).

[4] Dr. J. H. Hertz, *The Pentateuch and Haftorahs*, London: Soncino Press, 1936 (commentary on Exodus 34:6).

Rabbi Simlai (3rd Century CE) taught that *chesed* was the beginning and end of *Torah* - the Five Books of Moses. He explained: "The beginning of the *Torah* [in the Garden of Eden] is doing lovingkindness, as it is written, 'And the Lord God made for Adam and for his wife garments of skin, and clothed them' (Gen 3:21). And the end of Torah [at the time of the death of Moses] is doing lovingkindness, as it is written 'And He buried [Moses] in the valley' (Deut 34:6)." (Talmud Sotah 14a)

According to the rabbis, the doing of *chesed* is equal to all the ancient acts of sacrifice. Yochanan ben Zakkai (1st century CE) said to his disciple Rabbi Joshua, when they beheld the Temple in ruins: "My son, do not grieve. We have another way of atonement as effective as the Temple sacrifices, and it is doing acts of lovingkindness, as it is said 'For I desire *chesed* and not sacrifice' (Hosea 6:6)."

Is mercy sufficient?

In the Bible, *chesed* often appears as one half of a pair, most commonly coupled with the word *emet* – truth. We see this throughout the Five Books of Moses[5] and in the Prophets[6] and also in later biblical writings.[7] This coupling is particularly popular in the Psalms e.g "All the paths of the Lord are mercy (*chesed*) and truth (*emet*)." (Ps 25:10) "I have not concealed your mercy and your truth from the great congregation… Let Your mercy and Your truth continually preserve me." (Psalm 40:11, 12). These couplings suggested to the rabbis that neither mercy or truth is sufficient on its own, and each needs the other to be effective and fruitful.

Sometimes *chesed* is coupled with other words connected to truth such as *mishpat* (judgement) or *tzedakah* (righteousness). This reinforces the notion that mercy or compassion requires truth or judgement for its sustained fulfilment.

The rabbis used the Hebrew word *din* to describe strict law, while they used the word *rachamim* to describe the quality of mercy. The rabbis often spoke of the need to combine *din* with *rachamim*, judgement with mercy, in order to achieve true justice.

The rabbis commented on the phrase "When the Lord God made earth and heaven" (Gen 2:4): "This may be compared to a king who had some empty glasses. The King said: 'If I pour hot water into them, they will burst. If, however, I pour cold water, they will contract and crack.' What then did the king do? He mixed hot and cold water, and poured it into them, so that the glasses would remain unbroken. In the same way, the Holy One blessed be He said, 'If I create the world on the basis of mercy

[5] e.g. Gen 24:27 and Gen 47:29.
[6] e.g. Joshua 2:14, 2nd Samuel 2:6.
[7] e.g. Proverbs 20:28.

alone, its sins will multiply and destroy it. If I create the world on the basis of judgement alone, the world cannot endure. Therefore I will create it on the basis of judgement and mercy together, and then may it stand!'" (Midrash Rabbah Genesis 12:15).

God also expects us to exercise judgement combined with mercy: "He has told you, O man, what is good and what the Lord desires of you - only to do justice (*mishpat*) and to love mercy (*chesed*), and to walk humbly with the Lord your God". (Micah 6:8)

What is the prayer of God?

Rabbi Yochanan taught that we know that God prays because God says that he will cause all people, Jew and non-Jew, to "rejoice in the House of My prayer." (Isaiah 56:7) Rabbi Yochanan said in the name of Rabbi Lose: "It does not say '*their* prayer' but '*My* prayer'. Hence we learn that the Holy One, blessed be he, says prayers.

What does God pray? Rabbi Zutra ben Tovyah said in the name of Rav, God prays: "May it be My will that My mercy suppress My anger, and that My mercy may prevail over My [other] attributes, so that I may deal with MY children with the attribute of mercy and, on their behalf, stop short of the limit of strict justice" (Talmud Berachot 7a).

When we recognise our own sins and shortcomings, we often beg God to judge us in mercy and not in strict justice. However too often, when we think of our enemies, we are tempted to ask God to exercise His stern judgement and not to indulge His mercy and compassion. We learn about this on the Day of Atonement when we read the whole book of Jonah. The story describes how Jonah rebelled against God's command to speak to the people of Nineveh, because Jonah was reluctant for the people of Nineveh (the enemy of Israel) to benefit from God's mercy. Then God taught Jonah that all God's creatures are God's concern. If God's mercy extends even to the great sinners of Nineveh who found forgiveness when they repented, then there is hope for all of us too.

A balance between mercy and judgement.

What is the difference between *chesed* and *rachamim* in rabbinic thought? David Blumenthal explains that *chesed* is the mercy that motivated Creation. *Rachamim* is the mercy that motivated Revelation.[8]

Chesed is an overflowing boundless unconditional love. The covenant of the creation is a largely a one-way covenant that expresses the grace and lovingkindness of God who gives love, while demanding little in return.

[8] See David R. Blumenthal, "Mercy", in A. Cohen and P. Mendes-Flohr (eds.), *Contemporary Jewish Religious Thought*, New York: Free Press, 1988, 590.

Chesed is mercy that goes beyond any other concern. It is beyond any consideration of justice or righteousness.

Rachamim is mercy that is coupled with judgement, and is concerned with justice. It is the love that was expressed at Sinai when God gave us guidance, directions and moral standards. The Sinai covenant is more of a two-way partnership, and places demands and expectations on both parties. The relationship at creation resembled a parent-baby relationship. This is transformed at Sinai into a more mutual and mature relationship. God remains the senior partner, but humanity has more responsibility for this relationship.

Jewish mysticism "Kabbalah" took human responsibility even further. Kabbalah has the bold notion that it is not only we that rely on God's justice and mercy. God also relies on us to exercise our judgement and mercy. When we act compassionately and justly we help heal the rift in the divine realm.

Jewish mysticism is strongly committed to monotheism, to the complete faith that there is only one God, and that God alone is to be worshipped. However kabbalah does give us a language and imagery to express the many facets of our human experience of the one God. We speak of the mercy and love of God, as well as the power and judgement of the one God. It is similar to a child's experiences of his mother as sometimes being totally supportive and full of unbounded love, and yet the child can also experience his mother as being strict and limiting. The loving mother gives her child boundaries (expressing her *rachamim*) out of concern that the child should not harm himself. She gives teaching and directions in order to help the child grow.

Kabbalah is famous for its description of the ten sefirot, the ten spiritual emanations of the flow that comes from God and mediates our relationship with the divine. On the "right" side (so to speak) is *chesed* which is the "lovingkindness" of God. It is divine goodness in its uncontrolled flow. On the "left" side comes *gevurah* or *din* which is the Power of God, chiefly manifested as the power of stern judgement. This limits the flow of lovingkindness so that creatures can endure, and not be engulfed in the splendour of the divine grace. Out of the combination of *chesed* and *din* comes (in the middle) *rachamim*, the compassion of God, to which falls the task of mediating between the two preceding sefirot. *Rachamim* is sometimes known as *tiferet* (beauty). Both these terms refer to the harmonizing principle affecting the necessary balance between lovingkindness and judgement.[9]

---

[9] Gershom Scholem, *Major Trends in Jewish Mysticism*, New York: Schocken Books, 1961[originally published 1946], 213; Louis Jacobs, *A Jewish Theology*, London: Darton, Longman and Todd, 1973, 28.

Sin comes into the world when the balance is lost, or when the elements become split or separated. Evil arises when strict, stern judgement is untempered by mercy. Justice needs to be tempered by mercy if it is to be good, and if the world is to endure.

But similarly, (though to a much lesser degree) the rabbis were concerned about separating mercy away from judgement, with the danger that we would be overwhelmed by an overflowing unbounded lovingkindness. The world needs some boundaries and restrictions if it is to endure.

We can translate this into parenting terms, or pastoral care terms. A good parent gives unconditional love to a baby expecting nothing in return. But true parental love is also concerned to see the child accept boundaries, and take on responsibilities, and eventually achieve independence. A love which is totally non-judgmental, totally unbounded, and always accepting of whatever a child does, is not going to help the child grow, and will not help the child relate to others and respect them and their rights. On the other hand, parenting which is always stern and judgmental will crush a child and stop it developing.

According to Maimonides our greatest glory and purpose is to emulate God, and live a life of mercy combined with justice and righteousness. He concludes his philosophic masterpiece, the *Guide of the Perplexed*, by quoting Jeremiah: "Let him that glories, glory in this - that he understands and knows Me. That I am the Lord who exercises mercy, justice, and righteousness in the world. For in these things I delight, says the Lord. (Jeremiah 9:23; Guide of the perplexed 3:54).

Pastoral care and counselling

Mercy, judgement and ethical behaviour are the bases of good counselling and care. My counselling-trainer, Father Louis Marteau, used to say that the counsellor's job was to help the client face as much truth as they could handle. If we, as counsellors, present too much truth in an uncaring way – (i.e. when we give too much clever interpretation, and too soon), then the client will not be able to hear it or handle it, and may reject us as well as our interpretation. On the other hand if we, as counsellors, give the client too little truth, then we are not fulfilling our duty. Our misplaced kindness may result in the client remaining in an unhealthy and unrealistic situation longer than necessary. We might imagine that we are acting out of kindness, but the wish to protect the client from any hurt may be motivated by the carer's fear of the client's rejection or retaliation. Of course there is something patronising in this description but it is a useful reminder that the carer's task is to help the client grow, and find a way in the wilderness.

Pastoral care and counselling combines two worlds. It has its dual origins in the world of psychology and in the world of religion. It can be the bridge that allows the two traditions to meet and enrich each other. The dual origins of pastoral counselling enable counsellors to care for clients faithfully and with love, while also maintaining a commitment to analytic truth and judgement.

I believe there is a great deal of faith and kindness in psychotherapy, but it is rarely expressed. The language of pastoral counselling can help therapists find appropriate ways to acknowledge their values and concerns. Religious people, in turn, can use pastoral counselling to avoid irrational sentimentality or judgmental rigidity. Pastoral counselling can help people deepen faith, refine feelings, and increase understanding.

Pastoral care and counselling requires the head as well as the heart. Pastoral work requires our knowledge and skill, as well as our mercy and compassion. It requires the pastoral worker to be present in love and in truth, so that the client can grow in integrity and wholeness. Perhaps the ideal is found in the words of the psalmist: "Mercy and truth are met together, righteousness and peace have kissed each other." (Psalm 85:11)

Mercy as Basic Principle of Pastoral Care in Islam *

Silvia Horsch
Germany, 2013

For a religious foundation of pastoral care from an Islamic perspective, there are various concepts and ideas derived either from the sources or from tradition. Mercy (*raḥma*) is one of these and it is perhaps the most compatible with Christian forms of pastoral care, although it is better to look at all facets of pastoral care in the Islamic tradition. This is not in order to justify the concept of pastoral care with which some Muslims may have problems because it does not derive from the Islamic tradition. After all, pastoral care is part of the Islamic tradition even though the term was only used later. On the contrary, the intention here is to cultivate for our times the wisdom contained in the Qur'an, the Sunna and the Islamic tradition as developed and practiced through the centuries.

Among these concepts are, for example, the Islamic conception of the soul (*an-nafs, ar-rūḥ*) and the soul's three stages (the one which commands the bad, cf. 12:53, the one which criticises itself, cf. 75:2, and the appeased soul, cf. 89:27), which are highly relevant for subsequent Muslim ethics and philosophy.[1] Due to the practical orientation of pastoral care, philosophical speculation about the soul is less relevant than the psychological dimensions, which are considered especially in the *taṣauwuf*. The purification of

---

* Lecture presented at the 25th International Seminar on Intercultural Pastoral Care and Counselling, 2013, in Mainz, Germany. The German version was published in E. Begic, H. Weiß and G. Wenz (eds.), *Barmherzigkeit: Zur sozialen Verantwortung islamischer Seelsorge*, Neukirchen-Vluyn: Neukirchener Verlag, 2014, 23-32. Translation to English by Miriam Krumbach.

[1] In the Qur'an *nafs* means both the self and the soul (cf. 6:93, where both meanings are possible). *Rūḥ* means the breath of life or the spirit that God breathed into Adams nostrils (cf. 15:29) and elsewhere it is linked with a prophetic mission or a divine revelation for example by an angel (cf. 16:102; 19:17). In later literature, *an-nafs* and *ar-rūḥ* are generally used as synonyms for soul, while *rūḥ* also means "spirit". See "Nafs" in the Encyclopaedia of Islam, Second Edition. Brill Online, available at http://referenceworks.brillonline.com/entries/encyclopaedia-of-islam-2/nafs-COM_0833/ (accessed 12 July 2013).

the soul (*tazkīya an-nafs*) from illnesses like anxiety, anger, envy and greed as a practical method of achieving an appeased soul is based on the Qur'anic demand to keep the soul pure and not to let it whither (91:6-10).[2] Purification is regarded as a precondition for the development of the soul as indicated by the verb *zakkā*, which means "purify" as well as "allow to grow".

Another basis for pastoral care is *iḥsān*, a term described in a famous Hadith as follows: "To serve Allāh as if you could see Him" – i.e. the awareness of God's omnipresence, which is expressed in good deeds.[3]

The prophet himself pronounced the care for the physical and psychic well-being of the faithful and of fellow human beings as an ethical duty.[4] Service towards others plays a central role in the correct notion of honest service towards Allāh (*iḥsān*). We should also think of *aṣīḥa*, good advice, the importance of which is likewise stressed in a Hadith: "Religion is a good advice" (*ad-dīn an-naṣīḥa*).[5] Further important terms are benevolence and good acts (*birr*), love (*muwadda*), patience (*ṣabr*), which is a virtue with which believers should treat people as well as with mildness (*ḥilm*). These last five terms are found again among God's names: *al-Barr* (the Most Benevolent), *al-Wadūd* (the Most Loving), *aṣ-Ṣabūr* (the Most Patient) und *al-Ḥalīm* (the Mild One, the Indulgent One).

Thus we have arrived at the basis of Islamic pastoral care – God Himself. Below, we will pursue the meaning of some of God's names and attributes which are relevant in the context of pastoral care.[6] But before that, allow

---

[2] Taṣauwuf or Sufism is counted among the disciplines of Islamic scholarship and is also called the "science of the purification of the soul". See Jens Bakker, *Normative Grundstrukturen der Theologie des sunnitischen Islam im 12./18. Jahrhundert*, Bonn: EB-Verlag, 2012, 589.

[3] This is the so called ḥadīṯ Ǧibrīl (Gabriel-Hadith), which tells of how the angel Gabriel explains to the Prophet and his fellows about the three dimensions of religion (dīn): islām (the five pillars), īmān (the six fundamental beliefs) and iḥsān. Al-Buḫārī, *Ṣaḥīḥ al-Buḫārī, 3 vols.*, Vaduz: Thesaurus Islamicus Foundation, 2000, Vol.1, 15f.

[4] A characteristic of this duty is that those who should receive care are specifically named in the Qu'ran and the Hadiths. These are parents, family, relatives, neighbours, orphans, the sick, the poor and old people, children etc. Thus everybody has the opportunity and the duty to follow this mandate in his surroundings. For the Islamic duty of care see Nigar Yardim, "Theologische Grundlagen der islamischen Fürsorge und Anforderungen an eine Notfallbegleitung für Muslime", in Th. Lemmen, N. Yardim and J. Müller-Lange (eds.), *Notfallbegleitung für Muslime und mit Muslimen: Ein Kursbuch zur Ausbildung Ehrenamtlicher*, Gütersloh: Gütersloher Verl., 2011, 20-24.

[5] Al-Buḫārī, *Ṣaḥīḥ al-Buḫārī,* Vol. 1, 7. In particular the prophets are described as good counsellors in the Qur'an, cf. 7:62, 68, 79, 93; 11:34.

[6] I am referring here mainly to al-Ġazālīs text *Al-Maqṣad al-asnā fī šarḥ ma'ānī asmā' Allāh al- ḥusnā*, ed. by Fadlou A. Shehadi, Beirut, 1971. An English transla-

me one more remark to aid our under-standing of these names. The names by which God calls Himself and which are bequeathed in the sentences of the Prophet also refer to God's qualities. They provide an opportunity of approaching an understanding of God through analogy (even if it is inadequate) because such qualities exist or may also exist in a human being to a certain extent.[7] As in the end God's essence remains inaccessible for human beings, so the highest step in the knowledge of God is recognizing that we know nothing of Him, or as the mystics al-Ǧunaid (died 298/910) expressed it: "Only God knows God".[8] There remains the method of getting to know God through his names and qualities, as inadequate as this may be. Therefore a central practice of the *taṣauwuf* is the meditation on the 99 most beautiful names which, according to a Hadith, belong to Allāh.[9]

Over and above the possibility of a deeper – even if always limited – understanding of God, these names are important for the practical character-building of the believer. Al-Ġazālī writes in his book about God's 99 names that a human being's blessedness (*sa'āda*) and perfection (*kamāl*) consists in being formed according to God's qualities (*at-taḫalluq bi-aḫlāqi llāh*) as far as that is possible for a human being.[10] The aim is not to achieve absolute perfection, which is reserved for God, but an approximation.[11] Irrespective of these considerations which date back to a (disputed) Hadith,[12]

---

tion with notes by David B. Burrell and Nazih Daher was published in 1992: *The Ninety-Nine Beautiful Names of God*, Cambridge: Islamic Texts Society, 1992.

[7] This of course does not apply to the qualities which can only belong to God. Among these are the ones which in the later kalām are called negative attributes (ṣifāt salbīya). They are: uniqueness, not having a beginning nor an end, being dissimilar to all created things, and to consist of Himself. For these attributes see for example M. Horten (transl.), *Muhammedanische Glaubenslehre. Die Katechismen des Fudālī und des Sanusi*, Bonn: Marcus & Weber, 1916, 7-19.

[8] Al-Ġazālī, *Al-Maqṣad al-asnā*, 47.

[9] Al-Ġazālī, *Al-Maqṣad al-asnā*, 181ff., and others point to the fact that this list and thereby also the number 99 do not cover all of God's names.

[10] Ibid., 42.

[11] However, it has been argued that this process implies a similarity between God and human beings which may contradict the concept of "God's dissimilarity with everything created" as it is laid down in the revelation and later elaborated in *kalām* ("There is nothing like unto Him." 42:11). Al-Ġazālī responds that the correct understanding of incomparableness excludes any notion of a similarity. A human being, who is merciful, patient or grateful (all of these qualities refer to names of God) remains always a human being who does not have a stake in the divine being, who is the only one who necessarily exits in himself (*al-mauǧūd al-wāǧib al-wuǧūd bi-ḏātihi*) (Ibid., 47).

[12] This refers to the Hadith: "You shall be fitted with the qualities of Allah" (*taḫallaqū bi-aḫlāq Allāh*, cf. Al-Ġazālī, *Al-Maqṣad al-asnā*, 162), which cannot be found in any of the known collections. Al-Ġazālīs' explanations of the individual names contradict this problematic idea of a godlikeness of human beings (which can

a number of qualities related to God's names (like mercy and patience) are recommended to the believers in the Qur'an and the Hadiths.

As these qualities are also, and even especially, important in the context of pastoral care, the remembrance (*at-taḫalluq bi-aḫlāqi llāh*) of God and His names has a twofold significance. Firstly, for those whose soul is troubled it is a path to achieving calm ("Sure, remembering Allāh, the hearts rest." 13:28) and then also to strengthening the character during the course of getting closer to God in a way which sees this calmness become firm and ready for future problems and tests. For those who care about the soul of others, it offers the possibility of a consolidation of the qualities which are indispensable for dealing with those seeking comfort and psychological assistance.

In addition to the names mentioned above, the following are of special importance in the context of pastoral care;[13] names related to mercy, grace and benevolence: the Most Gracious (*ar-Raḥmān*), the Most Merciful (*ar-Raḥīm*), the Most Clement, (*ar-Ra'ūf*), the Most Loving (*al-Wadūd*), the source of All Goodness (*al-Barr*), the Most Gracious (*al-Laṭīf*, also: the one who knows the emotions of the heart); and names related to forgiveness and the prayer of the faithful: the All-Forgiving (*al-Ġafār, al-Ġafūr*), the Acceptor of Repentance (*at-Tauwāb*), the Pardoner (*al-'Afū*), the Responsive (*al-Muǧīb*) and the Nigh (*al-Qarīb*).[14]

Mercy, grace and benevolence

It is well known that the two names *ar-Raḥmān* and *ar-Raḥīm* are both derived from mercy (*raḥma*); they are by far the most frequently found names in the Qur'an. They are part of the Basmala, the introductory formula, "In the name of God, the Most Gracious, the Most Merciful", which with one exception stands at the beginning of all the *suras* of the Qur'an.

Mercy is a quality which God prescribed Himself (cf. 6:12 and 54) and which, as it is written in a Hadith, precedes His anger.[15] As with some of

be achieved). In the case of many names he stresses that they are not really applied to human beings but are only "a sort of a distant metaphor" (*nau'min al-maǧāz ba'īd*, ibid., 174).

[13] This enumeration is by no means exhaustive. More names may be added. For a list of the 99 names and their translation see Amir Zaidan, *Al-'aqiidah. Einführung in die Iimaan-Inhalte*, Wien: Islamologisches Institut 2011, 146-152.

[14] This last name is not enumerated amongst the 99, but is mentioned in the Qur'an 2:186.

[15] Al-Buḫārī, *Ṣaḥīḥ al-Buḫārī*, Vol. 3, 1507: "When Allah produced the creation, He wrote Himself above His throne (*al-'arš*): 'Truly my mercy precedes my anger.'" Many commentators connect this Hadith and variations on it with these two verses

the other qualities of God, there is an analogy with human beings, human beings are also merciful or can at least be so. The inadequacy of this analogy is also shown in a Hadith: "Allāh made mercy consisting of 100 parts, kept back 99 parts and sent one part down to the earth. With this part the creatures are merciful towards each other, and thus a mare raises her hooves above a colt afraid she may hurt it."[16]

As al-Ġazālī writes, God's mercy is both perfect – it aims to satisfy the needs of the needy ones and does satisfy them – as well as comprehensive as it includes those who deserve it and those who do not deserve it. The two names are not synonymous. *Ar-Raḥmān* has a broader meaning. It is only used for God and thus is closer to the proper name *Allāh* (cf. 17:110) and it refers to a mercy which is far beyond the capabilities of a human being and includes the hereafter: "*Ar-Raḥmān* is the one who exercises mercy towards his servants (*ʿaṭūf*), first by creating them, second by guiding them to faith and the methods of blessedness, third by making them happy and fourth by allowing them to see Him [in paradise]."[17] Therefore *ar-Raḥmān* is also translated as "the beneficent of big benefits" and *ar-Raḥīm* "the beneficent of small benefits".[18] The name *ar-Raʾūf* is a superlative and *raʾf* (compassion, pity) is more intensive than *raḥma*.[19] *Al-Wadūd*, the Most Loving, is the one who wishes all his creatures well and does good deeds. Even here there exists a similarity with *ar-Raḥīm*, but the difference is that mercy assumes the existence of a needy object which is not necessarily the case with love.[20]

The "share of the servant" (*ḥaṭṭ al-ʿabd*) in these names consists in mercy especially towards those in need, their active support and an attitude of empathy, hallmarked by tactfulness and sympathy "as if you were sharing their loss and their miseries".[21] In particular mercy belongs to the qualities which are warmly and emphatically recommended to believers. A well known Hadith, which traditionally will be the first a student will hear his new teacher say, is "The merciful exercises mercy towards the merciful. Be merciful towards those who are living on earth, then He who is in heaven will be merciful towards you."[22]

Full of love are those who wish other people what they wish for themselves or who even put others before themselves. *Muwadda* (love) will be

of the Qur'an. See Feras Hamza et al., *An Anthology of Qur'anic Commentaries, Vol. 1*, Oxford: Oxford Univ. Pr., 2008, 301.

[16] Al-Buḫārī, *Ṣaḥīḥ al-Buḫārī*, Vol. 3, 1228f.

[17] Al-Ġazālī, *Al-Maqṣad al-asnā*, 66f.

[18] Cf. Zaidan, *Al-ʿaqiidah*, 146.

[19] Ibid., 152.

[20] Ibid., 132.

[21] Ibid., 67.

[22] This is why it is called *al-ḥadīṯu l-musalsalu bi-l-auwalīya*, i. e. "the Hadith which is always listened to first in an uninterrupted line (of teachers)."

perfect if neither trouble nor anger nor harm suffered prevents altruism (*īṯār*) and the doing of good (*iḥsān*). The example for the perfection of this trait is the Prophet Muḥammad, who after being hurt in a battle with the people of Mecca said a prayer for them: "Allāh, guide rightly my people because they are ignorant."[23]

Altogether the Prophet, whose outstanding character is also mentioned in the Qur'an, is the ideal embodiment of these qualities ("And indeed, you are of a great moral character." 68:4). Many sources report his mercy and indulgence towards people, his ability to adapt to different people and his special love for children. In the Qur'an the Prophet Muḥammad's mission is described as mercy for the worlds (21:107). Love of the Prophet, which is part of true faith according to a Hadith, is an incentive for many Muslims to emulate the Prophet. ("None of you believes truly unless he loves me more than his own parents, children and all people.")[24] In fact he identified the perfecting of the good qualities of his character (*aḫlāq*) as one or the reasons for his mission.[25]

Al-Barr (the Most Benevolent) is one more of God's names which refers to a quality recommended to human beings, and especially towards one's own parents (cf. 17:23). Mercy again is particularly stressed in connection with elderly parents and should be and can be expanded, not only in the context of pastoral care, to all older people: "And out of mercy lower to them the wing of humility and say, 'My Lord, have mercy upon them as they brought me up when I was small.' " (17:24) A name which combines the aspect of benevolence with knowledge is *al-Laṭīf*, the Most Gracious, the sensitive one, the one who knows the emotions of the heart. *Luṭf* (which is only inadequately translated as benevolence) is a combination of "friendliness (*rifq*) in acting and subtlety (*luṭf*) in perception" and "this perfection in knowledge and acting only befits Allāh."[26] God as the creator knows all the subtleties and hidden facets of creation and He knows the emotions of the heart: "Whether you conceal your words or publicise them; indeed, He is All-Knowing of that which is within your breasts. How could He who created not know, when He is the Subtle (*al-Laṭīf*), the Acquainted (*al-Ḫabīr*)"? (67:13f.) God has conveyed something about the nature of human beings in the Qur'an, knowledge which is of immediate significance for pastoral care: "... mankind was created weak", which is why Allah wants to make it easier for him (4:28). Mankind is "anxious" (70:19), "ever hasty" (17:11) and forgetful. Adām, the first human being, already forgot (20:115). That is why he needs reminding. While God is aware of all this and knows every single person, their emotions, concerns and worries,

[23] Al-Ġazālī, *Al-Maqṣad al-asnā*, 132f.
[24] Al-Buḫārī, *Ṣaḥīḥ al-Buḫārī*, Vol.1, 8f.
[25] Mālik b. Anas, *Al-Muwaṭṭā'*, Vaduz: Thesaurus Islamicus Found. 2000, 357.
[26] Al-Ġazālī, *Al-Maqṣad al-asnā*, 109f.

people are only capable of empathizing with others to a certain degree. Considering the weaknesses of human beings, you should meet them with indulgence and clemency (*ḥilm*) and not let yourself be provoked into hasty reactions by negative emotions like dissatisfaction or anger.

Forgiveness and prayer

At first sight the names *al-Ġafār*, *al-Ġafūr* (the All-Forgiving), *at-Tauwāb* (the Acceptor of Repentance) and *al-ʿAfū* (the Pardoner) look like synonyms, but each of them stresses its own aspect. *Al-Ġafār* is the one who makes good visible and hides evil, thus he hides the sins of the believers in this world and does not punish them in the hereafter. Therefore people should hide for others those things they would not want to have disclosed in themselves.[27] "The person who hides one [i.e. mistake] of a believer, for him Allah will hide one [i.e. a mistake] on the day of resurrection."[28] *Al-Ġafūr* is a superlative form and identifies forgiveness in complete perfection.[29] *At-Tauwāb* (the Acceptor of Repentance) refers to the fact that God facilitates the repentance of believers by showing them some of His signs and granting them His warnings so that they are able to recognise the danger of their sins. Those who are ready to forgive again and again receive their share of this name.[30] *Al-ʿAfū* denotes the one who erases the sins, which is a higher good than hiding them. The one who realises that God gives his benefices even to those who are disobedient receives his share of this name because he excuses those who harm him and in addition does good unto them.[31]

The names which refer to God's forgiveness are particularly important where people are looking for psychological assistance due to their own moral lapses – in the fields of professional pastoral care this refers particularly to prisoners.

The attitude towards sinners in Islam is based on the fundamental distinction between a person and what he does. While certain deeds can (and must) be detested because they are sins, this abhorrence must never be assigned to the person himself. This is expressed in the behaviour of the Prophet himself who punished a Muslim who (habitually) drank alcohol, but prohibited the people to curse him – perhaps this man loved Allāh and His Messenger.[32] Similarly those practising pastoral care (but not only

---

[27] Al-Ġazālī, *Al-Maqṣad al-asnā*, 85.
[28] Al-Buḫārī, *Ṣaḥīḥ al-Buḫārī*, Vol 1, 459.
[29] Al-Ġazālī, *Al-Maqṣad al-asnā*, 114.
[30] Ibid., 150f.
[31] Ibid., 151.
[32] Al-Buḫārī, *Ṣaḥīḥ al-Buḫārī*, Vol 3, 1368.

them) who deal with people who have burdened themselves with (potentially heavy) guilt are asked to convey their esteem of these people as persons in spite of their sins.

There are many passages in the Qur'an and in the Hadiths which speak of God's infinite willingness to forgive.[33] The prerequisite for forgiveness is repentance and this consists of the awareness of the damage done to oneself and to others, the deliberate intention of refraining from these sins in future and the appropriate behaviour, also related to the past, as an attempt to atone as far as possible for the harm done.[34] In the context of the forgiving of sins, God's mercy is again significant: "Say, 'O my servants who have transgressed against themselves [by sinning], do not despair of the mercy of Allah. Indeed, Allah forgives all sins. Indeed, it is He who is the Forgiving *(al-Ġafūr)*, the Merciful *(ar-Raḥīm)*.' " (39:53)

The request for forgiveness leads to one more of God's names: *Al-Muǧīb* is the one who answers someone's prayers, who even "does beneficences to the needy before they cry to Him. [...] He knows the needs of the needy ones before they beg [for their fulfilment]. He has known from eternity."[35] In sura 2 it is said, "And when My servants ask you, [O Muhammad], concerning Me – indeed I am near. I respond to the invocation of the supplicant when he calls upon Me." (2:186) God's name *al-Qarīb* (the Nigh) is derived from this verse, which is not included in the list of the 99 names but does belong to the names of God.[36] As applied to human beings, the name *al-Muǧīb* above all means that they should be responsive to God and – following from this – also to other human beings within the framework of the capabilities which God has bestowed on them. To be responsive in this sense is to help those who ask or if one is not able to help directly, to answer in a friendly manner.[37]

The above has clearly shown that the dimensions of Allāh's names towards which human beings can strive to share a part is one of the many sources for a theological foundation of pastoral care, although of course it would need to be considered further than can be presented here. As is true

---

[33] In the Qur'an *širk* (association) is the only sin mentioned which God will not forgive. See 4:48.

[34] For a more detailed explanation of repentance see Al-Ġazālī, *Muḥammad al-Ġazālīs Lehre von den Stufen zur Gottesliebe: Die Bücher 31-36 seines Hauptwerkes*, transl. and commented by Richard Gramlich, Wiesbaden: F.Steiner, 1984, 24-49. For more about guilt and forgiveness and the consequences for pastoral care see Misbah Arshad, "Schuld, Vergebung und Seelsorge im Islam", in B. Uçar and M. Blasberg-Kuhnke (eds.), *Islamische Seelsorge zwischen Herkunft und Zukunft: Von der theologischen Grundlegung zur Praxis in Deutschland*, Frankfurt a.M.: Peter Lang, 2013, 39-58.

[35] Al-Ġazālī, *Al-Maqṣad al-asnā*, 129.

[36] Cf. ibid., 181.

[37] Ibid., 129.

for all the other concepts discussed here, pastoral care in Islam has to be understood in an all-embracing sense. For the qualities named here are warmly recommended to Muslims in their dealings with all those around them and particularly with those they are closest to. Ideally nobody should need a professional pastoral counsellor because he or she can appeal to family and friends both when in physical as well as in psychological need and there he or she will find mercy, leniency, empathy, but also the remembrance and the good advice (*naṣīḥa*) which are needed. In Islam it is assumed that those who know the person best will also be able to provide the best help, as can be seen in the Qur'an's recommendation to turn to the family for mediation if there are problems in a marriage. (4:35) In reality this is often not possible. On the one hand there may be cases which overburden friends and family, for example in emergencies like a serious accident, or where violence or suicide is involved. On the other hand Muslim families and couples have to grapple with the strains of everyday modern life just like other people and in many cases with the special challenges of being immigrants.[38] Often they lack the basic religious knowledge which would be necessary for the correct interpretation of illness, distress and death.[39]

That is why the training of professional Muslim pastoral carers is urgent, but can only be part of an answer to the problematic situation. Just as important is the active practice of the above mentioned character traits in families and congregations – and, it is to be hoped, also in Islamic religious education at school and the seeking out of role models from all walks of life who embody these traits. The forming of an Islamic character is a part of an education that does not see learning only as the acquisition of knowledge and skills for later working life and *soft skills* and "emotional intelligence" only as a means towards a successful career. The basis for preventative pastoral care is, on the one hand, the continuous care of the soul in terms of purification from anxiety, anger, envy and meanness, qualities which damage not only one's relation to God but also interpersonal relationships and cause harm to others. On the other hand, it is the encouragement of the positive qualities that have been discussed.

---

[38] See Ibrahim Rüschoff and Malika Laabdallaoui, *Ratgeber für Muslime bei psychischen und psychosozialen Krisen*, Köln: Edition Bukhara, 2005.

[39] For more about this basic knowledge see Nigar Yardim, "Theologische Grundlagen", 24-34.

Appendix

The "International Seminars on Intercultural Pastoral Care and Counselling" from 1986 to 2015

Listed here are the International Seminars on Intercultural Pastoral Care and Counselling [1] with their themes, dates and main speakers, starting in 1986.

During the 9th seminar 1995, the *Society for Intercultural Pastoral Care and Counselling* (SIPCC) was founded and took over the responsibility to organise these seminars. Since then, most of the Seminars were accompanied by a "Pre-Conference", related to the topic of the Seminar. In addition, SIPCC conducted a great number of consultations and study trips to promote issues of intercultural pastoral care and counselling. In 2007, SIPCC was hosting the World-Congress of ICPCC in Krzyzowa, Poland, together with other organisations.

1) Hope and Wholeness in a Threatened World

1986, June 16-20, Düsseldorf-Kaiserswerth, Germany. Attendance: 93.
Prof. Dr. Howard Clinebell, USA

2) Pastoral Care and Liberation

1988, June 20-24, Düsseldorf-Kaiserswerth, Germany. Attendance: 103.
Dr. Masamba ma Mpolo, Zaire; Dr. Lothar Hoch, Brazil; Dr. Salim Sharif, India; Reinhard Miethner, Germany

[1] The naming of the seminars changed in the early years, reflecting the sharpening of its focus: Starting as "International Seminar", changing to "International Seminar on Pastoral Care and Intercultural Theology" and then "Intercultural Seminar on Pastoral Care and Counselling", after the founding of SIPCC in 1995 the name was "International Seminar on Intercultural Pastoral Care and Counselling".

3) Healing and Healing Community

1989, Sept 18-22, Mülheim/Ruhr, Germany. Attendance: 132.
Prof. Dr. G.H. Ott, Germany; Dr. Emmanuel Lartey, Ghana; Dr. Flora Wuellner, USA; Prof. Genadios Limouris, Greece; Prof. Dr. Walter Hollenweger, Switzerland/United Kingdom.

4) Justice, Peace and Integrity of Creation: A Challenge for Pastoral Care
1990, June 18-22, Mülheim/Ruhr, Germany. Attendance: 81.
Dr. Matthew Fox, USA; Mary Thomas, India; Joseph Walk, Israel.

5) The Individual and the Community: The Process of Adjustment and Change

1991, Sept 22-27, Groß-Dölln, Germany. Attendance: 111.
Christel Hanewinckel, Germany; Dr. Jürgen Ziemer, Germany; Dr. Daisy Nwachuku, Nigeria; Dr. Karel Schwarz, Czechoslovakia; Prof. Dr. Liesel-Lotte Herkenrath-Püschel, Germany.

6) "A time to love and a time to hate": An Intercultural Dialogue on Marriage, Gender Issues and Sexuality

1992, Sept 27 - Oct 2, Mülheim/Ruhr, Germany. Attendance: 104.
Prof. Dr. Ronaldo Sathler-Rosa, Brazil; Dr. Wilhelmina Kalu, Nigeria; Dr. Gnana Robinson, India; Susanna Schmotz, Germany.

7) Economy and Violence: A Challenge for Pastoral Care

1993, Sept 29 - Oct 4, Mülheim/Ruhr, Germany. Attendance: 92.
Dr. Michael Chang, Malaysia; Prof. Dr. Archie Smith, USA; Olgierd Benedyktowicz, Poland; Rev. George Euling, Papua New Guinea.

8) "Everything is breaking down – can you help me?" Pastoral Care and Counselling as Response to Value-Changes of Society and Culture

1994, Sept 18-23, Prague, Czech Republic. Attendance: 165.
Jan Urban, Czech Rep.; Dr. Karel Schwarz, Czech Rep.; Dr. Dick Tielemann, Netherlands; Tomas Jezek, Czech Rep.

9) Pastoral Care and Counselling in "Post-Modern Time": Human Images and Life-Stories in Various Cultures and Religions

1995, Oct. 15-20, Mülheim/Ruhr, Germany. Attendance: 90.
Dr. Robert Solomon, Singapore; Prof. Dr. Ronaldo Sathler-Rosa, Brazil; Rev. Hilary Johnson, UK; Phra Somniuk Natho, Thailand; Rev. Lee, Song-Soo, Korea; Rev. You, In-Sook, Korea; Rev. Charles Konadu, Ghana; Prof. Dr. Edwin T. Decenteceo, Philippines; Dr. Nalini Arles, India.

10) Traditions: Shadows of the Past – Sources of the Future

1996, Oct. 13-19, Ustron, Poland. Attendance: 124.
Prof. Dr. Jozef Tischner, Poland; Prof. Dr. Zdzislaw Mach, Poland; Prof. Dr. Janusz Maciuszko, Poland; Jacek Leociak, Poland.

11) The Emergence and Pacification of Violence and the Multiple Meaning of Sacrifice

1997, Sept. 8-13, Mülheim/Ruhr, Germany. Attendance: 99.
Prof. Dr. Raymund Schwager, Austria; Prof. Dr. Hans-Martin Gutmann, Germany; Prof. Dr. Ronaldo Sathler-Rosa, Brazil; Prof. Dr. James Newton Poling, USA; Dr. Nalini Arles, India; Prof. Dr. Ursula Pfäfflin, Germany; Rev. George Euling, Papua New Guinea; Dr. Nieke Atmadja, Indonesia and Netherlands; Dr. Rose Zoe-Obianga, Cameroon; Pracha Hutanuwatr, Thailand.

12) Stories of Hope

1998, Sept. 20-26, Lakitelek, Hungary. Attendance: 115.
Prof. Dr. László Tökéczki; Prof. Dr. Bela Buda.

13) Cities: Fragmentations of Human Life? Community Life in the Fragmentations of Urban Societies

1999, Sept. 13-18, Berlin, Germany. Attendance: 79.
Prof. Dr. Wolfgang Grünberg, Germany; Prof. Dr. Michael Mata, USA; Dr. Nalini Arles, India; Prof. Dr. Ronaldo Sathler-Rosa, Brazil; Dr. Daisy Nwachuku, Nigeria.

14) Human Dignity, Culture and Health: Opportunities for Pastoral Care and Counselling

2000, Sept. 24-29, London, United Kingdom. Attendance: 95.
Canon Paul Oestreicher, UK; Prof. Scheila Hollins, UK; Prof. Kathleen J. Greider, USA; Stuart Bell, UK; Rev. Dr. Malcolm Brown, UK; Dr. Frances Ward, UK; Prof. Julian Müller, South Africa.

15) Global Economy and Every Day Life

2001, Sept. 2-7, Wuppertal, Germany. Attendance: 75.
Rev. Septemmy E. Lakawa, Indonesia; Dr. Thoma Köster, Germany; Dr. Helmut Henschel, Germany; Dr. Manfred Linz, Germany.

16) Why Do We Serve Others? The Ethics of Caring: Multifaith Perspectives

2002, Sept. 8-13, Basel, Switzerland. Attendance: 110.

Prof. Dr. Christoph Morgenthaler, Switzerland; Dr. Jalaluddin Rakhmat, Indonesia; Dr. Carola Meier-Seethaler, Switzerland; Edouard Selig, Switzerland; Rabbi Marcel Ebel, Switzerland; Dr. Shekar Seshadri, India; Ron Maddox, UK; Rev. Mark Sutherland, UK.

17) Young People and the Experience of Violence: Implications for Pastoral Care and Counselling

2004, Sept. 5-10, Kecskemét, Hungary. Attendance: 75.

Prof. Dr. Pamela Couture, USA; Dr. Uri Bloch, Israel; Rev. Bonar Lumbatobing, Indonesia; Dr. Ismail Altintas, Turkey/Germany; Prof. Dr. Hans-Martin Gutmann, Germany.

18) Intercultural and Inter-Faith Communication

2005, Oct. 2-7, Düsseldorf-Kaiserswerth, Germany. Attendance: 75.

Petra Appelhoff, Germany; Dr. Mohammed Heidari, Germany; Rev. Dorothee Schaper, Germany; Prof. Dr. Elisabeth Rohr, Germany; Dr. Ferdinand Schlingensiepen, Germany; Dr. Reinhard Kirste, Germany; Prof. Dr. Emmanuel Lartey, Ghana/USA; Uri Bloch, Israel; Daniel Schipani, Argentina/USA; Leah Dawn Bueckert, Canada/USA; Ismael Altintas, Turkey/Germany; Prof. Dr. Julian Müller, South-Africa.

19) "Truth Will Make You Free": Spaces of Exchange in Missionary Work and Pastoral Care and Counselling

2006, Sept. 17-22, Hamburg, Germany. Attendance: 72.

Prof. Dr. Theodor Ahrens, Germany; Prof. Dr. Hans-Martin Gutmann, Germany; Prof. Dr. Klaus Hock, Germany; Dr. Nalini Arles, India; Anke Flohr, USA; Pastor Edmund Sackey-Brown, Ghana/Germany; Prof. Dr. Leif Gunnar Engedal, Norway.

20) Identity in Times of Changes: Challenges for Pastoral Care, Churches and Religions

2008, Aug. 31 - Sept. 6, Bratislava, Slovakia. Attendance: 80.

Doc. PhDr. Ján Bunčák, Slovakia; Doc. PhDr. Emil Komarik, Slovakia; Pfr. Dieter Brandes, Germany; Dr. Jan Albert van den Berg, South Africa; Rev. Julius Pudule, South Africa; Rev. Eberhard v.d. Heyde, Germany; Rev. Dinesh K. Chand, India; Prof. Dr. Julius Filo, Slovakia; Dr. Mary Rute Esperandio, Brazil; Rev. Helmut Weiß, Germany; Prof. Dr. James Farris, Brazil.

21) Differences as Opportunity: Care and Counselling in Multi-Cultural and Multi-Religious Societies – The Example of Haifa, Israel"

2009, Sept. 4-8, Haifa, Israel. Attendance: 29.

Nasser Shakour, Israel; Prof. Dr. Kathleen Greider, USA; Rabbi Iris Yaniv, Israel; Robi Damelin, Israel; Ali Abu-Awwad, Palestine; Rabbi Prof. Dr. Daniel Hershkowitz, Israel; Professor Arnon Soffer, Israel; Dr. David Cohen; Israel; Boris Gauchman, Israel.

22) Dynamics of Migration Today

2010, Sept. 12 – 18, Strasbourg, France. Attendance: 67.

Mdm. Murielle Maffessoli, France; Rev. Julius Itumeleng Pudule, South Africa; Prof. Dr. Gabriele Münnix, Germany; Prof. Dr. Valburga Schmiedt-Streck, Brazil; Mrs. Maria Ochoa-Llido, France; Rev. Imad Haddad, Palestine; Prof. Dr. Elisabeth Parmentier, France; Prof. Dr. Kathleen Greider, USA; Prof. Dr. Ronaldo Sathler Rosa, Brazil; Brenda Ruiz, Nicaragua; Sabine Förster, Germany; Prof. Dr. Daniel Schipani, Argentina/USA.

23) In the Power of the Holy Spirit

2011, June 13 – 18, Hamburg, Germany. Attendance: 42.

Dr. Daniel Chiquete, Mexico; Pastor Matthias C. Wolff, Germany; Joan Brüggemeier, Germany; Professor Dr. Werner Kahl, Germany; Bishop William Appiah, Ghana; Dr. Palmer Appiah-Gyan, Germany; Peter Arthur, Germany; Prof. Dr. Daniel Schipani, USA.

24) Caring for Creation, Caring for People. Climate Changes and Natural Disasters as Challenges for Spiritual Care, Theology and Socio-Political Development

2012, July 15-21, Moshi, Tanzania. Attendance: 102.

Prof. Jesse N.K. Mugambi, Kenya; Dr. Julius Keyyu, Tanzania; Dr. Sabina Mtweve, Tanzania; Marcia Towers, Guatemala; Prof. T. David Ito, Japan; Prof. Brenda Ruiz; Nicaragua; Dr. Alfred Stephen, India; Rabbi Amnon Daniel Smith, United Kingdom; Professor Dr. Daniel Louw, South Africa; Prof. Dr. Emmanuel Lartey and Rev. Antoinette Kemp, USA; Rev. Godluck E. D. Kitomari, Tanzania.

25) Islamic Spiritual Care: A Trialogue Between Muslims, Jews, and Christians

2013, Sept. 28 - Oct. 4, Mainz, Germany. Attendance: 106.

Prof. Dr. Isabelle Noth, Switzerland; Rev. Imad Haddad, Palestine; Rev. Marudut Manalu, Indonesia; Rev. Dr. Uwe Rieske, Germany; Rev. Frank Stüfen, Switzerland; Dr. Peter Waldmann, Germany; Rabbi Danny Smith; United Kingdom; Esnaf Begic, Germany; Ahmet Özdemir, Germany; Dr. Abdul Nasser Al-Masri, Germany; Prof. Dr. Cemal Tosun; Turkey; Ahmed Faizal bin Ramly, Malaysia; Emina Čorbo-Mešić, Germany; Dr. Silvia Horsch-Al Saad, Germany.

26) The Other Religion and Tradition as Blessing: Exploring Spiritual Potentials for Care and Counselling

2014, Sept. 14-19, Mennorode, Netherlands. Attendance: 79.

Prof. Dr. Christa Anbeek, Netherlands; Dr. Dominiek Lootens, Belgium; Brecht Molenaar, Netherlands; Rev. Nahana Mjema, Tanzania; Prof. Dr. David Ito, Japan; Prof. Brenda Ruiz, Nicaragua; Prof. Dr. Martin Walton, Netherlands; Prof. Dr. Ruard Ganzevoort, Netherlands; Prof. Dr. Manuela Kalsky, Netherlands; Dr. Mohamed Ajouaou, Netherlands; Mohammad Imran Sagir, Germany; Dr. Ari van Buuren, Netherlands.

27) Religious Sources for Building Community and Peace

2015, June 11-17, Wrocław, Poland. Attendance: 50

Prof. Dr. Marek Jerzy Uglorz, Poland; Linda S. Golding, USA; Prof. Dr. Cemal Tosun, Turkey; Bishop Ryszard Bogusz, Poland; Rev. Dr. Maung Maung Yin, Myanmar; Rev. Imad Haddad, Palestine.

About the Contributors

Emina Čorbo-Mešić, author at the public broadcaster SWR and lecturer for the interreligious dialogue at Evangelische Hochschule Ludwigsburg (Protestant University), 2010-2012 chairperson of the Councel of Coordination for Christian-Islamic Dialogue (KCID) in Germany.

Elliot N. Dorff, Ph.D., ordained Rabbi (Conservative Judaism), Distinguished Professor of Philosophy and Rector at the American Jewish University in California, Visiting Professor of Jewish Law at the University of California, Los Angeles.

Mary Rute Gomes Esperandio, Psychologist, Ph.D. in Theology, Post-Doctorate in Psychology of Religion at The Indiana University South Bend, Professor in the Post Graduate Program in Theology and in the Post Graduate Program in Bioethics at the Pontifical Catholic University of Parana – Curitiba, Brazil.

Karl H. Federschmidt, Dr. theol., served as hospital chaplain, parish minister, and lecturer for Ecumenical Theology and Religious Studies at Kirchliche Hochschule (Protestant University) and at the University of Wuppertal, Germany. Currently he teaches religious education at a vocational school in Düsseldorf, Germany.

Joseph George, Th.D., Professor in the Department of Christian Ministry at the United Theological College (UTC), Bangalore, India, specialized in pastoral counselling. Besides teaching, he is engaged in clinical training programmes as well as practicing counselling.

Kathleen J. Greider, Ph.D., ordained United Methodist minister, Research Professor at Claremont School of Theology, Senior Staff Counselor and Clinical Supervisor at The Clinebell Institute for Pastoral Counseling and

Psychotherapy, and Fellow of the American Association of Pastoral Counselors.

Eberhard Hauschildt, Dr. theol., ordained Lutheran minister, Professor of Practical Theology and Executive Director of the Institute of Hermeneutics, Rheinische Friedrich-Wilhelms-Universität at Bonn, Germany.

Silvia Horsch-Al Saad, Ph.D., 2008-2012 scientific staff at the Institute for Arabistic at Free University Berlin, she currently does post-doctoral studies at the Institute for Islamic Theology, University Osnabrück, Germany.

Emmanuel Y. Lartey, Ph.D., L. Bevel Jones III Professor of Pastoral Theology, Care and Counseling at Candler School of Theology, Emory University, Atlanta, GA, USA. An ordained Methodist minister from Ghana, he was for several years Director of Pastoral Studies at the University of Birmingham, England.

Dominiek Lootens, Dr. Theol., pastoral supervisor and educator at Caritas Flanders, Belgium, and lecturer at the PTHV (Catholic University for Philosophy and Theology) in Vallendar, Germany. Since 2015 he is vice-president of SIPCC.

Daniël J. Louw, Ph.D., Professor at University of Stellenbosch, South Africa, and Dean of the faculty of theology (2001-2005). President of the International Academy of Practical Theology (IAPT) (2003–2005), President of the International Council for Pastoral Care and Counselling (ICPPC) (2011–2015).

Julian Müller, Ph.D., Professor em. at University of Pretoria, South Africa. He has taught Pastoral Care and Counselling and is currently involved in research and postgraduate supervision as a Senior Research Fellow at the Centre for the Advancement of Scholarship, University of Pretoria.

Daisy N. Nwachuku, Ed.D., Professor of Counselling Psychology and Pastoral Counselling at the University of Calabar, Nigeria. Former Head of Department, Educational Foundations, Guidance and Counselling. Founder and Executive Director of Robert Institute for Mission and Development (RIMAD).

Jalaluddin Rakhmat, Dr., lecturer for International Political Communication at Bandung Institute of Technology, Indonesia, and member of the

German Orient-Institute. He also works as author, counsellor, and leader of a training centre for Sufism at Jakarta, Indonesia.

Indigo Jonah Raphael, MA. in Hebrew and Jewish Studies (Leo Baeck College), MA. in Healthcare Chaplaincy (University of Leeds), ordained as a Progressive Rabbi in 1996, worked as a Rabbi in Liberal Judaism congregations, as Liberal Judaism Chaplain and as a Tutor at Leo Baeck College, now works as a Hospital and Hospice Chaplain in Multi-Faith Teams in London and as a Celebrant and a Life Coach.

Ursula Riedel-Pfäfflin, Dr., ordained Lutheran minister, Professor em. of Practical Theology and Gender Studies, Evang. Fachhochschule (University of Applied Sciences for Social Work) at Dresden, Germany. She also works as a trainer and supervisor in systemic counseling.

Ronaldo Sathler-Rosa, Ph.D., Professor of Pastoral Theology, Methodist University of Sao Paulo, Brazil, Honorarium Member of the Society for Intercultural Pastoral Care and Counselling, retired Methodist Pastor.

Daniel S. Schipani, Dr. Psy., Ph.D., ordained Mennonite minister, Professor of Pastoral Care and Counseling at Anabaptist Mennonite Biblical Seminary, Elkhart, Indiana, USA. He lectures widely in North and Latin America and Europe and is the author or editor of twenty-five books on pastoral and spiritual care and practical theology.

Archie Smith, Jr., Ph.D., ordained American Baptist minister, Distinguished former Professor of Pastoral Psychology and Counseling at the Pacific School of Religion at Berkeley, California. He also is a licensed marriage, family, and child therapist.

Daniel A. Smith, M.A., ordained Rabbi (Reform Judaism) and psychotherapist, Lecturer of Pastoral Care and Community Skills at the Leo Baeck College, London. 1996-1999 he was Chairman of the British Reform Assembly of Rabbis.

Robert Solomon, M.D., Ph.D., worked as a medical doctor and served as a pastor in Tamil churches in Singapore. He taught pastoral theology at Trinity Theological College, where he also was Principal. 2000-2012 he was Bishop of the Methodist Church in Singapore.

David Stevens, Dr. of Science, member of the Standing Advisory Commission on Human Rights (1988-1992), General Secretary of the Irish Council of Churches (1992-2003). From 2004 until his death in 2010 he was leading the Corrymeela Community, Belfast.

Martin Walton, Ph.D., Professor by special appointment in chaplaincy studies at the Protestant Theological University in Groningen, Netherlands. He serves as coordinator of the Northern Netherlands Network for Spirituality, Ethics and Care.

Edwina D. Ward, Ph.D., former Head of Practical Theology Department and Senior Research Associate for the School of Religion, Philosophy and Classics at the University of KwaZulu-Natal, South Africa. She currently practices pastoral counselling and spiritual direction in a private capacity.

Helmut Weiß, ordained Lutheran Pastor, Supervisor in the German Association of Pastoral Psychology, was many years teaching CPE. Since 1995 he is President of the Society for Intercultural Pastoral Care and Counselling (SIPCC), Düsseldorf.

Solomon Victus, Ph.D., Professor in the Department of Social Analysis and serves as Dean and Vice-Principal of Tamilnadu Theological Seminary (TTS), Madurai, South India. Ordained Minister of the Church of South India (CSI).

CPSIA information can be obtained
at www.ICGtesting.com
Printed in the USA
BVOW03s2143071217
502271BV00001B/18/P